The Theory of Democracy Revisited

GIOVANNI SARTORI
Albert Schweitzer Professor
in the Humanities
Columbia University

CHATHAM HOUSE PUBLISHERS, INC.
Chatham, New Jersey

THE THEORY OF DEMOCRACY REVISITED

CHATHAM HOUSE PUBLISHERS, INC.
Box One, Chatham, New Jersey 07928

Publisher: Edward Artinian
Design: Quentin Fiore
Composition: Chatham Composer
Printing and Binding: Hamilton Printing Company

LIBRARY OF CONGRESS CATALOGING-IN-PUBLICATION DATA

Sartori, Giovanni, 1924-
   The theory of democracy revisited.

   Includes indexes.
   1. Democracy.   I. Title.
JC423.S274   1987   321.8   86-31013

ISBN 978-0-93454-048-3

Manufactured in the United States of America
10 9 8 7 6 5 4 3 2

Foreword

The introduction to this work is in volume 1 and is not repeated here. Instead, the table of contents is given again in full. The division of the work into two volumes implies that volume 2 does not require the prior reading of volume 1. While I have gone to considerable pain to make *The Theory of Democracy Revisited* divisible into two relatively self-contained arguments, the cross-referencing is made to the work as a whole. Aside from their differences in content, the two volumes reflect a somewhat different emphasis: The first volume is more analytic, the second more historical. Even so, it is my hope that whoever looks into one of the volumes will be tempted to look into the other one as well. Indeed, both volumes seek to reestablish a mainstream theory of democracy, and both equally and extensively deal with how democracy is being discussed.

Contents

PART TWO: THE CLASSICAL ISSUES

The Classical Issues

9. What Is Democracy? Definition, Proof, and Preference

There is certainly a stage at which it is pointless to ask further questions or demand more reasons, but in the process of reaching that stage we may expect to find common ground with others in making our appraisals, and this common ground is of great importance.

—H.R.G. Greaves

9.1 Are Definitions Arbitrary?

Answering the question What is democracy? amounts to giving a definition of the word democracy. The next question is: What is a definition?[1] According to John Stuart Mill, "The simplest and most correct notion of a definition is a proposition declaratory of the meaning of a word, namely, either the meaning which it bears in common acceptation, or that which the speaker or writer . . . intends to annex to it."[2] Mill did not attach much importance to the difference between the meaning specifically given to a word by the speaker or writer and its common meaning. But, since Mill's time, some philosophers (whom we shall identify, for expediency, as the Oxford philosophers) do. They make a clear-cut distinction between a stipulative definition and a lexical or lexicographical definition.[3] In the former case, the speaker announces: I propose to use this word in this sense, and this is *my* definition of it. This, being my own "deliberate, arbitrary, self-conscious choice of a name for a certain thing,"[4] is a stipulation. In the latter case, the speaker reports how a word is generally used, that is, what people usually mean when they use it. This, being the kind of definition that dictionaries are supposed to give, is called lexicographical, i.e., written in lexicons.

The distinction between lexical and stipulative definitions implies this further distinction: Lexical definitions may be true or false, depending on whether the report on how a word is commonly used is accurate or inaccurate; stipulative definitions cannot be divided into the true and the false—they are (it is often emphasized) *arbitrary.*[5] For instance, I can stipulate that "black" shall mean "white" by pointing to a Caucasian and asserting that whenever I say "black," I mean the color of a Caucasian. The point is not that I am *in fact* permitted to utter whatever nonsense comes across my mind. The point is, according to this view, that my decision to call "black" what others call "white" is a perfectly *legitimate* decision as long as two conditions are observed: *(a)* that the stipulation be explicitly stated; and *(b)* that the stipulator always uses the word "black" in the same way. But how are the listeners to respond when they see something that they call "white" and somebody else says, instead, "black"? The Oxford philosophers meet the question by suggesting that we are entitled to approve or disapprove of a stipulation on the basis of its usefulness. In other words, although stipulations cannot be divided into true and false, they can be divided into useful and muddling. At first sight this criterion may seem to work. In the above example, everyone would probably agree that to say black when everyone else says white is not useful but merely confusing. The problem is easily settled, however, because the example is both pointless and of unbeatable simplicity. But when we develop a chain of arguments, I am at loss at finding a single instance in which the utility criterion works—I mean, blocks muddlers and muddlings. For instance, nearly all the stipulations of Marcuse are, in my opinion, confusing and "misuses of no use." But non-useful under *what criterion of usefulness?*

Remember, in particular, that "there is a special connection between politics and the debasement of language," for in politics more than in any other realm language is less an instrument for expressing thought than a means "for concealing or preventing thought."[6] The special difficulty that the student of politics encounters is, thus, that in his subject matter it is indeed "useful" to becloud problems.[7] Indeed, an important part of politics—and not necessarily its wicked part—may be described as the art of fudging political issues. So, let us repeat the question: What is the definition of "useful"? Useful for whom or for what? To press the question, suppose that one were to say that political science is useful for political practice and that in practical politics it is useful—as I have just conceded—to muddle issues. Could the Oxford philosophers object? I fail to see how. How can they prevent their criterion, as stated, from working in the reverse, from inviting obfuscation because it is useful? Thus, if definitions are nothing but arbitrary stipulations subjected to the sole condition that they should be useful in some stipulated (i.e., arbitrary) sense of the term, then the conclusion must follow that democracy means whatever appears useful from the stipulator's viewpoint.[8] But this is a conclusion that I am not prepared to underwrite.

Someone may retort that I have forgotten that only stipulative definitions are arbitrary and that there are still the lexical ones. But falling back on dictionary definitions is of no real help. Let us begin by taking a group of dictionaries. If I consult enough of them, I shall discover that democracy means so many different things to different people that I shall have to conclude that it even has contradictory meanings. What is the next step? If I wish to play it safe, there is no next step. My inquiry will end with a report like the following: Democracy means eastward what autocracy means to the West, and vice versa. Is this conclusion acceptable? If it is, then there can be no democratic theory. Indeed, if this is the argument, then it is useless to think. All we have to do is to take a census of what people are taught to believe and produce statistics that will enable us to determine the winning majority. Still worse, to say that the question is to be resolved by percentages is to imply that the question is deferred, ultimately, to an *argumentum baculinum,* to the argument "it is I who has the stick." Whoever is on the side of those who conquer the world will have told the truth. For at this moment all the dictionaries will define democracy according to the victor's definition, and in this way one of the stipulations will become lexically true.

Let us reconsider the whole question from the beginning, by asking: What is the truth value of definitions? In particular, what is the truth value of definitions of democracy? No theory of democracy has a basis on which to stand unless this question is settled. It is true that the mood of philosophy no longer is as "stipulativist" as it was in the 1940s and 1950s;[9] but political scientists and theorists still find a very great convenience in the stipulative message taken at its face value.[10] It spares them a great deal of work; it affords a wonderful alibi for terminological carelessness; it makes originality or, better, what I call "novitism," the easiest thing in the world. Hardly any student of politics currently fails to mention that definitions are neither true nor false but simply constitute stipulations that specify the use of linguistic expressions. Of course—but is this all?

As Mill's definition of "definition" attests, he did know that meanings can either be lexical or stipulative, yet he considered the difference of no import. Was it an oversight? I think not. Let us ask: Whence do dictionaries derive the meaning of words? That is, what kind of definition is the lexicographical? Obviously, dictionaries are only inventories of stipulations that have been generally adopted. What we find in lexicons are still stipulations. The only difference is that whereas a lexical definition refers to old conventions, a stipulative definition suggests a new one proposed for future observance. Yet in both cases we are dealing with conventions. Thus, if stipulative definitions are arbitrary, then so are lexicographical ones. It follows that to grant that dictionary definitions can be true or false is begging the question, for only our report as to how certain people actually use a certain word may be true or false, not the definition itself, which remains a stipulation and is therefore to be adopted or rejected only on the basis of utility.

It may be argued that there are other differences between lexical and stipulative definitions. First, while the lexical definition is not normative (it does not say that the term democracy, for instance, ought to be used in a certain way), the stipulative definition is legislative or normative, since it tells us how the term should or should not be understood. But this is specious. I can easily "legislate," if I so wish, by following the lexicographical or reportative path of relying on standard authors as authorities. Another difference between the two kinds of definitions is found in the fact that the lexical one is impersonal — a we-answer—whereas the stipulative one is subjective, namely, an I-answer. Yet, this difference is only apparent. Taken at its face value, what *I* say is always and only what I say, that is, all definitions are "I-definitions." But if what I say has any value, regardless of its verbal formulation it must be more than an I-definition that simply gratifies my ego.

Thus, the more we probe into the matter, the more it appears that the distinction is a frivolous one. There is, ultimately, only one kind of definition, the stipulative; and this kind of definition can only be divided into old and new linguistic conventions. If we take the conventionalistic position, we must be consistent; we cannot stop halfway. We cannot maintain that only stipulative definitions are arbitrary. Dictionaries will not help us escape the conclusion that all definitions are arbitrary. This conclusion cannot be mitigated by maintaining that a lexicographical definition is less arbitrary than a stipulative one in that the area of arbitrariness of the former is limited by the need for some common understanding and by the requirements of public discourse. Either the same limitation (the need for common understanding) applies to stipulations or the thesis that "in stipulation we freely make any word mean anything we choose"[11] purely and simply amounts to a program of wholesale destruction of language. It is either the case that the distinction between lexicographical and stipulative definitions is trivial and of little consequence or, if it is of consequence, we are undermining language, communication, and, I believe, thinking. If it is perfectly all right to call a dog "cat," or vice versa, just as long as the stipulation is made clear, then I do grant that a stipulative definition is immensely different from a non-stipulative one. But in such a case we are legitimizing and producing a world of incommunicados.

9.2 A Criticism of Conventionalism

The issue is, in the final analysis, what test we are to adopt for accepting a definition. Let it be clear from the outset that we are not concerned with the origins of speech. How the first meaningful utterance appeared—that is, how a certain meaning became associated with a certain articulate sound—is both obscure and immaterial. Even assuming that language originated from random and arbitrary emission of vocalizations and that, therefore, convention was the basis of language for *Homo Neanderthalensis,* can it follow from this that more than a million years later (at the least) convention still is the *sole* basis of language? It certainly cannot. If we have come to attribute prominence to stipulative arbitrariness, it must be for ulterior reasons—reasons that I propose to challenge by examining the following four questions:

1. Are definitions rules of the language game?
2. Is the useful-confusing criterion adequate?
3. Are definitions like axioms?
4. Has conventionalism an alternative?

In regard to the first question, I hold that the conventionalists are inconsistent; in regard to the second, that the criterion of utility, understood as a practical way to solve cognitive problems, is totally inadequate; in regard to the third, that the whole position is based on a false analogy; and in regard to the fourth, that we have been trapped by a false dilemma.

First, *inconsistency.* One of the reasons that gives prominence to the otherwise banal notion that language is "conventional" is the analogy between language and games. The discovery thus is that definitions are rules of linguistic equivalence, which are like "game rules." I shall assume, for the sake of the argument, that this is correct.[12] But if this is correct, then the game theorists of language contradict themselves. For there is no sense in speaking of rules and then asserting that it is perfectly legitimate to break them. If we maintain that everybody has the right to make whatever stipulations he wants, there are no rules; and if there are rules, then we cannot maintain that their infringement is legitimate. The right of a player who wishes to change the rules is not the right to tamper with the game as it stands but to withdraw from the game and (if he can find another universe of players) invent a new game. Note, however, that the rules of the new game would be as intransgressible as the ones of the former game. Suppose that the game is chess and that a chess player finds himself in a game where his opponent uses the king's moves for the queen's. According to the philosophers who refer to a game model, it is quite correct for the second player to do this as long as he announces it and does it consistently. But the first player will decide instead that his opponent does not know how to play chess and therefore cannot be permitted to play. In my opinion, the first player is right, and the philosopher is wrong. He who moves the king as if it were the queen is not creating another game but destroying that game. My first point, then, is that inasmuch as definitions are game-like *rules,* we must ask that they be duly observed. To encourage their violation is flagrant inconsistency.

Second, *inadequacy.* When we say that we adopt a definition because we find it useful, what do we mean? My guess is that most scholars would reply: useful for science, useful for the progress of knowledge. But then, clearly, we are speaking of *cognitive usefulness.* And once we admit this, I wonder how much difference there is between the true-false and useful-useless criteria. There certainly is one difference, namely, the difference between a realistic and a nominalistic theory of knowledge, between the "correspondence theory" of truth and the "coherence theory" of truth.[13] This is indeed a grand debate — but hardly for the non-philosopher. For the practitioner the problem boils down to *warranted assertibility,* and the query as to whether truth is a correspondence between mind and thing, an *adequatio intellectus et rei* (as in the Thomistic formula) or only the truth of the statements made (as the nominalists contend), has very little bearing on his actual proceedings. Of course, the scholars who believe in the correspondence theory of truth are surer of themselves, whereas the scholars who take a relativistic or nominalistic view of truth may even shy away from the word completely. Nonetheless, even they have a truth value in mind. For if we refuse to recognize that "useful" is simply a cautious way of dealing with truth, the utility criterion simply ceases to work. If we wish to solve a cognitive problem, we have to rely on a cognitive criterion. Whether we call it truth or usefulness, the latter term is only an understatement of the former. To advocate utility per se is to smuggle into the discussion a test that is wholly inadequate. Unless "useful" signifies "cognitive usefulness," it cannot help us to determine that a certain definition is useful while another is not.

Third, *false analogy.* In another one of its versions, conventionalism assimilates definitions to axioms. If this were correct, then it would indeed follow that definitions are, like axioms, arbitrary starting points. But before asking whether definitions are like axioms, let us first ask whether definitions are the starting point of an enquiry. So, what is the place of definitions? The fact that definitions are often found at the outset of a discourse does not demonstrate that they constitute its logical beginning. This placement may be only a didactic device. Another reason for placing a definition at the start is that it represents the conclusion of a process of analysis and investigation that others have already carried out. Conversely, a new analysis may well lead to a definition whose logical place is at the end. Thus, definitions are like axioms in axiomatic theory; they are not (like axioms) in non-axiomatic theory. And whether a theory can be axiomatic is hardly a matter of personal liking; it depends on whether we dispose of a "formalized" language or have instead to perform with a natural language. Geometry has long been the model, if not the dream, of a rigorous, calculus-like theorizing in which we start from a set of definitions — axioms and postulates — that are neither true nor false because they are the arbitrary beginning from which everything else follows deductively. However, the model of geometry cannot be shown to apply to how theory is intended in the realm of human affairs.[14] No matter how differently "theory" may be conceived, no theory of democracy is, or has ever been, calculus-like. Certainly, all the definitions given in this text are *not* like axioms: They are not premises, they obtain only a limited deductive power, and they are not supposed to be "arbitrary." In a natural language to say that a definition is arbitrary is to say that it is an unwarranted and uncalled-for definition.

Fourth, *false dilemma*. The winning argument of the stipulativist seems to be that conventionalism has no alternative. Words can have only conventional meanings, and thus definitions must be arbitrary, because it cannot be otherwise: Either one takes the conventionalistic stand or one is bound to fall back into the old delusion of "real essences" and "absolute standards."[15] No — and it is surprising to see present-day skilled logicians become victims of an outdated Greek dualism. The Greeks did dichotomize between nature (*physis*) and convention; but it is clearly the case that here we have a pair of contraries, not contradictories: between nature and convention *tertium datur* (the law of the excluded middle does not apply).[16] Everything that is human-made is not "nature"; yet, can it be altered (remade, dismissed) as a sheer matter of will and free choosing? Convention originally means "to come together," to convene (from the Latin *convenire*), and its meaning extension is "to agree." So, could we convene and agree to remake "stipulatively" a whole linguistic system? Even if it were possible, it would be nonsensical.

In order to stress innovation in defining the stipulativist largely overshoots the mark and affords an incorrect report of the ongoing process of knowing. If we look at how a scientific knowledge actually and normally performs, so-called linguistic conventions hardly result from the anxiety of being new and original at all costs; they result from the imperative of reducing ambiguities and sharpening the analytic power of concepts. In any case, linguistic conventions are the outcome of a long, thoughtful, and purposeful process of choice among the known and accepted meanings of a word plus an occasional element of argumented, not arbitrary, innovation. Hence, to the extent that definitions are traced back to stipulations, such stipulations are not arbitrary. If they are, or when they are, they are discarded. Arbitrariness is so far from being the typical feature of the defining process that it is in fact the criterion by which we decide that a definition is wrong or useless.

Throughout the process of construction and development of language the central characteristic is its interconnectedness. Language is a truly immense *system* and, indeed, a highly systemic system. Words (and the concepts they evoke) are not discrete entities; they belong to semantic fields consisting of sets of neighboring and associated terms that are such — i.e., *hang together* — because the redefinition (change of meaning) of one of its terms involves the redefinition of some, or even all, of the associated terms.

Take, to illustrate, "power." The set of associated terms is, at a minimum, influence, authority, coercion, force, sanction. Depending on how power is defined, all the neighboring terms also change meaning. In particular, if power is redefined (given a new meaning), all the other terms need to be redefined in order to make sure that *(a)* no "field meaning" is lost; and *(b)* the readjustment of the semantic field involves an analytic gain (a reduction, not an increase of ambiguity or vagueness). Another good example, one which we have discussed at length, is the semantic field covered by the terms political class, ruling class, elite, power elite, rulership, leadership, and the like. Since these terms constitute a system in which — as the concept of system implies — each linguistic unit interacts with all the others, it will not do (although it is incessantly done) to stipulate "I decide 'elite' to mean . . . " unless we equally engage in rearranging accordingly the whole field. And the reason for accepting or rejecting a new (stipulated) meaning of "elite" is precisely whether or not the *field* — not the term or concept in isolation — obtains, as a result, greater clarity and precision.

Does the foregoing add up to a resuscitation of metaphysical essences and absolute standards? Certainly not. It only amounts to establishing that we think via words, that words are our mental eyeglasses, and that their *semantic projection* embodies a way of conceiving and perceiving things (objects, processes). In short, *words mold thought.* Hence the process of selecting a given term and defining it has nothing to share with arbitrariness. To the contrary, this process can be cognitively useful if, and only if, it passes the *semantic field test,* as expressed by the following rule: Whenever the definition given to a term unsettles the semantic field to which the term belongs, then it has to be shown that *(a)* no "field meaning" is thrown overboard; and *(b)* the overall "field ambiguity" (fuzziness, unboundedness, disorder) is not being increased.[17]

Three points are worthy of recapitulation. First, we are not concerned with the origin of language but with existing, highly elaborate, and structured *language systems.* Second, arbitrariness in defining simply destroys the intersubjectiveness of language, thus transforming an instrument of communication (which also incorporates existing knowledge) into a sheer instrument of miscommunication. Third, the dilemma "either conventionalism or metaphysics" is both unsound and misleading. It is not via arbitrary indiscipline but via a great deal of semantic and intellectual discipline that language evolves and is "usefully" refined for heuristic needs.

9.3   *Words as Experience Carriers*

We can now turn from the issue in general to our specific concern, which is to show that is is frivolous to answer the question, What is democracy? either by saying that democracy is what a large number of people agree to call democracy, or by private stipulation, that is, by putting forward a convention of one's own that is legitimate *ex definitione* because it is a stipulation. No. The question, What is democracy? cannot address the term in isolation but also, if only implicitly, its semantic field, that is, the set of concepts that implement or complement "democracy." On the other hand, it should be well understood that my case is now strictly confined to the vocabulary of politics. My subject matter is not the dynamics of language *in general*—a controversy that must be left to the linguists themselves—but only one aspect of this evolution and, still more narrowly, the shaping of the key terms of politics.

The single reason that best explains why the mainstream theory of democracy settles, over time, for firm (not fickle) linguistic "conventions" is that all the terms that importantly enter the definition(s) of democracy *have been shaped by experience* and reflect what we have learned as historical experimenters. Argumentatively, there are many possible, i.e., logically conceivable democracies; but there are not many *historically possible* ones. If the present-day meaning of democracy departs from its Greek meaning and has little to do with a self-governing people, the transformation reflects the repeated historical failures of such self-governing. Similarly, terms such as liberty, oppression, coercion, legitimacy, and so forth, acquire with the passing of time a *firmness of meaning* that results from the fact that they are filled with historical content and substance.

Cicero's dictum was *historia magistra vitae,* history is the teacher of life. The dictum can be extended and converted into saying *historia magistra definitionis,* that history also governs definitions. As Burdeau nicely put it, man is assimilated history, history incorporated in his being.[18] This is so, however, because of language, because language is, among other things, a storehouse of past testing and learning. Again, John Stuart Mill said it very well: "Language is the depository of the accumulated body of experience to which all former ages have contributed their part." Thus, for Mill, language is a "keeper-alive," a "conservator," of former practice[19]—as indeed it is. So, *word cheats* do exist and are easy to identify: They are the people who, willfully or out of sheer unawareness, dismiss the fact that words are experience containers, *experience carriers.*

Reverting to democracy, my contention can be summed up as follows: The core meaning of the term is neither stipulative nor arbitrary, since it is historically rooted and derived. More precisely, words such as democracy are shorthand reports intended to convey ideas about how we are to behave *as experienced people* in matters regarding which each generation starts by having no experience. If this is so, if the term democracy is a carrier of historical experience whose meaning is stabilized by an endless trial-and-error process, it follows from this not only that the demand for freedom of definition is hard to distinguish from the right to be ignorant, but also that the stipulative theory of language fails to grasp the fundamental property of language. Even assuming (without conceding it) that at the origins of speech we find conventions, we ourselves are not beginners, and we do not start with a *tabula rasa.* We are not "noble savages" trying to discover how to build a house but inhabitants already dwelling at its thirtieth floor, that is, with some thirty centuries of records behind us. How can it be, then, that we are entitled to define and redefine "democracy" at whim? The question, How can we be governed without being oppressed? has been asked since the beginning of Western civilization. "Democracy" (liberal democracy) is our current way of answering it. But in so answering we are recalling structures and patterns of behavior molded by millennia of trial and failure; and if we are not, then we are just repaving the way to failure.

Of course, we cannot stay content with inherited knowledge. But this is no reason for recommending or practicing its cancellation. Whether we realize it or not, our ideas are only "ours" in infinitesimal part. They can be, however, very naive, unworkable and, indeed, stupid ideas. And history happens to be the only large-scale experimental laboratory that we have. It is history, then, that tests our ideas—a testing reflected in the history of concepts. We are well advised, therefore, to keep in mind that every concept has a history and that in this history (either its persistence or transformation of meanings) the vicissitudes of terminology are connected with the fate of societies and their polities.

It is clear, I trust, that I am not implying in the least that the political theorist or scientist should look at history in the manner of the historian. My suggestion is not to look at history as a record of "unique" experiences that never repeat themselves (as the historian is inclined to do) but, instead, of experiences perceived in their similarities and, hence, in their repetitive features. We know that every pear is unique, that each individual is different, and that even if every day we swim in the same river, its water is never the same. Despite these warnings, the botanist has the class "pear," we speak of human beings in general, and water is always, in its chemical components, water. Similarly, and *mutatis mutandis,* there is enough repetition in history to allow us, if we know how, to learn a good deal from the past. Maybe it is true that we learn from experience that human beings never learn from experience. Yet we have no choice. In the following chapters my primary emphasis is, then, on the historical performance of democracy under the assumption that the concept (and its semantic field) acquires meaningfulness and definiteness along the course of incorporating and reflecting such performance. I know that we live looking ahead and that, in the final analysis, we are interested in what democracy can and should be rather than in what it has been. However, the past is not only *pastness;* and I shall deal with its *presentness.*

But before pursuing this exploration, I am here required to explore how "defining" democracy relates to "proving" and/or to "preferring" democracy.

9.4 *The Search for Proof*

To define is not the same as to give reasons for. One may acquire a perfect understanding of democracy and yet be unconvinced by democracy. On this consideration the argument moves to the issue of justification and, ultimately, of proof.[20] Indeed, the major concern of political philosophy, and of many political theorists, has long been the search for the proof that a particular political system is "true" or "good" (just). A search whose classic formulation is: Do political systems have foundations?

If the query is taken at face value, most present-day philosophers would reply: No, there are no political foundations to be discovered. As Weldon put it: "There is nothing behind or beyond actual political institutions which those institutions express, copy or realize."[21] This refutation addresses a Platonic interpretation of "foundations," namely, the assumption that there exists a superworld of ideal prototypes that men attempt to copy in their world. But the search for foundations need not be associated with Plato's metaphysics; it may, for instance, address moral claims and seek, therefore, moral foundations.[22] In any case, the problem remains whether it is possible to give adequate or convincing reasons to demonstrate that our arguments in favor of democracy (for instance) are correct or true, whereas the arguments in favor of autocracy are incorrect or false. In answering we must guard against saying no for the wrong reason, namely, that man cannot be convinced by reasons. This is immaterial, for we are not concerned here with the effectiveness of reason. A second preliminary warning is that, in much of the literature on the issue, questions of proof and questions of preference easily get mixed up. Since I propose, instead, to treat them separately, my first question will be, Is democracy *true*? It is only after having answered this question that I shall address the next one, Is democracy *preferable*?

There are at least two fundamentally different meanings of "truth," empirical and rational. Let us begin by asking whether, and in what sense, democracy can be declared empirically true. In the empirical sense, truth means *factual truth;* it bears on the existence or non-existence of the fact(s) denoted by a statement. Empirical truth is thus based on observation or, more precisely, on the controlled acceptance of observed facts as real facts. In this sense we can surely make true assertions about democracies, to wit: In these polities free elections regularly occur; secret trials do not occur; and so forth. By extension, a theory of democracy is empirically true when it hinges on inductive reasoning and to the extent that all its factual assertions are verified or withstand falsification. In a fuller and even more interesting sense, a theory of democracy is empirically true when it *succeeds in application,* that is, when its working out in practice corresponds to what the theory expects or predicts. Ultimately, then, true democracy is a democracy that can successfully be put into practice and that functions as an ongoing political system. There can be many true democracies, in the empirical sense, just as long as they pass the test that they must function and succeed in the real world. Conversely, all democracies whose practice fundamentally perverts their professed goals, and whose accomplishments are very different from their declared aims, are empirically false.

Let us pause to ask: What is it that the above proves? For instance, does it demonstrate in any way that democracy obtains a "truth" that nondemocracies, i.e., autocracies,[23] cannot obtain? I think not. When saying that a true democracy is one that functions, we are only establishing which definitions (theories) of democracy should be adopted, for real-world consumption, of those that have been proposed and are argumentatively plausible. To establish this is no mean achievement. Yet one can seek "true autocracy" exactly in the same way. In this case the conclusion would be that, of all the possible autocratic systems, the one that achieves its aims most effectively is the true autocracy. So, when I say that a true democracy is one that functions, I have not proved anything vis-à-vis autocracy.

Can we do better—on proof grounds—by turning to *rational truth,* that is, to truth as established by the principle of non-contradiction? In the logical or strictly rational sense, a string of propositions is true when it is logically coherent; correlatively, a theory is true to the extent that its sentences follow one another, without break of continuity, from premise to consequence. Thus, a "rationally true" democracy is one *more geometrico demonstrata,* a democracy "without contradictions." This approach characterizes, we have seen, the French-type democracy.[24] It can also be said that the present-day democratic left characteristically seeks to "rationalize democracy." But what is the proof merit of a well rationalized or rationally true democracy? With respect to the issue at hand, are we better off on rational than on empirical grounds? If anything, I suspect that we are worse off. The exercise cannot demonstrate, again, that democracy obtains a truth that nondemocracies do not obtain. Just as I can hypothesize a well-reasoned, non-contradictory democracy, my opponent can outline with even greater ease a rational autocracy that meets the same standards. On the other hand, a logically or rationally true democracy is by no means a true democracy that actually exists and functions. As we have seen, the democracies nurtured by the French *raison* have in fact turned out to be, empirically, least or non-working democracies.

There is little point in pressing the issue of truth any further. While we may legitimately speak, in specified senses, of political systems as being true-false, it appears that this key does not help us in proving, warranting, or demonstrating that a given political system is "founded" whereas another one is not. Does this conclusion entail that political systems have no foundations whatsoever? It is obvious that the answer depends on how we define "foundation." I certainly would not subscribe to the Platonic meaning. As makers of history, we can copy nothing; we have to invent. The body politic is not given, it is constructed. Yet, constructions imply foundations. And the foundations of our political inventions consist, it may be argued, of their *working principles,* that is, of the basic rules that govern their functioning and solve their conflicts.

Thus far, the working principle of democracy has been referred to, at various points, as the majority principle. But since we are now addressing a foundation, in this regard and deep down the majority principle is not *the* founding principle. At the beginning of the construction, the maxim from which the majority principle is derived, is: The people are always right. To be sure, the maxim can be formulated in a less provocative form, as the one that "people have a right to make their own mistakes." Even so, the criterion that we have agreed to accept for the solution of controversies in a democratic society is that the reason of the many is always *the right reason,* by definition.

Evidently this is not a true rule, either empirically or rationally. If we try to verify it empirically, observation will show how often the voice of the people is wrong. And I gladly leave to others the task of trying to prove that the rule is rationally demonstrable.[25] For myself, I shall merely note that the proposition "The people are always right" is simply the founding rule of the game by which we consent to abide because it expresses the *pactum societatis* that allows a democracy. In a parallel fashion, the ultimate founding principle of autocracy is: *The ruler is always right.* And it goes without saying that this rule is also empirically false and, again, rationally indefensible. It simply expresses a Hobbesian despair, the notion that a *pactum subiectionis,* accepting submission, is better than a war of all against all.

The objection will be made that the foundations of political and social systems consist in the *values* they embody and profess, not in the procedural rules to which they submit. I am willing to agree with this; but if this is the case we step into a hornet's nest. Values, and especially terminal values, are generally assumed to be beyond the reach of any kind of proof. Even though we need not subscribe to an emotive theory of values, that is, to the theory that value evaluations express only emotions, only affect,[26] nonetheless there is more than a grain of truth in the observation that values are believed rather than demonstrated, desired rather than explained, cherished rather than justified. So-called value cognitivism does hold that value statements have truth content; but this is a view in troubled waters.[27] The prevailing view is the non-cognitive one. As Oppenheim finds in his analysis, "there can be no objective foundation for our most basic moral and political convictions."[28]

All in all, we are seemingly coming to a dead end. Democracy (no less than its opposite) cannot be founded, proved, or demonstrated on empirical grounds, on rational grounds, nor on the grounds that democratic values are objectively superior, in their intrinsic worthiness, to all other values. Are we, thus, about to conclude that our search for proof has failed? Not quite. Up to now, "proof" has been referred and confined to something that has to be justified or warranted with respect to polities taken one by one, *in themselves.* Our search for proof baffles us, then, when it addresses a political system per se and taken in isolation. However, why not *compare* one polity to another? Granted, comparisons do not provide absolute but only relative (i.e., comparative) proof. I am prepared to grant further that comparisons do not really or properly provide proof but can only justify and sustain preferences. Not only have I no difficulty in making this ulterior concession, but I also find it a helpful clarification. Let us say, then, that what is really at stake is not proof but *preference.* Consequently, the question becomes: Can preferences about polities be warranted? In itself, democracy may well be a political form that does not satisfy the rational mind or a polity whose values cannot be shown to have objective and absolute primacy. What of it? The problem of securing justification and proof for a political system arises, after all, because we are asked to make a choice among alternatives. What we really need to know is, Why choose this instead of that? And this is a comparative question.

9.5 *A Comparative Evaluation*

Suppose that I am asked to warrant the assertion that democracy is preferable to, or better than, autocracy. And let me begin by inquiring whether the case can be made without involving values, that is, whether preferences inevitably and immediately entangle us in value issues.

As already indicated democracy establishes a *pactum societatis,* that is, a coexistence among citizens (equal as citizens), whereas autocracy resolves itself in a *pactum subiectionis,* in creating subjects, an order based on subjection. This consideration immediately brings out that in the two cases a very different *risk factor* is involved. This is easily seen if we revert to the founding premise "The people are always right." While this axiom is empirically false and rationally indefensible, nonetheless it is hardly a menacing axiom because we know that, in fact, "the people" stand for a long process of both innumerable adjustments and innumerable checks—at least in liberal democracies. The people actually resolve themselves in a multi-actor, multi-step and multi-filtered decision-making process.

The same cannot be said of the founding premise "The ruler is always right." The ruler is a concrete actor; and under the assumption that he is always right, he is, by definition, unchecked. In autocracy, then, the power addressees are exposed to an overweening and, indeed, frightening *sic volo, sic iubeo*—so I wish, so I command. And very little reassurance can be found in the consideration that the absolute ruler is but one man and that there are but twelve daylight hours a day. One man in just twelve hours a day has in fact well succeeded—all too many times—in exterminating millions of human beings. Today, this "but one man" can, in a matter of seconds, press a button that would destroy human life altogether. To put it in a very restrained fashion, autocracy amounts to a *blind risk,* and a blind risk of incommensurable magnitude. While democracy (liberal democracy) is replete with safety mechanisms, autocracy characteristically and conspicuously lacks safeties.

The democratic leader says: "I am their leader and therefore I have to follow them."[29] The autocrat says, or would have to say: "I have made myself your ruler and therefore you must obey me." Certainly, the democratic formula has drawbacks. However, not only does it express the nobility of the democratic venture, but it is a reassuring one. Contrariwise, the autocratic formula is as menacing as can be: We are told that we must purely and simply submit to a *quia nominor leo,* to the fact that lions exist. They certainly do; but if we are able to cage them, why allow them to be on the loose? Nobody likes being eaten by a lion. The first point, thus, is that the preferability of democracy can be warranted on the risk element alone and, therefore, without having to call on values and value controversies. It is important that this be established before moving into the treacherous ground of "value evaluations." As we do, the preliminary move is to make sure that we sort out values that are both elemental and broadly comparable across time and space.

For the purpose of this discussion, I shall settle for the following: respect for human life, personal safety, and individual freedom. Correlatively, the question is: Can it be rationally, i.e., convincingly shown that life, safety, and freedom are the "good things" entitled to priority over all others? Value relativists[30] have long contended that there is no way of answering questions of the sort. However, they win their case too easily, for they generally require us (others) to demonstrate propositions expressed in the form "freedom is best." But why should we? I take it that the appropriate and sufficient question is whether "freedom is better than." That is to say that we are not required to confront propositions expressed in absolute form but only propositions expressed in comparative form. Furthermore, we should also be on guard against requiring worldwide publics to understand "values" in the highly abstract and sophisticated way in which ethics and, indeed, Western ethics conceives them.

So, can it be rationally and demonstrably argued that respect for human life, personal security, and individual freedom are *(a)* values preferred by most, and *(b)* highly preferable values? The first query addresses a matter of fact; the second one does not. Let us then begin with asking whether it is empirically true that, across the world, we find that human beings share some basic, if elemental, value attitudes, and specifically the value preferences just mentioned. Most observers will reply negatively on the basis of the evidence that across time and space different people partake of different value feelings, and that history is both a cemetery of values and a storehouse of conflicting values. But is this valid evidence? Does it bear on the point? I think not.

Comparative questions can be addressed only to a universe that is in a position to answer them. If I ask someone whether he prefers to travel on horseback or by car, he cannot reply, or his reply is meaningless, unless the respondent has at least seen a car and a horse. It is not only pointless but totally misleading to inquire about preferences vis-à-vis people who neither have, nor ever had, alternatives, that is, anything to compare. And the plain facts of the matter are that innumerable people cannot prefer something to something else because they have no "else" in sight; they simply live with, and encapsulated within, the human (or inhumane) condition they find. Hence, in order to ascertain whether human beings share, across the world, some ultimate value preferences, we must establish first to which universe the inquiry is applicable. If this crucial, preliminary condition is not met, it is obvious that our finding will be that the world of values is not a cosmos but a chaos.

But this is both an invalid and a deceiving evidence. Let it be added that the problem is not only to reduce our universe to people for which terms of comparison exist, but also to make sure that we are not asking them questions that pass above their heads. Possibly not even one out of four of the present-day inhabitants of our planet perceive the world in the analytic and abstract fashion that sorts out "values" as distinguishable entities. To be meaningfully conceived in their distinctiveness, values assume a fairly high capacity for abstraction and, furthermore, a vision of the world that dichotomizes between fact and value—and many cultures do not.

On the empirical issue—whether certain values are actually preferred— we are thus forced to conclude on the sober note that we can assuredly dismiss much of the counterevidence, but on grounds that imply that we do not possess adequate confirming evidence either. If so, the empirical formulation of the issue inevitably shades into the argumentative camp, that is, into the second one of our questions: Is it possible to justify rationally the proposition that life, security, and freedom are highly preferable values? *Highly preferable,* it will be immediately asked, in what sense? Well, at least in the sense that they *(a)* are to be preferred to their lack; and *(b)* constitute the good things that precede and condition whatever worthiness we may seek. Admittedly, the crucial part of the argument is the latter one, namely, how to warrant that life, security, and the freedom that assures them are to be preferred as *high-priority* values.

Bearing in mind that "values" are abstract reconstructions, the argumentative argument (so to speak) is pursued best by asking concrete questions, such as the following ones: Are there people who prefer uncertainty as to whether they will still be alive tomorrow (natural death aside) to the assurance that they will, or who prefer prison to home, bodily harm to the prohibition of torture, dispossessions to possessions, and, overall, who prefer being impeded in whatever they would choose to do by the sheer whim of some almighty lord? Such people, I grant, are certainly conceivable. But, statistically inevitable exceptions aside, they are conceivable under the condition that such people do not even grasp the sense of the aforesaid alternatives. And the fact that someone who has never tasted liberty and the protection of the law and has lived all his life an animal life is not able to answer such queries certainly does not mean that he would not want the values in question if he knew them. Therefore, aside from the consideration that innumerable human beings actually do not know that their destiny could be any different from what it is, I am at a loss in finding any rational way of sustaining that a person may prefer death, torture, prison, and arbitrary dispossession of home or harvest to their avoidance.

The retort might be that my argument does not fully meet the issue in that it sustains one line of priority but not others. The objection might thus be that it is fairly easy to argue that freedom wins over unfreedom; but how does one argue that freedom has priority, for example, over equality? I shall not enter this discussion here because I shall do so at length later.[31] It is, however, appropriate to explain that I have not included equality, in the case as I have presented it, on two grounds. First, freedom is here defined in connection with life and safety, i.e., in its most concrete and elemental manifestation. This is right because the discussion at hand requires us to stay with "value feelings," that is, to address values in their most immediate and least articulate state of being. Were I to assess how liberty and equality relate to each other, I would have to embark precisely on the kind of abstract analysis to which I am objecting. Consider, second, that if equality were to be entered in my argument, the test would have to take this form: Given a universe in which everybody has experienced liberty and equality in their distinctiveness (and conflicting characteristics), and in which everybody has experienced the loss of both, which of the two values would most of its members rather regain, or regain first, liberty or equality? It would be nice to dispose of such test conditions—but where are they to be found?

The argument remains, then, that if we know how to avoid the wrong questions and tests, it is quite feasible to justify, if only generically, the preference for democracy also on a value basis. That political projects and paradigms have, ultimately, axiological foundations does not entail that we must shut ourselves in a shell of inexpressible and indefensible value choices. In particular, neither value noncognitivism nor value relativism requires us, in order to uphold democracy, to fall all the way back to the "completely sceptical argument" of Wollheim, namely, that since

> it is impossible for anyone to discover what is the right course of action for the community, or where the true interests of its inhabitants reside . . . it follows that everyone in the community should be allowed to do what he wants to do as far as is socially possible. The only society in which this can happen is the one in which everyone has some control in the government: therefore Democracy is favored.[32]

I trust that we can do better than that. To recapitulate my stance from the beginning, I have distinguished the question, Is democracy in itself true? from the question, Can the option for democracy be rationally warranted? On the basis of this distinction, my conclusion is that political systems pose a problem of choice; that choice presupposes comparison between better and worse (not between good and true or between bad and false in the absolute sense); and that the relativity of values calls precisely for their relative (comparative) weighing. Hence it is perfectly possible to warrant preferences. Political choices do allow a rational argument, and political alternatives are— even when value related and value hinged—subject to warranted advisability. We cannot, strictly speaking, "prove democracy," but we can convincingly argue, I submit, that democracy is preferable.

Notes

1. It is immaterial to my present discussion to distinguish among various types of "definition." I have done so in G. Sartori, ed., *Social Science Concepts: A Systematic Analysis* (Beverly Hills: Sage, 1983), pp. 28-34. For an introductory overview, see L.S. Stebbing, *A Modern Introduction to Logic* (London, 1930), chap. 22: "The Theory of Definitions."

2. J.S. Mill, *System of Logic* (London, 1898), bk. 1, chap. 8, p. 86.

3. As a general source, see R. Robinson, *Definition* (Oxford: Clarendon Press, 1954), esp. chaps. 3 and 4.

4. Ibid., p. 60.

5. See, for all, Robinson: "Lexical definitions have a truth-value but stipulative definitions have not. . . . It is an arbitrary choice" (ibid., pp. 62, 63). If "arbitrary" simply meant "not necessitated by logic" the point would be pointless, for logic does not address word meanings (there is no logical necessity in calling "pear" a pear). Arbitrariness means, with the Oxford philosophers, free choice, *liberum arbitrium.*

6. G. Orwell, "Politics and the English Language," in *Selected Essays* (Harmondsworth: Penguin, 1957), pp. 154, 157.

7. It could be argued that economic producers have a similar interest, for they too are "hidden persuaders." The difference remains that economic fraud is subjected to legal controls, which neither do nor can exist in the sphere of politics (in free societies).

8. Hence, it "is futile to puzzle ourselves as to whether the American or the Russian use of 'democracy' is the true or correct one." T.D. Weldon, *The Vocabulary of Politics* (Harmondsworth: Penguin, 1953), p. 23.

9. For an overall, excellent discussion, pro and con, of the Oxford linguistic philosophy, see R. Rorty, ed., *The Linguistic Turn* (Chicago: University of Chicago Press, 1967).

10. It is fair to recall that Robinson lists no less than fifteen "rules of stipulation that we may usefully lay upon ourselves" (*Definition,* pp. 80-92), beginning by asserting that "the supreme rule of stipulation is surely to *stipulate as little as possible*" (p. 80), and concluding by admonishing that we should "remind ourselves to be responsible in stipulation" (p. 91). However, what is the justification of these rules? Robinson replies that "if they are justified [their justification] can only be . . . to lessen the disadvantages of stipulation" (p. 92). If so, I miss the sense of advocating a stipulative approach.

11. Ibid., p. 65.

12. Although it can convincingly be argued that it is not. See Michael Scriven,

"Definitions, Explanations and Theories," in *Minnesota Studies in the Philosophy of Science* (Minneapolis: University of Minnesota Press, 1958), 2:139-50.

13. For a full discussion, see, e.g., Arthur Pap, *Elements of Analytic Philosophy* (New York: Macmillan, 1949), chap. 14: "Theories of Truth."

14. See the discussion on "theory," chapter 1, section 5.

15. See Weldon's *The Vocabulary of Politics*, chap. 2, sects. 2, 3.

16. On contraries and contradictories, see chapter 7, section 1.

17. With regard to the notion of semantic field and related points see, more fully, my chapter in *Social Science Concepts*, esp. pp. 15-22, 51-54. The strong meaning of "semantics" to which I adhere was developed by Sapir and Whorf. See esp. Edward Sapir, *Language* (New York: Harcourt, Brace, 1921); and B.L. Whorf, *Language, Thought and Reality* (Cambridge, Mass.: MIT Press, 1956).

18. See G. Burdeau, *Méthode de la Science Politique* (Paris: Dalloz, 1959), pp. 121-23.

19. *System of Logic*, bk. IV, chap. IV, 6 (pp. 448 and 455, in 1898 ed.).

20. Justification is a lesser requirement than proof. However, a justification without any kind of proof is not much of a justification either.

21. *The Vocabulary of Politics*, p. 36.

22. See, e.g., S.I. Benn and R.S. Peters, *Social Principles and the Democratic State* (London: Allen & Unwin, 1959). Their contention is that all political arguments may be subsumed under a single moral heading whose constant criterion is "impartiality." It will be seen that I do not pursue this line of interpretation.

23. Autocracy is proposed as the best opposite of democracy in chapter 7, esp. section 5.

24. See chapter 3, section 6.

25. The fact is that along the rationalistic tradition we rarely come across theories of democracy. The rationalistic ideal, from Plato on, has been sophocracy or "noocracy," the aristocracy of the wise, and not irrational, unreasonable, and fickle democracy. In the Platonic approach, it is not the philosopher (he who loves knowledge, *sophía*) but the *philódoxos* (he who follows opinions, *doxai*) who can be *demóphilos*, that is, a supporter of democracy. Speaking in general, "reason" submits to Truth and not to will, to Knowledge and not to opinion, and its ideal is a definitive and coherent *ordo ordinatus* rather than an ever changing, unstable *ordo ordinans*.

26. In its extreme form this is the view set forth by A.J. Ayer, *Language, Truth and Logic*, 2d ed. (London: Gollancz, 1946), esp. chap. 6.

27. To be sure, value statements can be empirically true when they correctly report the actual value beliefs of the people by whom they are preferred. Likewise, value expressions may either be, among themselves, congruent or contradictory. The problem remains to give truth foundations to values as "principles of preference."

28. F.E. Oppenheim, *Moral Principles in Political Philosophy* (New York: Random House, 1968), p. 184. While Oppenheim opts for "value noncognitivism" to a greater extent than I would, his question, "Is it possible to demonstrate that certain basic principles of political ethics are objectively true or false?" (p. viii) is well discussed. For an emphasis, within logical positivism itself, on the role of reason in axiology, see E. Maynard Adams, "Empirical Verifiability Theory of Factual Meaning and Axiological Truth," in *The Language of Value*, ed. R. Lepley (New York: Columbia University Press, 1957), pp. 94ff. In general, a useful reader is W. Sellars and J. Hospers, eds.,

Readings in Ethical Theory (New York: Appleton-Century-Crofts, 1952). With specific reference to our subject, see the overview by A. Koch, "The Status of Values and Democratic Political Theory," *Ethics*, April 1958, pp. 166-85. That moral "subjectivism" is not the only viable position is the main thread of J.S. Fishkin, *Beyond Subjective Morality: Ethical Reasoning and Political Philosophy* (New Haven: Yale University Press, 1984). A major contemporary attack on ethical subjectivism is R.M. Unger, *Knowledge and Politics* (New York: Free Press, 1975). Unger's implausible conjecture is that shared objective values that emanate from human nature itself will emerge as "domination" is eradicated by a society of "organic groups."

29. The origin of the phrase is debated. To the best of my knowledge, the first to pronounce it was the French radical politician Ledru-Rollin, the father of universal suffrage in France.

30. The expression "value relativism" is here by necessity used in a broad, vague manner. For an extensive analysis of its various formulations, see A. Brecht, *Political Theory* (Princeton: Princeton University Press, 1959).

31. See chapter 11, section 2, but esp. chapter 12, and chapter 13 sections 5-7.

32. R. Wollheim, "Democracy," *Journal of the History of Ideas,* 19 (1958): 241.

10. Greek Democracy and Modern Democracy

It is clear that all the conditions of liberty have changed; the very word "liberty" does not have the same meaning in modern times as it had in ancient times. . . . It is always useful to study antiquity, but it is puerile and dangerous to imitate it.

— E. Laboulaye

10.1 *Homonymy, Not Homology*

The term *demokratía* was coined some twenty-four hundred years ago.[1] From then on, even though it was eclipsed for a very long interval, it has remained part of the political vocabulary. But in so long a lifetime "democracy" has naturally acquired diverse meanings, referring, as it has, to very different historical settings as well as to very different ideals. Thus, with the passing of time, both its denotative and connotative uses have changed. It would be strange if this were not so; and it is therefore surprising how little attention is paid to the fact that today's concept of democracy has only a very slight resemblance, if any, to the concept that was developed in the fifth century B.C. When we use the same word, we are easily misled into believing that we are referring to a same or similar thing. However, with regard to "democracy" this involves passing over more than two thousand years of change.

Ancient democracy was conceived in intrinsic, symbiotic relation with the *polis*. And the Greek *polis* was by no means the city-state that we are accustomed to call it—for it was not, in any sense, a "state." The *polis* was a city-community, a *koinonía*. Thucydides said it in three words: *ándres gar polis*—it is the men that are the polis. It is very revealing that *politeía* meant, in one, citizenship and the structure (form) of the *polis*. Thus, when we speak of the Greek system as a democratic state we are grossly inaccurate, both terminologically and conceptually.

"State" comes from the Latin past participle *status*, which as such simply means a condition, a situation or state of being (as in today's expression social status). Machiavelli was the first author to reify "state" as an impersonal entity and to employ the term in its modern political denotation — and this somewhat incidentally and sparingly. In Machiavelli's time political forms were still generally designated as either *regnum* or *civitas* (when republican). Subsequently, Hobbes favored the term "commonwealth"; and Bodin, who transformed the medieval *imperium* into "sovereignty" (the distinguishing characteristic, for us, of the state), did not use the word state either. The word gained slow political acceptance, I suggest, because there was no need for it unless and until *Herrschaft* (domination) acquired some kind of impersonal and distant fixity. If all there was, was a king and his court, *regnum* (kingdom) was fitting. Similarly, if all there was, were magistrates walking across the streets and living next door, *civitas* was adequate. The only consistent and persistent use of "the state" in the seventeenth century was, in the wake of Botero's *Ragion di Stato* of 1589, in the literature on the reason of state; and this was the case because that literature did attend to a reified entity: the survival imperative (and capability) of any and all body politic.[2] Be that as it may, as "state" gained currency as a political term it became less and less coextensive with *res publica* (the politically organized society as a whole) and more and more narrowly identified with the structures of command (authority, power, coercion) that impinge upon society.[3]

Thus, had the Greeks conceived of a state as we conceive it, the notion of a "democratic state" would have seemed to them a contradiction in terms. What characterized the democracy of the ancients was precisely that it was *stateless* — even more stateless, we may say, than any other possible form of the *polis*. Hence, ancient democracies cannot teach us anything about building a democratic state and about conducting a democratic system that covers not merely a small city but a large expanse of territory inhabited by a vast collectivity. Nor is this all. The difference between ancient and modern democracies is not simply one of geographic and demographic dimensions requiring completely different solutions but also one of ends and values.

Modern men want another democracy, in the sense that their ideal of democracy is not at all the same as that of the Greeks. It would be strange, indeed, if this were not so. In more than two thousand intervening years Western civilization has enriched, modified, and articulated its value goals. It has experienced Christianity, humanism, the Reformation, a "natural rights" conception of natural law, and liberalism. How can we possibly think that when we advocate democracy today, we are pursuing the same aims and ideals as the Greeks? How can it escape us that democracy, for us, embodies values of which the Greeks were not and could not have been aware? Yet a considerable literature currently recalls the Greek experiment as if it were a lost and somewhat recuperable paradise. The matter must be looked into.

10.2   *Direct or* Polis *Democracy*

Saying that ancient democracy was the counterpart of the *polis* is also to say that it was a "direct democracy"; and we actually have no current meaningful experience with a direct democracy of the Greek kind. All our democracies are indirect; that is, they are representative democracies in which we are governed by representatives, not by ourselves.

Of course, we must not take the notion of direct democracy (and of self-government) too literally and assume that in the ancient city the rulers and the ruled were identical. Not even Cleon, who was an advanced demagogue for his time, ever went so far as to maintain that the system was perfectly expressed and only amounted to the whole body of the *demos* in the assembly. Leadership existed even then, and officials were chosen by lot or elected to fulfill certain functions. Yet, within the untidiness of all human affairs, the democracy of antiquity was undoubtedly the closest possible approximation to a literal democracy in which governors and governed stood side by side and dealt with each other face to face. Regardless of how we appraise the intensity of self-government in the *polis*,[4] in any case the difference between direct and indirect democracy is radical. In this juxtaposition, direct democracy affords continuous participation of the people in the direct *exercise* of power, whereas indirect democracy largely amounts to a system of *limitation* and *control* of power. In present democracies, there are those who govern and those who are governed; there is the state, on one side, and the citizens, on the other; there are those who deal with politics professionally and those who forget about it, except at rare intervals. In ancient democracies, instead, these differentations had very little meaning.

Two questions arise: Is direct democracy preferable? Is it still possible?[5] From a logical vantage point we should start with the question of its possibility, for if we discovered that, today, direct democracy is impossible, it would be pointless to discuss its desirability. But we are not that logical. Besides, there is also desire or nostalgia for the impossible. So, is the recurrent longing for the classical world justified?

The preferability of direct democracy is one of those questions that rationalizations would answer in one way, and experience answers in another. In principle it can well be held that he who exercises power himself should be better off than he who delegates it to someone else, and that a system based on participation is safer or more fulfilling than one based on representation. But history attests that the Greek democracies and the medieval communes that somehow replicated them had a turbulent as well as ephemeral existence. This evidence is highly significant because in most if not all respects the *polis* was an ideal laboratory for an experiment in the application of pure and simple democratic principles. Not only were the ancient cities very small,[6] but the citizens lived symbiotically with their city, being tied to it, as it were, by a common destiny of life and death. Despite these optimum conditions, democracy based on direct participation turned out to be very fragile even in its unreproducible testing ground: the compact community unified by a converging religious, moral, and political *ethos* that was the *polis.*

Let us not forget that Aristotle, who was a realistic observer and witness of the events that led to the downfall of the liberties of antiquity, placed democracy in the class of the corrupted forms of *politeía.* While Pericles, in the famous funeral oration recounted by Thucydides, called democracy a "government [in favor] of the many,"[7] Aristotle called it "a government of the poor";[8] and this shift of focus does not result from the inference that the many are not likely to be the wealthy. Aristotle's *demos* was not everybody, but a section of the whole: the social stratum of the poor. Aristotle was thus led to assert that even if the wealthy were a majority, they would still produce an oligarchy, whereas a government of the poor, even if a government of the few, was a democracy.[9] Does this mean that Aristotle entertained a socioeconomic understanding of democracy? The technical point is that Aristotle's typology of political forms consists of three basic categories (government of the one, the few, the many) each admitting two possibilities (monarchy or tyranny, aristocracy or oligarchy, *politeía* or democracy). His six classes thus require two criteria: the number of rulers, and other-regarding versus self-serving interests. So, Aristotle had to inject the poor into the matter in order to obtain the "bad many" (democracy), just as he had to enter the rich in order to obtain the "bad few" (oligarchy). Technicalities aside, the full significance of Aristotle's conception is that it reflects the parabola of Greek democracy. In the fourth century B.C. cleavage in the *polis* had become extreme. Either the rich governed in their own interest or the poor governed in theirs (and this was the democracy that Aristotle had before him). The fact that he defined democracy as a government of the poor for their own advantage impresses us by its topical flavor. Actually, Aristotle said what he saw: the breaking up of Greek democracy by the class struggle. And there is nothing surprising in that outcome.

Real self-government, as the Greeks practiced it, required the citizen's devoting himself completely to the public service. Governing oneself meant spending one's life governing. "The citizen . . . gave himself to the State totally; he gave his blood in war; his time in peace; he was not free to put aside public affairs to take care of his own . . . on the contrary, he had to neglect them to work for the good of the city."[10] The degree of involvement in politics required by the formula was so absorbing that a profound imbalance was created among the functions of social life. Political hypertrophy brought about economic atrophy: The more perfect their democracy became, the poorer the citizens became. The vicious circle was thus entered of seeking a political solution to economic need: In order to make up for the insufficient production of wealth, one had to confiscate wealth. It would thus seem that the democracy of antiquity was fated to be destroyed in the class struggle between rich and poor because it produced a political animal at the detriment of *homo oeconomicus*. The Greek experience generated a "total citizen" that overreached himself.

The consideration that suggests itself on the basis of the foregoing is that indirect systems of government have advantages that we are too inclined to underrate. For one thing, a multi-stage and multi-filtered process of political decision making contains, precisely by virtue of its indirectness, precautions and restraints that directness cannot obtain. Second, direct democracy entails zero-sum politics, whereas indirect democracy allows for positive-sum politics. Third, in ancient democracy the war between rich and poor was inevitable, growing, as it did, out of a functional imbalance of the system; whereas today warlike politics is not inevitable, for no such imbalance subsists.[11]

The first point can be highlighted by noting that Greek democracy was a most simple and, in this sense, primitive construction: It essentially consisted of "voice"; it did not permit or even conceive "exit"; and it eminently and disastrously lacked filters and safety valves. In particular, the Greek system was unable to screen trivial noises from important signals, immediate whims from long-run needs. The second point, zero-sum politics, is by now a familiar one. The third point requires, instead, some enlargement. Aristotle remarked that a man who has to work in order to live cannot be a citizen. And Rousseau, after having recalled that among the Greeks "the slaves did the work" (for "the chief occupation [of the people] was their own freedom") exclaimed: "What! Freedom cannot stand without leaning on servitude? Perhaps. The two extremes touch each other."[12] Today, such extremes no longer touch each other. Indeed, the affluent society often carries with it the conviction that humankind has reached the stage in which we are all in the process of being *freed from* work. If so, should we not reverse Aristotle's dictum? Should we not say that we can now be, without economic loss, full-time citizens? Well, no. My sense is that no work produces no affluence and that poor work leaves us in poverty. Nor can we exclude that the hypertrophy of politics that is again in demand might not re-create the imbalance that fated the democracy of the ancients. When everything is loaded on politics, other activities (functions) inevitably become unloaded; and there is little evidence, to date, that any of this reloading is for the better.[13]

There remains the question of feasibility. Since I have already discussed it at length at many points of the book, let me simply recall that direct, real self-government cannot be presumed; it requires the actual presence and participation of the people concerned. It is impossible to have direct democracy at a distance and meaningful self-government among absentees. The gist is that the greater the number of people involved, the less effective is their participation—and this to a vanishing point.[14] Thus, when vast territories and entire nations are involved, direct democracy becomes an unusable formula. I have also and concurrently held that an electronic, "referendum democracy," while technically feasible, would be disastrous and, in all likelihood, suicidal.[15]

In conclusion, I would say that democracy based on personal participation is possible only under certain conditions; and, correspondingly, that when these conditions do not exist, representative democracy is the only type possible. The two systems are not alternatives to be chosen between on the basis of personal likings. Certainly, as I have stressed from the outset, democracy in the social sense is built on a network of small communities and is based on the vitality of participating groups. However, all of this remains in daily sufferance unless it is guaranteed by a "sovereign democracy" that is very definitely *not* a direct democracy. And we are only deluding ourselves if we consider referenda and popular initiatives of legislation as modern equivalents and substitutes of direct democracy. Even if the so-called forms of direct integration of representative democracy functioned as their early advocates had hoped,[16] they certainly would not bring about a "semi-direct" democracy. The matter admits to degrees but is not amenable to half-and-half solutions.[17]

When we declare, then, that there are two types of democracy, one based on the direct exercise of political power and the other on the control and limitation of power, we are not discussing interchangeable systems but the modern large-scale solution of a problem left unsolved by the ancients. Should we say that in order to realize democracy at all, modern man has had to be satisfied with less democracy? Perhaps. But I would rather say that although modern man expects less of "literal democracy," i.e., of popular sovereignty, he actually asks infinitely more of "liberal democracy," which is the other thing that he calls democracy. For the difference between the two systems is chiefly one of *ideals*. Participation in the exercise of power does not imply individual liberty. My liberty vis-à-vis state power cannot be derived from the infinitesimal portion of that power by means of which I concur, with innumerable others, in the creation of the rules to which I shall be subject. So, the limitation and control of power that our liberal democracies provide is not a lesser achievement vis-à-vis Greek democracy. For we have largely solved a problem that the Greeks did not have or did not face: providing a secure freedom for every individual.

10.3   *Individualism and Freedom: Old and New*

There is as much difference between the ancient and the modern conceptions of democracy as between the ancient and modern conceptions of freedom. This is hardly a piercing insight, and yet the respective characteristics of the modern and the classical notions of liberty are not easily pinpointed. The debate was opened in 1819 by Benjamin Constant.[18] Within his line of argument—followed, among others, by Tocqueville and Laboulaye—the extreme position was perhaps the one expressed by Fustel de Coulanges: "The belief that in the ancient cities man enjoyed liberty is one of the strangest errors one can commit. He did not have the remotest idea of it. . . . Having political rights, voting, nominating magistrates, being able to be appointed archon— that is what was called liberty; but men were not less slaves of the State for all that."[19] In essence: Measured by modern standards, men of antiquity were not free (vis-à-vis their polity) according to our notion of individual freedom. The question thus turns on how *individual liberty* is to be conceived and understood. That individual liberty was unknown to the Greeks is, probably, one of those assertions that will never cease to be challenged, especially on the ground that Greek, and particularly Athenian, civilization was a multiform unfolding of individual vitality, of the richness of an individualistic spirit. Nonetheless, between this "individualistic spirit" and the respect for the individual as-a-person that Constant had in mind, there is a wealth of difference.

To the *polites* the distinction between public and private spheres was unknown and would have been unintelligible. As Werner Jaeger put it: "A purely private moral code without reference to the State was inconceivable to the Greeks. We must forget our idea that each individual's acts are ruled by his conscience."[20] Hannah Arendt went deeper: "Free will . . . [is] a faculty virtually unknown to classical antiquity. . . . In Greek as well as Roman antiquity freedom was an exclusively political concept."[21] To be sure, a "political concept" in the Greek sense of being *polis* located and *polis* derived— not in the sense in which we speak today of political freedom as, indeed, an *anti-polis* freedom (a freedom *from* political constraints). But in order to firm up these points it is well to go back to the vocabulary of the ancients.

When Aristotle defined man as a political animal, he intended (in our present-day vocabulary) that man was part and parcel of his specific social whole, that he was society embedded. Conversely, what Aristotle did not intend was man conceived as an individual characterized by, and entitled to, a private self, to being himself. For the Greeks, "man" and "citizen" meant exactly the same, just as participating in the life of the *polis,* of their city, meant "to live." This is not to say, of course, that the *polites* did not enjoy individual liberty in the sense of a private space existing de facto. But the meaning and value that this notion had is exactly revealed by the meaning of the Latin *privatus* and its Greek equivalent, *ídion*. The Latin *privatus,* i.e., private, means "deprived" (from the verb *privare,* to deprive), and the term was used to connote an existence that was incomplete and defective in relation to the community. The Greek *ídion* (private), in contrast to *koinón* (the common element), conveys the sense of privation and lack even more strongly. Correspondingly, *idiótes* was a pejorative term, meaning he who was not *polítes*—a non-citizen and therefore a vulgar, unworthy, ignorant man who was concerned only with himself.[22]

The difference that Constant adressed was, then, that the Greeks did not entertain a positive notion of the individual; they did not, in short, conceive the individual *as a person.*[23] Jellinek well summarized the point: "In ancient times man was never definitely recognized as a person. . . . Only the nineteenth century has scored a general victory with the principle: 'man is a person.' "[24] The ancients did not, and could not, recognize the individual as a person and, concurrently, as a "private self" entitled to respect, for the obvious reason that this conception came with Christianity and was subsequently developed by the Renaissance,[25] by Protestantism, and by the modern school of natural law.[26] What the Greek individualistic spirit lacked, then, was the notion of a *legitimate* private space conceived as the moral as well as the juridical projection of the single human person. Therefore, the Greek experience of political freedom did not and could not signify an individual liberty based on *personal rights.* This is what Constant and the others meant.[27] When they denied that the Greeks entertained the idea of individual liberty, they were saying that the ancients did not pay heed to the *value* expressed by respect for the individual as a person, a notion that has since gained concrete safeguards from the rule of law, "juridical defense,"[28] and the declarations of rights.

The fact that an impassioned individualistic impetus flourished throughout Athenian democracy does not therefore contradict the assertion that the individual was actually undefended and remained at the mercy of the collective body.[29] That democracy did not respect the individual; rather, it tended to suspect him. Distrustful of outstanding individuals, fickle in its praise, pitiless in its persecution, it was a city in which ostracism was a precautionary, not a punitive, measure—a punishment for no crime. It was a democracy from which Ermodore of Ephesus was banished because one citizen was not permitted to be better than the others. In such a system the individual's position was precarious because, as Laboulaye observed, "the only guarantee for the citizen was his part of sovereignty," and this explains, he added, "how it happens that in Greece and Rome it was possible to pass overnight from the greatest liberty to the severest slavery."[30]

Why is it, then, that the difference between modern liberty and ancient freedom is often so ill perceived? One of the reasons is that many authors seldom make clear which Greeks and which period they are talking about. In the first place, Athens is not Sparta—it is its antithesis. As Plutarch told us: "In Athens each person could live as he pleased, in Sparta no one could."[31] In the second place, if in talking about the Greek vicissitudes we consider only Athens, and only Periclean Athens, we can easily prove anything we wish;[32] for the age of Pericles was one of those extraordinary and felicitous moments of history in which a harmony springs from a fortuitous combination of elements and events. But when we assert that the individual citizen of the *polis* did not enjoy the independence and security that we consider freedom, we are basing our judgment, as is only proper, on the entire parable of all the Greek democracies. I have said democracies (in the plural); but here a further caution is needed for we must remember that, paradoxically, Rousseau and his school idealized and cherished the Spartans and the Romans far more than the Athenians.[33]

To bring out the full implications of the direct type of Greek democracy, let its definition be: Democracy was that system of government (city) in which decisions were made collectively. This entails that in the classical formula of democracy the community allows no margin of independence and no sphere of protection to the single individual, whom it absorbs completely. The *polis* is sovereign in the sense that the individuals that compose it are completely subject to it. Hobbes understood it well: "The Athenians and Romans were free; that is, free commonwealths: not that any particular men had the liberty to resist their own representative but that their representative had the liberty to resist or invade other people."[34] A free city is one thing; free citizens, quite another. And the passage from the former to the latter does not occur so long as it is the *polis* that defines the *polites*. When Greeks and Romans alike said "man," they intended the citizen of his *civitas*. Therefore, the basic difference between the ancient and modern conceptions of freedom lies precisely in that we believe that a man is *more* than a citizen of a state. In our conception, a human being cannot be reduced to his or her citizenness. For us, a man is not merely a member of a collective *plenum*. From this it follows that our problems cannot be solved by a system that provides only that the exercise of power be collective. Modern democracy is meant to protect the freedom of the individual *as a person*—a freedom that cannot be entrusted, as Constant said, to the "subjection of the individual to the power of the whole."[35]

In order to grasp at the Greek idea of democracy, we must erase from our mental picture of it everything that was added later. This mental experiment is not easily done. Yet it is the only sure way of understanding the past as it really was. It really was, I submit, a past that we would not want back at all. When all the subtractions required by our mental experiment are made, we are left with an ethico-political idea of liberty that can mean very little, if anything, to us. Let us not get lost in minor and dubious distinctions, as when we discuss whether the ancients had political and not civil liberties, or vice versa. The essence is, very simply, that their ideas of civil, political, juridical, individual, and any other liberty were not the same as ours. Nor could it be otherwise, since we are separated from the ancients by value acquisition of which they were not aware.

10.4   The Modern Idea and Ideal

One reason that helps us lose the sense of historical distance springs from the careless habit of carelessly modernizing the vocabulary. Thus, the Greek *polis* is turned into "state," *politeía* into "constitution" (an equally objectionable and misleading translation), and, coming to the point, the present-day popularity of "democracy" leads us to forget, or at least bypass, the fact that for more than two thousand years the term democracy had practically disappeared from usage[36] and had entirely lost any laudatory connotation. Let Thomas Aquinas stand, on the point, for all: "When indeed a wicked regime [*iniquum regimen*] is carried out by the many [*per multos*], it is called democracy."[37] During this long period, Westerners spoke of republic; and to say *res publica* is not the same as to say democracy.

Semantically speaking, *res publica* expresses the idea of a thing belonging to everybody, or of the affairs of everybody—an idea that departs quite substantially from the one of a power belonging to the people. *Demokratía* lends itself (as in Aristotle) to being interpreted as the power of a part (opposing another), whereas *res publica* does not; and while the former term refers to a definite subject (the people), the latter is suggestive of the general interest and the common good.[38] Historically speaking, moreover, the two concepts had parted company to such a degree that the meaning of "republic" had become the very antithesis of that of democracy.

In 1795 Kant severely criticized those who had begun to confuse the republican constitution with the democratic, observing that as far as the *forma regiminis* is concerned, every government is "republican or despotic" and that democracy, in the proper sense of the word, "is necessarily a despotism."[39] We should not assume that in linking democracy with despotism he was reacting against the excesses of the French Revolution. Kant had welcomed the events of 1789; besides, the identification of democracy with despotism was an accepted notion of the time. Actually, Kant was in no way original in his blunt rejection of democracy as being a form of tyrannical rule. Madison and Hamilton, thousands of miles from Koenigsberg and in a far different context, did not think differently from Kant on the subject. Madison always said "representative republic" and never "democracy" because for him the latter meant the direct democracy of antiquity, that is, "a society consisting of a small number of citizens who assemble and administer the government in person." And Madison too was expressing a common judgment when he wrote that "democracies have ever been spectacles of turbulence and contention; have ever been found incompatible with personal security or the rights of property; and have in general been as short in their lives as they have been violent in their deaths."[40] The Philadelphia Assembly was not thinking in terms of a democracy either, and what was to become the constitution (properly called) of the first modern democracy was considered by its framers to be a republican, not a democratic, constitution.[41] Even the French Revolution had a republic as its ideal, and although in those turbulent years it also pressed for a democracy—the democracy that became known as Jacobin democracy— this was a secondary aim that was cloaked under the name *république*.[42] Only Robespierre used the word democracy, and then only at the end, in his speech to the Convention on 5 February 1794, thereby ensuring its bad reputation (at least in Europe) for another half-century.[43]

The fact is, then, that when we superimpose "democracy" on "republic," we are creating a false historical continuity that keeps us from realizing that, in adopting "republic," Western civilization had settled for an ideal more moderate and prudent than democracy; a mixed ideal, so to speak, of the political optimum that discards the *thing of somebody* (no matter whether the one or the demos) in favor of the *thing of nobody*. So, a careless handling of terminology hides the completeness of the break between antiquity's attempt at democracy and its modern reincarnation, and keeps us from asking what deserves asking: How was it possible for an ideal that (as we well know) can be so deeply inspiring to be in eclipse for so long a period of history?

If, as I believe, the history of language reflects history *tout court,* the oblivion into which the term democracy fell is highly significant. It testifies eloquently, in itself, that the collapse of the ancient democracies was as final as it was memorable. This suggests, in turn, that for the word again to come into use, something new had to come into existence. Although the word is Greek, the thing that we are now indicating by it originated outside of Greece, and on premises that the alleged "liberal temper" of Greek politics completely ignored.[44] Above all, modern democracies are related to, and conditioned by, the discovery that dissent, diversity, and "parts" (the parts which became parties) are not incompatible with social order and the well-being of the body politic.[45] The ideal genesis of our democracies is in the principle that difference, not uniformity, is the leaven and the nourishment of states—a point of view that gained ground in the wake of the Reformation after the seventeenth century. We have to be vague here because it is extremely difficult, if not impossible, to ascribe this new conception of life to a particular thinker, event, or movement. The maturation of this approach was slow and tortuous; and, as is often the case in history, the mental grasp of what was being achieved sluggishly limped after reality.

Certainly this new understanding of the good life came in the wake of the Reformation. In particular, the experience of the Puritan sects marked an important step in this process, but not for the reasons that are often given—such as that the Puritans championed freedom of conscience and opinion. In fact, they championed the freedom of *their* conscience and were, in all other matters, no less intolerant than their foes. Plamenatz made the point nicely:

> The first champions of liberty of conscience were neither ardent reformers nor ardent Catholics. They were mostly quiet men. . . . Both Catholics and Protestants asserted it against the state and against all churches except their own. Where they were a minority they often found it expedient (whatever their mental reservations) to claim it for everyone. . . . There is nothing inherently liberal or equalitarian about Protestantism as such, about the mere claim to defy authority for conscience sake. For what we claim for ourselves we may deny to others.[46]

The importance of the Puritan experience essentially resided in the fact that it encouraged the depoliticizing of society by breaking the tie between the spheres of God and Caesar, thereby shifting the center of gravity of human life to voluntary associations independent of the state, in the sense that the internal bond among the associates became stronger than that which linked them with the body politic as a whole. Having granted this, it does not follow that Puritanism was the decisive and primary agent in the process of creating the liberal-democratic *Weltanschauung*. In this regard, the contribution of the Puritans has been overemphasized.[47] Indeed, "to the majority of seventeenth-century Puritans, both English and Americans, 'democracy' and 'liberty' were despicable."[48] However, what is important is not to discover who was the originator (assuming there was one) but to understand the importance and the novelty of the event. By and large, until the seventeenth century diversity was considered a source of discord and disorder causing the downfall of states, and unanimity was regarded as the necessary foundation of any polity. From then on, the opposite attitude gradually took hold, and it was unanimity that came to be viewed with suspicion. It is through this revolutionary reversal of perspective that the civilization we call "liberal" has been built piecemeal, and it is by this route that we reach present-day democracy. Ancient empires, autocracies, despotisms, old and new tyrannies, all are monochromatic worlds,[49] while democracy is multicolored. But it is *liberal* democracy, not ancient democracy, that is based on dissent and diversity. It is we, not the Greeks, who have discovered how to build a political system on a *concordia discors,* on a dissenting consensus.

As we pass from the germination of the ideal to its realization, it is only about the middle of the nineteenth century that popular sovereignty begins to materialize as a positive and constructive element of the political process. This, too, we should note, is a novelty. With all due respect to nostalgic reconstructions, what really happened in Athens, as well as in Megara, Samos, Messene, Miletus, Syracuse—to name just a few eloquent cases—has been reported by those who were there and is indeed different from what ex post facto idealizers of a Golden Age contend. With the passing of time, "popular power" in Greek society functioned increasingly as a steamroller, since whatever the crowd approved became law, with no limits on their exercise of an unruly, limitless power.[50] Bryce could thus legitimately comment: "Impatient of restraints, even such restraints as they had by law imposed upon themselves, they [the people] ruled as a despot ruler exemplifying the maxim that no one is good enough to be trusted with absolute power."[51] The modern notion of popular power, as it was empowered and structured by constitutionalism, is completely different,[52] and it is by virtue of this difference that our democracies have long beaten, in longevity, the ones of antiquity. If popular sovereignty has risen once again, after its long demise, it is because in the decision-making processes of the liberal-democratic systems the purely democratic element is the most noticeable, but it is by no means the sole factor at play.[53]

10.5   A Reversal of Perspectives

I have stressed that modern democracy does not simply consist of the Greek ideal plus some subsequent additions. But how is it that the discontinuity between ancient democracy and ours so easily escapes us? One of the reasons is that, as a result of saying, for purposes of brevity, *only* "democracy," we forget or subordinate what we have left unsaid; democracy (the expressed word) thus becomes dominant, and liberalism (the implied concept) subordinate. This is the exact upending of the truth. For no matter how much a short-range historical perspective can magnify what is merely close to us, the present-day progress of democracy over liberalism is slight compared to the progress made by modern liberalism over ancient democracy. However little we are aware of it, the democracy that we believe in, and practice, is liberal democracy.

We may put it this way: If, according to the Greek criterion of freedom, the Greeks were free, by the same token we certainly would not be. The *polites* was subordinate to the *polis,* the *civis* lived for the *civitas*—not the other way around. Considering the circumstances, this made perfect sense. The citizen and the city were, at the time, inextricably tied together by commonality of destiny, by life-and-death concerns. When a city was conquered, its inhabiants were either sold as slaves or passed by sword. Let us now make the necesary substitutions. The square where the *demos* gathered has disappeared, and the governing carried on by the people themselves (six thousand at most) has been replaced by a governing state. Under these new conditions, the citizen that lives for his city becomes a subject that *lives for the state.* The precept now is that the citizen is made for the state, not the state for the citizen. And this is exactly the formula of the polities in which there is neither democracy nor freedom, the formula used today to justify absolute governments. Nor is this a strange turnaround. If a principle that was once valid for a democracy is now used by tyrannies, this is so because the real world has made a full turn.

In the city-communities of antiquity, liberty was not expressed through opposition to state power—for there was no state—but through participation in the collective exercise of power. But once we have a state that is distinct from, and ordained over, society, the problem is reversed, and a power *of* the people can only be a power taken away *from* the state. Whatever respect we have for the individual-as-person (and even if we attach very little value to it), the fact remains that the microdemocracy of antiquity was not faced with the problem of the relation between citizens and state, whereas modern macrodemocracy is. The Greeks were able to be free, in their own way, by starting from the *polis* to reach the *polites.* But this is not the case for us. When the *polis* is supplanted by a megapolis, we can remain free only if we start from the citizen, only if the state is derived from the citizen. Hence, to call for the "freedom of antiquity" is only to call, if inadvertently, for unfreedom.

It is important, then, to realize that when we indicate a free political system by the word democracy, we are using this one term for the sake of brevity, and that shorthands give rise to ominous simplifications and omissions. It is but a small step from abbreviation as a useful expedient to abbreviation as a cancellation of twenty-five centuries of trials, corrections, and innovations. In daily practice, "democracy" will do; in the theory of democracy, it will not do. The theory indeed demands that the blanks be filled, that is, that we make again *explicit* everything that—in saying "democracy" only—remains *implicit*. It does make little sense for us to give our concept of democracy the meaning it had for the Greeks in the fifth century B.C. At least, it makes little sense unless and until the differences between *ante-liberal* democracy and *liberal-democracy* are clearly and adequately drawn.

Notes

1. Herodotus is often held to have been the first to say "democracy" (see *History,* bk. III, 80-83). Actually the term does not appear in his text but in its translations. But we do find in Herodotus a *demos*-commanded or *many*-commanded polity neatly contrasted to monarchy and oligarchy. It is also the case that Herodotus associates the rule of the *demos* to *isonomía,* equal law (see chapter 12, n. 14, herein); an association that does remain preponderant, throughout the Greek experience, with respect to that between *demokratia* and *eleuthería* (freedom).

2. On the reason of state, the classic work is F. Meinecke, *Die Idee der Staatsräson in der neueren Geschichte* (München-Berlin, 1924). In France the modern use of "state" was especially divulged via the translation of Pufendorf, that is, because Barbeyrac chose to translate *civitas* as *état.* Such are the vagaries of history. Interestingly, "State" is not an entry in the *Encyclopédie* of Diderot and d'Alembert. On Machiavelli's *stato,* see chapter 3, n. 2, herein. An excellent general overview is N. Matteucci, "Stato," in *Enciclopedia del Novecento* (Roma: Instituto Enciclopedia Italiana, 1984), 7:93-113.

3. Society comes to us from the Latin *socius,* which means companion, associate. It can be said, therefore, that while society "associates" people, the state "stands upon" a people.

4. For how self-government relates to intensity, see chapter 4, section 3. The specificity of the Greek experience resides, however, in its face-to-face nature, as well pointed out by P. Laslett, "The Face to Face Society," in *Philosophy, Politics, and Society,* ed. P. Laslett (Oxford: Blackwell, 1956).

5. It should be understood that in this chapter "direct democracy" is always referred to its ancient Greek formulation. Other meanings have been discussed in chapter 4, section 3, and chapter 5, sections 6-7. Direct democracy is also spoken of as "immediate" (by Max Weber), "pure" (e.g., by Madison), "simple" (by Paine).

6. The estimates are controversial, but it is generally believed that the male population of the city of Athens at the time of Pericles did not number more than 45,000 free adult citizens, probably around 40,000. See W. Warde Fowler, *The City-State of the Greeks and Romans* (London: Macmillan, 1952), p. 167. See also the more elaborate counts by Alfred E. Zimmern, *The Greek Commonwealth* (Oxford, 1911), pp. 169-74.

7. Thucydides, *The History of the Peloponnesian War,* trans. R. Crawley (New York: Dutton, 1950), p. 123.

8. See *Politics,* esp. 1279, 1280. Plato too had remarked in passing that "democracy comes into being after the poor have conquered their opponents" (*Republic,* VIII, 557). Remember also Callicles' remark in *Gorgias,* 483: "The makers of laws are the majority who are weak; and they make laws and distribute praises and censures with a view to themselves and to their own interests" (Jowett's trans.).

9. See *Politics*, 1290. That the few may be poor, and the many rich, is here exemplified with reference to Colophon. Elsewhere Aristotle states, however, that "in a democracy the poor have more power than the rich, because there are more of them" (*Politics*, 1317b).

10. N.D. Fustel de Coulanges, *La Cité Antique* (Paris, 1878), p. 396. Chap. 11 of bk. 4 affords a vivid description of the "amount of work that this democracy exacted from its people."

11. For the distinction between peacelike and warlike politics, see chapter 3, section 2; for positive-sum and zero-sum politics, see chapter 8, esp. section 3.

12. *Contrat Social*, III, 15. Rousseau's own solution was in the recommendation that the city should be "quite small." It was on this essential condition that the citizen could have looked after his own freedom and have time for the rest, without falling into the "unhappy position where one cannot preserve his own freedom except at the expense of that of others, and where the citizen can be perfectly free only when the slave is extremely slave."

13. Reference is made to the discussion on "participationism" in chapter 5, sections 6-7, where other drawbacks are also spelled out.

14. See esp. chapter 4, section 3; chapter 5, section 6; and chapter 8, section 6.

15. See chapter 5, section 7.

16. See, e.g., G. Rensi, *La Democrazia Diretta* (Roma, 1926). Rensi distinguished between "pure" democracy (the Greek one) and "modern direct democracy," meaning by it a democracy operating on the basis of referendums, popular initiatives, and popular revisions of legislation.

17. See, *contra*, M. Duverger, *Droit Constitutionnel et Institutions Politiques* (Paris: Presses Universitaires de France, 1955), p. 226, who includes "semi-direct" democracy in his classification.

18. In a famous speech delivered at the Atheneum of Paris: *De la Liberté des Anciens Comparée à celle des Modernes*. See, in general, A. Zanfarino, *La Libertà dei Moderni nel Costituzionalismo di Benjamin Constant* (Milano: Giuffré, 1961). For an extensive interpretation of this distinction, see Stephen Holmes, *Benjamin Constant and the Making of Modern Liberalism* (New Haven: Yale University Press, 1984), chaps. 1 and 2.

19. *La Cité Antique*, p. 269, and passim, bk. III, chap. 18. Fustel's straight denial was directed at Grote's *History of Greece* (1856), which had described the Greek city as a bulwark of individual liberty. In the German theory of the state, Fustel's position was followed by Stahl, Von Mohl, and Bluntschli, and criticized by Jellineck. In Italy G. de Ruggiero followed Jellineck (*Storia del Liberalismo Europeo* [Bari: Laterza, 1925], p. 177), while Croce, in reevaluating Constant, remarked that the problem "is singularly minimized or rendered altogether insignificant by the treatment of the difference between ancient and modern freedom which is made by Jellinek in his *Allgemeine Staatslehre*." B. Croce, *Etica e Politica* (Bari: Laterza, 1943), p. 296.

20. *Paideia: The Ideals of Greek Culture*, trans. Gilbert Highet (New York: Oxford University Press, 1946), 1:326.

21. H. Arendt, *Between Past and Future* (New York: Meridian, 1963), p. 157.

22. It is very telling, therefore, that while the original derogatory connotation of *idiótes* has remained in our word "idiot," the association with "private" has been completely severed.

23. "Person" is Kant's wording in his practical (moral) imperatives. While the notion of person becomes related to the one of individual human being as early as the thirteenth century (radically detaching itself from the Latin *persona*), Kant's principle that persons are not to be treated as "means" but equally as "ends in themselves" renders better than any other, I submit, the respect for the individual that Western civilization has come to cherish.

24. *Dottrina Generale dello Stato* (Italian trans., Milano, 1921), 1:573-74. Jellinek reaches this conclusion despite his previous criticism of Fustel de Coulanges (see n. 19 above).

25. Jacob Burckhardt, *The Civilization of the Renaissance in Italy* (1860; trans., London: Phaidon Press, 1955), ascribes "individualism" to the Italian Renaissance to a point of overstatement. Reinhold Niebuhr makes the point as follows: "If Protestantism represents the final heightening of the idea of individuality within the terms of the Christian religion, the Renaissance is the real cradle of . . . the autonomous individual. . . . Ostensibly Renaissance thought is a revival of classicism. . . . Yet classic thought has no such passion for the individual as the Renaissance betrays. The fact is that the Renaissance uses an idea which could have grown only upon the soil of Christianity. It transplants this idea to the soil of classic rationalism to produce a new concept of individual autonomy, which is known in neither classicism nor Christianity." *The Nature and Destiny of Man* (New York: Scribner's, 1941), 1:61.

26. The modern, let it be emphasized, not the former ones. As A. Passerin d'Entrèves, *Natural Law* (London: Hutchinson's, 1951), notes sharply: "Except for the name, the medieval and the modern notions of natural law have little in common" (p. 9). In effect, medieval "organicism" largely canceled the New Testament's emphasis on the individual's supreme worth, as well shown by W. Ullmann, *The Individual and Society in the Middle Ages* (Baltimore: Johns Hopkins University Press, 1966).

27. On a slightly different tack Isaiah Berlin makes the point as follows: "There seems to be scarcely any discussion of individual liberty as a conscious political ideal (as opposed to its actual existence) in the ancient world . . . the notion of individual rights was absent from the legal conceptions of the Romans and Greeks." *Four Essays on Liberty* (London: Oxford University Press, 1969), p. 129.

28. This is Mosca's *difesa giuridica*. C.J. Friedrich finds it a "quaint" expression for "rule of law" (in the 1946 ed. of *Constitutional Government and Democracy* [Boston: Ginn], p. 592). However, as I note later (chapter 11, section 7), the reason for using different labels is that Mosca did not have in mind the Anglo-Saxon rule of law.

29. For this reason, Burckhardt remarked (quoting Böckh), "The *polis* must have made its people unhappy." It encouraged the individual "to bring out to the utmost the potential of his personality in order to demand later its most complete renouncement. In the entire history of the world," Burckhardt concluded, "it is difficult to find another nation which paid so dearly for its actions as the Greek *polis*. In fact, along with their high cultural development the Greeks must have also developed the sensitivity to realize the sufferings that they inflicted upon each other." *La Civiltà Greca* (Italian trans., Firenze: Sansoni, 1955), 1:339-40.

30. *L'Etat et ses Limites* (Paris, 1871), p. 108.

31. Cit. in M. Pohlenz, *Griechische Freiheit* (Heidelberg: Quelle & Meyer, 1955), p. 28.

32. Pohlenz makes reference to Pericles' epitaph when he asserts that "in every

respect the description of Pericles marks the reverse of the Spartan kosmos. The latter is dominated by coercion, and the individual is completely claimed by the state. In Athens there reigns a freedom where the individual is shut in as little as possible" (ibid.). See also G. Glotz, *The Greek City and Its Institutions,* trans. N. Mallinson (New York: Knopf, 1929): "In the age of Pericles, Athenian political life showed a perfect equilibrium between the rights of the individual and the power of the state. Individual liberty was complete" (p. 128). Glotz, however, exaggerates. See, *contra,* the overall judgment of W. Jaeger, which applies also to Athens: "The *polis* is the sum of all its citizens and of all the aspects of their lives. It gives each citizen much but it can demand all in return. Relentless and powerful it imposes its way of life on each individual and marks him for its own. From it are derived all the norms which govern the life of its citizens. Conduct that injures it is bad, conduct that helps it is good." *Paideia: The Ideals of Greek Culture,* 1:106.

33. As will be seen in chapter 11, section 4.

34. *Leviathan,* chap. XXI. Of course, "representative" is used, here, loosely.

35. *De la Liberté des Anciens Comparée à celle des Modernes.* I quote from A. Brunialti, ed., *Biblioteca di Scienze Politiche* (Torino, 1890), 5:455.

36. Schmalz (*Antibarbarus,* I, 415, sub *democratia*) noted that in the Latin writers of the classical period up to the fourth century A.D., the term *demokratía* appears only three times, and in passages and authors strictly of secondary order. It is not until the early Middle Ages that the term is used sometimes by those who referred to Aristotle's *Politics,* but rarely, and by writers of little importance, with the exception of Marsilius of Padua and Thomas Aquinas. The common practice is to follow Ciceronian paraphrases, like *civitas,* or *potestas popularis,* or *imperium populi.* Machiavelli will say *principato popolare* (popular principality), Guicciardini will write *vivere popolare* (popular living), and in Giambattista Vico one finds no trace of the word democracy. See, for an analysis of the history of the term, R. Wollheim, "Democracy," *Journal of the History of Ideas* 19 (1958): 225-42.

37. *De Regimine Principum,* bk. I, in *Selected Political Writings* (Oxford: Blackwell, 1948), p. 6.

38. Thus, classic writers in the English language have nearly always rendered *res publica* by "commonwealth"; a term that came into disrepute in the aftermath of Cromwell, but was soon reestablished in its etymological meaning.

39. *Perpetual Peace,* sect. II, The Primary Requisite of a Perpetual Peace: "The form of government of every state must be republican."

40. *The Federalist,* No. 10. See also Nos. 1, 9, 37, 70. Hamilton followed the same line of thinking as Madison, even if exceptionally, in a letter of 1777, he wrote "representative democracy" to mean "representative republic."

41. In those years, the only author who used "democracy" in a favorable sense was Paine; but only to mean that the "simple democracy" of the ancients provided "the ground" upon which representation was to be engrafted; and "representation engrafted upon democracy," Paine stressed, "is preferable to simple democracy even in small territories. Athens, by representation, would have surpassed her own democracy" (*Rights of Man,* 1791-92, pt. II, chap. 3). Jefferson too, later, used the phrase "representative democracy," but rarely and with the warning that a "republican government" had nothing in common with "pure democracy."

42. It is worth noting that Rousseau also placed "Republic" above "Democracy."

See *Contrat Social*, II, 6: "Therefore I call Republic any state which is governed by law . . . for then only the public interest governs. . . . Every legitimate government is republican." With respect to the forms of government (democratic, aristocratic, monarchic), Rousseau maintained that each form fits a particular type of country, but that democracy is best suited "to states which are small and poor" (*Contrat*, III, 8; see also III, 4). For the concept of democracy in the Encyclopedists, see R. Hubert, *Les Sciences Sociales dans l'Encyclopédie* (Paris, 1923), pp. 254-55.

43. However, Robespierre himself treats "democracy" as a synonym of "republic." Ferdinand Brunot in his monumental *Histoire de la Langue Francaise* (Paris: Colin, 1905-48), vol. IX, lists 206 words or expressions that characterize the political spectrum during the years of the revolution. Although "democratic" is mentioned, it appears as one to the terms less frequently used, and mainly to rival "aristocratic"— another revolutionary neologism recorded in a dictionary of 1791 (cit. in Brunot, p. 652) as follows: "*Aristocratic:* combination of syllables . . . which produce a strange effect on an animal called *democratic.*" R.R. Palmer, *The Age of the Democratic Revolution—The Challenge* (Princeton: Princeton University Press, 1959), points out that "there are only three texts of the period . . . where the author used 'democracy' in a favorable sense, as often as eleven times within a few hundred words; and these three texts are those of Paine, Robespierre, and the man who became Pius VII" (p. 19). In addition, see R.R. Palmer, "Notes on the Use of the Word 'Democracy' 1789-1799," *Political Science Quarterly* 2 (1953): 203-26, where Palmer notes that "it was in Italy . . . that the word 'democracy' in a favorable sense, was most commonly used in the years 1796 to 1799. This . . . is due also, one suspects, to the fact that since republics were an old story in Italy the new ideals could not be symbolized by the word 'Republic' as in France" (p. 220). On the Italian use of the term, see G. Calogero, T. De Mauro, and G. Sasso, "Intorno alla Storia del Significato di 'Democrazia' in Italia," *Il Ponte* 1 (1958): 39-66.

44. Reference is made to E.A. Havelock, *The Liberal Temper in Greek Politics* (New Haven: Yale University Press, 1957). I say "alleged" because Havelock's "liberal" is again an instance of the modernization to which I object.

45. In my *Parties and Party Systems: A Framework for Analysis* (New York: Cambridge University Press, 1976), chap. 1, passim, I trace back "pluralism" (as it is now understood, not in the meaning intended by the early English pluralists) to this seed.

46. In L. Bryson et al., eds., *Aspects of Human Equality* (New York: Harper, 1956), pp. 92-93. On religious toleration during the Reformation, see Joseph Lecler, *Toleration and the Reformation*, 2 vols. (London: Longman, 1960).

47. The assessment is difficult also because the Puritan mold of our world has not left an outstanding written testimony of itself; a fact that renders all traces of controversial interpretation. As William Haller has well shown in his classic works *The Rise of Puritanism* and *Liberty and Reformation in the Puritan Revolution* (New York: Columbia University Press, 1938 and 1955), the seed cast by the Puritans was transmitted to history especially by Milton's *Areopagitica* and *The Tenure of Kings and Magistrates.* But in Milton we have the fusion of the Puritan cause with the highest culture of the Renaissance. In the second place, the close derivation of our democracy from the Puritan experience, as maintained esp. A.S.P. Woodhouse, *Puritanism and Liberty* (London: Dent, 1938), and by Vittorio Gabrieli, *Puritanismo e Libertà: Dibattiti e Libelli* (Torino: Einaudi, 1956), is based mainly on the writings of the Levellers and unduly

neglects the theocentric and theocratic character of the Puritan sermon. On the other hand, against the tendency to overstate the contribution of the Puritans is the undue stress in the opposite direction by Benedetto Croce and by a considerable sector of Italian culture, which forgets the Reformation to such a degree as to defer the "theoretic" foundation of liberalism to Romanticism and German idealism. This excess stems from Hegelianism, but is also explained by the Counter-Reformation, that is, by the fact that the Catholic countries were sealed off until the arrival of the Romantic revolution.

48. Richard Schlatter, *Richard Baxter and Puritan Politics* (New Brunswick: Rutgers University Press, 1957), p. 4. See also L.F. Solt, *Saints in Arms: Puritanism and Democracy in Cromwell's Army* (Stanford: Stanford University Press, 1959).

49. Medieval fragmentation is no exception to this generalization, for it was armored, across the board of its hierarchies, by an organic, theologically sustained, conception of life that lead, in turn, to iron-clad corporate incorporations. The Middle Ages were organizationally multicentered but culturally unicentered and monochromatic.

50. See Plato, *Republic,* 563: "At length . . . they cease to care even for the laws, written or unwritten; they will have no one over them" (trans. B. Jowett). See also Aristotle (*Politics,* 1292a, 1293a), Isocrates, and Demosthenes, who all attest that no sooner had the laws lost the chrism of sacredness, which came to them from tradition, that they were overthrown by a popular government which, as early as 406 B.C. (according to Xenophon), could proclaim that it was absurd to believe that the demos did not have the right to do as it pleased.

51. J. Bryce, *Modern Democracies* (New York: Macmillan, 1924), 1:183.

52. See chapter 11, esp. section 3.

53. For the necessary qualifications, see esp. chapter 2, section 3; and chapters 5 and 6, passim.

11. Liberty and Law

> *The more corrupt the Republic, the more the laws.*
> —Tacitus

11.1 *Freedom and Freedoms*

Liberalism is a label that is harder to pin down than democracy. Among the many reasons for this, the obvious one is that "liberty" is far more elusive, denotatively, than "people." It was easy to concoct demo-cracy; we never have coined the word free-cracy. And the difficulties of our theme are compounded by the fact that the term freedom and the assertion "I am free to" stand for the kaleidoscopic scope and variety of human life itself. Fortunately, it will be sufficient for us to consider this chameleon-like word in one specific context: freedom in politics. Our main task is thus to separate the specific issue of *political freedom* from general speculations about the nature of *true freedom.* Lord Acton remarked that "no obstacle has been so constant, or so difficult to overcome, as uncertainty and confusion touching the nature of true liberty. If hostile interests have wrought much injury, false ideas have wrought still more."[1] While I agree very much on the harm brought about by uncertain, confused, and false ideas, I would hold that the problem before us is not to discover "the nature of true liberty" but to remove all the extraneous incrustations that prevent us from examining the question of political freedom *by itself,* and as one empirical question among others.[2]

We must begin, therefore, by putting some order in the contexts in which we variously speak of psychological freedom, intellectual freedom, moral freedom, social freedom, economic freedom, legal freedom, political freedom, and other freedoms as well.[3] These are related to one another, of course, for they all pertain to one and the same man. However, we have to distinguish between them because each one is concerned with examining and solving a particular aspect of the overall question of freedom. Hence, the first clarification to be made is that political freedom is not of the psychological, intellectual, moral, social, economic, or legal type. It presupposes these freedoms—it also promotes them—but it is not the same as these.

298

The second clarification has to do with the level of discourse. In this connection, the error is to confuse the empirical with the philosophical levels. Philosophers have very often speculated about political freedom, but only rarely have they dealt with it as a practical problem to be approached as such. Aristotle, Locke, and Kant are among the relatively few exceptions, among the small number of major philosophers who have not made the mistake of offering philosophical answers to practical questions. Locke, particularly, had this virtue. His treatment of the problem of freedom in the *Essay Concerning Human Understanding* is different from, and unconnected with, the one we find in the second of the *Two Treatises of Government*. In the former, he defines liberty as acting under the determination of the self, whereas in the latter he defines it as not being "subject to the inconstant, uncertain, unknown, arbitrary will of another man."[4]

Instead, most philosophers are concerned with True Liberty or with the Essence of Liberty—either the problem of the freedom of the will or the question of the supreme form of liberty (conceived variously as self-expression, self-determination, or self-perfection). This is what philosophers are supposed to do, and nobody blames them for that. But they should be reproached when they project their metaphysics of liberty into the political sphere and, unlike Locke, do not notice that in this context we are discussing another problem, a separate problem. The point is still far from being established. In reviewing the relationship between political philosophy and the science of politics, Friedrich—after having rightly criticized the mixing of philosophical questions and "the empirical realm of government and politics"—concludes that "any discussion of freedom and liberalism must, if it takes its argument seriously, confront the issue of 'freedom of the will.'"[5] I do not see why. Of course any discussion about the freedom cherished by the West is based on a *Weltanschauung*—on a conception of life and values. To be more exact, it presupposes that we somehow believe in the value of individual liberty. But I am reluctant to consider the connection any closer than that.

In the first place, even if we were to ascertain that man is not, ontologically, a free agent and that he is not really or ultimately responsible for his actions, should we, on such account, renounce a social order regulated by norms accompanied by sanctions? I do not quite see how we could. The one thing that would change is the meaning of penalty, which would lose its value as a deterrent and/or its justification as punishment. The convict would become a martyr of society, paying for offenses that he was not (morally or otherwise) responsible for. But he would still be condemned, since all societies must somehow dispose of whoever violates the rules of coexistence on which they are based.

The second reason for keeping the philosophical problem where it be-longs is that, unless we do, we are bound to misunderstand, for example, in what sense Spinoza maintained that liberty was perfect rationality, or Leib-niz that it was the spontaneity of the intelligence, or Kant that it was au-tonomy, or Hegel that it was the acceptance of necessity, or Croce that it was the perennial expansion of life. These conceptualizations make perfect sense when understood in their context; but their meaning and truth value have to do with the search for a freedom that is essential, final, or, as Kant would have it, transcendental. Notice, on the other hand, that none of these con-ceptualizations refers to a "relational" freedom. It follows that if we try to use the aforesaid concepts to deal with political bondage, which is a rela-tional problem, we distort their meaning to no avail. Indeed, when the ideas on freedom of Spinoza, Leibniz, Kant (as a moral philosopher), Hegel, or Croce are lowered to an empirical plane and attached to problems that their conceptualizations did not consider, they become not only erroneous but harmful. Harmful on account of the false witnessing that these philosophers have arbitrarily been called on to bear. So, the second point is that political liberty *is not* a philosophical liberty. It is not the practical solution to a phil-osophical problem, and even less the philosophical solution to a practical problem.

Finally, we must deal with the stages of the process of freedom. The phrase "I am free to" can have three different meanings or can be broken up into three phases. It can mean *I may,* or *I can,* or *I have the power to.* In the first sense freedom is permission; in the second sense it is ability; and in the third sense it calls on some other condition (material or otherwise) to sustain it. The third meaning is the newest, the last of the series, and will be taken up later. I shall here confine myself to the two primary meanings of freedom: I may, and I can. Clearly, *freedom as permission* and *freedom as ability* are connected, since permission without ability and ability without permission are equally sterile. Yet they should not be confused, because no one type of liberty can by itself cover both grounds. Certain kinds of liberty are designed primarily to create the *permissive conditions* of freedom. Political freedom is of this kind, and very often so are juridical freedom and economic freedom (as understood in a market system). In other contexts the emphasis is instead placed primarily, if not exclusively, on the roots and sources of free-dom—on freedom as *ability.* This is notably the case of the philosophical approach to the problem of freedom, and of the notions of psychological and intellectual freedom.

The distinction between *I may* and *I can* corresponds to the difference between the external sphere and the internal sphere of freedom. When we are interested in the externalization of liberty, that is, in free *action,* freedom takes the form of permission. When, on the other hand, the problem is not of external freedom, then we are concerned with freedom as ability. Terms like "independence," "protection," and "action" are generally used to indicate *external liberty,* whereas "autonomy," "self-realization," and "will" usually refer to the freedom that exists *in interiore hominis.* The conclusive point thus is that political liberty is not an internal freedom; it is an instrumental and *relational freedom* whose essential purpose is to create a situation of freedom, the conditions for freedom.

11.2   *Political Freedom*

Cranston remarks that "the word liberty has its least ambiguity in political use in times of centralized oppression."[6] This is very true and suggests that we better rely, in matters of political freedom, on the advice coming from those who have experienced unfreedom. People who never have known dictatorships and tyrannies easily yield to a rhetoric of freedom far removed from the terribly simple realities of real oppression where it really exists. The Western world is replete, to an unprecedented scale, with refugees who are told—when they report on the homelands they have escaped—that they are biased, that they exaggerate. Yet they are the ones who have left, often at peril of life, their homes, friends, belongings, while the Western intellectuals who believe to know better have been securely living wherever it pleases them to live. There is no question in my mind as to who really knows better—it is he who pays in person.

Hobbes and the English people of his troubled time did know how perilous life could be. And Hobbes claimed to report on the "generally received meaning," in England, of the word when he wrote: "Liberty, or freedom, signifieth, properly, the absence of . . . external impediments of motion."[7] Most authors emphasize, with regard to freedom, its very great variance of meaning. But if political freedom is disentangled from other freedoms, what is striking is its continuity and persistence of meaning over time. Wherever the state materializes as a supraordinate entity, and whenever the Western individual asks for liberty, he basically means what Hobbes says: absence of external impediments, removal of external constraints, lessening of coercive bonds. That is to say that political freedom is characteristically freedom *from,* not freedom *to.* We are now accustomed to call it "negative" freedom; but since this predication easily acquires a derogatory sense and helps presenting political freedom as an inferior kind of liberty, I prefer to say, more accurately, that it is a defensive or *protective freedom.*

Critics have repeated to the point of saturation that this idea of freedom comes from an erroneous individualistic philosophy based on the false assumption that the individual is an atom or a monad. But, in the first place, I would question that this notion is philosophical in the sense that only a small number of intellectuals are really interested in the individual. If we consider, for instance, the French Revolution (an event that admittedly escaped from the control of the *philosophes*), its entire parabola took on the meaning of a vindication of liberty *against* power. During the years from 1789 to 1794, the Third and Fourth Estates were asking for individual and political liberty in opposition to the state, not for a social and economic liberty to be achieved by means of the state. The idea that it is a purpose and concern of the state to dispense liberty would have appeared extravagant, to say the least, to the French people of the time. It would have appeared extravagant to them not because of their philosophical individualistic beliefs but for the much more earthly reason that they had been crushed for centuries by monarchs, lords, bishops, warriors, and all sorts of corporative binds.

In truth, I think that we need not call on monads and the atomistic philosophy of man in order to explain why political freedom tends to be understood at all times—especially when oppression heightens—as freedom *from,* that is, as a defensive freedom. The truly important point is that political freedom is not an issue, or at issue, unless we approach the relation between citizen and state *from the point of view of the citizen.* If we consider this relation from the point of view of the state, we are no longer concerned with the problem of political freedom. To say that the state is "free to" is merely to say that reference is made to a discretionary power. The tyrannical state is free *to* rule at its pleasure, and this means that it deprives its subjects of their freedom.[8] Let it be very clear, then, that *(a)* to speak of political freedom is to be concerned with the power of subordinate powers, with the power of the power addressees; and *(b)* the proper focus to the problem of political freedom is in asking, How can the power of these minor and potentially losing powers be safeguarded? We have political liberty, i.e., a free citizen, as long as conditions are created that make it possible for his lesser power to withstand the greater power that otherwise would, or at any rate could, easily overwhelm him. This is why the concept of political freedom primarily assumes an adversary connotation. It is freedom *from* because it is freedom *for* the weaker.

Of course, Hobbes's "absence of external impediments" should not be taken literally, lest it bring to mind an anarchic claim. The absence of restriction is not the absence of *all* restrictions. What we ask of political freedom is protection against arbitrary and limitless (absolute) power. By a situation of liberty we mean a situation of protection that permits the governed effectively to oppose the abuse of power by the governors. It might be objected that this clarification still does not clarify much. For what is meant by "abuse" of power? Where does the legitimate exercise of power end and the illegitimate begin? This is certainly a point of considerable disagreement. The answers to the questions, Protected from what? and Unrestricted to what extent? depend on what is at stake at any given time and place, and on what is most valued (and how intensely it is valued) in a specific culture. "Coercion" does not apply to every kind and degree of constraint; nor does "protection" imply defense against everything. In the first place, people must feel that what is involved is worth protecting (the threat of constraint has to be directed against something that they value); and, second, nobody worries about protecting what is not in danger. The above questions afford sufficiently precise answers provided that we place them in context, that we know what is being threatened and which threat is feared or disliked the most. In the end, non-impediment is always concretely rendered as: Nobody is impeded with respect to x, y, and z. In the liberal-democratic civilization these x's and y's have been derived from Christian moral principles, from natural rights, a felicific calculus, and a rights-based ethic. And this is as it should be.

The next question is whether freedom *from* is an adequate concept of freedom. To answer this query we must refer to a broader picture. Clinton Rossiter has summed up the general idea that we have of liberty today as consisting of four notions: independence, privacy, power, and opportunity. "*Independence* is a situation in which a man feels himself subject to a minimum of external restraints. . . . *Privacy* is a special kind of independence which can be understood as an attempt to secure autonomy . . . if necessary in defiance of all the pressures of modern society." However, says Rossiter, at this point we have only mentioned "one-half of liberty, and the negative half at that. . . . Liberty is also a positive thing . . . and we must therefore think of it in terms of *power* . . . and also in terms of *opportunity.*"[9] There is one imperfection in Rossiter's slicing, namely, that when he says "power" he seems to mean "ability to," in the sense of capacity. To shun ambiguity, I will include the concept of capacity in the list and place the concept of power at the end. Thus, *complete freedom* may be said to imply the following five traits: *(a)* independence; *(b)* privacy; *(c)* capacity; *(d)* opportunity; and *(e)* power.

Now we can frame our question more accurately: What is the relation between the first half of liberty (independence and privacy), and the second half (ability, opportunity and power)? The answer, it seems to me, is simple and clear: It is a relation between conditions and consequences and, therefore, a *procedural relation*. This is the reason why the above concepts constitute a sequence in which independence comes first and should not come last. Unfortunately, the procedural point is often missed. Rossiter himself, in putting his "pieces back together into a unity," does not convey in the least that there is an order and a sequencing in that unity. He concludes: "The emphasis of classical liberalism, to be sure, is on the negative aspects of liberty. Liberty is thought of almost exclusively as a state of independence and privacy. But this is precisely one of those points at which classical liberalism no longer serves, if ever it did serve, as a wholly adequate instrument for describing the place of the free man in the free society." Now, in granting that classical liberalism is not "wholly adequate," let us never forget that consequents arise from antecedents, and that classical liberalism still "serves" as the *ex ante* condition of the freedoms that it neglected. While a condition does not itself ensure that a given effect will follow, the sure thing is that if a condition does not precede what it conditions, then nothing can in fact follow; and this is what makes *the sequencing* of all the aforesaid freedoms (without exclusions and leapfrogging) as crucial as it is.

Political freedom is by no means the only kind of freedom, nor is it by any necessity the one that should rank highest in value. It is, however, the primary liberty on procedural grounds, for it is the sine qua non of all other freedoms. Hence, to speak of "independence from" as an inadequate notion of liberty, as we tend to do, is simply wrong. The other freedoms as well, if they are considered singly, are just as inadequate. Adequacy is provided by the whole series, and by the whole series arranged as a string, *in a given order.* It is not sufficient that our minds be free if our tongues are not. The ability (capacity) to direct our own lives is of very little use if we are prevented from doing so. How, then, are the so-called positive liberties adequate, if an all-powerful master blocks their unfolding? To assert that negative liberty is not sufficient is to assert the obvious; not to assert that we need freedom *from* in order to be able to achieve freedom *to* is to omit the essential.

If we chose to call political freedom "negative" (instead of "defensive"), then it is well to recall that liberty also requires "affirmation," that it cannot be a passive, inert freedom. As all freedoms, liberty too postulates activity. From this vantage point it has been argued that liberty is not only freedom *from* but also, and concurrently, *participation in* (the affairs of the polity). True; but false when we forget that participation is made possible by a state of independence, and not vice versa. Even our subjective rights, as Jhering wrote in a famous pamphlet, add up to nothing if we do not exercise them, indeed if we do not "fight" for them.[10] However, it is pointless to speak of exercising rights that do not already exist. The same holds good for political freedom. It is pointless to speak of "exercise" unless independence is there already. Totalitarian dictatorships require and promote a great deal of activity and, indeed, incessantly mobilize their subjects into action. But, so what? By mobilizing their populace from above, present-day dictators actually deviate and impede self-motion (participation) from below, that is, "independent freedom."

All things considered, it seems to me that we should resist the temptation to treat political freedom — liberty — as if it were, in itself, a complete freedom. Those who inflate liberty by speaking of it as participation end up by disfiguring its basic feature.[11] If we so often fail in seeking more liberty, it is also because we expect from participation more than it can give. Of course, liberty as nonrestraint is not an end in itself, and political freedom requires positive action and active resistance.[12] Where there is wholesale apathy, liberty is easily lost. But the bedrock is that the relation of forces between citizens and state is unequal; that vis-à-vis the state their power is easily destructible; and therefore that their freedom is typified by the presupposition of defense mechanisms. Unless it is shown that, in relation to the state, the citizens are not the weaker party, the political concept of freedom hinges on this argument: Only if I am not prevented from doing can I be said to have the power to do it.[13]

There is no reason to be oversensitive when we are told that this conception is incomplete. It is. Indeed, each specific form of freedom can amount only to a partial freedom because it concerns only the specific problem that it attempts to solve. What really matters is that political liberty cannot be bypassed. We cannot pass over freedom in the negative sense if we want to achieve freedom in the positive sense. If we forget for one instant the requirement of not being restrained, our entire edifice of liberties is in jeopardy. Once the procedural import of political freedom is established, we may well raise the question of its importance to us today. The assertion that liberty is not enough, meaning that "real freedom" is something else, is totally beside the mark. But, of course, every epoch has its urgencies and particular needs. So, we may well maintain *hic et nunc* that since today liberty is assured, it requires less attention than the freedoms that consist of enabling means. We shall come to this in due course.[14] Meanwhile, a final point is in order.

Thus far, I have underscored the multiplicity of freedoms. I have done so because I believe that no core meaning can be found so long as the metaphysical-philosophical conceptions of freedom are mingled with the empirical ones. But if the former are set aside, then yes, a nuclear, unifying meaning among the empirical progression of freedoms does emerge: It is *freedom of choice.* Political liberty (independence from) protects and permits the individual to choose; and the successive freedoms all add sustaining conditions to greater and more effective choice. Privacy is to choose without being pressured, by looking quietly into oneself; capacity is, among other things, a broadening of available choices; opportunity is the coming within reach of alternatives among which to choose; and power is, in the context of freedom, the equalizing condition, the condition that makes for an effective *equal freedom to choose.* When the word freedom is used generically what is generally intended is, then, freedom of choice. But freedom of choice is also an unfinished business of sorts. For freedom of choice is not a relational freedom; it simply confronts an actor with alternative courses of action. Political freedom is, instead, a relational freedom; it occurs among actors whose freedoms must coexist in reciprocity.

II.3   *Liberal Freedom*

It will be noted that so far I have spoken of *political* freedom and not of the *liberal conception of freedom.* The two concepts have become closely interlinked. However, since it is trendy to consider the liberal idea of freedom antiquated, it is wise to keep the problem of political freedom separate from the liberal solution of it. It is easy to argue that the freedom of liberalism, being a historical acquisition, is perishable. But are we prepared to make the same assertion about political freedom per se? Are we prepared to say that even liberty is a transient good or need? If so, let us say so. Political freedom (the idea) and liberal freedom (one of its incarnations) cannot be killed with one stone. Rather, it is at the very moment that we reject the liberal solution of the problem of freedom that this problem again demands, more pressingly than ever, a solution.

When the chips are down, what we ask of political freedom is protection. How can we obtain it? In the final analysis, from the time of Solon to the present day, the solution has been sought in obeying laws and not masters. As Cicero eloquently phrased it, *legum servi sumus ut liberi esse possimus,* we are servants of the laws in order that we might be free.[15] Locke said it even more concisely: "Where there is no law there is no freedom."[16] Paine too wrote that "the government of a free country . . . is not in the persons but in the laws."[17] And Rousseau, it will be seen shortly, stood firmly, on the point, with Cicero and Locke. The problem of political freedom always lands at the search for *rules* that do curb power.[18] This explains the very close connection between political freedom and juridical freedom. But the formula "liberty under law" and, thereby, by means of laws, can be conceived and implemented in different forms. The protection of the laws has been understood, by and large, in three ways: the Greek way, which is already a legislative interpretation;

the Roman way, which approaches the English rule of law;[19] and the way of liberalism, which is constitutionalism.

The Greeks understood well that if they did not want to be ruled tyrannically, they had to be governed by laws.[20] But their idea of law oscillated between the extremes of sacred laws, which were too rigid and immutable, and conventional laws, which were too uncertain and shifting. In the course of their democratic experience, the *nómoi* (laws) soon ceased to mirror the nature of things *(physis)*, and the Greeks were unable to stop at the golden mean between immobility and change. As soon as law lost its sacred character, popular sovereignty was placed above the law, and, by that very act, government by laws was once again fused and confused with government by men. The reason for this is that the legal conception of liberty presupposes the rejection of the Greek *eleutheria*—of a freedom that extends into the principle that what pleases the people is law. Looking at the Greek system from the vantage point of our knowledge, we see that what their conception of law lacked was the notion of *limitation*—a notion that, as was discovered later, is inseparable from it.

That is the reason why our juridical tradition is Roman, not Greek. The experience of the Greeks shows us how *not* to proceed if we want liberty under law. The Romans, it is true, posed for themselves a more manageable problem. As Wirszubski remarked, "The Roman Republic never was . . . a democracy of the Athenian type; and *eleutheria, isonomia,* and *parrhesia* that were its chief expressions, appeared to the Romans as being nearer *licentia* than *libertas.*"[21] Actually, Roman jurisprudence did not make a direct contribution to the specific problem of political freedom. But it did make an essential indirect contribution by developing the idea of legality whose subsequent version is the Anglo-Saxon rule of law.

The third juridical solution to the problem of political freedom is that of liberalism—which was developed in English constitutional practice, found its most successful written formulation in the Constitution of the United States, and is expounded in the theory of *constitutional garantisme* and, in this sense, of the *Rechtsstaat,* the state based on law.[22] What did liberalism specifically contribute to the solution of the problem of political freedom? It was not the originator of the modern idea of individual freedom, although it added something important to it.[23] Nor was it the inventor of the notion of liberty in the law (as expressed in Cicero's formula). But it did invent the way to institutionalize a balance between government by men and government by laws.

The originality and value of the approach of classical liberalism is best seen by comparing it with previous attempts. Basically, the legal solution to the problem of freedom can be sought in two very different directions: either in rule by legislators or in the rule of law. In the first approach, law consists of written rules enacted by legislative bodies, that is, law is legislated law. In the second approach, law is something to be discovered by judges; it is judicial law. For the former approach, law consists of statutory, systematic lawmaking; for the latter, it is the result of piecemeal law finding *(Rechtsfindung)* by means of judicial decisions. From the first viewpoint, law may be conceived as the product of sheer will; from the second, it should be the product of legal reasoning. The danger of the legislative solution is that a point may be reached in which men are tyrannically ruled by other men in spite of laws, that is, in which laws are no longer a protection. On the other hand, the second solution may be inadequate on three counts. First, because the rule of law does not, per se, necessarily safeguard the political dimension of freedom (e.g., the Roman rule of law concerned the elaboration of the *jus civile,* not of public law). Second, when the rule of law actually consists of discovering the law, that is, when judges perform under this belief, then it may well become too static (let alone too fragmentary). Third, judges may well perceive themselves not as law *finders* but as law *makers* — and, if so, the "rule of judges" can be even more disruptive than the "rule of legislators."

Liberal constitutionalism is the technique of retaining the advantages of the aforesaid solutions while lessening their respective shortcomings. On the one hand, the constitutional solution adopts rule by legislators, but with two limitations: one concerning the method of lawmaking, which is checked by a severe *iter legis;* and one concerning the range of lawmaking, which is restricted by a higher law and thereby prevented from tampering with the fundamental rights affecting the liberty of the citizen. On the other hand, the constitutional solution also sees to it that the rule of law is retained within the system. Even though this latter component of the constitutional rule has been gradually displaced by the former, it is well to remind ourselves that the framers of liberal constitutions did not conceive of the state as being a *machine à faire lois,* a lawmaking machine, but conceived of the role of legislators as a complementary role according to which parliament was supposed to integrate, not to replace, judicial law finding. It should also be stressed, conversely, that the independence of the judiciary was conceived by the framers of the liberal constitutions as an independence *from* politics, not as another route to policy making.

To be sure, this was the *design* that the drafters of the liberal constitutions had in mind — not necessarily the achievements of the documents they drafted. There are, also, many significant differences among constitutional systems. If we refer to the origins, the unwritten English constitution was largely built upon, and safeguarded by, the rule of law;[24] the American written

Constitution, in spite of many departures from the British constitutional practice, still leaned heavily on the rule of law; whereas written constitutions in
Europe were preceded by the codifications enacted by Napoleon and were
thus based from the outset on the legislative conception of law. But these initial differences have been gradually reduced, since there is at present a general
trend—even in the English-speaking countries—in favor of statutory law.
Despite this trend, we cannot say as yet that present-day constitutions have
lost their *raison d'être* as the solution that combines rule-of-law and rule-of-
legislators. Even though our constitutions are becoming more and more un-
balanced on the side of statutory lawmaking, as long as they are considered
a higher law, as long as we have judicial review, independent judges dedicated
to legal reasoning, and, possibly, the due process of law,[25] and as long as
a binding procedure establishing the method of lawmaking remains an effective brake on the bare-will conception of law—as long as these conditions
prevail, we are still depending on the liberal-constitutional solution of the
problem of political power.

Constitutional systems, both past and present, are therefore *in fact* liberal
systems. One might say that liberal politics is constitutionalism[26]—a constitutionalism that seeks the solution of the problem of *political* freedom in a *dy-
namic* approach to the legal conception of freedom. This explains why we
cannot speak of political freedom without referring to liberalism—liberalism,
I insist, not democracy. The political freedom that we enjoy today is the freedom of liberalism, the liberal kind of liberty, not the precarious and dubious
liberty of the ancient democracies. This is also the reason why, in recalling
the characterizing principles of the democratic deontology, I have mentioned
equality, isocracy, and self-government, but not the idea of liberty.

Of course, it is possible to derive the idea of liberty from the concept
of democracy, but somewhat indirectly and via a detour. The idea of liberty
does not follow from the notion of popular power but from the one of equal
power, of isocracy. It is the assertion "we are equal" (in power) that can be
interpreted as "nobody has the right to command me." Thus, it is from the
postulate of equality that we can deduce, if we so wish, a freedom *from*. However, this inference is made by modern rather than by ancient thinkers. In the
Greek tradition, democracy is much more closely associated with *isonomía*
(equal law) than with *eleuthería* (liberty), and the ideal of popular power is
by far preponderant in the inner logic of development of the Greek polity.
Moreover, liberty meant to the Greeks something different from what it means
today.[27] It is crucial to note, then, that neither our ideal nor our techniques
of liberty pertain, strictly speaking, to the line of development of the
democratic idea. Modern liberal democracies do extol the idea of a liberty

of Man, which includes the liberty of each man. But this is an acquisition of democracy, not a product of it. Unless this is borne in mind, we can be easily misled into believing that our liberty can be secured by the method that the Greeks adopted. This is not so, for our liberties are assured by a notion of legality that constitutes a *limit* and a *restriction* on pure and simple democratic principles. Kelsen, among others, saw this very clearly when he observed that a democracy "without the self-limitation represented by the principle of legality destroys itself."[28] Although modern democracy has incorporated the notions of liberty and legality, these notions, as Bertrand de Jouvenel rightly points out, "are in terms of good logic, extraneous to it."[29] They are extraneous to it in terms of good historiography as well.

II.4 *The Supremacy of Law in Rousseau*

I have indicated three ways of seeking legal protection for political freedom: the legislative way, the rule-of-law way, and the liberal or constitutional way. But it is held that there is another relationship, which would be the fourth in my list, between liberty and laws: *autonomy,* i.e., giving ourselves our own laws. And since liberty as autonomy is supposed to have Rousseau's *placet,* many people take it for granted that this is the democratic definition of liberty and contrast, on this basis, the minor liberty of liberalism with the greater democratic liberty, autonomy. I question, first, whether those who equate liberty with autonomy are justified in associating this notion with Rousseau. In the second place, which is the supposedly minor liberty: political freedom or the liberal solution of it? The two are evidently, albeit erroneously, being treated as one. In the third place, I wonder whether it is correct to contrast freedom *from* with autonomy, for it is hard to see in what sense autonomy can be conceived of as a political kind of freedom. Let us begin by ascertaining what Rousseau exactly thought and said.

We can have doubts about Rousseau's solutions but certainly not about his intentions. The problem of politics, Rousseau affirmed loud and clear, "which I compare to the squaring of the circle in geometry [is] to place law above man."[30] This was for him *the* problem because, he said, only on this condition may man be free: when he obeys laws, not men.[31] Rousseau was more sure of this certainty than of any other. "Liberty," he confirmed in the *Letters from the Mountain,* "shares the fate of laws; it reigns or perishes with them. There is nothing of which I am surer than this."[32] And, as Rousseau said in the *Confessions,* the question he constantly asked was, "Which is the form of government which, by its nature, gets closer and remains closer to law?"[33]

This was the problem that Rousseau had every reason to liken to the squaring of the circle.[34] While in the *Letters from the Mountain* he observed that when "the administrators of laws become their sole arbiters . . . I do not see what slavery could be worse,"[35] in the *Social Contract* his question was, "How can a blind multitude, which often does not know what it wills, because only rarely does it know what is good for it, carry out for itself so great and difficult an enterprise as a system of legislation?"[36] For Rousseau this question had only one answer: to legislate as little as possible.[37] He had been coming to this conclusion with more and more conviction for some time. Already in the Dedication of his *Discourse on Inequality* he had stressed the fact that the Athenians lost their democracy because everybody proposed laws to satisfy a whim, whereas what gives laws their sacred and venerable character is their age.[38] This is precisely the point: The laws that Rousseau referred to were Laws with a capital *L*—that is, few, very general, fundamental, ancient, and almost immutable supreme Laws.[39]

Rousseau held that the people are the judges and custodians of the Law, not the makers and manipulators of laws. He by no means had in mind the idea of a legislating popular will.[40] On the contrary, he proposed to liberate man by means of an impersonal government of Laws placed high above the will from which they may emanate, that is, related to a will that acknowledges them rather than creates them, sustains them rather than disposes of them, safeguards them rather than modifies them. Whoever appeals to the authority of Rousseau must forget our formal definition of law. His Laws were substantive, that is, laws by reason of their content; and they were as firm as the laws conceived by the theory of natural law.[41] But how can this be without a transcendent anchorage?

Rousseau's solution was the *volonté générale*,[42] a concept that turns out to be less mysterious than it seems—notwithstanding all the fluctuations to which it is subject—if we remember that it is an expression of the crisis of natural law and at the same time of the search for an *Ersatz,* for something to take its place. In the shift from Grotius's *ius naturale* to the Law sanctioned and accepted by the general will, the foundations are different, but the new protagonist (the general will) has the same functions and attributes as the old (nature). Rousseau's general will is not the will of all, that is, it is not "the sum of individual wills,"[43] nor is it a *sui generis* individual will freed of all selfishness and egoism. It stands somewhere between the two.[44] And to better unveil its mysterious nature, we must go back to Diderot's definition of *volonté générale* in the *Encyclopédie:* "The general will is in each individual a pure act of understanding, reasoning in the silence of the passions."[45] Rousseau did not accept that definition. Why? I do not think that what disturbed Rousseau was the rationalistic flavor of Diderot's definition, that is, his reducing the general will to a "reasoning in the silence of the passions." For, although Rousseau's general will is nourished and strengthened by love and by feelings, it is guided by reason.[46] That is, it is still a rational will— "will" as it could be conceived before the Romantic outburst, certainly not that voluntaristic will which precedes and dominates reason.[47]

In order to get the point straight, it must be understood that Rousseau envisages, throughout his works, two radically different hypotheses: either educating man "according to nature" (in *Emile*) or "denaturing" him into the citizen (in the *Social Contract*). When society is too large and corrupt, only the individual can be saved. Therefore, in *Emile* Rousseau proposes to abolish even the words "country" and "citizen," and exalts love for one's self. In this hypothesis, man must devote his attention entirely to himself. But when the city and society are small and still patriarchal—this is the second hypothesis—then one must save the community; this is the problem of the *Contract*. Here the citizen must cancel the man, the patriot must collectivize his love for himself, and the individual must give his self to the whole; he dies as a "particular" and is reborn as a moral member of the collective body. Rousseau is coherent, but his hypotheses are alternative and mutually exclusive.[48] In the "nature man" the sentiment dominates, but in the "denatured" one (the citizen) passion and love become a catalyst of a society that acts according to reason; and the general will is the *deus ex machina* of this construction.

So, what was it that Rousseau could not accept of Diderot's definition of the general will? I take it that it was Diderot's answer to the question *ou est le dépôt de cette volonté générale?*—where is the general will located? Rousseau could not accept the location of the general will "in each individual." He could not settle for this individualistic approach because he had to rebuild somehow, within society itself, an equivalent of the transcendence formerly afforded by the *Deus sive natura* formula. The general will had to be the anthropomorphic substitute for the order of nature and for the "natural reason" that mirrored that order. So much so that in Rousseau the laws were derived from the general will just as they were previously derived from natural law. He wrote: "Whenever it becomes necessary to promulgate new ones [laws], this necessity is perceived universally. He who proposes them only says what all have already felt."[49] This is like saying that laws are not produced *ex homine,* but are recognized and proclaimed *ex natura:* The general will does not, strictly speaking, make them and want them, but bears them within itself. If it were really a will, when inert it would not exist, and when mute it would not will; while for Rousseau the general will is "always constant, unchangeable, and pure" and cannot be annihilated or corrupted.[50] Which comes back to saying that it is an entity of reason that does not suffer the vicissitudes of human will, or of particular wills.[51]

The general will can be compared to the "spirit of the people," to what the Romantics and the historical school of law later called *Volksgeist;* not because the two concepts are similar, but because they both attempt to fill the void left by natural law. Both notions were motivated by the need to discover some objectivity in subjectivity, some absoluteness in relativity—in short, a fixed point of reference. The Romantics sought transcendence within immanence by locating the former in History (with a capital *H*), in the collective, anonymous, and fatal flux of events; Rousseau tried to find transcendence in Man by placing it in a common ego that unites all men. And just as the Romantic school of law enfeebled its case when, in order to insert its transcendent *Volksgeist* in the orbit of immanence, it had to call upon a privileged interpreter, in the same way[52] and for the same reason Rousseau revealed the weak point of his construction when, in his search for a link between the general will and what the citizens want, he allowed the majority to be the interpreter of the *volonté générale.*

Indeed, here Rousseau stands in deep contradiction, for the majority's will is subjective and merely stems from the will of all, whereas Rousseau's general will is an objective moral will made up of qualitative elements; it must be "general" in essence, at its origin, and for its objective.[53] Although Rousseau kept his general will in the orbit of calculable qualities—he even indicated that it is derived from a sum of the differences, i.e., after the pluses and minuses of individual wills are canceled out[54]—counting can only reveal the general will, it cannot produce its essence.[55] The popular will is additive, the general will is one and indivisible. Even if we grant that in the process of popular consultations an interplay of compensations eliminates individual passions, in order to achieve the quality of general will we need much more: *bonne volonté* (goodwill), patriotism, and enlightened popular judgment.[56] These are demanding conditions that amount to forbidding restrictions on popular sovereignty.[57] If the general will "is always good and always tends to the public interest," it does not follow, Rousseau added, "that the deliberations of the people are always right."[58] He later explained: "The people always desire the good, but do not always see it. The general will is always in the right, but the judgement which guides it is not always enlightened."[59] The people would like the good but that does not mean that they recognize it. Therefore, it is not the general will that resolves itself into popular sovereignty but, vice versa, the popular will that must resolve itself into the general will. Rousseau did not ask whether the people rejected or accepted a bill, but whether it did or did not express the general will.[60] In substance, his polity hangs on a general will that supplants popular power.

Was Rousseau's "democracy" a democracy at all? One may well doubt it. His "people" were not a demos in any accepted (past or future) sense of the term.[61] Nor did Rousseau privilege "democracy" as the best form of government. While he frequently employed the word, his general category for the properly constituted, legitimate government — the one governed by law — was "republic." However, almost everybody asserts that Rousseau does father some kind of democracy. If so, Rousseau was indeed the proponent of a monumentally *immobile democracy*, a democracy that was supposed to legislate as little as possible and could survive only on condition that it kept its actions to a bare minimum. Rousseau devoted all his ingenuity to controlling the forces that his ideal would have let loose. His democracy was the exact antithesis of Jacobin democracy; it was a watchdog system. He rejected representatives, wanted a direct and, as far as possible, a unanimous democracy, and required that the magistrates should have no will of their own but only the power to impose the general will. The result was, clearly, a static body, a democracy bent upon impeding, not upon promoting, change and innovation. It is true that Rousseau spoke of "will," but he did not mean by it a *willing will*. The general will was not a *dynamis*, but the infallible instinct that permits us to evaluate the laws and to accept as Law only the Just, the True Law. Rousseau's aim was to free man from his bonds by inventing a system that would obstruct and curb legislation. This was because he felt that the solution of the problem of securing freedom lay exclusively in the supremacy of law and, furthermore, in a supremacy of law concerned with avoiding the legislative outcome of the Athenian democracy, that is, the primacy of popular sovereignty over the law.

That Rousseau was no revolutionary is generally acknowledged. Indeed, we owe him one of the most sarcastic refutations of revolutionarism: "I laugh at those people . . . who imagine that in order to be free all they have to do is to be rebels."[62] Rousseau was not a reformer either. Quite aside from his many declarations to the effect that he "had always insisted on the preservation of existing institutions,"[63] the fact is that for Rousseau change was almost always change for the worse. In his time, only Corsica was considered changeable for the better; but such events, he cautioned, are "rare" events, indeed single-shot "exceptions . . . that cannot even occur to a same people twice."[64] As a rule, changes are dangerous; this is so because Rousseau expounded — in polemics with the optimism of the eighteenth century — a pessimistic conception of history.[65] He did not share the Enlightenment's belief in progress; his emphasis was, instead, on the inevitability of decadence. "Sooner or later it must happen that the Prince [the government] oppresses the Sovereign and breaks the social treaty. This is the inherent and inevitable vice which, from its inception, tends without respite to destroy the body politic, just as old age and death end up destroying man's body."[66] His view was, in essence, that the best that could be hoped for was the delaying of the inevitable. On such a view, one can neither be a revolutionary nor even much of a reformer.[67]

But this, important as it is, is a sideline. What matters here is that Rousseau did not present a new conception of freedom. He enjoyed going against the current and contradicting his contemporaries on most scores, but not on this one point: the legalitarian concept of liberty that had found fresh nourishment and support in the natural rights of the natural law revival of the seventeenth and eighteenth centuries.[68] Rousseau never for a minute had the idea of freeing man by means of popular sovereignty, as we are told by many of his current devotees. The assertion that liberty is founded by law and in law found in Rousseau, if anything, its most intransigent supporter. Rousseau was so uncompromising about it that he could not even accept the legislative conception of law within a constitutional framework (as proposed by Montesquieu), for this solution allowed for changing laws, while Rousseau wanted a basically unchanging Law.

11.5 *Autonomy: A Criticism*

It will be asked: Did not Rousseau speak of liberty as autonomy at all? We do find in the *Social Contract* this sentence: "Obedience to laws that we have imposed on ourselves is liberty."[69] But when he declared that everybody is free because in obeying the laws that he himself has made he is submitting to his own will, Rousseau was by no means speaking of the autonomy of which we speak today as if it were his discovery. In the first place, Rousseau related his idea of autonomy to the contract, that is, to the hypothesis of an original pact in which ideally each party to the contract submits to norms that he has freely accepted. The fact that Rousseau had in mind a democracy that was not in the least inclined to change its Laws shows how important it was for him to keep this liberty tied to its original legitimacy, and clearly indicates that he did not mean this idea to be used as we are using it. There is an essential condition that qualifies Rousseau's formula, namely, that the people are free so long as they do not delegate the exercise of their sovereignty to legislative assemblies.[70] So his conception has very little to do with a non-contractarian obedience to laws that are made for us by others.

In the second place, Rousseau's thesis is closely related to the smallness of his democracy. A participatory small democracy, if we wish — but not participatory in any exalted and exalting meaning. His model for his time was, after all, Geneva; and Geneva was a clear-cut aristocratic and indeed oligarchic republic in which only some 1500 people out of some 25,000 were entitled to participate in the lawmaking. Nor did Rousseau ever show, in all his writings on Geneva, the slightest interest and concern for the "natives," that is, for three-quarters of the population. Aside from Geneva, Rousseau had incessantly in mind Spartans and Romans – again, oligarchic and/or aristocratic republics. But even if his dubious exemplar cases are set aside, the fact remains that Rousseau's ideal state was confined to the small city, and that he never thought that his democracy was applicable to large republics.[71] Now, it is still plausible to maintain that some 1500 citizens of a small city who govern themselves directly submit only to the rules that they have accepted and, therefore, obey nothing but their own wills; but when the "natives" are included, when the citizens become millions and are dispersed over a vast territory, when they are not the self-makers of their laws, does the thesis still make sense? Not for Rousseau.

In the third place, by tracing to Rousseau the concept of liberty as autonomy, we take the premise from which he started and forget the conclusion that he reached. When Rousseau went back to a liberty that is submission to laws we have prescribed ourselves, his problem was to legitimize law. If man renounces his natural liberty in order to achieve a superior civil liberty, he does so because the society he enters subjects him to norms he has accepted, that is, to just Laws that liberate, not oppress him. But once Law is legitimized and true Law is established, Rousseau's liberty is liberty under Law. Man is free because, when Laws and not men govern, he gives himself to no one. In other words, he is free because he is not exposed to arbitrary power. This was Rousseau's concept of liberty. And so it was understood by his contemporaries. Even in the Declaration of Rights of 1793, article 9 stated: "The law must protect public and individual liberty against the oppression of those who govern." This article has a strange ring if we recall that the Terror was in full blossom. Yet what we have read is a definition of liberty that could well have been drawn from Rousseau.

The truth is that "autonomy" originated with Kant and that it was Kant who brought the concept to the fore. Except that for the author of the *Critique of Practical Reason,* the notion of autonomy had little to do with democratic liberty or any other kind of political or even juridical liberty.[72] Kant distinguished between "external" and "internal" freedom. And the prescription by ourselves of our own laws (autonomy) is in Kant the definition of moral liberty, that is, of our *internal freedom* – a completely different matter from the question of *external coercion.* In the moral sphere we are concerned with whether man is free or not in the interior forum of his conscience, while in politics we are concerned with ways of preventing man's exterior subjugation. That politics is conceived by Kant, ultimately, as instrumental to morality does not alter the point that Kant's ethics does not address the problem of political freedom. This also explains why the word autonomy rebounded from Kant back to Rousseau as soon as it took on a political meaning. But to which Rousseau? To the real Rousseau, or to the one remodeled by the Romantics and subsequently by the idealistic philosophers?

With the assurance that is characteristic of him, Kelsen flatly asserted, "political freedom is autonomy."[73] But Kelsen, as well as many other scholars, has adopted this thesis far too lightly. The autonomy in question is a concept of a speculative-dialectical nature that stems from a philosophy—Hegelian idealism—that has indeed little to do with liberalism and democracy.[74] I can understand that many present-day democrats have been fascinated by the idea of autonomy. Still, a concept that has performed, and is all too easily brought to perform, the function of justifying and legitimizing obedience bodes ill for defending our liberties.

Autonomy as a concrete expression of political freedom ended with ancient democracies. The formula of the Greek liberty was—we read in Aristotle —"to govern and to be governed alternately . . . to be under no command whatsoever to anyone, upon any account . . . otherwise than by rotation, and that just as far only as that person is, in turn, under his also."[75] This self-government can certainly be said to be "autonomy." How well did it protect liberty? Not too well even then. As Aristotle himself immediately pointed out, under this formulation "whatever the majority approves must be the end and the just"—and this is exactly the conception in which laws easily cease to protect liberty. However, if it pleases us to speak of autonomy in this connection, then it should be acknowledged that the supposedly new and most advanced conception of liberty advocated by present-day progressives was already known to Aristotle. New, it certainly is not. Is it obsolete? Yes, I am afraid it is. For only a *micropolis,* and indeed a very small one, can solve the problem of political freedom by having, as in Aristotle's concise formulation, "all to command each, and each in its turn all." Certainly our ever-growing megapolis cannot.

Autonomy applies not only to individuals but also, in the current usage of the term, to institutions and organizations. Thus far, reference has been made to individual autonomy, and my contention has been that the notion of self-determination (obeying one's own norms) well defines moral freedom and the freedom of each individual, but ill defines political freedom. If reference is made, however, to institutional autonomy, then we have a different

referent that involves different problems. Take so-called local autonomies—
at whichever level. By virtue of its being autonomous a local body can be
said to be free—but in what sense? And does it follow that whoever falls under
the jurisdiction of such autonomous-free body is, by the same token, a free
individual? It surely does not follow. The city can be totally free and its citizens
totally slaves.

As is always the case, a good way of defining institutional autonomy is
to determine its contrary. Specifically, the contrary of local autonomy is centralization. That is to say that full centralization implies zero autonomy, full
autonomy implies zero centralization, and that increases of local autonomies
are increases of decentralization (just as, conversely, decrements of autonomy
are increments of centralization). From this vantage point, local autonomies
result from the distrust of concentrated power and are therefore an expression of freedom *from* the centralized state. The liberty connected with administrative decentralization, with the German *Selbstverwaltung,* or with self-
government of the Anglo-Saxon type, does not mean, then, what Rousseau
or Kant had in mind and do not establish, in themselves, any individual autonomy. Local autonomies may be nothing more than "autarchies,"[76] and serve
as safeguards of liberty chiefly because they bring about a polycentric diffusion of political power.

It may be said that the notion of autonomy in its political application
must not be interpreted in its literal sense but in a feeble and looser way, and
that it is in this sense that it helps to connote the democratic brand of liberty.
Norberto Bobbio observes that "the concept of autonomy in philosophy is
embarrassing, but . . . in the context of politics the term indicates something
easier to understand: it indicates that the norms which regulate the actions
of the citizens must conform as far as possible to the desires of the citizens."[77]
But if this is the case, why use the word autonomy? The problem of having
norms that conform to the desires of the citizens is the problem of consensus
as addressed by the theory and practice of representation. Bobbio also points
out that while a state of liberty in the sense of nonrestriction has to do with
action, a state of autonomy has to do with will.[78] This is indeed the point.
For the sphere of politics concerns volitions *insofar as they are actions,* not
pure and simple will. The internal problem of freedom of will is not the political problem of freedom, for the political problem is the external problem
of freedom of action. Therefore, as long as we interpret liberty as autonomy,
we do not cross the threshold of politics.

In politics, and beginning from the procedural beginning, the problem
of liberty is the problem of coercion, of being protected from coercion. It
can thus be posited that liberty grows as coercion diminishes, and vice versa.

That is equally to say that coercion and liberty are good contraries. Let us now ask: Is coercion also a contrary of autonomy? The reply is, surely, no. For instance, it makes perfect sense to assert that I can be coerced and still remain autonomous, that is, inwardly free. Indeed, this is the reason why we say that force can never extinguish in man the spark of freedom. Conversely, I can be coercion-safe and yet non-autonomous, that is, incapable of self-determination. Clearly, to be coerced and to be autonomous are by no means mutually exclusive states of being. And if they can go together, autonomy cannot protect me from coercion. That my will remains free (autonomous) even when I am physically imprisoned (coerced) leaves me exactly where I am — in prison. My internal freedom, my autonomy, does not solve the problem of my external freedom, of my liberty.

To reiterate the point logically, the contrary of autonomy is heteronomy. And heteronomy stands for passivity, anomie, characterlessness, and the like — all of which are notions that concern not the subject-sovereign relationship but the problem of an inner-directed responsible self. But, it may be asked, is heteronomy the one and only "good contrary" of autonomy? Do we not hear speak, for instance, of autonomy versus control? We certainly do — but as manners of speech endowed with little conceptual underpinning. When autonomy is employed as a synonym for other terms (as when it simply means independence), we are wasting, if not losing, its distinctive meaning. And its distinctive meaning is the one pinpointed *a contrario* by the notion of heteronomy. So, the semantic field of "autonomy" bears, as I was saying, on internal, not external, liberty, on the power to will, not the power to do.

Needless to say, the argument can be pursued on the normative plane. In this case we are not actually maintaining that somewhere there are people who are free by virtue of their own lawmaking, or that some place exists where liberty actually consists in the rule of oneself by oneself. In this case autonomy is only an ideal. Even so, I still very much doubt whether the ideal of self-obedience is really suited to the democratic creed. It seems to me that the democratic deontology is authentically expressed in the ideal of self-government, not of autonomy. When the notion of autonomy takes the place of the notion of self-government, it obscures and weakens it. It obscures it because after its cross-breedings among Kant, Rousseau, and Hegel, the idea of autonomy can easily demonstrate (in words, of course) that we are free when we are not. The German and Italian literature of the 1930s attests *ad nauseam* to how well autonomy can be turned into a practice of submission justified by high-level explanations about "true freedom."[79] There is more. When we speak of self-government, we can ascertain whether it exists and know what we have to do in order to approach it; whereas when we speak of autonomy, verification is circumvented, and we can idly rest in bed and think of ourselves as free.

There is, of course, a type of autonomy that could be considered a *libertas major* even in the sphere of politics; but it would be found in a society that functions by spontaneous self-discipline wherein internalized self-imposed rules would take the place of compulsory laws emanating from the state. We can keep this concept in reserve for a time when the state will have withered away; but as long as the state exists, let us not be duped into believing in a superior democratic liberty conceived of as autonomy. I do believe in autonomy as moral freedom, in the sense indicated by Kant; I do not believe in autonomy as an external freedom. Liberty from, and freedom as autonomy, cannot be substituted for each other; nor is autonomy the "positive" liberty because it is not a political freedom at all.

11.6 *The Principle of Diminishing Consequences*

I have also wanted to discuss in some detail the concept of autonomy because it affords a typical example of a more general vice, namely, of a verbal overstraining that ignores what I call the law of diminishing consequences or, as we may also say, the principle of the dispersion of effects.

Thus, from the premise that we all (as infinitesimal fractions) participate in the creation of the legislative body, we boldly evince that it is *as if* we ourselves made the laws. In like manner, and in a more elaborate way, we make the inference that when a person who allegedly represents some tens of thousands contributes (he himself acting as a very small fraction of a parliament) to the lawmaking process, then he is making free the thousands of people whom he is representing because the represented thereby obey norms that they have freely chosen (even though it might well be that even their representative was opposed to those norms). How absurd! These chains of acrobatic inferences in a frictionless space are worthless, and this for the good reason that the driving force of the causes (premises) is exhausted long before it reaches its targets (end states). In empirical terms, from the premise that I know how to swim, it may follow that I can cross a river but not that I can cross the ocean. The "cause," ability to swim, cannot produce everlasting effects. And the same applies, in the empirical realm of politics, to the "cause," participation and elections.

There are at times no limits to the services that we ask of political participation. Yet from the premise that effective, continuous participation of the citizens in the self-government of a small community can produce the "result" liberty (precisely a liberty as autonomy), we cannot draw the conclusion that the same amount of participation will produce the same result in a large community; for in the latter an equally exhaustive and exhausting participation will entail (at an exponential rate) diminishing consequences. A similar warning applies to our way of linking elections with representation. Elections do produce representative results, so to speak; but it is absurd to ask of the "cause," elections, unending results. Bruno Leoni made the point lucidly when he wrote:

> The more numerous the people are whom one tries to "represent" through the legislative process and the more numerous the matters in which one tries to represent them, the less the word "representation" has a meaning referable to the actual will of actual people, other than the persons named as their "representatives." . . . The inescapable conclusion is that in order to restore to the word "representation" its original, reasonable meaning, there should be a drastic reduction either in the number of those "represented" or in the number of matters in which they are allegedly represented, or both.[80]

I do not know whether we can go back to the "drastic reduction" suggested by Leoni. But there is no doubt that if we keep on stretching the elastic (but not infinitely so) cord of political representation in defiance of the law of the dispersion of effects, it will snap. The more we demand of representation and the more we burden it, the less closely are the representatives tied to those they represent. Let us therefore beware of treating representation as another version of autonomy and of the formulas that make us believe (by logical demonstration) that we are free when actually we are not.

Keeping our feet on the ground—as we are required to do by the law of diminishing consequences—the choosing via elections of representatives cannot be read *as if* we made the laws through them. Nor are we free because we have actually wanted the laws enacted by our representatives; we are free because we limit and control their power to enact them. If the liberty that we enjoy lay in our personal share in lawmaking, I fear that we would be left with very few liberties, if any. For, as John Stuart Mill very neatly put it, "The self-government spoken of is not the government of each by himself, but of each by all the rest."[81]

11.7   *From the Rule of Law to the Rule of Legislators*

There are two reasons for having made a particular point of the connection between liberty and law. The first one is that we have pushed far too far the so-called informal approach. Nowadays, most political scientists believe that laws can accomplish little, or in any case much less than had previously been deemed possible. In concurrent fashion, philosophers (especially the ones of idealistic persuasion or derivation) have become neglectful of the liberty-law nexus as their concerns have turned to "higher freedoms." Yet, even a typically anti-juridical, idealistic philosopher such as Benedetto Croce brought himself to write that "those who build theories attacking law, can do so with light heart because they are surrounded by, protected by, and kept alive by laws; but the instant that all laws begin to break down they would instantly lose their taste for theorizing and chattering."[82] Nevertheless, the widespread skepticism about the effectiveness of the juridical protection of liberty is not unjustified. This is so because our conception of law has changed, and as a consequence, law no longer affords the guarantees that it did in the past. This is no reason for leaving, or creating, a void where law used to be, but it is certainly a reason for staying alert and not letting ourselves be lulled by the idea that the laws stand guard over us while we sleep twenty-four hours a day. And this is my second motive for dwelling on the relationship between law and political freedom.

Montesquieu, who was still relying on the protection of natural law, could very simply assert that we are free because we are subject to "civil laws."[83] Our problem begins exactly where this statement terminates. For we must ask the question that Montesquieu (as well as Rousseau) could ignore: Which laws are "civil laws"? To begin with, what is law? In the Roman tradition, *ius* (the Latin word for law) has become, over the centuries, inextricably connected with *iustum* (what is just);[84] and in the course of time the ancient word for law has become the English (and the Italian and French) word for justice. In short, *ius* is both "law" and "right."[85] That is to say, law has not been conceived as any general rule enforced by a sovereign (*iussum,* i.e., command), but as that rule which embodies and expresses the community's sense of justice (*iustum*). In other words, law has long been thought of not only as any norm that has the "form" of law but also as a "content," i.e., as that norm which also has the value and quality of being just.

That has been the general feeling about the nature of law until recently.[86] Yet, on practical grounds the problem is that law is not given; it has to be made. Only primitive or traditionalistic societies can do without overt lawmaking. The question thus becomes: Who makes the law? How? Furthermore, who interprets the laws? In order for us to be governed by laws, or by means of laws, the lawmakers themselves must be subject to law. This is obviously a formidable, strenuous, ever precarious undertaking. The problem has been tackled, within the constitutional state, by arranging the legislative procedure in such a way that the "form of law" also implies a control of its content. A large number of constitutional devices are, in effect, intended to create the conditions of a lawmaking process in which *ius* will remain tied to *iustum,* in which law will remain the right law. For this reason legislation is entrusted to elected bodies that must periodically answer to the electorate. And for the same reason we do not give those who are elected to office *carte blanche,* but we consider them power holders curbed by and bound to a representative role.

But the constitutional solution has, by succeeding, reacted on our conception of law; we now have a different understanding of its nature. The analytical jurisprudence (that calls up the name of John Austin), on the one hand, and the juridical positivism (of the Kelsen type), on the other, have ended by giving law a purely formal definition, that is, identifying law with the *form of law.* This shift comes about as an obvious consequence of the fact that the existence of the *Rechtsstaat*[87] appears to eliminate the very possibility of the unjust law and thereby allows the problem of law to be reduced to a problem of form, not of content. Unfortunately, however, the formalistic school of jurisprudence completely overlooks this dependence, that is, the fact that the formal definition of law presupposes the constitutional state. Therefore, the high level of systematic and technical refinement achieved by this approach cannot save it from the charge of having erected an unsafe juridical edifice open to easy conquest.

The implication of this development—with regard to the political problem that constitutional legality tries to solve—is that today we have taken to applying "constitution" to any type of state organization[88] and "law" to any state command expressed in the form established by the sovereign himself. Now, if law is no longer a rule qualified by a value (a *ius* that is *iustum*), and if the idea of law is, on the one hand, restricted to the commands that bear the mark of the will of the sovereign and, on the other, extended to any order that the sovereign enforces, then a law so defined can no longer solve our problems. In the formal conception, law is available to any content and a law without righteousness is nonetheless law. Therefore, legislation can be crudely tyrannical and yet not only be called legal but also be respected as lawful. It follows from this that the conception of law established by Austin, Kelsen, and their numerous followings undermines law as the safeguard of liberty; even "law" becomes, or may be used as, a trap word.

If the analytic-positivistic approaches of modern jurisprudence are not reassuring—for those who are concerned about political freedom—it must be added that the *de facto* development of our constitutional systems is even less so. What the founding fathers of liberal constitutionalism[89] had in mind, in relation to the legislative process, was to bring the rule of law into the state itself, that is, to use McIlwain's terms, to extend the sphere of *iurisdictio* to the realm of *gubernaculum* (government).[90] English constitutionalism actually originated in this way, since the *garantiste* principles of the English constitution largely are generalizations derived from particular decisions pronounced by the courts in relation to the rights of specific individuals. And since English constitutional practice, even if constantly misunderstood, has constantly inspired the Continental constitutionalists, the theory of *garantisme* as well as of the *Rechtsstaat* (in its first stage) had precisely this in mind: to clothe the *gubernaculum* with a mantle of *iurisdictio*. Regardless of differences of juridical hinterlands, there is little doubt that liberal constitutionalism as a whole looked forward to a government of politicians that would somehow have the same flavor and give the same security as a rule-of-law system. But after a relatively short time had elapsed, constitutionalism changed — although less rapidly and thoroughly in the English-speaking countries — from a system based on the rule of law to a system centered, in fact, on the rule of legislators.[91] Bruno Leoni summarized this development very clearly:

> The fact that in the original codes and constitutions of the nineteenth century the legislature confined itself chiefly to epitomizing non-enacted law was gradually forgotten, or considered as of little significance compared with the fact that both codes and constitutions had been enacted by legislatures, the members of which were the "representatives" of the people. . . . The most important consequence of the new trend was that people on the Continent and to a certain extent also in the English-speaking countries, accustomed themselves more and more to conceiving of the whole of law as *written law,* that is, as a single series of enactments on the part of legislative bodies according to majority rule. . . . Another consequence of this . . . was that the law-making process was no longer regarded as chiefly connected with the theoretical activity on the part of the experts, like judges or lawyers, but rather with the mere will of winning majorities inside the legislative bodies.[92]

It seems to us perfectly normal to identify law with legislation. But at the time when Savigny published his monumental *System of Actual Roman Law* (1840-49), this identification was still unacceptable to the chief exponent of the historical school of law. And we can appreciate its far-reaching implications today very much more than was possible a century ago. When law is reduced to state lawmaking, a "will conception" or a "command theory" of law gradually replaces the common-law idea of law, that is, the idea of an incremental lawmaking process derived from custom (the *lex terrae)* and defined by the law-*finding* of judicial decisions.

There are many drawbacks — we are now discovering — in our legislative conception of law. In the first place, the rule of legislators is resulting in a real mania for lawmaking, a fearful inflation of laws. Leaving aside how posterity will be able to cope with hundreds of thousands of laws that increase, at times, at the rate of thousands per legislature, the fact is that the inflation of laws in itself discredits the law. This is not to say that governments should govern less. It is to say that it is both unnecessary and, in the longer run, counterproductive to *govern by legislating,* i.e., under the form and by means of laws. This is to confuse governing with lawmaking, and thus is a misconception of both. Jurists are now increasingly asking for delegification, that is, for myriads of "small laws" to be converted into administrative acts and regulations. Now, if the contention that innumerable laws are to be declassified into administrative regulations is borne out, then it is clearly the case that they should have never been born as laws.

There are further drawbacks. It is not only that the excessive quantity of laws lessens the value of law; it is also their bad quality. Inevitably, "legislative bodies are generally indifferent to, or even ignorant of, the basic forms and consistencies of the legal pattern. They impose their will through muddled rules that cannot be applied in general terms; they seek sectional advantage in special rules that destroy the nature of law itself."[93] The point here is not that the framers of the liberal constitutions placed overly high hopes on the lawmaking talents of lawmakers. The point is that the system was not designed to have legislators replace jurists and jurisprudence. When the classical theory of constitutionalism entrusted the institutional guarantee of liberty to an assembly of representatives, this assembly was not being assigned so much the task of changing the laws as that of preventing the monarch from changing them unilaterally at his discretion. As far as the legislative function is concerned, parliaments were not intended as technical, specialized bodies; and this because they were not intended as law-producing machines.

We shall address later the present-day deterioration of laws with respect to their *generality,* that is, the problem of sectional legislation.[94] At the moment I simply wish to mention that sectional legislation brings to the fore a "command characterization" of law. As Hayek notes, "a general rule that everybody obeys, unlike a command proper, does not necessarily presuppose a person who has issued it. It also differs from a command by its generality and abstractness. . . . However . . . laws shade gradually into commands as their content becomes more specific."[95] But the point of more immediate concern is that mass fabrication of laws ends by jeopardizing the other fundamental requisite of law: *certainty.* Certainty does not consist only in a precise wording of laws or in their being written down; it is also the long-range certainty that the laws will be lasting. Lasting, to be sure, in the sense and to the extent that a legal order is such precisely because it allows the addressees of its norms to plan their course of life, to be forewarned as to where the red and green lights are placed.[96] So, certainty is a concern because the present rhythm of statutory lawmaking calls to mind what happened in Athens, where "laws were certain (that is, precisely worded in a written formula) but nobody was certain that any law, valid today, could last until tomorrow."[97]

Finally, and most important, the theory and practice of "legislated law" (the legislative conception of law) accustoms us to accept any and all commands of the state, that is, to accept any *iussum* as *ius*. Legitimacy resolves itself in legality, and in a merely formal legality at that, since the problem of the unjust law is dismissed as meta-juridical. On these premises, either one of two developments may occur. The first is that judges cease to perceive themselves as law-finders (in the process of administering justice) and become more and more *judge-legislators* in the manner of *politician-legislators;* both categories increasingly take the law in their hand as if there was nothing more to it than having a winning hand. If so, the "republic of deputies" (as the French called their Republic) finds here an equally dismembering antagonist in the "republic of judges." The second development, the one that centrally addresses our concerns, is that once we become accustomed to the rule of legislators, the *gubernaculum* also obtains a free hand vis-à-vis *iurisdictio.* This implies that the legal suppression of constitutional legality is within easy reach. When fascism established itself in power, the passage occurred quietly, almost unnoticed and, indeed, with little break of continuity. It has happened, and it can happen again.

I shall not go so far as to say that the transition from a rule of law to a rule *by* laws which nears, albeit in disguise, a rule by men, has already deprived us of the substance of juridical protection. But I do wish to stress that we have arrived at a point where such protection crucially depends on the survival of a system of constitutional guarantees. For our rights are not safeguarded by the positivistic, merely formal conception of law. We are no longer protected by the rule of law but (in Mosca's terminology) only by the devices of "juridical defense." In recent decades there has been a widespread call for a "democratization" of the constitution—a call that attests, more than to anything else, to the erosion of *garantisme.* The ideal of these reformers is to transform law into outright legislation, and legislation into a rule of legislators freed from the fetters of a system of checks and balances. Thus, their ideal calls for constitutions that they are no longer, properly and strictly speaking, constitutions. We seemingly fail to appreciate that the more the achievements of liberal constitutionalism are undermined by so-called democratic constitutionalism, the closer we are to the solution at which the Greeks arrived and that proved their downfall, namely, that men were subject to laws so easily changed that they became laws unable to assure the protection of the law.

There are then many causes for alarm. Whereas law, as it was formerly understood, effectively served as a solid dam against arbitrary power, legislation, as it is now understood, may become no guarantee at all. For centuries the firm distinction between *iurisdictio* and *gubernaculum,* between matters of law and matters of state, made it possible for legal liberty to make up, in a number of respects, for the absence of political freedom. Nowadays the opposite is true: It is political freedom that supports the legal protection of individual rights. For we can no longer count on a law that has been reduced to statutory law, to a *ius iussum* that is no longer required to be (according to the formal or positivistic conception) a *ius iustum.* Or, rather, we can rely on it only insofar as it remains tied to the constitutional state in the liberal and *garantiste* meaning of the term.

On a different tack a further cause for alarm has yet to be mentioned. "Today—I read—law and liberty are commonly thought to be antithetical."[98] If this be the case, our present-day thinking needs to be thought through. At first blush it may well appear that every law is an infraction of liberty (as Bentham put it), for laws generally command and prohibit more than permit. But, remember, the freedoms that we have been investigating are *relational freedoms,* freedoms among a multiplicity of individuals, groups, and organizations. This implies that every freedom of each actor is defined by the unfreedom of others to interfere with it. For example, my freedom of speech entails the unfreedom of everybody else to muzzle me. So too with my freedom to vote, my freedom to move, my freedom to marry, and so forth. Furthermore, every freedom of each actor finds its limit (its unfreedom, if you wish) in the harm principle: It cannot be exercised to the point of harming, injuring, and (beyond some point) disturbing others. So, all relational freedoms are qualified by *(a)* unfreedoms of reciprocity, and *(b)* the unfreedom to harm. The latter is a self-evident principle. The former, the principle that freedom must be reciprocated by an unfreedom, may be formulated as follows: with respect to *A, B* is unfree to impede *A*'s doing something to the same extent to which, conversely, *A* is unfree to impede *B*'s doing. From here it needs little reflection to see that it is only within a legal system of general laws that our relational freedoms can be equally enjoyed by all without each harming others. To perceive laws as infractions of liberty is to misperceive that without laws the freedom of *A* would result in the oppression of *B.*

Reverting from the general case to the specific one of political freedom, it bears reiteration that today, as yesterday, liberty and law are bound together. "How are we to escape enslavement? By virtue of the law. This route, the only one, has been discovered more than two thousand years ago. . . . Nothing better has been found since."[99] True. The only way that we know to construct a non-oppressive political system is to depersonalize power by placing the law above men. But the bond between liberty and law has never been as precarious as it is at present. When the rule of law resolves itself into the rule of legislators, the way is open, in principle, to the most subtle form of oppression: the one "in the name of the law." And the remedy is, I am suggesting, to return to the constitutional state with renewed awareness. There is nothing legalistic in this thesis because it is political freedom, in my argument, that sustains legality—not vice versa. What protects our liberties today are "rights," not the law-as-form on which jurists rely; and our rights are the constitutionalization of a freedom *from*. It is in this sense, and strictly under these conditions, that I have stressed that only liberty under law (not liberty as autonomy), only a constitutional system as an impersonal regulating instrument (not popular power as such), have been, and still are, the guardians of free societies.

I asked earlier what place in the scale of historical priorities has political freedom for us today. I answer that to the extent that *iurisdictio* becomes *gubernaculum* and legality supplants legitimacy, to the same extent freedom *from* cannot be taken for granted and again becomes a concern. The pendulum of history swings back and forth. We have been told for too long and too loudly that the political and liberal notions of liberty are obsolete. They are certainly not obsolete, and they are a first priority, in all the unfree societies—which are just about as numerous, as the twentieth century approaches its end, as they were in the past. And the unfree societies should neither be forgotten nor given, by the general theory of democracy, bad advice. The foregoing does not mean in the least—let it be said once more—that the question of freedom is exhausted by the liberal solution of the political problem of liberty, or that it is unimportant to supplement liberty as nonrestriction with freedoms *to* and substantive powers *to*. But it is equally important to realize that it is freedom *from*, not freedom *to*, that marks the boundary between political freedom and political oppression. When we define liberty as "power," then the power *to* be free (of the citizens) and the power *to* coerce (of the state) are easily intermingled—an intermingling that advantages the power of the strongest, the power of overpowering. To the question whether there are many freedoms to be sought I answer yes, of course; but to the question whether there is, aside from the liberal kind, another *political* freedom I answer no: The so-called social and economic freedoms presuppose the liberal technique of taming power.

Notes

1. *Essays on Freedom and Power* (New York: Meridian Books, 1955), p. 53.

2. On the problem of freedom in general, a precious source are the two volumes of M.J. Adler, *The Idea of Freedom* (Garden City, N.Y.: Doubleday, 1958 and 1961). However, in this work the concepts of each author are treated in a historical vacuum, and one easily misses that different theses were eventually held for the same reason, and/or that many differences amount to the same thing said under different circumstances. Two important symposia are R.N. Anshen, ed., *Freedom: Its Meaning* (New York: Harcourt, Brace, 1940); and L. Bryson, L. Finkelstein, R.M. MacIver, and R. McKeon, eds., *Freedom and Authority in Our Time* (New York: Harper, 1953). See also M.R. Konvitz and C. Rossiter, eds., *Aspects of Liberty* (Ithaca: Cornell University Press, 1958); and C.J. Friedrich, ed., *Liberty* (New York: Atherton, 1962). Hannah Arendt, "What Is Freedom?" in *Between Past and Future,* is excellent.

3. I set aside freedom from fear, from want, from need, or the formula "freedom as self-expression," since it is seldom clear in what context they belong. With the exception of freedom from need (which is clearly economic), freedom from fear and from insecurity can be understood as instances of psychological freedom but also as related to political freedom. Still worse, freedom as self-expression can be just as much a psychological freedom as a moral and/or intellectual one; and has also been mixed up with "power" by C.B. Macpherson, esp. in *Democratic Theory: Essays in Retrieval* (Oxford: Clarendon Press, 1973), chap. 3.

4. See *Essay Concerning Human Understanding,* esp. vol. 1, bk. II, chap. 21; and *Two Treatises of Government,* bk. II, chap. 4, sect. 22.

5. In R. Young, ed., *Approaches to the Study of Politics* (Evanston: Northwestern University Press, 1958), pp. 174, 184.

6. *Freedom: A New Analysis* (London: Longman, 1954), p. 11.

7. *Leviathan,* chap. 21. See also chap. 14. Even though this definition is placed in the context of "natural liberty" (indeed, it "may be applied no less . . . to inanimate creatures than to rationall"), it overlaps also into the context of civil liberty, of the "liberty of subjects." Hobbes said "motion" also on account of the strict mechanistic formulation of his philosophy.

8. I disagree, thus, with H.J. Morgenthau's thesis ("The Dilemmas of Freedom," *American Political Science Review,* September 1957) that political freedom is confronted with a dilemma: freedom for the holder, or for the subject of political power? That a power holder is unfree when he is not allowed unrestricted powers is a pointless point.

9. "Patterns of Liberty," in Konvitz and Rossiter, *Aspects of Liberty,* pp. 16-18. My subsequent quotation is from p. 18.

10. In Jhering's phrase, "Law is not a logical concept, but an energetic and active one." *Der Kampf um's Recht (*1873), chap. 1.

11. Reference is made both to the liberty of the ancients (chapter 10, herein), and to the earlier discussion of present-day participationism (see chapter 5, sections 5-7, and chapter 8, section 6).

12. "Les libertés sont des résistances" (liberties are resistances), used to say Royer-Collard, a doctrinaire of the French Restoration. Harold Laski was altogether Hobbesian in the matter ("liberty is essentially an absence of restraint") and made a very similar point: "Liberty cannot help being a courage to resist the demands of power at some

point that is deemed decisive." *Liberty in the Modern State* (London: Faber & Faber, 1930), pp. 11 and 250.

13. It should be understood that in the expression "political liberty" I include also the civil liberties (freedom of speech, of press, of assembly, etc.). Civil liberties too are liberties that come under the category of freedom *from,* since they delimit the sphere of action of the state and mark the boundary between the use and abuse of political power. Our political rights stem from civil liberties as their prosecution and, above all, as their concrete guaranty. That is to say that political rights are civil liberties that have been extended and protected, and civil liberties are the *raison d'être* (though not the only one) for the existence of political rights. A conceptual analysis is Richard E. Flathman, *The Practice of Rights* (Cambridge: Cambridge University Press, 1976).

14. The argument is especially pursued in chapter 12, section 7, and in chapter 13, sections 6 and 7.

15. *Oratio pro Cluentio,* 53.

16. *Two Treatises of Government,* Second Treatise, chap. VI, 57. See also chap. XVIII, 202: "Wherever law ends, tyranny begins."

17. *Rights of Man,* pt. II, chap. 3, last paragraph.

18. Notice that, as formulated, my assertion neither contradicts nor can be contradicted by the assertion that liberty consists of not being regulated. As Adler points out, while the obedience to laws and the exemption from regulation theses "may appear to be giving opposite answers to the question 'How is law related to liberty?' they are really not taking that question in the same sense" (*The Idea of Freedom,* 1:619). To be sure, if an author does not address political freedom but other freedoms (e.g., self-realization), then he is likely to hold that any regulation is inimical to the freedom that he has in mind. This confirms, however, the importance of isolating political from extra-political freedoms.

19. The similarity of development between Roman and English constitutionalism was perceived by Rudolf von Jhering in his *Geist des Römischen Rechts,* and by Bryce in his *Studies in History and Jurisprudence.*

20. See Aristotle: "Men should not think it slavery to live according to the rule of the constitution; for it is their salvation." *Politics,* 1310a.

21. C. Wirszubski, *Libertas* (Cambridge: Cambridge University Press, 1950), p. 13.

22. Constitutional *garantisme* is more precise than "state based on law" because the latter can be understood as a mere system of administrative justice. In fact, the administrative notion of *Rechtsstaat* has prevailed upon the constitutional one. On the various ways in which the state based on law links with the "just state," see Gottfried Dietze, *Two Concepts of the Rule of Law* (Indianapolis: Liberty Fund, 1973).

23. See chapter 10, herein.

24. A classic exposition remains A. V. Dicey, *The Law of the Constitution* (1885). Blackstone was the eighteenth-century author who established, more than anyone else, what was the English constitution. That Coke and, even more, Blackstone made the common law appear much more "common" and custom-based than it actually was, is immaterial to my argument.

25. I say possibly because the "due process of law," as understood in the United States, has no equivalent in Europe, and also goes beyond not only the *lex terrae* of the old English law but beyond the English interpretation of the rule of law as well.

26. As Duverger aptly recalls, "when Laboulaye gave the title *Cours de Politique Constitutionnelle* to a collection of Benjamin Constant's works, he meant to say in substance *Course in Liberal Politics*. 'Constitutional' regimes are liberal regimes" (*Droit Constitutionnel et Institutions Politiques*, p. 3). Constant himself had collected those writings, in 1818-19, saying that "they constitute a sort of course in constitutional politics."

27. This is my argument in chapter 10, esp. section 5.

28. *Vom Wesen und Wert der Demokratie* (Tübingen, 1929), chap. 7.

29. *Du Pouvoir* (Genève: Bourquin, 1947), p. 290.

30. He added: "[otherwise] you can be sure that it will not be the law that will rule, but men." *Considerations sur le Gouvernement de la Pologne*, chap. 1.

31. It is the constant thesis in all of Rousseau's writings. In the *Discours sur l'Economie Politique*, compiled probably in 1754 for the *Encyclopédie*, he wrote: "Law is the only thing to which man owes his freedom and the justice he receives." In the Dedication to the *Discours sur l'Origine et les Fondements de l'Inégalité parmi les Hommes* (called the *Second Discourse*), he wrote: "No one of you is so little enlightened as not to realize that where the vigor of the law and the authority of its defenders end, there can be no safety or freedom for anyone." In the Geneva first draft of the *Contrat Social* (circa 1754), law was described as "the most sublime of all human institutions." In the "brief and faithful" condensation of his *Contrat Social* in the *Lettres Ecrites de la Montagne* Rousseau repeated: "When men are placed above the law . . . you have left only slaves and masters" (pt. 1, no. 5).

32. Pt. II, no. 8. Rousseau had said before: "There is . . . no freedom without laws, nor where there is anyone who is above the law. . . . A free nation obeys the law, and the law only; and it is through the power of the law that it does not obey men. . . . People are free . . . when they see in whoever governs them not a man, but an organ of the law" (ibid.). In pt. II, no. 9, he writes: "All that the citizen wants is the law and the obedience thereof. Every individual . . . knows very well that any exception will not be to his favor. This is why everyone fears exceptions; and those who fear exceptions love the law."

33. *Confessions*, bk. IX. It is a rephrasing of this question: "What is the nature of a government under which its people can become the most virtuous, most enlightened, most wise, in short the best that can be expected?"

34. Rousseau enjoys this comparison, which is also found in a letter to Mirabeau dated 26 July 1767.

35. Pt. II, no. 9.

36. *Contrat Social*, II, 6 (hereinafter abridged *Contrat*).

37. See B. de Jouvenel in the splendid *Essai sur la Politique de Rousseau* that introduces his edition of the *Contrat Social* (Genève: Bourquin, 1947), pp. 123-26. See also *Du Pouvoir*, pp. 295-304.

38. The criticism against the legislative fickleness of the Athenians is resumed in *Contrat*, II, 4. See also III, 11.

39. The state, says Rousseau, "needs but a few laws" (*Contrat*, IV, 1). Let us remember that one of his models was Sparta, that is, the static constitution by antonomasia. Addressing the citizens of his favored Geneva, he wrote: "You have good and wise laws, both for themselves, and for the simple reason that they are laws. . . . Since the constitution of your government has reached a definite and stable form, your func-

tion as legislators has terminated; to assure the safety of this building it is necessary that you now find as many obstacles to keep it standing as you found aids in building it. . . . The building is finished, now the task is to keep it as it is" (*Lettres de la Montagne*, pt. II, no. 9). The exhortation to "maintain and reestablish the ancient ways" is found also throughout the *Considérations sur le Gouvernement de la Pologne* (esp. chap. III). One must also keep in mind that Rousseau's concept of law is based on custom, which he judges as the most important aspect of law (see *Contrat*, II, 12).

40. In the Dedication to the *Second Discourse* Rousseau states that the republic he would have chosen is the one in which "individuals are happy to accept the laws." In the *Considérations sur le Gouvernement de la Pologne* (chap. II), Rousseau distinguishes between the common "lawmakers" and the "Legislator," laments the absence of the latter, and recalls as examples Moses, Lycurgus, and Numa Pompilius. See also *Contrat*, II, 7, where he invokes the Legislator, "an extraordinary man in the state," who must perform "a particular and superior function which has nothing in common with the human race," for "it would take gods to make laws for human beings."

41. The relationship between Rousseau and natural law is studied in detail by R. Derathé, *Jean-Jacques Rousseau et la Science Politique de son Temps* (Paris: Presses Universitaires de France, 1950).

42. The wording is not Rousseau's, in fact the expression was common enough. See the careful reconstruction of the concept in Jouvenel's *Essai sur la Politique de Rousseau*, pp. 105-20, 127-32.

43. *Contrat*, II, 31.

44. Here the caveat is that we should not look at Rousseau's general will through romantic glasses and for how it has reached us after the idealistic mediation. As Derathé points out, "the general will is essentially a juridic notion which can be understood only through the theory of the moral personality which had been formulated by Hobbes and Pufendorf" (*J.J. Rousseau*, pp. 407-10). N.O. Keohane, *Philosophy and the State in France* (Princeton: Princeton University Press, 1980), puts forward a more intriguing interpretation. In her view, "The roots of the general will lie deep in the office of the absolutist king . . . [it] transforms the monarchical will that . . . holds together the whole polity into the absolute sovereignty of the fused individuals" (p. 461; see also pp. 442-45).

45. *Encyclopédie*, "Droit Naturel," sect. 9. For an analysis of how Rousseau related to Diderot's conception of the general will, see R.D. Masters, *The Political Philosophy of Rousseau* (Princeton: Princeton University Press, 1968), pp. 261-69. While Masters does not bring out my point, his work is of great exegetical value.

46. Rousseau asserts that in the civil society man must "consult his reason before listening to his inclinations" (*Contrat*, I, 8), and that to submit to the civil society means to be subject to a "law dictated by reason" (II, 4). Consider also the following passage in *Contrat*, II, 6: "Private citizens see the good which they repudiate; the public wants the good which it does not see. . . . It is necessary to compel the first to make *their will conform with their reason*; one must teach the other to *know what it wants* [my italics]." And in *Emile* (I) Rousseau says: "Whoever wants to preserve in a society the priority of the natural sentiments does not know what he wants."

47. See in this connection A. Cobban's *Rousseau and the Modern State* (London: Allen & Unwin, 1934), and Derathé's *Le Rationalisme de Rousseau* (Paris: Presses Universitaires de France, 1948). Cassirer goes as far as maintaining that "Rousseau's

ethics is not an ethics of sentiment, but it is the purest and most definite ethics of the law ever formulated before Kant" (*Das Problem Jean Jacques Rousseau* [1932], Italian trans., p. 84). This is going too far. The counter-argument is in the monumental work of P.M. Masson, *La Réligion de J.J. Rousseau* (Paris, 1916), 3 vols.

48. Hence, his politics may well be a continuation of his ethics, and yet the "ethics of the sentiment" (emphasized by Masson) and the "ethics of politics" fall wide apart. See, however, N. Keohane, "Rousseau and the Morality of Enlightment," *Political Theory,* November 1978.

49. *Contrat,* IV, 1.

50. Ibid. It is true that in Rousseau there is also a "subjective" position through which the will can decide about the laws (see *Contrat,* II, 12); but that admission is always accompanied by the position that reason discovers their "objective" necessity (*Contrat,* II, 11).

51. Patrick Riley proposes a complementary interpretation, namely, that Rousseau sought a "cohesive will" close to the "corporate 'will' of a whole society." While I agree that a corporate vision may have inspired Rousseau, I am puzzled by Riley's point that Rousseau created "the philosophical paradox of *willed nonvoluntarism.*" (*Will and Political Legitimacy* [Cambridge, Mass.: Harvard University Press, 1982], p. 100). Aside from the mystic stream of Christianity (very much a sideline with the victory of Thomism), the Western philosophical tradition did not conceive a voluntaristic will in which *stat pro ratione voluntas* (the will replaces reason) until Romanticism; and I find no paradox in a reason-monitored and even reason-blocked will.

52. The analogy is that for Rousseau too the legislator is a "revealer," as Groethuysen has pointed out in his *Jean Jacques Rousseau* (Paris: Gallimard, 1949), p. 103.

53. See esp. *Contrat,* II, 4, 6.

54. *Contrat,* II, 31. Here one perceives the distance between Rousseau and Hegel, between the philosopher of the eighteenth century and the Romantics. In Rousseau's conceptualizations we do not find, for there could not be, any of those ingredients used by the Romantics for building their organismic, collective entities, we do not find the "soul" or the "spirit" of the people. For this reason it was impossible, for Rousseau, to fully disconnect the general will from a numerical count.

55. In fact, Rousseau hastens to specify: "Often there is quite a difference between the will of all [*la volonté de tous*] and the general will" (*Contrat,* II, 3). That "often" reveals Rousseau's difficulties and oscillations. On the one hand he was concerned to find a passage between Law and Sovereign, but on the other hand Rousseau was not at all resigned to accept this consequence: that "a people is always free to change its laws, even the best ones: for if it wants to harm itself, who has the right to stop it?" (II, 12).

56. B. de Jouvenel renders the distinction very well: "The will of all can bind everyone juridically. That is one thing. But it is quite another thing to say that it is good. . . . Therefore, to this will which has only a juridic value he counterposes the general will which is always correct and always tends towards public welfare." *Essai sur la Politique de Rousseau,* p. 109.

57. Note that Rousseau's "people" is completely different from the *populace.* The people consists of the "citizens" and the "patriots" only. Both in the project of the Constitution of Poland as in the one of Corsica, Rousseau prefigures a meticulous *cursus honorum* which amounts to a qualification for sovereignty. And from the *Let-*

tres de la Montagne one can see very clearly that equality, for Rousseau, is an intermediate condition between the beggar and the millionaire represented by the bourgeoisie. Between the rich and the poor, between the oligarchs and the *populace*, Rousseau's "people" is not far removed from Hegel's "general class." See also n. 61, below.

58. *Contrat*, II, 31.

59. *Contrat*, II, 6.

60. *Contrat*, IV, 2.

61. In Geneva "the people" with a say amounted to a 6 to 7 percent of its inhabitants (see next section). Rousseau went as far as to assert, with regard to Venice, that it is an "error" to consider its government "a veritable aristocracy," for "if it is true that the people have no part in the government, it is the nobility who is the people itself" (*Contrat*, IV, 3). See n. 57 above.

62. *Considérations sur le Gouvernement de la Pologne*, chap. VI.

63. Third *Dialogue*. In 1765 he wrote to Buttafoco: "I have always held and shall always follow as an inviolable maxim the principle of having the highest respect for the government under which I live, and to make no attempts . . . to reform it in any way whatever."

64. *Contrat*, II, 8. Corsica was "reformable" only because it was a very young state (*Contrat*, II, 10). And the project on the reform of Poland was throughout a reminder of the use of prudence in carrying out reforms.

65. See R.D. Masters, "Nothing Fails like Success: Development and History in Rousseau's Political Teaching," *University of Ottawa Quarterly*, July-October 1979, pp. 357-76.

66. *Contrat*, III, 10. He repeats in *Contrat*, III, 11: "Even the best constituted state will come to an end."

67. Groethuysen said: "Rousseau's ideas were revolutionary; he himself was not" (*J.J. Rousseau*, p. 206). I would say that although Rousseau's *ideas* were not revolutionary in intent, and as he intended them, they did have a revolutionary potential in that they were easily convertible into oppositional *ideals*.

68. One must discern at least three phases in the evolution of the idea of natural law. Until the Stoics, the law of nature was not a juridic notion, but a term of comparison that denoted the uniformity and the normality of what is natural. With the Stoics, and the Romans above all, one can already speak of a theory of natural law. But the Roman conceptualization did not contain the idea of "personal rights," which is at the base of our idea of constitutional legality and which belongs to the third phase. In addition to Passerin d' Entrèves, *Natural Law*, a masterful overview is N. Bobbio, "Il Giusnaturalismo," in *Storia delle Idee Politiche Economiche e Sociali*, ed. L. Firpo (Torino: U.T.E.T., 1980), vol. 4, chap. 8.

69. *Contrat*, I, 8. See also I, 6.

70. *Contrat*, III, 15.

71. One can quote at length, for this is a very firm point. Even in the *Considérations sur le Gouvernement de la Pologne*, that is, in a context in which Rousseau has to soften and adjust his conception to a large state, he maintains that the "grandeur of nations, the extension of states" is the "first and principal source of human woes. . . . Almost all small states, whether republics or monarchies, prosper for the very reason that they are small, that all the citizens know each other. . . . All the large nations, crushed by their own masses, suffer whether . . . under a monarchy or under

oppressors" (chap. v). Also see *Contrat*: "The larger a state becomes, the less freedom there is" (III, 1); "the larger the population, the greater the repressive forces" (III, 2).

72. The link between Kant and Rousseau is generally found in a passage of Kant's *Perpetual Peace* where one reads that external, i.e., juridical freedom is "the faculty of not obeying to any external laws other than the ones to which I have been able to consent." As the quotation shows, the point is on "consented government," not on autonomy. Indeed, in the same writing Kant asserts that democracy is "necessarily despotism."

73. *General Theory of Law and State* (New Haven: Yale University Press, 1945), pt. II, chap. 4.

74. *Pace* de Ruggiero's masterful *History of European Liberalism*, Hegel cannot be raised to the central figure of liberal thought, nor can I accept de Ruggiero's conclusion (under the aegis of autonomy) that "the State, the organ of compulsion par excellence, has become the highest expression of freedom" (p. 374, Italian ed.). I pursue the point in chapter 13, section 2.

75. *Politics*, 1317b.

76. For the difference between self-government, *Selbstverwaltung* (which German scholarship wrongly equated with self-government), and autarchy, see Giuseppino Treves, "Autarchia, Autogoverno, Autonomia," in *Studi in Onore di G. M. De Francesco* (Milano: Giuffré, 1957), 2:579-94.

77. *Politica e Cultura* (Torino: Einaudi, 1955), p. 176.

78. Ibid., pp. 173, 272. The point had been clearly made by Montesquieu: The philosopher asks of freedom "the exercise of the will," whereas in politics "liberty cannot but consist of being empowered to do [*pouvoir faire*] what one ought to will" (*L'Esprit des Lois*, XII, 2, and XI, 3).

79. Isaiah Berlin knows his authors when he stresses, with regard to notion of a "higher self" (a notion that goes to implement the one of autonomy) that "what had begun as a doctrine of freedom . . . became the favoured weapon of despotism" (*Four Essays on Liberty*, p. xliv).

80. *Freedom and the Law* (New York: Van Nostrand, 1961), pp. 18, 19.

81. *On Liberty*, chap. 1 (p. 5 in the Norton critical ed., New York, 1975).

82. *Filosofia della Pratica* (1909), 4th ed. (Bari: Laterza, 1932), p. 333.

83. *L'Esprit des Lois*, bk. XXVI, chap. 20: "Freedom consists above all in not being compelled to do something which is not prescribed by law; and we are in this situation only as we are governed by civil laws. Therefore we are free because we live under civil laws."

84. Greek had no real equivalent of the Latin *ius*. The Greek *diké* and *dikaiosúne* render the moral but not legal idea of justice; which means that they are not equivalent to the *iustum* (just) which derives from *ius*.

85. The etymology of *ius* is debated. Two points will suffice. First, the later terms *directum,* from which comes the Italian *diritto,* the French *droit,* the Spanish *derecho,* etc., are not the same as the English "right," since the latter is concrete and/or appreciative whereas the former concepts are abstract and neutral nouns indicating the legal system as a whole. Second, the associations of *ius* with *iubeo* (to order), *iuvo* (to benefit), *iungo* (to link), and *iustum* (just), all appear at a relatively late stage. However, the linkage between *ius* and *iustum* did characterize the medieval order. As A.J. Carlyle says, "The . . . most fundamental aspect of political thought in the Middle

Ages was the principle that all political authority was the expression of justice . . . [that] all civil and positive law flow from justice as a stream flows from its source." *Political Liberty* (New York: Oxford University Press, 1941), p. 12.

86. For a swift historical survey, see C.J. Friedrich, *The Philosophy of Law in Historical Perspective* (Chicago: University of Chicago Press, 1958). Specifically on the origin and nature of the rule of law, an excellent, brief analysis is F.A. Hayek, *The Constitution of Liberty* (London: Routledge & Kegan Paul, 1960), esp. chap. 11.

87. Reference is made to the *Rechtsstaat* as a synonym of constitutional *garantisme* (see n. 22). If the notion of state based on law is conceived in strictly formal terms, it becomes purely tautologic. "If we start with the preconception that our point of view must be exclusively juridic, on what other basis could the State based on law be founded except on law? What else could the State realize except law?" R. Treves, "Stato di Diritto e Stati Totalitari," in *Studi in Onore di G. M. De Francesco,* p. 61.

88. That is, simply to designate any "political form," or any way of "giving form" to any state whatever. Whether or not this loose meaning of the term constitution precedes legal formalism, it finds its technical justification in it. My objections are spelled out in "Constitutionalism: A Preliminary Discussion," *American Political Science Review,* December 1962, which has seemingly ignited an ongoing debate. See, always, in *American Political Science Review,* the "Comment" of W.H. Morris-Jones, and my "Rejoinder," both in the June 1965 issue, pp. 439-44; and, subsequently, G. Maddox, "A Note on the Meaning of Constitution," December 1982, to whom I respond on the June 1984 issue, pp. 497-99. It should be well understood that I never use "constitution" in the all-embracing, merely organizational sense, but to qualify a specific type of state in which governmental action is effectively restrained.

89. I say "liberal constitutionalism" where American authors are inclined to say "democratic constitutionalism" on account of the peculiar meaning of "liberal" in the United States. This question will be looked into in chapter 13, herein.

90. See his classic *Constitutionalism: Ancient and Modern* (Ithaca: Cornell University Press, 1940), esp. chap. 4. *Iurisdictio* and *gubernaculum* was the terminology used by Bracton toward the middle of the thirteenth century.

91. A notable exception to this trend may be the United States on account of its unique system of separation of powers. *Pace* Montesquieu, English constitutionalism separated the power to rule from the power to ascertain and apply the law, but hardly separated the exercise of power between parliament and government. The latter is a distinctive feature of the American presidential system only.

92. *Freedom and the Law,* pp. 147-49.

93. T.R. Adam, in Bryson et al., *Aspects of Human Equality,* p. 176.

94. See, in relation to the implementation of equality, chapter 12, section 5.

95. *The Constitution of Liberty,* pp. 149-50.

96. Since certainty is a technical term that addresses the problem of predictability, it should not be understood to call for unchangeable laws.

97. Leoni, *Freedom and the Law,* p. 79.

98. Norman P. Barry, *An Introduction to Modern Political Theory* (London: Macmillan, 1981), p. 161. This is not the author's own view, but his reading of a prevailing outlook. See n. 18, above.

99. B. Barret-Kriegel, *L'Etat et les Esclaves* (Paris: Calmann Lévy, 1979), p. 229.

12. Equality

It is precisely because the force of circumstances tends always to destroy equality that the force of legislation must always tend to maintain it.

—Rousseau

12.1 A Protest Ideal

To have inequality, all that is demanded of us is to let things follow their course. But if we are to seek equality, we can never afford to relax. As Tawney wrote, echoing Rousseau: "While inequality is easy since it demands no more than to float with the current, equality is difficult for it involves swimming against it."[1] Inequality can be attributed to acts of God; equality can result only from the acts of men. Inequality is "nature"; equality is denaturalization. A societal order permeated by the belief that each person should live within the ambit of his or her station stands, so to speak, on its own feet. But a society that seeks equality is a society that fights itself, that fights its inner laws of inertia. When equality is sought, differences in power, wealth, status, and life chances, as they are "naturally" found to exist, cease to be routinely accepted differences. By appealing, then, to liberty, and in its wake—but with greater impact—to equality, man asserts his claim to a city that is no longer subject to necessary and ascriptive forms of organization.

Equality stands out, first and foremost, as a *protest ideal,* indeed, as the protest ideal par excellence. Equality symbolizes and spurs man's revolt against fate and chance, against fortuitous disparity, crystallized privilege, and unjust power. Equality is also, as we shall see, the most insatiable of all our ideals. Other strivings can conceivably reach a point of saturation, but there can hardly be an end to the race for equality—among other reasons because the attainment of equality in one respect seemingly generates inequalities in others. If, then, one ideal exists that starts man on an endless race, it is equality.

As long as we can afford to stay with equality qua protest ideal (in the singular), the matter is neat. But as soon as we start spelling out a detailed list of inequalities—that is, of the equalities that fail us—we soon discover that the list becomes all the more endless the more we detail it. This is no doubt one of the reasons why we generally confine the list to a small set of "unjust inequalities" and, correlatively, of "rightful equalities." We thus begin by asking: Which equalities, on what grounds, are selected as just or rightful equalities? The question that immediately follows is: Which are the ways and means for dealing effectively with unjust inequalities? But as soon as we get to the means, a third query comes to the fore: Are such means congruent with those that serve other goals? Are the means of equality, for instance, compatible with the means of liberty?

Writers on the subject of equality are eloquent and persuasive in voicing a *cahier de doléances* when denouncing the evils of inequality. But their arguments become thinner and less convincing as they tackle the question of *how* the ideal of equality is to be realized. As an ideal expressing a protest, equality is appealing and easy to understand; as an ideal expressing proposals, as a constructive ideal, I can think of nothing as complicated as equality. Indeed, the more we proceed in proposing a greater equality, or more equalities, the more we risk entering a labyrinth.

12.2   *Justice and Sameness*

The first complicating factor—and this is no paradox—is that the notion of equality is in itself, or can be transformed into, the simplest notion in the world. We cannot answer the question, What is free? by indicating something and saying: This. Whereas we can reply to the question, What is equal? by pointing to billiard balls and saying: These are equal. The notion of equality, unlike that of freedom, lends itself easily to tangible illustration. Why is this a complicating factor? Plato already knew the answer: because "a perfectly simple principle can never be applied to a state of things which is the reverse of simple."[2] But there is more to it.

Equality may indeed be conceived simplistically in all too tangible fashion, but may also be conceived in highly complex and elusive fashion. In one sense, equality conveys the idea of *sameness*. In another sense, equality goes to connote *justice*. Two or more persons or objects can be declared equal in the sense of being—in some or all respects—identical, of being the same, alike. But justice too calls on the idea of equality. Brunetto Latini said it, as medieval writers often did, in all candor: "Just as justice is an equal thing, so injustice is unequal; and thus he who wants to establish justice tries to make equal the things that are unequal."[3] Brunetto Latini was not displaying a novel thought. He was merely simplifying, out of context, Aristotle: "Injustice is inequality, justice is equality."[4]

It might be observed that the concept of equality is not alone in displaying a variety of meanings ranging from simple to complex ones. Yes, except that the two aforesaid conceptions of equality are miles apart and yet difficult to disentangle—like two opposite faces of one body. Equality is Janus-faced, and unique in being such, in that it can associate itself with sameness and with justice simultaneously. The entanglement of equality-as-sameness with equality-as-justice largely arises from, and consists of, a semantic overlapping. The Italian *eguale,* the French *égal,* and the German *gleich* not only mean "equal" but also carry exactly the meaning of the English "same." To say in Italian, French, and German that two things are equal is to say that they are identical. In this respect, English-speaking people are more fortunate, i.e., less exposed to equivocations, for in English usage it is unusual to say that two objects, such as two cars, are equal to indicate that they are of the same make or type. Nonetheless, the association of the ideas of equality and sameness was introduced through translations into English of the writings of continental authors, as well as through the theory of natural law. In referring to the Declaration of Independence, Lincoln in his Springfield speech of 1857 explained that the authors of that notable instrument "did not intend to declare all men equal in all respects. They did not mean to say all were equal in color, size, intellect, moral developments or social capacity."[5] It is clear that Lincoln was referring here to "equal" in the sense of *alike,* of being identical, and that his explanation would have been superfluous had the two meanings of the word equal not mingled in English as well.

The extent and tenacity of this Gordian knot can be illustrated by the argument that men are entitled to equal rights and opportunities *because* they are in fact equal, in the sense of being, at least in some respects, the same as one another. With all due respect to the illustrious thinkers who propound this view, the argument does not hold. There is no "because" about it. The moral quest for equality neither implies nor requires *de facto* sameness. There is no necessary connection between the fact that men are or are not born alike (same) and the ethical principle that they ought to be treated as equals. If equality is a moral principle, then we seek equality because we think it is a just aim—not because men actually *are* alike, but because we feel that they should be treated *as if* they were (even though, in point of fact, they are not). This is attested, historically, by the fact that our most fundamental egalitarian principles (e.g., being equal in freedom, equal laws, equality before the law) were not derived from the premise that men are identical. The Greeks and the Romans affirmed equalities that are still fundamental to us without entertaining any notion that men were the same (alike, equal). So, the actual granting of a given equality is motivated only prima facie by the alleged reason that men are born equal. The moment we unravel equality in the moral sense from equality in the physical sense, we realize that the very opposite is true: We contend that it is *just* to promote certain equalities precisely to compensate for the fact that men are, or may be, *born different.*

But why, it may be reasonably asked, do we not resolutely set aside equality-as-sameness and stay with equality-as-justice? The reply is that such a resolve would not solve the imbroglio, for justice too calls upon the notion of sameness — especially when reference is made to *social* justice in its difference from *individual* justice. Individual justice is governed by the maxim *suum cuique tribuere:* To do justice is to see to it that each is given what he deserves, or that to which he is entitled. Social justice is quite another matter. Aristotle dealt with both; Rawls deals exclusively with social justice.[6] In Rawlsian terms, even if we say, "to each his due," we mean that each should have a fair share; and a fair share means that shares should be approximately the same, unless there is some justification for adopting a different sharing. More generally put, underlying every discussion of social justice (whether or not conceived as fairness) there is the recurrent theme of identical treatment, of a same measure. Even if we repeat, with Aristotle, that equal things should be treated equally but unequal things differently, we still assert that justice demands the *same* treatment for the *same* differences. With this I do not imply that the sameness, or the identical treatment, of the theory of justice is like the physical sameness of billiard balls. Yet the word is the same word; and "same" is a word with an unmistakable core meaning. Therefore, even if the explication of equality were derived only from an explication of justice, the moral meaning(s) of equality could still be confused with some sort of material identity.[7]

That the concept of equality constitutively remains Janus-faced is best confirmed by looking into how equality relates to liberty — for equality can either be the best complement of freedom or its worst enemy. The relationship between equality and freedom is a love-hate relationship, depending on whether we demand an equality that suits diversity or an equality that sees inequality in every diversity. And, certainly, the more equality is sameness, the more an equality so conceived feeds a distaste for variety, self-assertion and eminence, and thereby, in the final analysis, for freedom.

The Janus-like, enormous oscillation of meaning of "equality" is also reflected, as one would expect, in the practice of equality. With reference to the way in which democratic majorities wielded their power, Plato's ironic remark was, "I suspect that they are only too glad of equality."[8] In 431 B.C., Pericles said to the Athenians that "while the law secures equal justice to all alike in their private disputes, the claim of excellence is also recognized; and when a citizen is in any way distinguished he is preferred to the public service, not as a matter of privilege but as a reward of merit."[9] But at a century's distance Aristotle observed a very different implementation, for democratic justice had in fact become the "application of numerical, not proportionate equality; whence it follows that the majority must be supreme, and that whatever the majority approves must be the end and the just."[10] Aristotle's account recorded the fact that the ideal of equality was rapidly transformed in the *polis* into the arithmetical tyranny of the majority denounced, more than two thousand years later, by Tocqueville and Mill. In Tocqueville's account there is a "debased" taste for equality "which leads the weak to drag the strong down to their level."[11] Simmel made the complementary point: For many, he said, equality purely and simply means "equality with one's own superior."[12]

Equality originates, then, as a moral vindication and is, indeed, a moral ideal; but it is an ideal that is all too easily corrupted. It begins as the purest reclamation of justice, but it can end as an alibi for downgrading others in order to promote oneself. Furthermore, as the sub-equals wish to become equal with their superiors, the equals may in turn (and retaliation) wish to become supra-equal, that is, to emerge above their equals. If so, the practice of equality would defeat its principle: The rhetoric would seed, in reality, inequality seekers frantically engaged in toppling or surmounting their equals. As I was saying, equality has on its side the not inconsiderable advantage of *seeming* to be a clear and simple notion. In the long haul, however, this advantage is no advantage at all. The more equality is believed to be easy, the more it turns out to be either demeaning and self-destructive, or self-deceiving.

12.3   *Predemocratic and Democratic Equalities*

As long as equality is spoken of in the singular, we are dealing with only the preliminaries of equality. Let us now proceed to deal with *equalities* in the plural. Before doing so, I repeat the warning that introduced our earlier analysis of freedom, namely, that we neither are nor should be concerned with discovering—at a speculative level—the nature of true equality, of equality in the absolute. Equality in politics and via politics requires us to deal with the empirical problem of those particular equalities that human beings have sought to establish in the course of their history. Just as liberty actually comes down to the struggle to achieve particular liberties, so equality is defined, historically, as the repudiation of certain differences.

As we begin to inquire about specific equalities (in the plural), an important reminder is that a number of equalities precede democracy and are not connected with it. Equality and democracy coincide only in the sense that the egalitarian ideal can be raised to the status of the symbol par excellence of the democratic idea. This means that the demand for equality attains its greatest force and expansion within a democratic system; it does not mean that there are no equalities outside democracy or that all equalities are a democratic achievement. In the first place, during the twenty-five centuries that separate the first appearance of the Greek word *isótes* from the present-day meaning of "equality," there has been a long process of elaboration of the concept carried out by jurisprudence, by Christianity, by moral philosophy — in short, by the whole tradition of Western thought.[13] Democratic theory, as such, has contributed very little to this development. In the second place, we must not lose sight of the fact that, with the wane of the Greek *polis,* the idea of equality became detached from that of democracy and has traveled through history independent of the fortunes of the sovereign people. The fact is, then, that not all but only some species of equality belong to the democratic family as its legitimate and distinctive descendants.

Equality before the law—*isonomía*—as we now understand it, namely, as equal protection of general laws, was only a short-lived experiment in the Greek democracies.[14] Its far more solid foundation resides in the principle that every man is equal to every other in his intrinsic dignity and worth; a Christian and ethical concept affirmed only after the wane of the ancient republics. In like manner, when we declare that all men as such have equal and inalienable rights, we are affirming an important egalitarian principle—but one that acquired its force from the notion of natural law as reconceived in the seventeenth century.[15] Also, *isegoría* and *parresía,* the Greek equalities of assembly, vote, and speech, bear only a pale resemblance to our freedoms of association and expression. All told, *isonomía, isegoría,* and "rights" are equalities far more closely hinged on, and linked with, liberal liberty and constitutional protection than with ancient democratic practices. Last, but in no way least, it often escapes us—as many obvious things do precisely because they are so obvious—that freedom signifies, when it meaningfully exists, *equal* freedom, the *same* freedom for each and all. Freedoms are also manifestations of equality.

What, then, is the specifically democratic contribution to the notion of equality? The point of reference, or the turning point, is aptly provided by the various French *Declarations of Rights.* The Declaration of 1789, article 6, reads: "All citizens being equal [in the eyes of the Law], they are equally entitled to all the emoluments and positions of public office in accord with their capabilities and under the sole distinction of their virtue and intelligence." The Declaration of 29 May 1793, article 2, puts it very concisely: "Equality consists of everybody being entitled to the same rights." And even the Constitution of August 1795, article 3, says nothing more than "Equality consists of this, that the law is equal for all, regardless of whether it protects or punishes. Equality admits no distinction of birth, no inheritance of power." These texts say very clearly that the paramount concern of the French revolutionaries was equal rights and equal laws. They were also concerned, to be sure, with disposing of "inheritance of power" and, thus, with ensuring equal access to office—but not unqualifiedly. Indeed, the French revolutionaries were in the matter far more cautious than the Greeks had been, for their equal right to positions of public office was ranked in accord with the "capabilities . . . virtue and intelligence" of the candidates. And the noteworthy point is that in no sense did economic equality enter their purview. Like the earlier seventeenth-century English Levellers, the French revolutionaries expressly refused to abolish private property (reaffirmed as a natural and inalienable right in the Constitutional Act of 24 June 1793), and did not demand equal property; they demanded only equality in rights and laws. It was, then, only after Robespierre's downfall, the Napoleonic period, and the Restoration, that the liberal-democratic demand for equality progressively came to involve three specific claims:

1. *Equal universal suffrage,* that is, extension of the right to vote to everyone as a completion of their political freedom
2. *Social equality,* understood as equality of status and of consideration, thus implying that class and wealth distinctions carry no distinction
3. *Equality of opportunity*

Although these equalities have been affirmed in the context of liberal democracy, I would say that they are characteristic rather of its democratic than its liberal component.[16] It has taken a long time for liberalism to accept *political* equality in its full implementation (as equal universal suffrage), and its unqualified acceptance of enfranchisement remains somewhat disenchanted, as attested by the saying that it is better to count heads than to break them. Regarding *social* equality, there is little doubt that liberalism (historic liberalism) is far more concerned with political freedom than with problems of class and status. If social equality is, above all, *isotimía,* equal respect regardless of rank and status, then this "equality of estimation" (as Bryce called it) represents a typically democratic ethos.[17] As for the principle of equal *opportunities,* liberalism in the twentieth century adopts it as its own, but on two conditions: that it be understood as a development of individual liberty, and that it be realized by means that do not conflict with that end. And I would say that today this is the point at issue between liberals and democrats within liberal democracies.[18] The issue of equality of opportunity separates them, in part because the ideal allows for different interpretations, but especially because they tend to disagree on how to achieve it.

Equality of opportunity is not, however, the last equality to retain on our agenda. *Economic* equality is another egalitarian claim of our time. It should be ascribed, however, to the context of socialism. This is not to say that liberal democracy cannot appropriate many of the demands connected with the vindication of economic equality, for the principle of equalization of opportunities can also be developed in the direction of canceling out the unequal points of departure due to overgreat disparity of wealth. Nevertheless, there exists a watershed beyond which the formula for democratic economic equality differs sharply from the socialist-Marxist formula for economic equality.

The equalities of liberalism end, ideally speaking, where the aim of safeguarding and strengthening individual liberty ends. Democracy, therefore, takes up the task of "denaturalizing" the social order where liberal liberty leaves off. We know today that liberty per se does not equalize opportunities; this illusion of liberalism has by now been abandoned. Modern democracy seeks, thus, a set of "just equalities" that do not follow spontaneously in the wake of freedom. This is also to say that the democrat is prepared to make a trade-off: more equality, or greater equality, for less freedom—but not at a too-great expense of freedom. If we take this last step, we move beyond liberal democracy, and also beyond social democracy, into an overriding concern for material, economic equality.

12.4 Equal Opportunities and Equal Circumstances

As we have just seen, the historical progression of equality (equalities) can be brought under four classes or types: *(a)* juridico-political equality; *(b)* social equality; *(c)* equality of opportunity; *(d)* economic equality. The first two classes need not be discussed further. The latter two classes need, instead, further explication.[19] In order to do so I propose to subdivide "equality of opportunity" into equal access and equal start. It would also be analytically useful to subdivide "economic equality," but I have to settle for parsimony, that is, for handling economic equality as a residual category. This is permissible, in turn, because I narrow its meaning to one specific (and drastic) kind of "equalization of circumstances."

Let all of the foregoing be recapitulated in table 12.1 on the following page.

TABLE 12.I. TYPES OF EQUALITY

1. Juridico-political equality
2. Social equality
3. Equality of opportunity as *equal access,* i.e., equal recognition to equal merit (as in the career-open-to-talent formula)
4. Equality of opportunity as *equal start* (or equal starting points), i.e., as equal initial material conditions for equal access to opportunities
5. Economic sameness, that is, either the same wealth to each and all, or state ownership of all wealth

In accordance with the criteria of justice that inspire these equalities and with the powers that correspond to them, table 12.1 can be interpreted as follows:

1. To everyone the same legal and political rights, that is, the legalized power to resist political power
2. To everyone the same social importance, that is, the power to resist social discrimination
3. To everyone the same opportunities to rise, that is, the power to put one's own merits to account
4. To everyone an adequate initial power (material conditions) to acquire the same ability and rank as everyone else
5. To no one any (economic) power

Beginning from the last item—economic sameness or, conversely, no economic power—it is apparent that I have reduced it to the bottom line. This is so because I have divided "economic equality" into two separate meanings and moved one of them, in my table, to item 4. My reason for this is that we can no longer speak of economic equality indiscriminately. It is true that the demand for economic equality was forcefully carried to the forefront in the nineteenth century and the first decades of the twentieth by socialism and, in the end, by its Marxist brand. But unless we are happy with equality in poverty (and powerlessness), it cannot be said that Marxism has taught us how to cure the ills of economic inequality. Actually, the Marxist therapy represents the resurrection of the oldest and crudest of egalitarian medicines, the one already advocated by Plato and already criticized by Aristotle. In particular, Marx believed power to be a substantive entity—something "possessed" by virtue of "possessions"—in wholesale neglect of its relational nature; he thus momentously confused *one* of the *resources* of power with power itself.[20]

For a long time the theory of liberal democracy has dismissed, somewhat too cavalierly, the problem of economic inequalities with the argument (as Bryce worded it) that since democracy "is merely a form of government, not a consideration of the purposes to which government may be turned [it] has nothing to do with Economic Equality. . . . Political Equality can exist either along with or apart from Equality in property."[21] Now, it is true that democracy in the political sense is one thing and economic democracy quite another.[22] Yet the inferences drawn from this distinction by Bryce do not quite follow. In the first place, once democracy is established as a form of government, the content of its policies may well have a great deal to do with economic equalization. In the second place, we know that political equality can exist apart from economic equality; but how do we know that the obverse is also true, namely, that the attainment of equality in property (or nonproperty) has no bearing on political equality? Bryce pushes the implications of the distinction between political and economic equality too far. Marxists make the same error in reverse. In substance, they apply to the political implications of their economic equalization the same formula that Bryce used; this problem (which is, for a Marxist, the form of government) does not concern us. This is not only too easy but also highly treacherous — for the Marxist solution can be achieved only via a highly forceful and pervasive form of government.

Be that as it may, we must see clearly that what is fundamentally at stake here is a problem of *equalization of circumstances.* And this problem can be tackled not only by advocating the elimination of private property and economic sameness (item 5), but also by advocating a fair and fairly equal redistribution of wealth (item 4: equal starting conditions).

The objection could be that my two versions of "equality of opportunity" are too restrictive. To wit, equal access (item 3) has been focused on career opportunities,[23] while equal starts (item 4) have been reduced, in the final analysis, to economic means, to material redistributions. I may be asked, What about Medicare, or equal education? Is Medicare not a case of equal access to equal medical care? Similarly, is equal education not a joint case of equal access and equalization of starting points? I will certainly not deny that both cases can be construed as above and, generally, as cases of equality of opportunity. But they can also be construed differently. In any event, it is the subdivision between access and starts that untangles best the issues.

Equal access amounts, in essence, to non-discrimination in entry or promotion;[24] the access is made equal to equal abilities (not to all); and whether unequal abilities are the offsprings of nature or of nurture is not a problem that this formula does or can address. Thus this version of equality of opportunity does not, in fact, equalize circumstances. Equal access implies that what is recognized and rewarded is *actual performance* and thereby leads to equality in merit, capacity, or talent.

The notion of *equal start* addresses an entirely different and preliminary problem, namely, how equally to develop *individual potentialities.* To be sure, there is no contradiction between these two versions of equality of opportunity: Once each person is given the fairest possible start (by allowing all his potentialities to blossom), it can cogently follow that from this point onward individuals should be left to ascend via their merits and abilities. This is indeed the reason for calling both things "equality of opportunity."[25] But their logical connection requires equality of starting conditions to come first and equality of access to follow. In the real world this order is reversed, and the reason for this is obvious: The *means* for equal access are infinitely less difficult and less costly than the *means* for equalizing the starting conditions.[26] Openness of access does not demand redistributions; equal starts do.

If the opportunity to start equally is far removed from the equal opportunity afforded to equal talents, it is also far removed from economic sameness. Clearly, both "redistribution" (item 4) and "dispossession" (item 5) imply that the state or government must incessantly intervene, that political power is crucially involved. However, this intervention occurs in very different ways and with very different goals in mind: either to give everyone enough power (equal power resources) to afford equal opportunities to rise or to take away all power from everyone for the sake of equality (sameness) in itself. And there is an abyss between these two approaches, between equal power to rise and the enforcement of leveling, between granting equal rights, opportunities, and starting points on the presupposition that the beneficiaries neither are nor must become alike, and imposing sameness as a final solution to the problem of these rights and opportunities.

We now have, I trust, a sufficient and sufficiently detailed topical list of equalities. How do they relate to one another? Before addressing this query, we must enter into the analytics of equality, that is, into the *criteria* of equality.

12.5   *Egalitarian Criteria, Treatments, and Outcomes*

Any analytical grasp of the concept of equality crucially presupposes the question: Equal *with respect to which characteristic?* Equal in what?[27] There is no such thing (not even in our best imaginative efforts) as equality *in all,* i.e., with respect to all possible characteristics. Individuals are different in everything: health, longevity, beauty, intelligence, talents, charm, tastes, preferences, and more. As these general headings are underpinned, we easily arrive at lists of characteristics so extensive that they become truly countless. Even when we speak of equality unqualifiedly, we never actually envisage all conceivable differences but only relatively *few differences:* the ones that we perceive, at given moments in history, as *relevant,* ostensibly *unjust,* and, implicitly, *remediable.* For instance, differences in beauty are surely unjust; they now begin to be remediable; but they have not yet been declared relevant on a policy plane. Suppose, then, that we perceive a given difference in a given characteristic as unjust and remediable. How do we proceed to eliminate it? The answer hinges on the *criteria of equalization,* which are, at the minimum, the ones presented in table 12.2.[28]

TABLE 12.2. CRITERIA OF EQUALITY

1. *The same to all,* i.e., equal shares (benefits or burdens) to all
2. *The same to sames,* i.e., equal shares (benefits or burdens) to equals and therefore unequal shares to unequals—and here four subcriteria are prominent:
    a. Proportionate equality, i.e., shares monotonically allocated in proportion to the degree of extant inequality
    b. Unequal shares to relevant differences
    c. To each according to his merit (desert or ability)
    d. To each according to his need (basic or otherwise)[29]

Three clarifications are immediately in order. First, it would be a serious misreading to read the above criteria as implying "everything." Criterion 1 does not assume equal shares to all *in everything,* nor does criterion 2 assign *everything* in equal shares to equals. Second, shares of benefits or burdens may either consist of permissions and prohibitions or consist of actual allocations (favorable or disfavorable); but the nature of the shares is immaterial to the criteria. Third, most criteria listed under item 2 can be called, generically, criteria of "proportionate equality."[30] Whether this heading should be reserved only to a monotonic proportionality depends on how much detail one wishes to enter in the argument.

Criterion 1—*equal shares to all*—is eminently the principle of the legal systems that provide equal laws and equality under the law. Notice that the clause *to all* is crucial to this criterion. If there are exclusions among the rule-receiving population, then either a rule is not egalitarian or it is egalitarian under one of the breakdowns of criterion 2. Reverting to the example of legal systems, here the clause "to all" is rendered by the principle of the "generality" of laws. That is to say that laws are equal, and we are treated equally under them if, and only if, laws are general. Sectional laws, laws that benefit or burden particular sections or blocs of a population (defined by state boundaries), are not equal under this criterion.[31]

What are the limits of criterion 1? In our example, they are well rendered by the dictum *dura lex, sed lex*. In order to be what it is, a law not only imposes hardships (is *dura*) but eventually unjust hardships (because general rules cannot do justice to individual cases). Laws are not, cannot be, person-regarding, i.e., sensitive to persons and their differences.[32] On the other hand, the counterpart of this insensitivity is that the criterion cannot be, so to speak, gerrymandered. When we say *to each the same,* there is no way of manipulating or twisting such a principle. Thus, as long as we stay with criterion 1, we stand on safe ground. It is true that a rule such as "chop off all heads" would treat us in a highly displeasing egalitarian fashion; but under our criterion there is about one chance in a million for a rule of that sort to be enacted, for, if it truly applies *to all,* even the head of the rule issuer would have to go. The point is not, then, that this criterion ensures good rules (where "good" stands for congruence with our value beliefs) or even less "equalizing rules" (in their results), but that the criterion eliminates a very large potential class of *hurtful rules,* that is, rules that we might wish to see applied to others but not to ourselves.

Criterion 2 — *equal shares to equals* and *unequal to unequals* — is no less cogent, or less defensible, than criterion 1. As Aristotle phrased it, "There is no inequality if unequals are treated in proportion to their mutual inequality."[33] Criterion 2 also turns out to have a far more extensive application than criterion 1. Its advantage consists of its flexibility, which allows not only that justice be done to subgroups but also, as we shall see, that equal results be attained. But this flexibility carries with itself an Achilles' heel. We are no longer saying "to all the same" but "*to each same,* the same." The question thus becomes: *Which sameness* is relevant? This is like opening a Pandora's box. Furthermore, and perhaps even more important, under criterion 2 there is no limit to the extent to which any conceivable rule, or any conceivable societal structure, can be declared equal — especially if we master the game of switching back and forth from one of its subcriteria to another. For instance, a medieval or caste-type society would fare very well not only under 2b (unequal shares to relevant differences) but also under 2d (to each according to his needs), provided that the difference between a warlord and a peasant appears relevant, or under the assumption that the needs of a superior caste are incommensurably greater than the ones of an inferior caste. What we lose, then, as we pass from criterion 1 to criterion 2, are the safeties and restraints provided by the clause that the benefits or burdens of a rule must equally apply, without exceptions, to all.

Despite the foregoing, it is clear that egalitarianism can neither be satisfied nor pursued under criterion 1 alone. A classic illustration would be direct taxation. A same tax for the millionaire and the beggar (criterion 1) makes no sense. Thus all fiscal systems apply equal burdens to equals (people in the same tax bracket), and unequal burdens to unequals (people of different wealth). Yet, even the least controversial case — fiscal proportionality — immediately becomes controversial the moment we get into the criteria of implementation. In my scheme, the subcriterion 2a — proportional equality — is defined monotonically. With respect to fiscal matters, this might do. Even so, should the proportion be progressive or not? And, if progressive, under what rate of progression? It will not escape us that, with this latter question, we may already be entering subcriterion 2b: unequal shares to relevant differences. If so, we may also be stepping into a hornet's nest. The illustration of this would be affirmative action in the United States, which certainly has an egalitarian (if remedial) motivation to its propounders and yet represents discrimination in reverse to its critics. In any event, the sure thing is that the criterion of affirmative-discriminative action is, in its current formulation, that the *relevant differences* "race" and/or "sex" should enjoy *unequal benefits,* with unequal burdens consequently falling on the groups that do not qualify as racially or sexually relevant.[34] The issue, let it be stressed, is not only about the pros and cons of a bloc-regarding equality (women *en bloc* or blacks *en bloc*) that damages individual-regarding and also person-regarding equality.[35] The most intractable issue is, in the longer run, why *these* and not *other* differences (of the same kind) should be deemed *relevant.*[36]

Let us deal quickly with the remaining subcriteria. Equality of merit, desert, or ability (2c) has already been sufficiently explicated. As for giving to each according to his needs (2d) I shall leave it at two considerations. The first is that if the needs are qualified as "basic" and the argument is that everybody should be ensured "minimal conditions" of a decent life (above sheer survival and yet below the level of desired and satisfying wants), then "this is an argument for equality only in a highly attenuated sense. It is really an argument simply for a more adequate welfare state, which is not quite the same thing. What is opposed is not inequality but human sufferings and insecurity."[37] On the other hand, and this is the second consideration, if need goes beyond the confines of what is "basic," there is no conceivable end to the arbitrariness that subcriterion 2d would permit.[38]

As the analysis of the criteria develops, it emerges that there are two fundamentally different ways of approaching equality, namely, as *equal treatment,* i.e., a same and *impartial* treatment; or as *equal outcome,* equal results or end states. Criterion 1 is, in effect, a criterion of equal treatment. The various criteria listed under criterion 2 variously address, instead, equal results (though they can justify unequal ones as well). The fundamentality of this distinction escapes many students of equality. Rees, for instance, asserts that absolute (maximal) equality "would literally treat everyone in the same way in every respect."[39] But a system of general laws does treat everyone in the same way in every respect (to the extent contemplated by that legal system). The fault lies, then, in saying treatment where one should say "outcome." The maximal egalitarian claim is not "all are treated equally in all" but "all are *made* equal in all."

Equal treatment and equal results are not only diverse in themselves; they also reflect divergent underlying approaches. The view underlying equal treatment is that human beings should be treated equally (with respect to x, y, and z) *in spite of* their being different, while the view underlying equal outcomes is that human beings *should not be different* and must be reinstated in their pristine nondifference. In spite of these diversities, it may at first be thought that the two stances follow each other as in a nice crescendo. On second thought, however, the crescendo is a dissonant one, for equal treatment does not lead to equal results and, conversely, equal end states require unequal treatment. The predicament, bluntly put, is this: *To be made equal (in outcome), we are to be treated unequally.*

That egalitarian treatment does not eliminate differences, i.e., does not engender equal results (in conditions or otherwise), is by now a recognized fact. Equal laws, important as they may be, simply leave us equal before the law; but the underprivileged and the privileged, the gifted and the ungifted, remain as they are. It is often less well understood, instead, that *equal end states* necessarily call for *unequal means,* that is, for discriminating (differential) treatments. Once we decide that given groups are disfavored with respect to the relevant characteristics x and y, in order to eliminate the inequality in question the disfavored must be overfavored, and, vice versa, the advantaged must be disadvantaged. If good and bad runners are to be given an equal chance to win the race, the first group must be held back and the second one pushed forward.[40] Contrary, then, to a widespread opinion, equal results require *unequal opportunities,* and it is certainly a fallacy to use results to assess equality of opportunity. Not only equal starts are not equal arrivals, but no opportunity is offered if its outcome is predetermined.

To be sure, there is a wide area of tradeoffs between equal treatment and equal results. A treatment can be made "less equal" in order to foster a "more equal" outcome; conversely, we may settle for "imperfectly equal" results in order to salvage "minimally equal" treatments. But if this is not understood, and if equality of outcome becomes the sole, overriding concern, then egalitarian ends will destroy egalitarian treatment — and this may well entail that the end destroy its means. In this connection, it is important to remember that the safeties (and restraints) are all in criterion 1. Once we reject the intrinsic value of the clause "the same *to all*," criterion 2, left alone to its own variety of devices, will permit and legitimize, in the name of equality, any conceivable arbitrariness and partiality of treatment. The central consideration is, however, that the pursuit of equal end states may jeopardize equal treatment to the point where no assurance remains as to the very pursuit of the alleged goal. Beyond the point of equality of access, policies of equalization are largely policies of *redistribution* and, ultimately, of *dispossession.*[41] Now, every concrete intervention of the sort presupposes a decision as to which inequalities (characteristics) are relevant, as opposed to characteristics that are not; and it has been seen that every redistribution founded on a given characteristic will hurt distributions descending from other characteristics. Therefore, an excess of unequal treatment is more likely to engender a war of all against all than to satisfy egalitarian demands. If every equality is attained at the expense of generating other inequalities, and if this becomes generally perceived, we are simply slipping into a vicious vortex.

12.6 The Maximization of Equality

The extent to which the intricacies — I called it the labyrinth — of equality are greater than the complexities of liberty is now apparent. This alone suffices to explain why we are fairly well in control of the techniques of liberty but still very much up in the air with the techniques of equality. Insofar as our accumulated body of knowledge and experience goes, with liberty we stand on firm ground, but with equality we do not. The ground is shaky, to be sure, not with respect to the equalities we do have (such as political and juridical equality), but with respect to the equalities we do not have, or have minimally.

Let us take a step back to table 12.1, which sorts out five types or classes of equality: 1. juridico-political equality; 2. social equality; 3. equal access; 4. equal starts; 5. economic sameness (equalization or rather, in current practice, state appropriation of wealth). The sequence of the first three items reflects the historical succession in which the equalities in question were affirmed. The latter two items represent, instead, alternative solutions for equalities that we either do not have or have in a most displeasing manner. Clearly, it is by no means fortuitous that our first three equalities were claimed and born in that order. One reason for this is that simpler things precede more complicated things. But the more important reason is that the newer equalities *presuppose* the equalities that precede them. The equalities that came later in time are also equalities built on and *sustained by* the preexisting ones. We thus arrive at the question: As the list grows, are equalities cumulative and cumulable all the way along the line? This question aptly introduces us to the issue of how equality can be maximized.

In the Marxist literature and its spillovers, juridical and political equality are declared "formal" equalities, "form" is construed as appearance (illusion or sham), and the distinction between formal and material equalities is thereby turned into one between apparent and real equalities. But this argument rests on a complete distortion of the technical meaning(s) of the term form—which is the meaning by which it correctly applies to equality. And the frequency with which we hear "formal equality" sneered at makes it important to redress the misunderstanding.

When we speak of "juridical form" we are singling out the very requisite of a legal order. The form of law and the formal nature of law constitute (at least *de jure condito,* in positive law) the characteristics by virtue of which a law is a law. There is also a second, broader and basically ethical, sense of the notion of form. Here the contention is that only if norms have a "formal formulation" will the addressee of the commands expressed by these norms be treated as a free agent. For this reason Kant formulated his categorical imperatives in such a way as to indicate what ought to be the *form of any moral action.* That is to say, Kant refused to indicate the specific content of moral prescriptions, lest moral experience become a matter of submission to external norms (a heteronomous ethic) rather than a matter of freedom, that is, the acceptance of rules imposed on us by ourselves (an autonomous ethic). Now, juridical and political equality, as well as equality of access, are formal equalities in these technical meanings of the term. To call them formal is not to say that they leave us defenseless in the face of inequality of privilege or that we are dealing with empty semblances of equality. Formal is the method, not the result. It is therefore totally beside the mark to disparage the formal conditions (including the juridical and political ones) that promote equal opportunities, or to say that these equalities are fictitious or scarcely important. How great is their importance is open to question, but it is out of the question that their importance vis-à-vis material equalities cannot be approached like Marxists do or have taught others to do.

The preliminary point thus is that the cumulation and cumulability of equalities has nothing to do with formal, i.e., non-substantive and deceiving equalities, being superseded and replaced by "real equalities." The relationship is not between appearance and substance, window dressing and the real thing. When we say that certain equalities are formal, we mean (when we know what we are saying) that they are, first of all, *equal treatments,* and that what makes the treatment equal is precisely the "form" in which it is expressed. It follows from this that we are not entitled to dismiss juridico-political equality by declaring it *not real.* This is, again, an entirely misleading formulation. If it is true that juridical and political equalities sustain (as requisite conditions) all other equalities, then they are as *real* as what follows from them. And if this is not true, as the critics contend, it behooves these critics to show how "real" equality can be achieved (without accompanying, frightening unpleasantnesses) in their absence. This they have never shown, either on paper or even less in accomplishments.

Whether the various equalities are cumulable or not depends, then, on whether and to what extent they are either complementary (compatible) or mutually exclusive (incompatible). Stated in logical form, the question whether one specific kind of equality can be superadded to another kind of equality hinges on whether they are mutually *contradictory.* But where do we look for the contradictions or noncontradictions in question? We must look, I suggest, at the *criteria* of equality, for it is only the neatness of criteria that affords a neat appraisal. We are thus required to revert to table 12.2. For the purposes at hand, let the criteria in question be abridged and reformulated as follows:

1. Equal shares to all
2. Proportionate shares in proportion to relevant differences
3. Disproportionate shares to counteract relevant differences
4. To each according to his ability
5. To each according to his need (left undefined)

The list affords a number of possible readings. As I read it, if any one of the above criteria is pushed to its extreme, then it is clearly destructive of, or at war with, all the others. We may thus say that in principle all our criteria are mutually contradictory, mutually exclusive. However, this is so under the clause "if pushed to its extreme." If this clause is removed, as in practice it is, then the interesting reading becomes that the criteria afford some combinations that seem compatible and others that seem incompatible. To illustrate, criteria 1 and 2 can be rendered complementary, for each can make concessions to the other without flagrant inconsistency. On the other hand, criterion 1 is very strongly at odds with criterion 3, and is largely incompatible with criteria 4 and 5 as well. Criterion 2 can adjust to 1 but blends far better with criterion 4, while it is strongly incompatible with 3. Criterion 3 can be easily associated with 5 but is otherwise in patent conflict with, or contradiction to, all the other criteria. What matters is not the detail of my reading but the general feeling one derives from a list of criteria assessed in terms of their compatibility (or incompatibility). No matter how the list is drawn, and regardless of the many different ways in which the complementarities can be argued, in any case we obtain an ensemble that is definitely *not additive:* Overall, equalities do not play in harmony.

We are now ready to confront the grand issue, namely, how we are to understand and consequently achieve *more equality*. The intellectual market displays three sets of replies: *(a)* there is one *major Equality* that includes all the others; *(b)* greater equality is achieved by *adding* all the single or partial equalities together; *(c)* increasing equality is attained by *better rebalancings* of inequalities.

The first thesis has the greatest appeal, but it is mistaken and can be highly destructive. Equality in the singular and written with a capital letter is a deontological symbol aimed at warming people's hearts. To infer from it that there is an essential, larger equality that includes all the small equalities is to invent another voracious Leviathan, a mythical "total Equality" that will swallow up the specific, concrete equalities. An all-subsuming synthetic Equality does not exist. Under its shadow we are smuggling in a specific equality, the one we cherish the most. But when a particular kind of equality is displayed as the solution to the overall problem of Equality, we can confidently expect this alleged final Equality to reopen the way to all the inequalities that it claims to have surpassed.

The second thesis grants that there is no such thing as a single essential Equality and therefore holds that equality grows by addition. The thesis is, then, that maximization of equality is achieved by adding together, one after another, all the separate kinds of equality. As we have implicitly seen, this thesis has merit but does not hold all the way: Some inequalities are mutually incompatible and, indeed, exclusive. Thus, at some crucial juncture the pile may collapse instead of growing further. The argument often is that since legal and political equalities have been achieved, no further attention should be paid to them; the real need is to proceed beyond them. But this is the argument that turns additions into subtractions. Equality of rights certainly does not bring, in itself, equality of possessions; but what if equality of possessions (or nonpossessions) leaves us without rights? If equal rights do not afford us equal power, giving the state the power to equalize all power may result in annihilating, not increasing, whatever power we possessed previously. All in all, the thesis that equality grows by addition does not provide an adequate model for handling the maximization of equality.

355

My own thesis is, hence, the third one: Greater equality consists of fuller and better rebalancings among inequalities. The problem of equality finds no solution when pursued *pars pro toto,* that is, when a partial equality is proclaimed as *the* total Equality; nor is it a matter of adding together as many equalities as are needed to ultimately make everybody equal in all respects. The problem of equality always is to achieve an efficient system of *reciprocal compensations among inequalities,* that is, a system of countervailing forces in which each inequality tends to offset another inequality. Overall, then, equality results from the interplay of a system of liberties-equalities that is designed to cross-pressure and neutralize one disparity with another.[42]

In the course of our discussion we have, in the main, attended to the question: Equality *in what?* But we have also held in mind, if unsystematically and implicitly, the question: Equality *for whom?* For, and across, individuals? Or for blocs (regardless of inequalities within each bloc)? It has been seen that equal treatments are not person-regarding; they are insensitive to whether the treatment "fits" the person. On the other hand, unequal treatments *may be* person-regarding[43] but lack the security afforded by the same treatment for all. When these (and more) elements are assembled together, they are suggestive of a game, or a war, that is never supposed to end with final winners and final losers. This is even more clearly shown by the analysis of the criteria of equalization. First, no single criterion unquestionably commands a superior claim upon the others. Second, some of these criteria complement each other, but other criteria are mutually exclusive. When they implement and, thereby, presumably reinforce one another, it would be self-defeating to have one replace the other. And when they contradict one another, it is even more important that their mutual antagonism be maintained rather than resolved. Contrary criteria (none of which can be shown to have supremacy) are required to correct each other; this requires, in turn, that they all subsist. Were one of the criteria to defeat the others, in victory it would only exaggerate its own shortcomings. As I put it earlier, what is logically an either-or becomes, in the realm of practice, a matter of tradeoffs. We can eat part of the cake and still have the cake in part.

I have just explained, I trust, what I mean by *rebalancing.* But I have also spoken of "fuller" and, more daringly, of "better" rebalancings. What do I mean by this? I understand it to mean, in essence, a greater effectiveness of whatever rebalancing is being sought and/or a greater adherence to the values of justice that prevail in any given society at any given time. In history, what each age regards as a progress toward greater equality reflects either an increased implementation of the same sense of justice or novel enactments redirected by a changed sense of justice. In the first case, the question, Equal with respect to which characteristic? is not even asked, for a society stands by the egalitarian values in which it has long believed. In the second case, a society desires to be equal with respect to new characteristics. Here it is the change toward new "just equalities" that supplies the feeling, if not also the reality, of achieving greater equality. It goes without saying that both progressions may occur simultaneously. In that case the process becomes more complicated, but the meaning of "better rebalancings" remains as described. In every case we always seek to eliminate *some* inequalities: the disparities that are resented, not the host of disparities that pass unnoticed or are accepted as a matter of course or are deemed to be irremediable. Thus, the counterbalancing of inequalities by no means implies a static bias. As I have just indicated, a system of reciprocal cancellation of inequalities is always organized, historically, in response to changing centers of gravity, that is, in response to changing values and priorities regarding what is deemed to be just.

12.7 Liberty and Equality

The nexus between liberty and equality has been lingering over our discussion, though somewhat elusively. It has been seen that for a very long time liberty implied "equality in liberty" and that equality in itself (especially in its distinction-opposition to liberty) obtained little salience. This is no longer the case. Today liberty and equality command separate recognition — and along this path equality may not only implement freedom but also destroy freedom. So we generally say. Still, this is a matter that must be looked into.

Let us start with the assertion that equality *presupposes* freedom. The assertion does not declare a value priority or that one is more important than the other. We are simply pointing to a procedural linkage, namely, that liberty must materialize, in time and in fact, *before* equality. Liberty comes *first,* then, on the simple consideration that equality without freedom cannot even be demanded. There is, to be sure, an equality that precedes freedom and bears no relation to it; but it is the equality that exists among slaves, among individuals who are equal either in having nothing or in counting for nothing, or both, equal in being totally subjected. However, the equality of slaves or of enslaved subjects is not a conquest of equality and has nothing to do, I would hope, with the equalities we cherish. It is difficult not to grant, then, that liberty comes *first* in the sense that he who is unfree does not even have a voice in the matter.

But, it will be asked, must liberty *sustain* equality all along? I shall not dwell on this issue, for, *mutatis mutandis,* it repeats the argument I have ex-

357

tensively made about freedom: Just as political freedom (freedom *from*) is the preliminary and enduring condition for all the powers of liberty, for all the freedoms *to,* for exactly the same reasons it is also the preliminary and enduring condition for all the powers of equality. Deprive equals of the liberty to "voice for," and they become equal in being voiceless and abused.

Yet no sooner does a situation of liberty open the way to the appetite for equality than the ideal of liberty finds itself at a disadvantage, and the appeal of equality proves stronger. This occurs for two major reasons. First, the idea of equality is more accessible, since equality can be given a tangible meaning (albeit a misleading one), whereas liberty cannot. Second, equality results in providing tangible benefits, material benefits, whereas the benefits of liberty are, as long as they are enjoyed, intangible. And the second consideration also goes a long way toward explaining why, of all the equalities that we have surveyed, economic equality turns out to be the foremost rallying cry of our time. Tawney not only explained the sense of this development but perceived its limit when he observed: "Though the ideal of an equal distribution of material wealth may continue to elude us, it is necessary, nevertheless, to make haste towards it, not because such wealth is the most important of man's treasures, but to prove that it is not."[44] This was written in 1931 but deleted in the 1952 edition. Why did Tawney omit it? Possibly because in the 1950s it was increasingly clear that there was more to economic equality than "equal distribution of wealth" and that, aside from incremental gains and additions, we were confronted with a fundamental alternative: economic equality *within* or *without* liberal democracy. The issue is taken up, then, by asking: When does equality implement liberty, and which is, instead, the kind of equality inimical to liberty?

In replying, we ultimately revert to the Janus-faced nature of equality, that is, equality conceived as sameness or as justice. When "equal" means "same," then liberty constitutes, at a minimum, a disturbance. If we seek *Gleichschaltung,* likeness or uniformity, we must dislike diversity; and if we dislike diversity, we cannot appreciate freedom—except by being flagrantly inconsistent. Conversely, the freedom seeker will perceive equality as an expansion of his principle and, more precisely, as embodying *rights of freedom.* His formula is not "unequal opportunities to become equal" but "equal opportunities to become unequal." To the freedom seeker there is as much injustice in enforcing sameness on what is different as there is in accepting hereditary inequalities. To equalize *all in all* is to create a situation as rife with privilege as the one that accepts inequality in all. His criterion is that unjustified equalities must be opposed as much, and for exactly the same reason, as unjustified inequalities.

It must be clear that the issue is not an issue of fact. Both sides can accept that individual differences (leading to individual inequalities) are *in part* facts of society and *in part* facts of nature. But neither camp really knows to what extent individual differences result from extant societal inequalities. We do know that animals are far more different—within a same morphology—than meets the eye. Thus, nature has its part in generating differences. We do see that the children of a same family, all brought up in the same way and in the same environment, both resemble and do not resemble one another. Therefore the cause of all differences cannot be in convention and nurture. But this kind of evidence does not settle in the least the question of which part—society or nature—produces which differences to what extent. If the debate, say, between libertarians and levelers is a heated one, this is so on grounds of principle or, as the fashion wants it, on ideological grounds. The libertarian admits that differences-inequalities are *also* generated by societal arrangements; the leveler asserts that they are *mostly* societal byproducts. Neither can warrant whether it is an "also" or a "mostly."[45] We are thus left to appraise the issue, as I have done, as hinging on value beliefs.

I was saying that, at the level of principles, equality combines with freedom only when equality loses its association with uniformity—with being, or being made, same. Even so, the frictions continue as we descend from principles to means. *How* is equality to be pursued? As soon as equality is construed as equalization of circumstances, it involves (at minimum) continuous redistributions, which in turn imply that a political hand intervenes to correct or replace the automatisms of market-type distributions. Thus, the more we seek to maximize equality, the more the question arises, What about liberty? Are we employing the means of liberty or instruments that endanger freedom?

Equal starts, let alone equal outcomes, call for unequal treatment. And the fact is that we are departing more and more from a juridical order based on general rules, i.e., on the criterion "the same to all." The worry or suspicion is that along this path we may end up with a "return to the rule of status, a reversal of the 'movement of progressive societies,' which in the famous phrase of Sir Henry Maine 'has hitherto been a movement from status to contract.' "[46] Whether discriminatory, sectional legislation will bring us back to an estate-type society is questionable. But it can hardly be doubted that the *gerechtestaat,* the just state that enforces justice, is in the process of destroying equal laws and equality under the law; and Rousseau for one would doubtless affirm that, along this path, the government of laws reverts to being an arbitrary, unsafe government of men.

So long as the equalization of circumstances is sought in equal starting points, the pursuit of equality and the requirements of liberty can find a balance and do, if uneasily, rebalance one another. Up to this point we remain *within* liberal democracy. However, this dialectic breaks down and rebalancing mechanisms no longer subsist in the polities in which the problem of economic equality is allegedly resolved once and for all by making the state the sole capitalist-type proprietor. The point need not call on the evidence afforded by the communist regimes; it stands, with unbeatable cogency, on its logical force alone, and is this: Whether property is private or public, in every case "power over a man's subsistence is power over his will."[47] As the state becomes the sole employer and the controller of all the means of production, a truly formidable and indeed crushing disparity of power is created between rulers and ruled. Trotsky well knew it: "In a country where the sole employer is the state," he wrote with reference to how the "oppositionists" were handled by Stalin, "this means death by slow starvation. The old principle: who does not work shall not eat, has been replaced by a new one: *who does not obey shall not eat*."[48]

When all the evils of private property and capitalist ownership are denounced, the fact remains that a multiplicity of employers allows exits and reentries; he who does not obey can still eat by working for another employer. But neither exits nor reentries are possible with one employer only. The critics of capitalism allege that in Western societies the capitalists are an enslaving force. If these critics were minimally consistent, they would have to admit that this is even more the case, a fortiori, when many (dispersed) capitalists are resolved into one, and, in addition, economic power joins forces with political power. Within Western societies state power and economic power are certainly not in the same hands, and while politicians and capitalists may collude, they also collide. And, certainly, no built-in impediment prevents the liberal-democratic state from keeping the propertied class under control. But how and by whom can an all-owning state be controlled? Under such conditions, are not the citizens deprived of the very possibility of resisting the state's will on the irresistible ground that a disobedient citizen confronts starvation?

There is definitely a point, then, beyond which equality destroys freedom and, with it, liberal democracy. If the state becomes all-powerful, it is by no means certain that it will be a benevolent, equality-dispensing state; on the contrary, it is highly probable that it will not. In that case, our equalities will go in one with our freedoms. How can we fail to perceive, then, the distinctiveness of freedom vis-à-vis equality? Yet the tendency has long been and still is to confuse problems of equality with problems of freedom. Take, for instance, the much repeated sentence: Equality is a form of freedom. Or take, still worse, the thesis that equality is a "larger freedom" and a "higher freedom," if not resolutely the "real freedom." It bears stressing that in all of this the element of truth is far smaller than that of error.

To begin with, equality is a form of freedom in the sense that it is a *condition* of freedom. And to say that one thing is a condition of another is not to say that they are the same thing. From the premise that equality is a condition of freedom, one cannot derive that by being made equal we become by that very reason free. It depends above all on what type of master has made us equal. Let us also recall that if equality is a condition of freedom, the converse is even more true: Freedom is a condition of equality. However, by reason of the fact that we are free, we are not also equal. But then, by what logic can it be held that if we are equal, we are, ipso facto, free? No — equality is *only* (nothing more than) a condition of freedom. In particular, it is a condition of freedom but by no means a *sufficient condition* of freedom. A dictatorial polity may enforce participation (everybody must vote) and simultaneously deny freedom of participation (nobody can vote for an alternative). Clearly, equal participation does not entail free participation. It may also be doubted whether equality is a *necessary condition* of freedom. Medieval liberties did exist without equality (by our standards). We are seemingly left, then, with equality as a *facilitating condition* of freedom. Be that as it may, all that needs to be established here is that equality is not a sufficient condition. For if equality is only a (non-sufficient) condition of freedom, then with even greater reason we cannot make of equality a larger freedom, let alone a higher freedom. As for the thesis that equality, and in particular economic equality, is "real" freedom or even the only real freedom, this thesis only adds the error of a mythical total Equality to the error of a single total Liberty. And the combination of two errors of such magnitude is an ominous one.

Nobody disputes that freedom and economic conditions are related. Freedom, it is said, begins at breakfast; and someone suffering from hunger may well call bread "liberty." However, this is only, and only in the short run, a way of asking for food. In the short run because in illiberal systems the problem is not solved by giving more bread but by taking away the right to ask for it. Moreover, and certainly, we are not free once our bellies are full. It is true that political freedom does not solve the problem of hunger; it is, however, equally true that bread does not solve the problem of political freedom. At the beginning of the French Revolution, Marat wrote to Desmoulins: "What good is political freedom for those who have no bread? It counts only for theorists and ambitious politicians."[49] The query was sensible, but the course of the revolution would have shown that the reply was wholly inadequate. One cannot help wondering whether Desmoulins himself, on his way to the guillotine, did not see his way to discovering that political freedom has its uses and that a very "unreal" freedom follows for those who call for equality confusing it with freedom. Let the point be firmly reiterated: Who will equalize the equalizers is not an equality issue — it is a liberty issue.[50]

It is often repeated that as liberty performs for the advantage of the few, in parallel fashion equality acts as the force of the many (in that it favors force by numbers). But the parallelism does not hold all the way. There is a crucial difference between the two cases, namely, that with the instruments of liberty neither the few nor the many can fully succeed in oppressing each other, whereas in the name and with the instruments of equality both the many and the few can find themselves in chains. The difference is, thus, that while the principle of liberty cannot be overturned — in actual operation — into its very opposite, the principle of equality can.

Notes

1. R.H. Tawney, *Equality,* 1st ed. (1931), chap. 1. The sentence was modified in the 4th ed. (London: Allen & Unwin, 1952), p. 47.

2. *Statesman,* 294 (trans. Jowett). Plato made reference, here, to law; but the remark applies even better to equality.

3. *Tesoro,* VI, 26. This is a fourteenth-century text.

4. *Nichomachean Ethics,* 1131a.

5. *The Collected Works of A. Lincoln* (New Brunswick: Rutgers University Press, 1953), 2:406-7.

6. See J. Rawls, *A Theory of Justice* (Cambridge, Mass.: Harvard University Press, 1971). The point is forcibly made by Anthony Flew, *The Politics of Procustes: Contradictions of Enforced Equality* (Buffalo: Prometheus, 1981), esp. chap. 3. Flew argues that since the theory of justice as such, without prefix or suffix, traditionally and essentially deals with "deserts and entitlements . . . of whatever else his [Rawls's] 'justice as fairness' may be a theory, it is not of justice" (pp. 81-82). An entirely different critique of Rawls is Brian Barry, *The Liberal Theory of Justice* (Oxford: Clarendon Press, 1973). While Rawls stands, at one extreme, for social justice, at the opposite extreme R. Nozick, *Anarchy, State and Utopia* (New York: Basic Books, 1974), may be said to stand for individual justice.

7. Among the notable studies on the concept of justice yet to be recalled, see G. Del Vecchio, *La Giustizia,* 3d ed. (Roma: Studium, 1946); C. Perelman, *The Idea of Justice and the Problem of Argument* (London: Routledge & Kegan Paul, 1963); H. Kelsen, *Was ist Gerechtigkeit?* (Wien: Deuticke, 1953). Three symposia largely dealing with equality are F.A. Olafson, ed., *Justice and Social Policy* (Englewood Cliffs, N.J.: Prentice-Hall, 1961); R.B. Brandt, ed., *Social Justice* (Englewood Cliffs, N.J.: Prentice-Hall, 1962); C.J. Friedrich and J.W. Chapman, eds., *Justice* (New York: Atherton, 1963). See also W.G. Runciman, *Relative Deprivation and Social Justice* (Berkeley: University of California Press, 1966); and M. Walzer, *Spheres of Justice: A Defense of Pluralism and Equality* (New York: Basic Books, 1983).

8. *Gorgias,* 483 (trans. Jowett).

9. Thucydides, *The History of the Peloponnesian War,* bk. xi., par. 37.

10 *Politics,* 1317b.

11. *Démocratie en Amerique,* bk. 1, pt. 1, chap. 3.

12. "Uber und Unterordnung," trans. Kurt H. Wolff in his ed. of *The Sociology of Georg Simmel* (Glencoe: Free Press, 1950), p. 275.

13. For the historical development of equality as a political demand, see Sanford A. Lakoff, *Equality in Political Philosophy* (Cambridge, Mass.: Harvard University Press, 1964).

14. Note, also, that the Greek *isonomía* overlapped with *isopoliteía* (equal citizenship) and that the *isopolítes* was the citizen as distinct from, and opposed to, the slave. In this association, *isonomía* qualified, more than anything else, the notion of citizenship.

15. The Stoics theorized a natural law, but not the "natural rights" that Grotius derived *ex principiis hominis internis* and that are at the basis of the modern idea of legitimacy. As A. Passerin d'Entrèves succinctly puts it (*Natural Law,* pp. 59-61), "The *ius naturale* of the modern [seventeenth and eighteenth century] political philosopher is no longer the *lex naturalis* of the medieval moralist nor the *ius naturale* of the Roman lawyer." See also E. Cassirer, *The Philosophy of the Enlightenment* (Princeton: Princeton University Press, 1951), chap. 6; and the still fundamental work of O. von Gierke, *J. Althusius und die Entwicklung der Naturrechtlichen Staatstheorien,* trans. *The Development of Political Theory* (New York: Norton, 1939). See, in addition, chapter 10, n. 26, and chapter 11, n. 68, herein.

16. In order not to be misled by the peculiar American meaning of "liberal," it must be underscored that with reference to liberal democracy the first word stands for "liberalism," and thereby for the historic acceptation of "liberal": he who believes in liberalism, not in democracy. See chapter 13, herein.

17. See the analysis of democracy in the social sense in chapter 1, section 3. That distinctions of wealth and class carry no distinction is a formulation in the negative. Rawls reformulates the negation into an affirmation: the morality of "equal respect and *concern*" (my emphasis).

18. The divide was forcibly stated by John Plamenatz, "Equality of Opportunity," in Bryson et al., *Aspects of Human Equality,* as follows: "The equality that matters in this world is equality of freedom, all other kinds of worldly equality being important only as means to it. There is equality of opportunity wherever any man has roughly as good a chance as any other of leading the kind of life he wants to lead" (p. 84). In brief, "Our equality is rooted in freedom and is not to be understood apart from it. It is not equality of status but equality of opportunity, and the opportunity is to 'be oneself' " (p. 94). A brilliant restatement is Ralf Dahrendorf, *Life Chances* (Chicago: University of Chicago Press, 1980). In Dahrendorf's argument, as we move away and beyond equality of opportunity, the choices available to society, and to individuals in society, are increasingly threatened.

19. A major, recent step forward in the literature on equality is Douglas Rae et al., *Equalities* (Cambridge, Mass.: Harvard University Press, 1981). Felix Oppenheim (see n. 27, below) is the most important single author on egalitarian rules and criteria. Two symposia with very valuable contributions are Bryson et al., *Aspects of Human Equality;* and J.R. Pennock and J.W. Chapman, eds., *Equality* (New York: Atherton, 1967). Rawls's theory of justice certainly has a central bearing on the theory of equal-

ity as well. This becomes very evident with his critics from the left. See, e.g., Norman Daniels, ed., *Reading Rawls: Critical Studies on Rawls' Theory of Justice* (New York: Basic Books, 1976).

20. The point hinges on Friedrich's important distinction between *(a)* corporeal or substantive power (power as "a thing had") and *(b)* relational power, i.e., "power over." See *Constitutional Government and Democracy* (1950 rev. ed.), pp. 22-24 and 584.

21. Bryce, *Modern Democracies,* 1:67.

22. See chapter 1, section 3.

23. Flew would sustain this narrowing, for "what has usually been meant by 'equality of opportunity' would be better described as open competition for scarce opportunities." *The Politics of Procrustes,* p. 45.

24. This is, however, no mean demand, for patterns of recruitment always tend to be importantly influenced by friendship, family connections, and exchanges of favors, let alone political, ideological, religious, and ethnic considerations, and importantly channeled via innumerable networks (from alumni groups all the way to mafias). Much of the recent belittlement of "formal" equality of opportunity fails to acknowledge how much substance is involved.

25. Thus, Rawls's *"fair* equality of opportunity" (my emphasis) comprises both "openness" to positions and "similar life chances," i.e., some equalization of starting points—at least in terms of compensatory education, of "roughly equal prospects of culture" (*A Theory of Justice,* p. 73), and on the basis of the consideration that "property and wealth must be kept widely distributed" (pp. 277-79). However, my strong distinction (between access and start) permits a better assessment of where authors actually stand, and also of the fact that equality of opportunity confronts us (beyond Rawls's careful smoothing) with clear-cut alternatives.

26. On the costs of equalizing the start, a much too neglected aspect of the problem, see Robert Amdur, "Compensatory Justice: The Question of Costs," *Political Theory,* May 1979.

27. For this discussion, see esp. F.E. Oppenheim, "Equality," *International Encyclopedia of the Social Sciences,* 5:102-7; "Egalitarianism as a Descriptive Concept," *American Philosophical Quarterly,* April 1970; and "Egalitarian Rules of Distribution," *Ethics,* January 1980 (largely utilized in *Political Concepts: A Reconstruction* [Chicago: University of Chicago Press, 1981], chap. 6). I am very indebted (if at times in dissent) to his insightful analyses. I also wish to thank Oppenheim for his helpful critical comments on an earlier version of this chapter.

28. I am assuming, for the simplicity of the argument, that a given difference in a given characteristic applies to discrete individuals. It should be understood, however, that egalitarian claims apply to a variety of units: not only to individuals but also to "segments" (when equality is sought *within* subclasses) and to "blocs" (where equality is sought *between* subclasses). This analysis is developed in great detail and sophistication by Rae et al., *Equalities,* passim.

29. To be sure, *c* and *d* are subspecifications of *a* and *b*. But the arrangement of the table simplifies the argument.

30. This was, by and large, Aristotle's understanding, whose basic distinction was between proportionate or proportional equality (to desert) and what he called "numerical equality" (basically, my criterion 1). But Aristotle's argument was highly sophisticated. See esp. *Nicomachean Ethics,* II, 5; V, 2, 3, 6, 8; and VIII, 7; but also

Politics, bks. II and V, *passim.*

31. Since every conceivable rule treats equals equally (this is what makes it a rule), the difference among rules is established, in this respect, by their greater or lesser inclusiveness. That is, only an all-inclusive rule truly treats all equally, whereas the smaller the population to which a rule is addressed, the greater the population treated unequally (either in advantages or disadvantages) by that rule.

32. D. Rae, "Two Contradictory Ideas of (Political) Equality," *Ethics,* April 1981, counterpoises "person-regarding equality" to "lot-regarding equality." In the light of this distinction, criterion 1 is, in general, lot-regarding: Each recipient is entitled to exactly the same things in the same amounts.

33. *Politics,* 1301b. This is indeed a very free translation by John Warrington (London: Dent & Sons, 1958), p. 134, but does not betray the spirit of the text.

34. In defense of what Nagel calls "compensatory discrimination," see Marshall Cohen, Thomas Nagel, and Thomas Scanlon, eds., *Equality and Preferential Treatment* (Princeton: Princeton University Press, 1977). For the critical views, see Nathan Glazer, *Affirmative Discrimination* (New York: Basic Books, 1975); and Daniel Bell, "On Meritocracy and Equality," *The Public Interest* 29 (1972). F. Oppenheim, "Equality, Groups and Quotas," *American Journal of Political Science* 21 (1977), suggests a neutral assessment for quotas.

35. See n. 28, above. Specifically, a bloc-regarding and "bloc-equal" equality is defined (structurally) by two features: "i. the subjects of equality are divided into two or more subclasses, and ii. equality is required between subclasses (blocs) and not within them." Rae et al., *Equalities,* p. 32.

36. To illustrate, why is it important to be black, Mexican, Puerto Rican, American Indian, Filipino, Chinese, Japanese (the categories spelled out in the quota guidelines), and not important to be Armenian, Cuban, Pole, Irish, Italian, and almost endlessly on? At the outset the reply is that "relevance" (the inclusions) is established by which ethnic groups are most disfavored. In the longer run, however, the excluded ethnic groups will perceive themselves as being the disfavored ones; and this will be all the more the case, the more compensatory discrimination (in favor of the other blocs) acquires salience and succeeds.

37. Charles Frankel, "Equality of Opportunity," *Ethics,* April 1971, p. 199.

38. Rawls extends the notion of need to what he calls "primary goods," defined as the rights and resources that "people in a well ordered society may be presumed to want whatever their final ends." (See "A Kantian Conception of Equality," *Cambridge Review,* February 1975, p. 97.) But this is either a pie-related argument (as in Frankel's point on the welfare state), or Rawls's "presumed to want" is an impossibly elastic yardstick.

39. John Rees, *Equality* (New York: Praeger, 1971), p. 98 and chap. 7, *passim.* Rees actually follows other authors.

40. I leave aside the complication that there is a major difference, along the way toward equal outcomes, between "allocation of objects" (e.g., everybody is entitled to one pair of boots per year) and the effects (benefits) of such objects upon their "recipients" (who may neither need nor like them). So, which is the point of equal result? Presumably, and ultimately, the recipient's equal end-state of well-being—indeed, a most elusive target.

41. In the argument of Rae et al., redistributions sustain only "compensatory

inequality" (i.e., remedial unequalitarian treatments). Beyond that point, what is required is a "redistribution of domains" such that the domain of allocation (what is available for division) corresponds to a "domain of account" (what ought to be divided). E.g., if the domain of account is property, then its corresponding domain of allocation is created by dispossessing private owners of property. See *Inequalities,* chap. 3, passim.

42. My formula, "rebalancing of inequalities," is intended descriptively. It differs, therefore, from Rawls's "compensatory reciprocity," which is a normative formula. But, clearly, the two formulations are complementary. I also take it that my argument parallels the one of Walzer's *Spheres of Justice.*

43. Whether unequal treatments actually are person-regarding depends on how finely and homogeneously the recipients are grouped together. Certainly, when the recipient is a bloc, neither individual nor person-regardiness obtains. As a rule of thumb, person-regardiness requires an ad hoc slicing of a population into multiple, relatively small groups.

44. *Equality,* 1st ed., p. 48.

45. The ulterior issue is how much of what is man-made can be man-unmade. See, on the point, Rees, *Equality,* chap. 1. In general, see Ralf Dahrendorf, "On the Origin of Inequality among Men," *Essays in the Theory of Society* (Stanford: Stanford University Press, 1969).

46. F.A. Hayek, *The Road to Serfdom* (London: Routledge, 1944), p. 27. Maine intended "status" in the medieval sense incorporated, until the French Revolution, into the division among "estates."

47. *The Federalist,* No. 79 (Hamilton).

48. L. Trotsky, *The Revolution Betrayed,* trans. Max Eastman (Garden City, N.Y.: Doubleday, 1937), p. 283 (italics mine). While Trotsky imputes this to Stalin, it is patent that "death by starvation" is the inherent, obvious resource of the structure. Trotsky himself had noted earlier that "*mutatis mutandis,* the Soviet government occupies in relation to the whole economic system the position which a capitalist occupies in relation to a single enterprise" (p. 43).

49. Letter of 24 June 1790.

50. Nothing is changed in the argument if the pitting of liberty against equality is transformed (as Rae et al. suggest in *Equalities,* p. 48) into the distinction between "equality in the narrow" and "equality in the broad." This reformulation—and, indeed, the entire work—does not even attempt to meet the formidable issue of which state will dispense, how, the "equality in the broad." The relation of liberty to equality is taken up again in chapter 13, section 4.

13. Liberism, Liberalism, and Democracy

It is very easy to reject liberalism if it is identified with a theory or practice of freedom understood as power of the bourgeoisie, but it is much more difficult to reject it when it is considered as the theory and practice of limiting the State's power . . . for freedom as power to do something interests those fortunate enough to possess it, while freedom as non-restraint interests all men.

—Norberto Bobbio

13.1 *Overlaps*

Liberalism and democracy, together with socialism and communism, are the labels that sum up the political contest of the nineteenth and twentieth centuries. Of these four labels, only "communism" is relatively clear, at least from 1918 onward.[1] However, the break between socialists and communists has also helped to make "socialism" less ambiguous. It is true that socialism may be Marxist, semi-Marxist, and non-Marxist, either maximalist or reformist (as in its Labor and Social-Democratic current incarnations). Yet, whoever is a socialist is not a Marxist-Leninist. Unless socialism is used as a camouflage word, that much has been made clear by the Russian revolution and what has happened in its wake.[2] But while "communism" helps disambiguate "socialism," the same cannot be said with respect to "liberalism" and "democracy." From the second half of the nineteenth century onward, the liberal and the democratic ideals blended with each other, and in their blending became misapprehended. The happy historical conjuncture that bound them together erased their respective characteristics, let alone their boundaries. Their attributions shifted, and continue to oscillate, depending on whether a writer is more concerned with keeping democracy in the orbit of liberalism or with underscoring the passing of liberalism into democracy. Many, beginning with Tocqueville, bring out how secondary, if not extraneous, freedom is to the internal logic of the idea of democracy; but it would not be difficult to draw up a long list of authors who rank freedom as the first principle of democracy. Kelsen, among these, firmly asserted: "It is the value of freedom and not of equality that determines in the first place the idea of democracy." As for equality, its role is modest: "Certainly," Kelsen granted, "the idea of equality also has its part, although . . . in an entirely negative, formal, and secondary sense."[3] At first glance it might appear that Tocqueville and Kelsen disagreed profoundly. But a closer look reveals that they were very much of the same mind.

The misunderstandings spring from the fact that we sometimes say democracy to indicate "liberal democracy" and at other times to indicate only "democracy." In the first case, democracy is given all the attributes of liberalism,[4] and the democratic ideal is therefore presented as an ideal of freedom; in the second case, liberalism and democracy are separated, and consequently the democratic ideal goes back to being equality. Both theses are correct and light up two facets of the problem: *(a)* that freedom is the requisite constituent element of liberal democracy, and *(b)* that it is by no means the requisite constituent element of democracy per se. When the Western polity is made to revolve around the ideal of freedom, the thesis is to anchor democracy to liberalism. When, on the other hand, it is made to revolve around the ideal of equality, the thesis is that democracy may or should depart from liberalism.

If we can speak of liberal democracy but also of a non-liberal democracy, in order to know what democracy we want we must first establish what liberalism is. Alas, hardly ever has a good horse been ridden so much to death. "Liberalism" seemingly attracts extravaganza. An initial complication is that, in becoming confused with the ideal of democracy, the concept of liberalism is promiscuously used in two senses: to indicate *only liberalism,* or *democratic liberalism.* In addition, we talk of social liberalism, of welfare liberalism, and the like. Clearly, whenever "liberalism" comes with a qualification, we are considering the descent of liberalism; and liberalism already combined with democracy (or variants of democracy) is of no use to us for the intent at hand. If the concept of liberalism is to explain the concept of liberal democracy, we must start with the *quid sui* of liberalism, with liberalism in its pure form. In order to examine a composite reality it is first necessary to break it down into its single component elements. The first point is, then, that we must concentrate on *pure and simple liberalism.*

"Liberalism" also applies, in adjectival form, to parties, movements, factions, programs, and policies. In this respect the complication is that while a fairly definite connection can be traced between communism and a Communist (I give a capital letter to the party name or membership) and between socialism and a Socialist, in most cases there is only a very tenuous link, if any, between liberalism and a present-day Liberal.[5] For instance, an American

Liberal would not be called a Liberal in most European countries—he would be called a Progressive, or a left-Democrat. Most continental European Liberal parties either are center or conservative parties, and in almost no case would Europeans call Liberal the left-wing element of their party (as is the case in the United States).

The volatility of the connection between liberalism in the historical sense and the party-policy meaning of Liberalism should not surprise us. Since it is not easy to identify the historical essence of liberalism, the term is up for grabs. At one end, the uncertainty about "liberalism" results in "Liberalism" being used, in party parlance, in an entirely contingent fashion. At the other end, if we do not know what the historical meaning of the term is, it is natural to take our bearings (as is done with Socialism and Communism) with reference to the party meaning. As a consequence, it is all too easy to make, or fake, liberalism into something it is not.

If party Liberalism, or rather Liberalisms, give us no reliable clue to understanding liberalism, it is not much better to rely on the meaning of liberalism that T.P. Neill calls "ecumenical." In this all-embracing meaning, which would include, according to Neill, "at least half of the human race," liberalism is simply the inborn attitude of a normal civilized Westerner toward life. Neill's generous estimate shows in itself that this cosmic meaning is much too vague to lead us anywhere. His approach is nonetheless interesting from another point of view, that is, for the distinction with respect to which he poses the problem. Neill writes: "It . . . seems proper and useful to distinguish between ecumenical liberalism and sectarian. The former refers to that liberalism which is identified with generosity of spirit or liberality of mind, the latter to a precisely defined and rigidly held body of doctrine. . . ."[6] What strikes me about this distinction is that it eliminates liberalism, for liberalism as the historical component of modern democracy is neither of the two. Neill offers us the alternative of ascending to an ecumenical stratosphere or descending to grassroots politics. To follow either alternative is to lose sight of what liberalism is, and has been, as a historical accomplishment and body of doctrine.

Classic liberalism (let us settle for this identification) is certainly more definite and corporeal than a mere ecumenical feeling, and at the same time much less contingent and variable than the sectarian (party or policy) Liberalisms. It is true that liberalism is also an attitude, a mental pattern, or, as Dworkin insists, a "political morality."[7] However, unless we start from a definite historical signification of the concept, it is difficult to understand how we can speak with any propriety of a "liberal mind." In recent decades the route generally followed by intellectuals of Liberal persuasion has been to extract abstract principles from the policy goals that they, as Liberals, had at heart.

This working back from policy ideals to their theoretical justifications has been very fruitful; but as the same approach is repeated from one author to another, in the end almost nothing remains of classic liberalism in what it has achieved in the real world and still accomplishes in it. It seems to me, therefore, that we again need to provide "liberalism" with historical anchorage — as I here propose to do.

Given the fact that sometimes we use democracy as a shorthand term for liberal democracy, while in other cases we intend only democracy, it behooves me to state that in this chapter "liberalism" means liberalism *only*, and "democracy" means democracy *only*. To be sure, if the fusion of liberalism and democracy were final, there would be no need to divide what has become united. But after their happy convergence in the last century, liberalism and democracy are coming again to diverge. If so, it becomes essential to go back to distinguishing their respective functions and jurisdictions in order to avoid working inadvertently for an illiberal democracy, or losing democracy out of hatred for liberalism. Most people, I dare say, like liberty plus equality, or equality and also liberty. How is it that they (and all of us) have managed in so many countries to lose both? Unless I am wrong about people's likes, the reply must be: by mistake.

13.2 *An Unfortunate Timing*

While the *thing* liberalism has been — according to Harold Laski, a witness above suspicion — the outstanding doctrine of the West for four centuries,[8] the *word* is much more recent. We speak of Locke or Montesquieu as "liberal" thinkers; they themselves did not. "Liberal" intended as a political word was coined in Spain in 1810-11 and began to circulate in Europe (in the French form *liberaux* or in the Spanish one *liberales)* in the 1820s in a somewhat derogatory sense, that is, with reference to the Spanish rebels of the time. It was not until the middle of the nineteenth century that the term was accepted in England as English and praiseworthy. "Liberalism" followed even later. It appears, therefore, that the name (the abstract noun) was established some three centuries later than the thing. This was unfortunate. Being born that late, it was too late for the name to have the time to take root. Moreover, for a number of other reasons, it was born at the wrong moment, indeed at the worst possible moment. The history of the word is thus an interesting side of the story and is worth telling, for few labels can compete with "liberalism" for having been born under an unlucky star.

The first misfortune was, I said, being born late, indeed too late. Too late not only because "liberalism" was coined after liberalism (as yet unnamed) was already producing its benefits, if not the essential part of itself, but above all because at that moment history had begun to move fast, so fast that the liberals did not succeed in making up for the long stretch of time that had been lost between the clandestine birth and the official baptism.

Thus, paradoxically, in some countries people began to speak of "liberalism" when they had ceased or were ceasing to be liberal. This was notably the case with German liberalism, *a l'avant garde* during the Enlightenment.[9] The German natural law school, Kant, Wilhem von Humboldt—all deserve an eminent place in the theory of liberalism. Yet, Humboldt's masterpiece, *The Limits of State Action,* written in 1791, remained unpublished until 1851, when the German liberals of the time had suffered—in the short-lived Frankfurt parliament of 1848-49—a lasting defeat. Elsewhere, especially in the United States, "liberal" never really arrived as a term endowed with historical status and substance. As Louis Hartz well phrases it, "Ironically, 'liberalism' is a stranger in the land of its greatest realization and fulfillment."[10] Americans never adopted "liberalism" as the distinctive label for the polity they had constructed. The United States was first perceived by them as a republic and subsequently as a democracy, flying as it were over the head of "liberalism" (the name). In order to identify the species that was born on American soil some two centuries ago, Dahl has to come up with the notion of Madisonian democracy. Yet so-called Madisonian democracy is liberalism pure and simple. Liberalism in the historical and European sense of the term has been, and still is, deeply rooted in American practice. Furthermore, the American Constitution—according to European standards—is the prototype of liberal constitutionalism in the classic and strict meaning of the term. Yet Americans hardly think of it as the typical "liberal" constitution. This is because Liberal and Liberalism are almost exclusively used in the United States in a sectarian and/or policy-related sense. Liberalism—thereby including Madisonian liberalism—as a structure-building enterprise and achievement is not what an American Liberal has in mind, nor the reason for his conceiving of himself as a Liberal.

In summing up, while a nameless liberalism has constituted between the seventeenth and the twentieth centuries the most fundamental drive of Western civilization, "liberalism" as a denomination *pleno iure* intended to epitomize that experience has achieved status and regard only for a few decades.[11] The case of France is, in this connection, symptomatic. Here, with Benjamin Constant and Tocqueville liberalism had leaped well ahead of its eighteenth-century versions and had displayed one of its most refined formulations; yet, in France the liberalism of Constant and his school was already challenged, if not overthrown, by the Revolution of 1848.

Why this premature decline, as result of which liberals today exist *de facto* but hardly *de iure?* I mentioned that the second misfortune was that in the nineteenth century history began to move fast. The pace of time accelerated so quickly that in the course of a few decades "liberalism" encountered two formidable competitors: the names "democracy" and "socialism." Two competitors are one too many—for politics hinges, in the long view of history, on elementary oppositions and polarizations. Up to the fall of the ancient regime, that is, until the absolute monarchies lasted, the antithesis had long been between monarchy and republic.[12] Afterward, once republics had been achieved, or at any rate once monarchy had been made harmless, the new antithesis—especially in the authors who had their minds on the experience of the French Revolution—was between liberalism and democracy. But soon enough the appearance of a third protagonist demanded a new alignment of the opposing fronts. This new protagonist was, in Europe, socialism.[13] And to the extent that socialism conveyed the workers' demands, the liberals and democrats were, and still are, reduced to maneuver on the same electoral space and, therefore, pressed to converge.

Tocqueville, perhaps better than anyone else, helps us to follow this development. In the first volume of *Democracy in America,* published in 1835, democracy and liberalism appeared to him to be inimical to one another. One reason for this is that he was examining the United States while using, implicitly, a French frame of reference. It must also be remembered that in France (and, for that matter, in all of Europe) democracy was still an intellectual hypothesis built on library reminiscences. Such was the democracy of Rousseau, and such it remained for those who drew inspiration from it. Consequently, Tocqueville closely identified democracy with equality and was led to stress the illiberal implications of democracy. In the second volume, which came out five years later, Tocqueville sounded the alarm even more, one of the reasons for this being that the English-inspired democracy that he had seen in America and that was more directly reflected in the first volume was one thing, and the prefigurations of democracy that he returned to see in France, and that was more directly introduced into the compiling of the volume of 1840, was another. Indeed, the "democratic despotism" that Tocqueville had seen foreshadowed in the American scene was a much more threatening prospect in the light of the gospel of Saint-Simon's followers, or of the phalansteries of Fourier—that is, when reformulated by a rationalistic and simplistic radicalism.

But, suddenly, in 1848, democracy and liberalism are enemies no more; they join forces. In a speech delivered on 12 September Tocqueville's antithesis is no longer between liberalism and democracy but between democracy and socialism. Attending the Constituent Assembly, Tocqueville said: "Democracy and socialism are linked only by a word, equality; but the difference must be noted: democracy wants equality in freedom, and socialism wants equality in poverty and slavery." Had Tocqueville changed his mind? Yes and no. Certainly at this point a momentous change did occur, for he abandoned the classical or pre-liberal meaning of the term democracy and gave it the new, the modern meaning: Tocqueville's democracy was now *liberal democracy*. But then, perhaps, what had changed was not his thought; rather, or far more, it was the situation. The Revolution of 1848 had shown the strength of what called itself "socialism."[14] And under the onslaught of those dramatic days, political alignments were quickly modified. Tocqueville, who in his visit to the United States had seen, after all, a truly liberal democracy, immediately sensed the meaning of the reexamination of conscience brought about by the 1848 events. Hence he divided his former concept of democracy into two parts. To socialism he attributed the illiberal part of democracy, democratic despotism;[15] whereas he associated its non-despotic part with liberalism. Liberty and equality were still contrasted to each other, but under new labels: The equality that is inimical to freedom was to be found in socialism, whereas the equality that is in harmony with freedom was to be found in anti-socialist democracy, in the democracy that accepts liberalism.

It must not be thought that these were mere verbal adjustments. Tocqueville made allowance in advance for what was to happen in the second half of the century. It is not that democracy drawn from historical memory was replaced in a flash, in 1848, by the liberal democracy that was the offspring of reality (and was already well under way beyond the Atlantic). What Tocqueville put on record was the birth of this alliance. Only later, and gradually, did people become aware that what was being born from the seed of liberalism was a democracy quite different from that monolithic city whose fascination had been felt by European readers of Rousseau. The convergence between liberalism and democracy was undoubtedly a felicitous one, and on the whole the operation was successful. But the partnership was unequal.

In the substance it is liberalism that has prevailed over democracy, in the sense that it has absorbed democracy far more than democracy has annexed liberalism; for democrats (with the exception of the radical, revolutionary wing that merged with socialism) have accepted the principle that freedom is the end and democracy the means. But the victory of liberalism (the thing) was not the victory of the word. No sooner had liberalism found a name for itself than it had to abandon it. Partly because the label democracy had a tradition that the other lacked; partly because, semantically speaking, "democracy" is more tangible than "liberalism" (which has no straightforward descriptive meaning); and partly to avoid emphasizing cleavage, it was the liberals who ended by giving up their own identity and presenting themselves as democrats. Prima facie it was a modest concession to political convenience, but one destined to have, in the long run, far-reaching consequences. What is not named, what remains unnamed, is no longer detected. Thus the notion of liberalism today is associated in most people's minds either with a species of the past or, conversely, without past.

The name liberalism has not taken second place only for the above reasons. We must still account for a third misfortune. In those years the first industrial revolution, with all its strains, miseries, and cruelties, was taking place; and the industrial revolution was accomplished in the name of economic freedom. Today we know that industrialization—no matter under what banner it was brought about, capitalism or socialism—has invariably been paid for by a ruthless exploitation of the industrial proletariat. Nevertheless, industrial progress in the West did come about under the auspices of free competition, of laissez faire, and of the gospel of the Manchester school. The unfortunate coincidence was, then, that the name should be coined at a time when the novelty was not *political liberalism* but *economic liberism.*[16] Yet the blame fell upon liberalism as an undivided whole. In the aftermath of this fortuitous and unfortunate coincidence liberalism (the undifferentiated label) came to have more of an economic association than a political one; it was eventually called "capitalist," earned the lasting hostility of the working classes, and even today most authors continue to speak of classic liberalism as a laissez-faire liberalism—thereby grievously muddling liberalism with economic "liberism."

Let it be stressed that this is very unfair to liberalism. Locke, Blackstone, Montesquieu, Madison, Constant were not the theorists of a laissez-faire economy. To them liberalism meant the rule of law and the constitutional state; and liberty was political freedom, not the economic principle of free trade or, still worse, the law of survival of the fittest. Had the term liberalism been invented not in the nineteenth century but a hundred years earlier or a hundred years later, this momentous quid pro quo (mistaking one thing for another) would not have occurred. Had it not been for an unfortunate coincidence, instead of using "liberalism" promiscuously to refer as much to the ideas of Montesquieu and Constant as to those of the Manchester school (how absurd, when we think of it), we would be using in all likelihood two different names, devised to put the problem of political freedom in one context and that of market freedom in another.

This is still not the end of the story. The Spanish *liberales,* when they invented the name, had England in mind. But in those years English philosophy had turned, with Bentham, to a strict utilitarianism and a narrow felicific calculus. Now, Bentham (or, better, the older Bentham) was a "liberal" in a sectarian meaning of the term but hardly contributed to the mainstream of liberalism, for "liberty, he thought, is nothing in itself, and is valuable only as a means to happiness."[17] Furthermore, and still more to the point, Bentham advocated a *tabula rasa* of the traditions and conventions on which English constitutionalism was actually founded. At the time, then, England was hardly a soil as fertile — for the theorization of liberalism — as was France. To be sure, Bentham and James Mill were followed by John Stuart Mill, who did rescue liberty from Bentham's uninspiring felicific calculus. However, the referent of John Stuart Mill no longer was liberalism but liberal democracy. Nor was John Stuart Mill as successful at the turn of the century as he is today; for the generations that followed him in time followed him little in spirit. Authors such as Thomas Hill Green and Hobhouse[18] sought inspiration from Hegel rather than from Locke and Mill, and disseminated an idealistic version of liberalism that left little trace of itself, in the longer run, in England, but certainly did confuse the matter throughout the Continent and also in America.[19] Even in this respect, then, liberalism has not been fortunate. For certainly it was no help to it to be christened at the moment when English philosophy was first in the process of becoming narrowly utilitarian and became subsequently exposed to the influence of German idealistic philosophy.[20]

Corresponding to the (terminological) untimeliness of liberalism, there is also its ill fortune at the hands of the historians. Setting aside the quasi silence on the part of American historians[21]—which is in itself a serious loophole — even Germany never produced histories of its own liberalism. When the great German historical school was flourishing, or at any rate when history came to be affirmed as "history of ideas," German liberalism was either extinct or narrowly focused on the problem of national unity. It so happened, then, that the first major historical account of liberalism was written in Italy, under fascism and in reaction to fascism, by Guido de Ruggiero. His *History of European Liberalism,* which appeared in 1925, was a truly outstanding achievement.[22] Yet de Ruggiero was a philosopher influenced in part by Benedetto Croce, who made liberalism into a highly abstract philosophical category;[23] and in part directly by Hegel. For both reasons, the concluding section of his book on liberalism *as such* was the least felicitous in his work, and the unitary concept of liberalism that he put forward was singularly out of focus: de Ruggiero made liberalism into an *étatiste* liberalism of the Hegelian type.[24] On the other hand, his coverage of the eighteenth century and the history of liberalisms (in the plural) of which most of the book consisted was masterful—and seemingly set the pace for what followed. Thus, Maurice Cranston provides, in his *Freedom: A New Analysis,*[25] a penetrating sketch of English, French, German, and American liberalisms without even attempting to present a unitary idea. Indeed, Cranston allows his taste for multiplying liberalisms so much scope as to declare that only English liberalism is unambiguous, since, in his view, even the French type should really be divided into two layers: the Lockeian and that of *étatiste* liberalism. I would say, however, that the alleged French *étatiste* liberalism is not acknowledged as a liberalism. A state-loving variety of liberalism appears only with German and, in its wake, Italian idealism, and it remains an open question whether this specimen may be properly classified as liberalism. Cranston's multiplication of liberalisms is challenged, among others, by Manning, who leaves us, however, with the untelling conclusion that "the essences of liberalisms can no more be defined than can the essence of liberalism as a whole."[26] At best, we are thus seemingly left to speak of the "elasticity" of liberalism.[27]

The elasticity, however, of what? Must we bow to the conclusion that *one* liberalism does not exist but only *many* different liberalisms? Is it furthermore the case that these liberalisms must be sliced into a number of phases: the classic, the democratic, the social, the *étatiste,* the humanistic, the socialist, etc.? I think not. By the same token it should be maintained that not democracy but only many democracies exist, one for every nation, and further that each of these democracies changes from generation to generation. Yet we do, in fact, speak of modern democracy in the singular. On the same grounds we are fully entitled to speak of liberalism in the singular—provided that we search for it and find it. Thus far I have stressed that classic liberalism—the ancestor—must be separated from its progeny (let alone its contingent and sectarian varieties). I now propose to proceed in this unpacking.

13.3   Property and Possessive Individualism

I have already underscored the need for distinguishing *liberism* as an economic system from *liberalism* as a political system. Note that when we say democracy *tout court* it is generally understood that reference is made to "political" democracy. When "economic" democracy is intended, we say it. Even Marxists make the distinction, if only to declare that the "political democracy" that we have is a superstructure of capitalism. Only liberalism, then, seemingly enjoys the dubious privilege of being treated in undifferentiated fashion. It is important, therefore, to dwell on the drawbacks thus resulting.

Macpherson's theory of "possessive individualism" suggests itself as a fitting illustration of the point—and this not only because it is the most subtle

Marxist interpretation of Lockeian liberalism and of how this origin flaws (in his view) liberal democracy, but also because his theory attracts audiences that are clearly unaware of the characteristically *political* nature of liberalism. The gist of Macpherson's thesis (and grievance) is a very simple one: A property-based, indeed a property-obsessed and capitalistic-oriented "possessive individualism," engenders a "possessive market society [which] is a series of competitive and invasive relations between all men."[28] Is this, as Macpherson contends, the basis, essence, and vice of liberalism and its progeny? In my view, this is a caricature of both the economics and the politics of the matter.

First, the economics. Leaving aside whether the notion of market (not of the marketplace, but of a *market system*) can be pushed all the way back to Hobbes and Locke,[29] the question is: How do we pass from "competitive" to "invasive"? Historically, "invasiveness" exists since we know of man's existence. Roman law was gradually elaborated precisely in order to curb invasiveness. Life in the Greek *polis* was pervasively invasive. In general, every unfettered power—be it of a king, a soldier, a stronger neighbor—invades not only the belongings but the very life of any lesser power. Contrariwise, "competitiveness" (also on Macpherson's account) is of relatively recent vintage. Hence it cannot be that a "competitive relation" entails as a somewhat automatic implication an "invasive relation." Indeed, the pairing of the two notions is telling in that it brings out that competition enters civilization precisely as a way of limiting, civilizing, and, in crucial respects, displacing invasiveness. A competitive system, as it has now developed, may well make our lives unbearably tense; yet we are permitted to pull out of competition; we can withdraw and, if we do, nobody is allowed, under the rules of competition, to "invade" us.[30]

The crucial point is that Marxists in general and Macpherson in particular read back into history a concept of private property that does not belong to the actual fabric of history. Nowadays it is easy to scorn the persistence with which "possessing" has long been vindicated by all quarters. It is easy because liberalism—and liberalism only—provides us with other kinds of defenses, with hitherto unprovided *political safeguards*. What is missed by facile critics is that from Roman times until the end of the eighteenth century, property meant, all in one and indivisibly, "life, liberty, and estate";[31] it did not mean "possession" for its own sake or for the sake of unlimited accumulation, let alone "capital accumulation."[32] In Locke's time, and still for some time, property was not part of a chrematistic (money seeking) economic system.[33] Even the Levellers maintained that freedom is a function of possession. Were they, for this, inconsistent or bourgeois revolutionaries? I would rather say that they understood what everybody understood. With a bare subsistence economy and endemic exposure to undifferentiated insecurity, to "own" signified, very simply, to improve life chances: Property was *protection*—indeed the way of removing existential insecurity from the bare surface of one's skin. To be sure, even then to "have" implied to "have power." But the economic power of property had yet to gain autonomy and to be perceived as such. The patrimonial state (and, from the top, all the way down the feudal echelon) was not an economic state; it needed resources for raising armies that were, in turn, its real power base. Until the liberal taming of politics, power meant *force* (not mere, and mild, influence), the force of arms and violence — not the force of property.

Hence the allegation that liberalism was founded on a "possessive market society" or that it is a superstructure of a capitalist-type economy[34] is simply untrue to the facts. Liberalism cannot be reduced to economic premises, or presuppositions, even at this most elemental juncture. If property is an economic concept related to an acquisitive society and to the industrial multiplication of production, then this is not the concept that upholds liberalism. In praising the individual (that much of Macpherson's thesis is true) liberalism sustains this individual with that *security* which is property—with a *property-as-safety* that has very little to share with the capitalistic notion of property or with an economic vision of life.

We are thus left with the market analogy or, more exactly, with the market substratum. Granted that Macpherson handles the issue skillfully, the point of interest is not whether his "models of society"[35] are analytically convincing, but resides in this shift: "Possessive market *society* . . . implies that where labour has become a market commodity, market relations so shape or permeate all social relations that it may properly be called a market society, not a market economy."[36] So, the economy pervades *the society*. Indeed it does. I would add that we largely owe the discovery and affirmation of the autonomy of society, as we conceive it today, to the laissez-faire economists.[37] The question remains, What about *the polity?* In what way is it shaped by, and submitted to, market possessivism? As long as Macpherson replies that in the possessive market society "there is no authoritative allocation of work" (whereas in the earlier customary or status society "the productive and regulative work of the society is authoritatively allocated"),[38] I can understand this reply only as a compliment, if an unintended one, to the liberating force of the liberal polity and its laws. On the other hand, when Macpherson hints that our legal systems mainly or centrally protect proprietorship and its possessive and invasive market implications—this is a wholesale misreading, indeed a wholesale distortion of the entire problem of constitutionalism and of how liberty and law relate to one another. Actually, in Macpherson's theory of democracy all the discussion that has taken us so long to survey[39] is cavalierly ignored. In the end we discover that Macpherson's theory says nothing and has nothing to say about the polity and about the vertical dimension of politics.[40] When he comes to politics, in his *Democratic Theory* he merely and monumentally confuses political freedom with power.

That Macpherson's way of handling the market theme is highly unconvincing does not imply that the market issue is, in itself, of small import. Historically speaking, I believe Marxists to be wrong: Political liberalism did precede commercialism, laissez-faire, and capitalism — in short, liberalism preceded liberism. However, it does not follow from this that a past disconnection attests to a future disconnectability. It is very appropriate to ask, therefore, whether the liberal solution to the problem of political (not economic) power can still be a "solution" within the context of a propertyless, nonmarket economic system. We shall turn to this question in the next chapter. Here the point to note is that if we reply in the negative, namely, that liberalism cannot survive in conjunction with a state-owned, all-planned, communist-type economy, this is by no means *because* liberalism is a by-product of market economy and/or of private property. The argument is, instead, that *any* concentration of all power (political and economic) implies that the individual and whatever individual liberty he may praise are crushed. The argument is, then, the very old one that subjects become citizens (with rights and a free voice) only within societal structures that *disperse power* and allow for a variety of intermediary and countervailing powers. We may well dislike market-type structures and mechanisms. The problem remains to replace them without losing sight of the fact that not only the freedoms of the propertied, but even more the freedoms of the propertyless, hinge on a system that disperses the control over production and employment.

To distinguish is not to separate — as my argument, I trust, shows. Therefore my plea that liberism should be distinguished from liberalism simply says this: Only because we first distinguish an economic system from a political system can we subsequently assess in what ways and to what extent they are related, interrelated, and/or subordinated to one another.

13.4 *Liberalism Defined*

In order to advance the inquiry we must note further distinctions. Economic liberism, we have seen, is not political liberalism. A second distinction is the one between liberty and liberalism. It can well be asserted that the "elementary desire to be free is the force behind all liberties, old and new."[41] It does not follow that this elementary desire is a natural one; rather, it is a cultural one. Many civilizations and most traditional societies neither express nor repress this elementary desire.[42] It equally does not follow that the desire in question necessarily leads to the liberal polity or to the liberal kind of solution. The elementary desire to be free found its first outlet—within Western culture—in the Greek *eleuthería,* in something that the Romans rendered as licentiousness (in opposition to *libertas*) and that is more easily projected in what we have come to call anarchy.[43] Furthermore, some two thousand years went by before deriving "liberalism" from *libertas* and "liberty." Had the derivation been obvious or natural, this enormous time lag would be inexplicable.

A third difference is the one between philosophical liberalism and the empirical theory and practice of liberalism. This distinction is thin and of little consequence before the so-called idealistic revision of liberalism, but of great consequence after Hegel and with respect to both the neoidealistic (Benedetto Croce) or some equally abstract Marxist and neo-Marxist philosophical reconstructions of liberalism. Croce conceived Liberty (capitalized) as a "pure category of the Spirit" from which he derived a philosophy of liberalism in which nothing was left of the techniques of taming absolute power, that is, of the *quid sui* of liberalism. On the opposite camp, Macpherson soars at a level of abstraction that is only slightly less rarefied than the one of Croce, constructs his argument, like Croce, on an ethical definition of freedom,[44] and lands at the same no-man's land: an account in which the distinctiveness and real-world substance of liberalism altogether disappear from sight.

Perhaps the best way of disposing of what may be called "metaphysical liberalism" is to insist on a fourth, related distinction: the one between political and extrapolitical (moral or other) freedoms. Since the point has already been discussed,[45] it will suffice to recall that liberalism deals with political freedom —freedom *for* the citizen *from* state oppression—and that if this is forgotten or deemed of no importance, liberalism is forgotten. If we are able and content with "realizing our self" in a prison, this attests to the infinite resources of man's *inner* freedom; but this is not what liberalism is about. The problem of liberalism is *outer* freedom, and thus its overriding concern is precisely that no man should be imprisoned without due process and due cause.

The foregoing prunings bring out, I submit, the distinctive core of liberalism. Remember that we are dealing with liberalism *only,* not with its subsequent transformations, additions, and combinations (with something else). Under this premise liberalism can be declared to be, very simply, the theory and practice of the juridical defense, through the constitutional state, of individual political freedom, of individual liberty. Two things will be immediately noted: *(a)* I have not given prominence to "individualism," and *(b)* I say "constitutional state" and not, as is at times suggested, "minimal state."

Regarding the first point, I deemphasize individualism not only because the concept is being unduly overdone but because "individualism" (in splendid isolation) either does not suffice to characterize liberalism or confines liberalism, far too narrowly, to one of its many possible conceptions. Certainly liberalism believes in the *value* of each and all human beings and conceives them, it has been seen, as *persons;* but liberalism stands even if the so-called abstract conception of the individual is knocked down and regardless of whether the individual is "possessive" or "social," society-maker or society-made. Regarding the second point, I do not wish in the least to ridicule the minimal state. It lasted, notably in England, until World War I; and if it was a "watchdog state," the imagery should not convey that it behaved like a barking guardian. To the contrary, "Until August 1914 a sensible, law-abiding Englishman could pass through life and hardly notice the existence of the state, beyond the post office and the policeman. . . . He had no official number or identity card. . . . He could travel abroad . . . without a passport. . . . The Englishman paid taxes on a modest scale . . . rather less than 8 percent of the national income."[46] But bygones are bygones; and the point is that while the constitutional state was born as a minimal state set up to uphold a liberty *from* government that expressed a basic distrust of power, one must not for this reason put the size of the liberal state ahead of its structure, that is, a contingent characteristic ahead of the essential. However much the constitutional state may have been conceived of as a small state, and also as a do-little or even a do-nothing state, this does not prevent its becoming, if need be, a large state that does something, and even a great deal — on this essential condition: The more it ceases to be a minimal state, the more important it is that it remain a constitutional state.

It will be argued, and I certainly shall not deny it, that liberalism has come a long way from where my definition leaves it. Thus far I have defined classic liberalism. So, what about *new liberalism,* or what is new in liberalism? I shall not pursue this ulterior question in any detail, for my intent is to provide the parameter, or the base point, with respect to which one can best assess whether the so-called new liberalisms remain within the orbit of the core meaning or depart from it. Also, the parameter may show that some alleged novelties are not such. For instance, it is often held that new liberalism has dropped the laissez-faire formula of "old liberalism." But this, according to my argument, is hardly a novelty; it is a wrong way of redressing the confusion between liberalism and liberism.

The expression "new liberalism" can also indicate the so-called justice state and welfare and/or social liberalism. In these instances we have gone on to consider the democratic development of liberalism and, in particular, not so much what liberalism has given of itself to democracy as what the idea of democracy has contributed to the liberal idea. New liberalism in this case is tantamount to saying democratic liberalism. There is no harm in using the former instead of the latter label. Still, unless we know what liberalism without adjectives is, we are in no position to establish to what extent social or welfare or "justice" liberalism remains liberalism. For instance, if the formula of the welfare state is understood as meaning that economic security and the "assisted society" are to be the paramount concern, then it is needlessly confusing to involve liberalism in this typically democratic development.

The retort might be that my case seemingly condemns liberalism to being conceived as an old and thereby outworn doctrine. This is hardly my intent, which is to bring analytic clarity into the matter. And a point about "oldness" is immediately in order, namely, that there is a democracy that is far older than liberalism. All who understand democracy literally—and this includes many present-day populists and participationists—go all the way back in time to ancient Greece. If oldness is assumed to outwear, then the propounders of etymological democracy, as I have called it,[47] are more outworn, more out of step, than anyone else. If, on the other hand, we take the view that not every legacy of the past is worthless and that old truths may be everlasting truths, then my definition of the core of liberalism carries no automatic implication of obsolescence. Under this premise and proviso the question, Who is older than who? is an interesting question. Indeed, it is important to have the sequence right.

As I was saying, democracy *tout court* is far older than liberalism. It is only if we speak of *liberal democracy* that we are speaking of a democracy that comes after liberalism and that is younger than liberalism. But even in this reference the thesis that modern democracy is born from liberalism is at times contradicted. Panfilo Gentile, for example, wrote that "it is commonly thought that first came liberalism and then *démocratisme,* as if . . . liberalism were only a timid predecessor. This opinion is by no means exact because . . . liberalism followed *démocratisme,* corrected it and went beyond it."[48] How do things stand, then? The complication lies in the fact that the English genealogy is different from the French. In the former case it was Lockeian liberalism that was transplanted to the New World and produced there the first modern democracy. But if we consider what happened in France (and reacted on the neighboring countries), this genealogical line can be reversed, since the liberal element was imported, whereas the native element was a democratic rationalism a la Rousseau.[49] However, if the anglophile Montesquieu came before the anglophobe Rousseau, afterward the roles were exchanged: Rousseau is older, Constant and Tocqueville are more modern. In effect, liberalism was accepted on the Continent and showed its best results after learning its lesson from the Jacobin democracy that preceded it.[50] This is what Panfilo Gentile meant to point out. So, while it is true—according to the main genealogical line, the Anglo-American one—that liberalism came first and democracy followed, it is equally true that in the nineteenth century liberalism was restated and refined on the basis of a previous democratic experiment that quickly went off course. The sequencing alerts us, then, to the fact that many people may be calling for a *post-liberal democracy* that is to supersede liberalism, without realizing that they are only working for a *pre-liberal democracy* that has long been superseded by liberalism.

The sum of the argument is that I do not feel that liberalism is really helped by rejuvenating it in some alleged novel version every year or so. Politicians will doubtlessly continue to appropriate "liberalism" and twist it to their conveniences whenever it happens to be the best vacant label in a given market of key words. Scholars, however, should be wary of going along with party or sectarian abuses of the term—such because they contribute to making liberalism (the core of liberalism) misapprehended. If certain aspects of classic liberalism are unsatisfactory or outworn, so be it. What matters is not to miss the part that defies the corrosion of time, that represents the lasting and unreplaced contribution of liberalism. Liberalism *has* curbed absolute and arbitrary power; it has defeated the circularity of despair expressed by the query, Who controls the controllers?; it has freed man from the fear of the Prince; it has, indeed, liberated man from plunder and dread (force-related dread, to be sure). Liberalism is unique in its accomplishments in a further respect: It is the only engineering of history that endows *ends with means.* Within its orbit—polity building—it is liberalism, not Marxism, which is a *theory with praxis,* a project that works (as devised and intended). All in all, then, my suggestion is that we should bother less about "new liberalism" and more about what is and remains new in liberalism.

13.5   *Liberal Democracy*

The basic relationship between liberalism and democracy is generally rendered—from Tocqueville to de Ruggiero, Kelsen, and Raymond Aron—as a relation between liberty and equality.[51] Thus, in order to isolate liberalism from democracy we say that liberalism calls for liberty and democracy for equality. Conversely, in order to unite them we say that it is the task of liberal-democratic systems to combine liberty with equality.

That liberty and equality can blend is shown by the very fact that Western-type systems are both liberal and democratic. How they converge is what we have been examining at no small length. Actually, it is not that liberalism is wholly a matter of liberty and democracy wholly a matter of equality. Rather, there are freedoms that are of little import for the democratic stance, just as there are equalities to which liberalism is insensitive.[52] As I have stressed, all equalities are not democratic acquisitions, just as all freedoms are not liberal conquests. If liberty and equality mark the demarcation between liberalism and democracy, it is because of a different underlying logic. Liberal democracy can be viewed as a skein with two threads. As long as the skein remains at rest, all is well; but if we begin to unravel it, the threads come apart.

If we pull the liberal thread, not every form of equality disappears; but liberal equality as such is above all intended to promote, by way of liberty, aristocracies of merit. Liberalism per se is wary of granting more than juridico-political equality because it distrusts any equality gratuitously bestowed from above. Croce gave us a concise picture of the liberal spirit in its purest form when he observed that for "liberalism, which is born and remains intrinsically anti-egalitarian, liberty, according to Gladstone's saying, is the way of producing and promoting not democracy but aristocracy."[53] Perhaps better said, liberalism strives for a "qualitative democracy." If, on the other hand, we start to pull the democratic thread, we attain an equality that neutralizes spontaneous processes of differentiation. As de Ruggiero remarked: "The art of stimulating from within the need to raise oneself is totally unknown to democracy, which contents itself with bestowing rights and benefits, which out of their being gratuitous are for this very reason depreciated and dissipated from the outset." Here one can neatly read the liberal's reproof. "It is a fact," he concluded, "that the rigid and unintelligent application of the principle of equality tends to cripple the efforts and the benefits of liberty, which of necessity are in the direction of differentiation and unevenness, and to spread, together with mediocre qualities, also the love of mediocrity."[54]

In the final analysis, equality has a horizontal urge, whereas liberty has a vertical impetus. Democracy is concerned with social cohesion and distributive evenness, liberalism esteems prominence and spontaneity. Equality desires to integrate and attune, liberty is self-assertive and troublesome. Democracy has little feel for "pluralism," liberalism is its offspring. But perhaps the fundamental difference is that liberalism pivots on the individual, and democracy on society. De Ruggiero well caught the reversal that comes about in the two perspectives when he observed that democracy ends by turning upside down "the original relationship which the liberal mentality established between the individual and society: it is not the spontaneous cooperation of individuals' energies which creates the character and value of the whole, but it is the whole which determines and shapes its elements."[55] Walter Lippmann was just about he last major American author to make the point even more forcefully: "In the discipline of a free society it is the inviolability of all individuals which determines the social obligations . . . it is here, on the nature of man, between those who would respect him as an autonomous person and those who would degrade him to a living instrument, that the issue is joined."[56] In the end, we arrive at this query: "How can we combine that degree of *individual initiative* which is necessary for progress with the degree of *social cohesion* that is necessary for survival?"[57] Daniel Bell turns the query into a set of contradictions that derive, in his words, "from the fact that liberal society was originally set up—in its ethos, laws, and reward systems—to promote individual ends, yet has now become an interdependent economy that must stipulate *collective goals*."[58] Quite so. But why leave this as a contradiction? Why not perceive it as an ever-to-be-solved undertaking?

The relationship between liberalism and democracy must also be considered on a more concrete level descending, as it were, from the Tocquevillian sphere of ultimate principles to the more mundane sphere of deeds. Here the distinction becomes that liberalism is above all the technique of limiting the state's power, whereas democracy is the insertion of popular power into the state. Therefore, with the passage of time there comes to be created between the liberal and the democrat (whatever the party labels may be) a division of roles, as a result of which the former feels more the political concern, whereas the latter has more of a welfare concern. Of course, and again, the caveat is that democracy has imparted something of itself to political liberalism, just as liberalism in its turn has imparted its own values to democratic sociality. Nevertheless, we may still make an approximate division of this sort: While the liberal is concerned with the *form* of the state, the democrat is primarily interested in the *content* of the norms emanating from the state. In relation to the form of the state, the problem is to establish *how* the norms should be created; in relation to the concern about content, the problem is *what* must be established by the norms. The liberal has a better grasp of the method of creating the social order, and he is the one who attends to "procedural democracy." The democrat is somewhat indifferent to method, is concerned above all with results and substance, and seeks to exercise power more than to watch over it.

If we break down the component parts of liberal democracy in this way, the distinction between democracy in the *political* sense and democracy in the *social* (and economic) sense becomes clear. In the political sense there is no appreciable difference between the democratic and the liberal state; the former is, for the most part, the latter under a new name. When, on the other hand, we speak of democracy in the social sense, we are speaking of what is properly democracy and not liberalism.

What is less clear is, however, what is meant by "social" and, thereby, by "social democracy." As we know, the latter label obtains two very different meanings. In one, and I would say primary sense, social democracy points to an *ethos,* to a way of living that is also a way of relating to one another.[59] In a second meaning social democracy is less a state of society and far more a way of governing society. In the first case social democracy is the extra-political substratum and foundation of political democracy. In the second it is a policy intended to create from above the circumstances that, in the judgment of the policy makers, will produce a democratic society. Therefore, in the primary sense it is the antecedent fact of any policy, while in the second sense it is the product of a policy. Despite this difference, when we speak of *social* democracy we are using "democracy" legitimately in both cases; whereas when we say *political* democracy, for the sake of exactness we ought to say "liberalism" or, at least, liberal democracy.

In résumé, the interplay between the liberal and democratic component elements in our systems can be portrayed thus: The first is especially concerned with political bondage, individual initiative, and the form of the state; the second is especially sensitive to welfare, equality, and social cohesion. What we have, then, is a composition, a compound. I have decomposed it not so much for the sake of analysis itself but because we have reached a point, in the development of our political and social systems, where we confront two futures: a democracy *within* liberalism, and a democracy *without* liberalism.

I am aware of how much the foregoing may appear weird to the English-speaking present-day Liberal. He cannot recognize himself in my account, I submit, because I deal with liberalism longitudinally—over time and in history—whereas his Liberalism is as highly updated as it is poorly retrodated. As I read him, it is almost as if liberalism started with Rawls. In my readings, it starts with Locke. If this is understood, I trust that I shall not be misunderstood. One of my reasons for reverting to liberalism and democracy in their respective historical identities and sequencing is that a horizontal Liberal who overly disconnects himself from the longitudinal one may indeed inadvertently contribute to a democracy without liberalism.

13.6 *Democracy within Liberalism*

Roughly speaking, in the nineteenth century it was the liberal element that prevailed over the democratic; in the twentieth century the pendulum has swung, and today it is the democratic component that prevails over the liberal. Tocqueville outlined the process as follows: "Our forefathers were ever prone to make an improper use of the notion that private rights ought to be respected; and we are naturally prone, on the other hand, to exaggerate the idea that the interest of a private individual ought always to bend to the interest of the many."[60] For once Tocqueville was not prophetic enough, for we are moving long beyond the exaggeration that he saw, or foresaw. But his "exaggeration" suggests a first general warning: If Western-type systems are the product of liberalism *plus* democracy, it follows that they incessantly pose a problem of internal rebalancings between their component parts. The assertion does not entail that the equilibria in question should be stable (let alone static), i.e., characterized by negative feedbacks that tend to restore the pre-existent state of the system; they can equally be unstable equilibria whose positive, amplifying feedbacks transform the system.[61] In reality, we always end up, in history, with different equilibrium solutions, that is, with equilibria consisting of different mixes and proportions of their ingredients. Yet, if a social-political system is to hang together, it must obtain at each point in time some equilibrium-type rebalancing. If all the actors in a given system generate disequilibrium, that is, if no countervailing behavior occurs, then that system simply breaks apart. The first point is, then, that the growth of the democratic component element of liberal democracy increasingly requires us to make allowances for the *opposite danger.*[62]

A second consideration is that a chronological order, i.e., the *before* and the *after,* is by no means an order of importance, i.e., a *less* and a *more.* If modern democracy is an *after* in relation to liberalism, this does not entail that it surpasses or supersedes liberalism, that liberalism is *less,* less important. Our preferences may well be set by what we enjoy last, and especially least. This is psychologically understandable, if not inevitable. Nonetheless, desire is ephemerally deceptive; it flies, as it were, over the head of what sustains our desires of the day. It should be well understood, therefore, that what democracy adds to liberalism is at the same time a consequence of liberalism. Thus, to speak of democracy as something that supersedes liberalism—in the meaning of the dialectical verb *aufheben*—may be very misleading.[63] Democracy is the completion, not the replacement, of liberalism.

If these points are kept in mind, then we are also in control of how to achieve "more democracy." There is nothing to be gained (other than the crippling of liberal democracy as a whole) by seeking a maximization of democracy in ways that destroy the liberal component of the system and obtain disproportionately little in exchange. We are thus advised to look for democracy where it really resides or can really blossom—and this implies that we pay special attention to the distinction between democracy in the social and economic sense, on the one hand, and in the political sense, on the other hand.

To maintain that democracy is *more* than liberalism is half true and half false. It is largely true if by this we mean that democracy is more than liberalism in the social sense; it is mostly false if we intend that democracy is more than liberalism in the political sense. The democratic state—if we reestablish the correct credentials—is the liberal-constitutional state; this means that *political* democracy merges with liberalism and has, in the main, been superseded by it. The exhortation "democratize the state" does not lead far, and much more often leads astray. The machinery of government is always open to improvements; but it is very hard to see what would be improved by the so-called democratic takeover of the liberal-constitutional state. Thus far, the takeover dictum has eventually enthroned constitutions that no longer provide constitutional safeties—that no longer are, I have argued earlier, constitutions.[64]

"More democracy" thus means, when intelligently understood, that democracy is not only a political form. It means, in the first place, that more social equality and economic welfare are to be sought. It also means that, at its roots, democratic life revolves around small groups, face-to-face relationships, a multigroup society, and "private governments."[65] As Dahl and Lindblom observe: "The nation-state can only provide the framework within which the good life is possible; it cannot fulfill the functions of the small groups. . . . To the extent that it attempts to do so, the nation-state must provide either an impoverished substitute for, or a grotesque perversion of, small group functions."[66] The foregoing may not appear an exalting task or prospect. In particular, many people will probably take exception to the thought that as a political form democracy (representative democracy, to be precise) cannot be much more than the entry of the demos into a juridical order geared to a cluster of techniques of liberty. Their unhappiness would be lessened, however, if they came to see that freedom from political fear is a truly enormous achievement and that the liberal-constitutional state is *the* precondition for everything else.

Squarely put, while liberalism is an instrument of democracy, democracy is not in itself a vehicle of liberalism. The formula of liberal democracy is *equality through liberty,* by means of liberty, not liberty by means of equality. Logically the inversion is plausible, but empirically it is not. On purely logical or purely conceptual grounds I myself am perfectly capable of either deriving equality from freedom or, conversely, freedom from equality. But the order and connection of abstract ideas is not an *ordo et connectio rerum,* the order and connection of things. This is even more the case with artifacts—things created by human workmanship. In whatever we construct something has to be done first in order for something else to follow. We have to make the bricks before building a brick house. This is a procedural order and a procedural necessity. And, here, the brick is liberty. That is to say, the liberty of liberalism and the equality of democracy relate to each other *procedurally* in this order. We may praise equality more than liberty, but this does not make what is first in order of preference also first in order of construction. From liberty we are free to go on to equality; from equality we are not free to get back to liberty. The itinerary is non-reversible—nobody has ever plausibly shown how to reverse it. It is certainly not fortuitous that democracy came back to life as a good polity (after millennia of condemnations) in the wake of liberalism. And it is an easy prediction that democracy will again perish if the end of a greater equality is pursued to the detriment of the means that allow us to lay claim to it.

That political democracy cannot be divorced from liberalism, and is actually resolved into liberalism, still leaves us with *extrapolitical* democracy. On this simple reflection two points suggest themselves. First, more democracy does not entail, by any necessity, less liberalism. Second, and consequently, there is no contradiction in asking simultaneously for more democracy *and* more liberalism.

Liberalism has depreciated, after all, as a result of its success. The constitutional state has succeeded so well in neutralizing power that people have begun to notice economic much more than political constraints. However, this situation is being noticeably changed. No modern state is a minimal state any longer. With the passing of time the state has become not only the "general regulator" of almost everything but also, and more and more, a mastodontic "mass employer." And the growing pervasiveness of political constraints can be measured by the increase in the number of decision areas that are collectivized, i.e., no longer left to individual choice.[67] Therefore, as Cranston rightly points out, "the constraints on which the liberal has concentrated have become *more* important; the constraints he has neglected *less* important. . . . It is therefore strange, if it is true, that liberalism has entered its 'decline as an ideology' just when this altered balance of social constraints make the liberal analysis more timely and correct than it was when it flourished. . . ."[68] This is true but perhaps not strange. Hardly ever, at least in political matters, do we realize in time that the time has come to face the opposite danger. Yet, if liberalism (classic liberalism) has depreciated because of its success, it may regain its value as a result of its present lack of success. For those who believe in a democracy *within* liberalism, this is indeed a hope at which to cling. For the time being, however, many people seemingly believe in a democracy *without* liberalism.

13.7   Democracy without Liberalism

I have argued the case for liberal democracy. Let us now see how the opposite camp argues the case against it. The thesis of the opponents is, in essence, monotonously simple: True democracy is not liberal democracy, for the latter is only a sham bourgeois and/or capitalistic democracy. Thus authentic democracy awaits us beyond liberalism and beyond its deceitful and repressive freedoms. How is all of this demonstrated? As in all wars — and this is a war — victory very much depends on the choice of the ground on which to do battle. It is not surprising, therefore, that the anti-liberal doctrine (as I shall call it) entirely reformulates the way of setting up the argument. The reformulation is often foggier than I make it, but its thread is unmistakably, in its shrewd form, of the following tenor: There is only, at base, a "chain of freedoms" that begins with purely formal freedoms and ends at complete, real freedom. The advantages of such a presentation are obvious at a glance. First, it is immediately evident which is the minor and which the major term of the series and, second, a progression is postulated such as to suggest a natural and somewhat necessary trajectory that links the initial to the final term.

I lay stress on the approach, since it is this which provides the conclusion without further ado. The winning move is to call "freedom" what is otherwise identified as "equality." When the problem is discussed in relation to the concepts of liberty and equality, it is by no means self-evident that one term matters less than the other. If anything, the liberty-equality dyad conveys that the issue cannot be settled on grounds of *Aufhebung*, of supplanting or superseding, precisely because we have to deal with *two* distinct problems. If we instead repeat the same word, presented on the the first occasion negatively ("formal" liberty in this antithesis stands for apparent liberty) and on the second occasion positively (liberty in the "real" sense, meaning effective, true), the conclusion is as obvious as it is inescapable: one freedom for another, if we have to reject the first, the formal one, in order to have the second, we choose "real" freedom. As anyone can see, the argument hangs entirely on two verbal manipulations: *(a)* the renaming of equality as "liberty"; and *(b)* the misconceiving of "formal" (with reference to politico-juridical freedom). Both stipulations are entirely arbitrary — and I take this to mean impermissible and mistaken.[69]

To make two things verbally alike only makes them *verbally* alike. No matter how insistently we use "liberty" to denote equality, the fact remains that we are confusing different things. In one instance (when we have our mind on the problem of equality) we refer to a *condition of liberty,* while in the other instance (when we think of liberty) we no longer refer to a condition but to the thing itself. This distinction is basic for a further reason:

Equality is a condition of liberty only under the ulterior clause that equality be desired for liberty's sake. If we have come to conjoin equality with liberty, this is because we are accustomed to view equality in the context of a liberal civilization, in a framework in which a liberal *animus* happens to pervade our egalitarian claims. So, equality cannot be identified with liberty, not only because it is only a condition of liberty, but also because this link between the two is contingent.

Passing on to the second point, to call formal the freedom that we enjoy in liberal-democratic systems—when formal is used in the sense of "unreal"—is to misconceive the juridical signification of the term form and to obfuscate the issue.[70] An unreal freedom is not a "formal" freedom but, to begin with, a non-existent freedom, a freedom promised but not provided. And no matter how often one may use the word unreal to denote our juridico-political liberties, the fact remains that whoever has enjoyed and then lost them (in Eastern Europe and, intermittently, in much of Latin America) longs for their reestablishment. Had liberalism produced only an empty formal liberty, how is it that its Western detractors protest so vehemently whenever their unreal freedom (in their claim) is (in their claim) infringed upon? To be sure, once the expression "formal liberty" is reconceived in its technical and, indeed, positive juridical meaning, then we are fully entitled to pursue ulterior and greater freedoms. This does not detract from the fact that a smaller freedom is just as real as a greater one—especially when the latter requires the former in order to exist.

So, when we recommend the rejection of politico-juridical rights and freedoms on the grounds that they are unworthy or false, what we are in effect rejecting, wittingly or unwittingly, is a legally disciplined and restrained exercise of power. And what greater freedom—*vulgo,* "real freedom"—can come out of this is indeed a well-kept secret. No one maintains that the subject of liberty is exhausted by the concept of freedom *from.* But after having granted that political freedom is, alone, an incomplete freedom, this much is certain: Eliminate the first freedom of the series, and the term liberty becomes devoid of meaning. There is an iron procedural path that marks the expansion of liberty, and it is such that political freedom is the sine qua non of all the positive liberty-equalities.

I have already said so, but the point bears hammering: There is no plausibility in the thesis that real liberty follows from the achievement of material equality, that is, of economic equalization. How is it that equality of possessions, or of lack of possessions, is held to imply real liberty? Those who hold this view evidently forget that man's power over man is not, or not only, a corporeal thing connected with property. Power is also, and more fundamentally, a relational phenomenon. Therefore the elimination of the power deriving from ownership can only produce the consequence that *all power takes on a relational form.* There is little to rejoice in that. If anything, in this form we have power at its worst, in its most menacing incarnation. This is by no means to deny—as we have seen at length[71]—that the problem of implementing our freedoms with the means (economic or other) that allow for their positive fruition is a very real one. What I do affirm is that there is nothing, in our quest for positive freedoms and substantive equalities, that justifies the repudiation of the liberty of liberalism. By dismissing it we are simply killing the chicken that lays the eggs.

All in all, my strong suspicion is that those who reject liberalism have never really grasped what it is all about. But while this is unfortunate, it is *de facto* immaterial. Many civilizations have fallen because they were, to begin with, misapprehended by their beneficiaries. However, my sense is that a growing number of East Europeans are in fact, even if unknowingly, rediscovering liberalism (as such). They are rediscovering, I mean, the political virtues—and, in my interpretation, essence—of liberalism: that unchecked power is insufferable and disastrous; that justices and courts must be truly independent; that constitutions are not merely whatever structure a state happens to have, but a specific *garantiste* structure that actually restrains and constrains the power wielders. This rediscovery is taking, to say the very least, effort, tears, and time. But if the Western civility (which either is liberal-democratic or is nothing) manages to survive long enough, then my hope is that liberal democracy will be sustained, and eventually rejuvenated, by Eastern liberalism. Be that as it may, it is certainly possible that the erosion of the liberal component element of Western liberal democracies will continue and that at some future point in time the balance will be upset beyond repair. If so, something is awaiting us beyond the democracy that we know. What?

Since "democracy" has become a universally sanctified term apparently destined to keep us company whatever road we take, let us initially join in the game and reply: What awaits us is a totalitarian democracy. If the expression sounds like a *contradictio in adiecto,* it is because we refer it to liberal democracy. But if we woke up one morning in ancient Athens, in all likelihood we would find that democracy invasive (far more than our competitive market societies), suffocating, and insecure (with respect to the individual rights to which we are accustomed). Certainly, moreover, we would not feel free from political fear. Whether we would call that experience totalitarian depends on how the word is defined—and matters little, for the point is, remember, that the democracy of the ancients was able to perform as a democracy because it was stateless, while our democracies are not, and cannot be, stateless.[72] This is the difference that makes all the difference. In the end, a non-liberal (pre- or post-liberal) state nominally performing in the name of the people — all the guarantees, remember, are gone — and thus claiming an absolute legitimacy would hardly carry the day as being, in any meaningful sense, democratic. Beyond liberal democracy, then, what one really glimpses is only the survival of the word, that is, of a democracy for rhetorical consumption, that thanks to the *fictio* of some presumed popular support can sanction the most despotic bondage. This means, in plain terms, that together with the demise of liberal democracy, democracy dies too — regardless of whether we are referring to it in its modern or in its ancient form, whether it is a democracy based on freedom of the individual or one that only requires that power be exercised by the collective *plenum*.

Notes

1. In the years 1872 to 1918, during the period that runs between the break of the First International and the Russian Revolution, communism and socialism were used more or less interchangeably, but with a decided prevalence of the latter name. It is only with Lenin that "communism" leaves the orbit of the broad Marxist interpretation of socialism. More exactly, it was in March 1918 that the Bolsheviks left to the Mensheviks the label "Russian Party of the Social-Democratic Workers," adopting for themselves that of "Russian Communist Party." See n. 39, chapter 14, herein.

2. To be sure, since the communist doctrine is supposed to pave the way to an ultimate "socialist society," in the end communism and socialism will again come to mean the same thing. However, for all present-day intents, across the Western world socialists neither accept the communist method nor its Soviet model. Only the communists speak of their stand, at times, as socialist.

3. *Vom Wesen und Wert der Demokratie*, chap. 9. In his *General Theory of Law and State* Kelsen was even more drastic: "democracy coincides with political . . . liberalism" (p. 288).

4. This is notably the case of the authors that tie the concept of democracy and that of "constitutional government" closely together by claiming that a democratic government is necessarily constitutional.

5. One might say that the same holds for the link between "democracy" and "Democrat." Yet, within the Western world the meaning of Democrat is not as changeable as that of Liberal. Also, the ambiguity of "Democrat" in most cases derives from the ambiguity of "Liberal."

6. *The Rise and Decline of Liberalism* (Milwaukee: Bruce, 1953), pp. 25, 23.

7. See Ronald Dworkin, "Liberalism," in *Public and Private Morality*, ed. S. Hampshire (Cambridge: Cambridge University Press, 1978). While Dworkin argues, against the skeptic, that "liberalism is an authentic and coherent political morality," such that it does "make sense to speak of 'its' central principle" (p. 115), his essay makes no attempt at grounding such "central principle" upon historical foundations. The "constitutive political position" that Dworkin singles out as being constitutive of liberalism

is, rather, constitutive of Liberalism conceived as the "political position" opposed to conservatism. See also Dworkin's "Neutrality, Equality and Liberalism," in *Liberalism Reconsidered,* ed. D. MacLean and Claudia Mills (Totowa: Rowman & Allanheld, 1983). I happen to agree with his central point that the political theory of liberalism requires the structure of social institutions to be "neutral" as regards the good life. My point remains that Dworkin does not show that his Liberalism is liberalism.

8. *The Rise of European Liberalism* (London: Allen & Unwin, 1936), p. 9.

9. This is well attested by the classic study of F. Meinecke, *Weltbürgertum und Nationalstaat* (1908), trans. *Cosmopolitanism and the National State* (Princeton: Princeton University Press, 1970).

10. *The Liberal Tradition in America* (New York: Harcourt, 1955), p. 11.

11. Perhaps England makes exception to this generalization. It is noteworthy, however, that for much of the second half of the nineteenth century "liberal" indicated little more than a member of Gladstone's party.

12. See Paine, who can stand for all: "What is called a *republic,* is not any *particular form* of government. It is wholly characteristical of the purport . . . for which government ought to be instituted . . . *res publica,* the public affairs, or the public good. . . . It is a word of a good original . . . and in this sense it is naturally opposed to the word *monarchy,* which . . . means arbitrary power in an individual person. . . . Every government that does not act on the principle of a republic, or, in other words, does not make the *res publica* its whole and sole object, is not a good government." *Rights of Man* (1792), pt. II, chap. 3, pp. 168-69 of *Basic Writings* (New York: Willey Book Co., 1942).

13. The coining of the word socialism has been vindicated by Pierre Leroux, who used it for the first time in 1833. Actually the word had already appeared in France in 1831 (in an anonymous article attributed to Alexandre Vinet), and even before in England in the Owenist review *Cooperative Magazine* of 1827. Besides, Leroux used the word to deplore "the exaggeration of the idea of association or of society," and therefore in a sense that has not caught on. The essential facts of the matter are, then, that the word was already in the air around the years of the Revolution of 1830; that it was coined by cooperativist circles, and within the group of Saint-Simon in particular, as a term in opposition to "individualism"; and that for several decades it was used in a very loose manner, in associations that included doctrines as diverse as those of Saint-Simon, Fourier, and Proudhon. The works that attracted most attention to the label have been *Organisation du Travail* of Louis Blanc (which came out in 1839), followed in 1848 by his *Le Socialisme: Droit au Travail;* Proudhon's *Qu'est-ce que la Propriété* and his *Philosophie de la Misère* (published in 1840 and 1846 respectively); and, finally, *Principes de Socialisme* of Considerant (printed in 1847), the most important exponent of Fourier's doctrines.

14. In 1848 also the word communism came into the open with the *Communist Manifesto.* However, the communists were then a sectarian variety of socialism, and remained all along—despite Marx—a minor stream of the proletarian movement. As for the word, "communism" derives from the line Babeuf-Buonarroti, and began to be used in the secret revolutionary societies in Paris in the years 1835-40. It was made public by Blanqui, who in 1840 spread the idea of a communist revolutionary dictatorship. Marx did not come in contact with the term directly through the French, but through Moses Hess and Lorenz von Stein; and it was Engels who adopted it before

Marx. See A. Cornu, *Karl Marx: L'Homme et l'Oeuvre* (Paris: Alcan, 1934), chap. 4. See also the amplified work, A. Cornu, *K. Marx, F. Engels, leur Vie et leur Oeuvre,* vol. 1 (Paris: Alcan, 1955).

15. One should keep in mind that at the time "socialism" had a political rather than an economic implication and that it was meant to be a declaration of war against liberalism, a drastic vindication of the priority of the state over the individual.

16. I transfer into English the Italian common and most useful practice of using "liberism" instead of "liberalism" to refer to the economic doctrine of laissez-faire.

17. J.P. Plamenatz, *Man and Society* (New York: McGraw-Hill, 1963), 2:27.

18. See, for all, Hobhouse's influential *Liberalism (1911)*.

19. As one can evince, e.g., from G.H. Sabine's standard *History of Political Theory* (New York: Holt, 1951), which presents Thomas Hill Green as a central figure of liberalism, and does not even mention Tocqueville and Lord Acton, let alone Constant. Clearly, Sabine attributes a disproportionate importance to the "idealist revision of liberalism," perhaps on account of the point that "the philosophies of Mill and Spencer taken together left the theory of liberalism in a state of unintelligible confusion" (p. 724).

20. The major effort to utilize the idealistic speculation for laying down a basis for liberalism (which is that accomplished, *pace* Sabine, by Benedetto Croce) has above all demonstrated how badly the two things go together. See Norberto Bobbio, *Politica e Cultura,* esp. pp. 238-68.

21. For instance, Vernon Parrington's *Main Currents in American Thought* (New York, 1927), illustrates, in the final analysis, only the evolution of the party or of the sectarian meanings of "liberalism" in the United States.

22. The book was translated by Collingwood and published in England in 1927. De Ruggiero also authored (and this attests to the recognition obtained by his *History)* the article "Liberalism" in the 1933 *Encyclopaedia of the Social Sciences.*

23. See chapter 3, section 3.

24. See chapter 11, n. 74, herein.

25. Op. cit., see chapter 11, n. 6, herein.

26. D.J. Manning, *Liberalism* (London: Dent, 1976), pp. 142-43. Actually, Manning does condense the liberal doctrine into three principles: "the principle of balance, the principle of spontaneous generation and circulation, and the principle of uniformity," and perceives what he calls "the symbolic form of the doctrine" as Newtonian (p. 143). This is only slightly less rarefied than Neill's "ecumenical liberalism" (above, n. 6). Moreover, both the Newtonian analogy and "uniformity" strike me as highly unconvincing characterizations.

27. J.S. Schapiro, *Liberalism: Its Meaning and History* (Princeton: Van Nostrand, 1958), p. 35.

28. The quotation is from *The Political Theory of Possessive Individualism: Hobbes to Locke* (Oxford: Clarendon Press, 1962), p. 271. The thesis is accentuated, in even more questionable forms, in Macpherson's *Democratic Theory.*

29. I think not, as will be seen in chapter 14, sections 2 and 3. As regards Macpherson's interpretation of Hobbes, a meticulous criticism is Keith Thomas, "The Social Origins of Hobbes's Political Thought," in *Hobbes Studies,* ed. K.C. Brown (Oxford: Blackwell, 1965), pp. 185-236. My own comments are implicitly referred, rather, to Macpherson's reading of Locke.

30. My point is confined to competition, since it responds to Macpherson's. The broader (and correct) picture is the one given by A.O. Hirschman, *The Passions and the Interests: Political Arguments for Capitalism Before Its Triumph* (Princeton: Princeton University Press, 1977). As Hirschman well shows, the capitalistic money-making pursuits became "honorable" in being called upon to counteract "passions" and their harms. The process that Macpherson renders as a warlike "invasiveness" pursued, instead, gentle customs and did harness the fury of passions.

31. If one cares to read, this was said very clearly. See, for instance and for all, the 1776 Virginia Declaration of Rights: "That all men are by nature equally free and independent, and have certain inherent rights . . . namely, the enjoyment of *life*, and *liberty*, with the means of acquiring and possessing *property*, and pursuing and obtaining happiness and *safety*" (my emphasis).

32. J. Baechler, *Les Origines du Capitalisme* (Paris: Gallimard, 1971), moves the origin of capitalism all the way back to the Middle Ages. However, on his account the roots of capitalism are political — they are to be found in medieval pluralistic "anarchy" — not economic. On the other hand, capitalism becomes "capital accumulation" (a completely different thing, as I shall underscore in chapter 14, section 3) in unison with the industrial revolution. In either way, Macpherson's interpretation is wrong both in timing and conceptualization.

33. Up to the beginnings of the industrial revolution, what we call economy was still largely intended in the Greek meaning of *oikonomía*, i.e., as law *(nomos)* of the home *(oikos)*, as "household management." Activities that flagrantly exceeded the household needs were called by Aristotle *chrematistic* and condemned as a *hybris,* an excess. Hobbes, for one, still believed that "endless acquisitiveness was bad in itself" (K. Thomas, in Brown, *Hobbes Studies,* p. 217). What we call economy today is thus much closer to "chrematistics" than to Aristotle's *oikonomía.*

34. Macpherson is altogether orthodox on the point: "liberal democracy is strictly a capitalist phenomenon." *Democratic Theory,* p. 173.

35. Namely, *(a)* customary or status society, *(b)* simple market society, *(c)* possessive market society. See *The Political Theory of Possessive Individualism,* pp. 46-61.

36. Ibid., p. 48 (italics in the original).

37. See G. Sartori, "What Is Politics?" *Political Theory* 1 (1973): 13-16.

38. *The Political Theory of Possessive Individualism,* pp. 53, 49.

39. Reference is especially made to chapter 11, herein.

40. See chapter 6, herein.

41. R. Dahrendorf, *The Reith Lectures 1974,* reprinted from "The Listener," 14 November 1974, opening statement.

42. This is buttressed by the fact that it is impossible "to translate . . . *eleuthería, libertas* or 'free man,' into any Near Eastern language . . . or any Far Eastern language for that matter." M.I. Finley, *The Ancient Economy* (Berkeley: University of California Press, 1973), p. 29.

43. Likewise, anarchy, not *libertas,* is the political projection of laissez-faire economics. This is another way of underpinning the distinction between liberism and liberalism.

44. Reference is made to Macpherson's "power as the ability to exercise and develop . . . human capacities" (*Democratic Theory,* p. 50). This is but one verbal variant of the freedom of self-realization, which has long been construed as an ethical freedom.

45. See chapter 11, esp. section 1, but also the discussion of freedom as autonomy in section 5.

46. A.J.P. Taylor, *English History 1914-45* (Oxford: Oxford University Press, 1965), p. 1.

47. See chapter 2, herein.

48. *L'Idea Liberale* (Milano: Garzanti, 1955), pp. 5-6.

49. For the incomprehension of "English liberty" (which explains the superposition of Rousseau's influence over Montesquieu), see Joseph Dedieu, *Montesquieu et la Tradition Politique Anglaise en France* (Paris, 1909), chap. 12; and R. Derathé, "Montesquieu et J.J. Rousseau," *Revue Internationale de Philosophie* 3-4 (1955): 367ff., who notes: "It is only in the nineteenth century, at the time of the Restoration, that the *Esprit des Lois* acquired in France an undisputed prestige. . . . During the eighteenth century the book had not been taken too seriously."

50. It is with reference to the French indigenous tradition that J.L. Talmon justly emphasizes that "diversity of views and interests was far from being regarded as essential by the eighteenth-century fathers of democracy. Their original postulates were unity and unanimity. The affirmation of the principle of diversity came later, when the totalitarian implications of the principle of homogeneity had been demonstrated in Jacobin dictatorship." *The Origins of Totalitarian Democracy* (London: Secker & Warburg, 1952), p. 44.

51. For an analysis of how Tocqueville related democracy to liberty, see Jack Lively, *The Social and Political Thought of A. de Tocqueville* (Oxford: Clarendon Press, 1962), esp. chap. 1.

52. See chapter 12, esp. section 3.

53. *Etica e Politica*, pp. 288-89. Croce's polemics were directed against democracy also because he identified the latter with the abhorred philosophy of the Enlightenment. See, however, this more balanced appraisal of 1936: "Liberalism is both friendly and inimical to democracy. A friend because its political class is an open class . . . which resolves itself in a government which in its very action educates the governed to the ability to govern. But it is an enemy of democracy when the latter tends to substitute quality by number and quantity, because it knows that in so doing democracy paves the way for demagogy, and without wishing to, for dictatorships and tyrannies, thereby destroying itself." *Pagine Sparse* (Napoli: Ricciardi, 1948), 2:407.

54. *Storia del Liberalismo Europeo*, pp. 395, 401.

55. Ibid., p. 395. Note that de Ruggiero says individual, not "individualism." Since he was at base a Hegelian, he can hardly be suspected of individualistic atomism.

56. *The Good Society* (New York: Grosset & Dunlap, 1943), p. 387.

57. Bertrand Russell, *Authority and the Individual* (London: Allen & Unwin, 1949), p. 11.

58. *The Cultural Contradictions of Capitalism* (New York: Basic Books, 1976), p. 176.

59. This is the meaning intended by Tocqueville and Bryce. See chapter 1, section 3.

60. *La Démocratie en Amérique*, vol. 11, bk. 1v, chap. 7.

61. The notion of unstable equilibrium suffices to point out that the equilibrium model is not necessarily biased in favor of conservatism.

62. See chapter 4, section 5.

63. *Aufheben* conveys all in one three meanings: *(a)* to lift up "progressively," *(b)* in the sense of "maintaining," and/or *(c)* in the sense of "annihilating." The fact that *Aufhebung* is actually untranslatable in English is a handicap so far as the understanding of the idealistic philosophy goes, but makes English-speaking people less prone to dialectic miraculosity.

64. See chapter 11, section 7.

65. See C.E. Merriam, *Public and Private Government* (New Haven: Yale University Press, 1944). He intended a self-government of voluntary associations outside the government.

66. *Politics, Economics and Welfare* (New York: Harper, 1953), p. 520.

67. See chapter 8, section 1, where politics is defined in terms of collectivized decisions.

68. *Freedom,* p. 81.

69. See chapter 9, sections 1 and 2, where I take issue with the stipulative theory of meaning. I equally do so in *Social Science Concepts,* esp. pp. 34 and 60-61.

70. The technical (legal and/or ethical) meaning of "formal" is spelled out in chapter 12, section 6.

71. In chapter 12, esp. section 7.

72. See chapter 10, sections 3 and 5.

14. Market, Capitalism, Planning, and Technocracy

The human condition is small brain, big problems.
— Charles E. Lindblom

14.1 What Is Planning?

Thus far, democracy has been envisaged as a political system, for that is what democracy is above all. However, democracy can also be envisaged as a politico-social and/or politico-economic system. This extension, or joint consideration, is especially prompted by the fact that democracy as we know it today has infinitely more tasks and functions than it had, say, fifty years ago. To a greater or lesser extent, and varying from place to place, the democratic state has increasingly become a do-everything state. Whether this happens under the pressure of circumstances or by virtue of deliberate choice, our political systems are intervening more and more in hitherto unregulated realms. More and more areas of decision are collectivized, that is, decided authoritatively for all. Much of this expansion is either sought or deemed acceptable. The battle begins, however, where the "visible hand" of the state enters a course of collision with the "invisible hand" of the market.

To be sure, states have always intervened in economic matters. Laissez faire resulted from interventions against trade impediments. Industrialization was sustained in most countries by protective interventions. And states intervene in the free market in order to "free it" from monopolistic and other ills or evils. What is crucially at stake, then, is not the extent of state intervention or regulation but whether our economic systems should remain, at base, market systems. Market or nonmarket—that is the question.

I have said: market versus nonmarket. But much of the discussion has been sidetracked, from the 1930s onward, onto the notion of planning. The question at center stage has been: Are democracy and state economic planning compatible? Since "planning," especially in English, is a remarkably loose term, one can with equal reason answer yes or no, depending on how the term is defined. For instance, in 1953 Dahl and Lindblom defined planning as "an attempt at rationally calculated action to achieve a goal"[1] This is by no means a technical meaning, and it is certainly not the meaning intended by the economists who coined the term (with reference to the Soviet Union). To them planning was "collectivistic planning" or total planning, that is, a centralized state management that replaced the market; and their view was that planning was highly irrational.[2] Between these two very different, if not contrasting, meanings, the term came gradually to denote what may be called "limited planning." Notice that this minor specimen was seldom called planning by the economists of the 1930s and early 1940s. French authors variously spoke of "directed" or, more softly, of "concerted" and "controlled" economy. Italian authors characteristically said "programmed" or "dirigiste" economy.[3] It was only from the late 1940s onward that "planning" (the English word) overcame the other labels, thus acquiring a third signification. Taking stock, our present-day discussions relate to three different referents and meanings, to wit:

Planning as rational organization
Limited planning
Total planning

As already noted, planning conceived as *rational organization* (as in the focus of Dahl and Lindblom) does not represent a technical connotation of the term and is handicapped by excessive looseness. Nevertheless, this meaning cannot be dismissed. First, it does reflect a widespread understanding of "planning," if for no other reason than that people find it so defined in dictionaries. Second, and more important, expressions such as "rational organization," rationally calculated action, rational coordination, and the like, do represent the underlying common thread of any and all demands for some kind of planning. Regardless of which planning (limited or total) is preferred, pro-planners find the market system irrational, at least in the sense that the automatisms of the market baffle the rational, deliberate control of our own destiny. Since a market system is a "spontaneous order" monitored by its feedbacks, it conflicts with a "rational order" shaped by targets. So, planning may well be conceived as a rational organization; but when planning is so conceived it does not denote a specific type of planning. Reference is not made here to a concrete specimen but to *reasons for* planning and, by implication, to a criterion for evaluating planning policies.

Let us turn to *limited planning,* that is, to one of the two technical meanings of the term. Since there are many degrees and forms of limited planning, there are many names for it. In addition to directed economy and programmed economy (the older labels), we hear of framework planning, indicative planning, planning by inducement, and the like. Whatever the labels, we must determine where the wide spectrum of limited planning begins and where it ends.

Planning begins as something *more* than mere government intervention and regulation. Every present-day government incessantly interferes with the economic process; and, of course, every government makes plans. But this is not yet "planning" in any technical sense of the word. Limited planning always coexists (by definition) with the market system, but is not yet in existence when a government simply enacts monetary or Keynesian policies and manipulates the automatic stabilizers of the economic process. All this is not yet planning because it does not add up to an organic plan that is both *coordinated* and *future oriented* toward targets — targets that cannot be attained by market mechanisms. By definition, planning does not consist of piecemeal responses to the contingencies of the day. Limited planning always coexists with the market system, but as a corrective of, and an antidote to, a market system. In varying degrees, planning is intended to compensate for the inadequacies or faults of market processes. Under a system of limited planning, the market still provides the "efficiency pricing" for all calculations and still reveals consumers' preferences. Yet we now have a politico-economic system monitored *in part* by consumer sovereignty but *in part* by a central agency that does not respond to market signals. Rather, the planning agency pursues development goals (industrial or other) or equalization goals.[4] The objection might be that despite efforts to draw one, the border that separates government intervention from limited planning is not clear-cut. Since limited planning always coexists, if more or less uneasily, with a market economy, the respective jurisdictions are necessarily porous ones. This does not detract from the fact that at some point important differences and importantly different consequences are involved.

Just as it is unnecessary to determine exactly where limited planning begins, it is equally unnecessary to determine exactly where it ends. A breaking point is reached at which the market is destroyed as an efficient mechanism for determining costs and prices (for the productive economy as a whole).[5] At that point, planning is no longer "limited." So, if it is true that, aside from the market, no other mechanism exists for efficiency pricing, enough has been said for tracing the ultimate frontier of limited planning.[6]

We are left with *total planning,* often called totalitarian planning, collectivistic planning, central authoritative planning, or command economy. These labels all stand for a centrally commanded economy in which a master mind displaces and replaces the market. This is the Communist or Soviet meaning of planning, and it may be reconstructed, by hindsight, as an unintended outcome of Marxian and, even more, Saint-Simonian premises. Marx concentrated his artillery on the abolition of private property, but this was a fairly common stance around the 1820s and 1830s among socialist groups.[7] The Saint-Simonians went further.[8] It was very clear to them that, along with property, what had to go was the market, replaced by a centrally directed economy; and they did work out detailed schemes of a nonmarket, centralized economic system. Thus the Saint-Simonians (not Marx) hit on the crucial point. In truth, Marx never envisaged the requirements, let alone the concrete implications, of a command economic system based on state ownership. More often than not, Marx advocated the centralization of all means of production in the hands of the state; but he also advocated (especially, though not only, in his 1871 writings on the Paris Commune) a decentralized self-management of the producers. In the long run it was the latter view that was consistent with his ultimate vision of a stateless, associational, "transparent" society where all the people continually exercise collective control over their own life.[9] In reality, Soviet planning is Stalin's creature.[10] Since Marx afforded no guidance, planning in the Soviet Union was improvised and imposed by the force of the sword. Soviet planning was, then, an unintended outcome. It was not intended by Marx, and it was intended differently (although Lenin and Stalin never knew it) by the only ancestry it had: the early Saint-Simonian planners of planning.

I said at the beginning that the issue ultimately boils down to the alternative market versus nonmarket. The standard retort will be that this is dichotomous thinking and that even in this matter differences are largely of degree. But the evidence for this objection is meagre. The critic can only point out that in actual practice even command economies tolerate a black market or indeed encourage a secondary, parallel "private market." But in order to prove that black or private markets attest to anything other than failures of total planning, one has to prove that they assist the calculations of the master mind. Do they? How in fact do the Soviet and Soviet-inspired planners decide what is to be done?

Certainly not on the basis of information provided by secondary "free" markets. Soviet planners can see by eyesight which consumer goods are scarce and which are in demand—and they tolerate a private market precisely because they are unable to supply them. It is equally certain that consumer preferences, even if known or surmised, are in no way sovereign. Total planning is the planning of an all-owner and all-seller state that is the sole decider of the allocation of resources, of what the wages are, and of what consumers have to accept (or do without). In short, total planning is a planning in the name of the sovereignty of the objectives. But, then, what about costs? Economists have endlessly pondered how a command economy could perform, so to speak, economically. By the middle of the 1930s the central objection was already spelled out in full force: It was theoretically and practically impossible for the collectivistic planner to *calculate costs*.[11] His costs and prices are, and can only be, arbitrary. To be sure, arbitrary not in the sense that they are established at whim but in the sense that they are *baseless;* they cannot be derived from any economically significant base or baseline.

This objection did not, at least in the Mises-Hayek line of criticism, stand alone; its political corollary was that collective planning found its inevitable complement in a totalitarian dictatorship. It was the political implication, namely, the contention that planning and freedom were incompatible, that prompted heated counterattacks.[12] However, if we remain among economists, that is, if the objection remains technical and confined to the cost problem, it cannot be denied that the Mises-Hayek objections brought about a great deal of rethinking in the social-democratic and socialist theory of planning.[13] To make a long and complex story short, today the consensus among economists largely is that if the cost (or efficiency pricing) problem of collectivized planning has a solution, it can only be a solution of this sort: In the absence of a real market, the planner must be able to "simulate a market."[14]

This response is intellectually appropriate but extremely difficult to implement. True, the computer revolution has seemingly removed the technological obstacle to a simulation of the market, and we have witnessed over the decades important mathematical developments in linear programming. Yet a sympathetic observer takes stock of the situation in 1976 as follows: "Communist planners acknowledge that they have not achieved synoptic economic planning. . . . Planning, they have declared, is to become more 'scientific.' More computers, more mathematical models . . . more centralization. . . . One result so far is that in seven years the administrative bureaucracy grew by a third."[15] The magnitude of the problem is such as to defy computer technology itself. For highly simplified calculations that do not even begin or attempt to simulate a market, a Soviet estimate is that 14,000 computers would be required and that it would take one hundred years to train the required technicians. Furthermore, and aside from computing capabilities, the problem remains that the task "of drawing up the necessary equations or a model of the economy is . . . probably beyond any profession's competence."[16] In the end we are back to the beginning. The 1935 objection still stands: Without a market system, resources cannot be rationally or efficiently allocated, and this because the collectivistic planner goes around in circles—he has no (economic) cost basis from which to go.

What is the fallback position? From the outset it consists of two different, though often intermingled, arguments. The first is that, *in fact,* some kind of latent and disguised market system does exist even under total planning and that the planner's calculations are in many indirect ways assisted by it. But I have never encountered any convincing proof of the existence or the bearing of such entity (unless the latent or disguised market in question is confused with the secondary, tolerated "private" market mentioned earlier— but this would be false witnessing). Nor can the argument be sustained under the form that the Soviet pricing system is assisted by Western market pricings. To the extent that this may be the case (especially with reference to the commodities that are in fact exchanged between East and West), we are simply confirming that, in and of itself, the Soviet planner swims in a sea of darkness. We are thus left with the second fallback position, which argues, in essence, that the way out is to *re-create,* in some amended form and to a sufficient extent, a real market. This is the only well-sketched route, and I shall come to it shortly.

Before proceeding further, let us recall that thus far I have merely, or mostly, sought to clarify the meanings and referents of "planning." It is argued that since the term planning denotes widely different phenomena, it is best to leave it undefined. On this view, only haziness and much futility have in fact followed. There are people who reject limited planning (definition 2) because they confuse it with total planning (definition 3). There are some, on the other hand, who accept total planning in terms of planning as a rational ideal (definition 1). There are still others who demand planning as a rationalization of economic processes, are presented with forms of state intervention that are neither economic nor rational, and yet are happy all the same because they behold the word and are unable to see into the thing. In parallel and equally confusing fashion the assertion is, on the one hand, that democracy and planning are incompatible, and on the other, that they are perfectly or even necessarily interlinked. Clearly, only if planning is spoken of intelligibly can it be discussed intelligently.

The *anti-planning* thesis applies to total planning; the thesis that planning is *necessary* best applies to "rationally calculated action" (a criterion, not a real-world specimen); and the *compatibility* between democracy and planning is a thesis that applies to limited planning. As these theses fit into place, we can also appreciate the fact that the "grand alternatives" are all still with us. They have been dismissed on the ground that governments have in fact a limited range of choice and do not actually make "great global choices among grand alternatives."[17] True, but only for Western governments; not true for much of the Third World, for China when Mao took over, and probably not true for Czechoslovakia, Hungary, and Poland (if they were permitted to choose). The dismissal of the grand alternatives applies only, and narrowly, to what goes on *within* democracies, to the exclusion of what may happen *to* democracy. Perhaps the wrong debate is not the one *about* the grand alternatives but the one *against* them.

14.2 *What Is the Market?*

Planning, it has been seen, must be defined in relation to the market. But what is the market or the market system? The market is called an "invisible hand"[18] and there certainly is far more in the market than meets the eye. On the other hand, a common contention is that market systems no longer exist, either because they are overly impure or because they have been replaced by a third kind, a mixed system.

Let us first address the notion of *mixed system*. If it says that market mechanisms are only one of the component elements of the realm of economics, this can be readily granted; but the point would be trivial. In order to make a point of heuristic value the contention must be that a mixed system is *mixed* and *not market*—that we are confronted with a *sui generis* entity. So, mixed with what? With planning? Assuming that reference is made to actual deeds, this would be a gross overstatement. Limited planning has been enacted, timidly, by a few democracies only.[19] So, mixed with what else? With state ownership, or tamperings, or sanctuaries? It is indeed the case that most present-day market systems are shrinking and highly interfered with; but does this add up to another, "third" kind of economic system?

Since much of the discussion equivocates between mixed system and impure-imperfect system, it is important to firm up the difference between the two. The market is generally called market *system*. This is correct, for the market doubtless displays systemic properties;[20] but it is imprecise, for precision requires us to say that the market is a *subsystem* of the economic system as a whole. Nobody has ever held that market and economic system are coextensive. Yet the argument that all concrete systems are mixed and that in such a mix the market is non-predominant centrally rests on the fallacy of measuring a subsystem *as if* it were a system. That the economic system is greater than its market subsystem is what the distinction between system and subsystem already implies (by definition). On the other hand, that the market subsystem falls short, even very short, of being the economic system does not establish in any way who or what is "predominant." If a boxer faces three dilettante assailants, will the ratio of three to one tell who wins? Probably not. Probably what counts more is the punch. But the relative magnitude of each subsystem vis-à-vis its master system fails to tell who has the punch.

Let it be underlined that not even on normative grounds has anybody ever held that the market subsystem ought to be all-subsuming, i.e., brought to coincide with the economic system. To begin with, public goods (at least some) are truly indivisible and thus permit free riding: They are accessible to everyone at no cost. This entails that public goods are not, and cannot be, supplied by market incentives. We are also confronted more and more with accumulations of "externalities," such as pollution, degradation and even destruction of the environment. Who pays for the repairs? Who bears the costs for cleaning a lake or the water supply? Then, to be sure, national defense is a state, not a market, concern. As we proceed in itemizing all the many needs that market mechanisms will not satisfy, we also see that the service sector—indeed, in postindustrial societies, the largest chunk of the economic system—is not necessarily well served by them. A number of public services may well be left in private competitive hands and thus left to operate on the basis of market rules; but many public services (especially utilities) are necessarily submitted to price controls, and still others can be provided only by the public hand. In the end we discover that the market is, above all and crucially, *the subsystem of the productive sector;* it relates producers of goods (not of services) to consumers of goods. How much is that, in magnitude, vis-à-vis the entire economic system? The statistics on the matter depend on where we draw the line of what is "productive." Let us say, for the sake of illustration, that the market subsystem corresponds to one-third of the economic system. Is a third too little? Or is it too much? Should the market-governed sector be reduced further, or should it be aggrandized? Above all, does this (or another) size ratio make for a mixed system? My view is that it does not.

It is also misleading simply to derive the notion of mixed system from the impurities, imperfections, limitations, or even failings of the market. Impurity (and related near-synonyms) refers us to the question, Impure with respect to which yardstick? The real world is always a messy approximation of our theoretical constructs. The real world is always characterized by stickiness (time lags) and friction (resistencies), and this adds up to saying that *market achievements always are suboptimal.* Hence it goes by definition that any concrete market system will be impure, that is, will not function as our mental simplifications—ideal types, models, or schemes—would have them function. The model is always departed from. In order to assert that market systems have in fact ceased to exist we must prove *excessive impurity* and, more precisely, prove that the excess element (the disturbances) overwhelms a "physiological impurity" to such an extent as to warrant this conclusion: We no longer have an impure or disturbed system but indeed another system. Does the impurity-imperfection argument meet such burden of proof? I believe not, for we are never exactly told which is the death threshold and which are the related test criteria.

As we wait for the notions of mixed system and market impurity to prove whatever they are assumed to prove, let us revert to the central question: What is the market — the market as a self-regulating system — and what does it do? What is certain is that in all the modern polities that do not abide by collectivistic planning it is the market subsystem that fundamentally establishes costs and prices — at the very minimum for the financial and good-producing economy, but with important spillover effects on the service and other sectors as well.[21] This means that the economic value of all commodities is basically determined by their exchange value; and this assumes, in turn, that the market processing is *the* method for pursuing efficiency pricing. Is this all? It already suffices to show, I believe, which part of the economic system predominates (has the punch) over the others. But this certainly is not all. Indeed, the mystery or miracle of the market has yet to be unveiled.

Hayek has attended to this unveiling perhaps more than any other author. We owe to him, to begin with, the perspective. Societies are held together by two kinds of order, where "order" means that the activities of the members are "mutually adjusted to one another." One of these,

> the kind of order achieved by *arranging* the relations between the parts according to a preconceived plan is called an *organization*. . . . It is an order we all understand because we know how it is made. . . . The *discovery* that there exists in society orders of another kind, which have not been designed by men but have resulted from the actions of individuals without their intending to create such an order . . . shook the deeply ingrained belief that where there was an order there must also have been a personal orderer . . . [and] provided the foundation for a systematic argument for individual liberty. This kind of order . . . is an order . . . that forms itself. It is for this reason usually called a *spontaneous* . . . order.[22]

There are many social spontaneous orders, to wit, *self-ordering orders*. The market system (subsystem) is, among them, the one that "spontaneously orders" exchanges and mutual adjustments among "economic animals": human beings as they strive for food, shelter, goods, wealth (in order to purchase all of this) and, ultimately, accumulation of wealth. Since it is spontaneous, the first implication — from an economic vantage point — is that the market is *costless;* a system hinged upon automatic feedbacks neither requires nor permits administrators for itself. A second implication is that the market is enormously *flexible* and ever-adapting; it never exhibits—as "organized orders" always do—change resistance, let alone sclerosis and senility. The market cannot be outdated; it outdates. The third implication is that a self-ordering, spontaneous order is a *free order*. But here we must watch for hasty inferences.

Let us preface the argument by noting that the expression "free market" has nothing per se to do with the freedom of individuals; it simply means that the market should be left to itself, to its own mechanisms. So, how does a "free order" relate to individual freedom? The straightforward reply is that a spontaneous order is not *coercive* in the sense in which organized orders are. An order is "spontaneous" precisely in that no single person or agency does or can run it. Since the market is in fact a system monitored by its feedbacks, it is in fact the case that no single person or agency does run it. In the market we are not told by anybody what we have to do; we are not, in this sense, coerced. Organized orders ultimately appeal to a man with a sword, but swords are impotent vis-à-vis a market system; they can only break it. So far, so good. But what about the ulterior and stronger claim that the market system actually enhances individual freedom? In order to assess it, we must bring another element into play.

Spontaneous orders are not all alike in all their characteristics. The market system is distinctively, and somewhat uniquely, an order that incessantly generates alternatives. And the point is this: Alternatives are the necessary complement of *freedom of choice*—the nuclear meaning of all concrete freedoms. But let us not misstate the argument. The market is (offers) a *structure of alternatives*. However, from the fact that the market is a structure of alternatives, one cannot derive that *all* participants in market transactions are *actually* and *equally* free to choose. Structures allow for things to happen; they do not, in themselves, make them happen. Going one step farther, we may say that a structure "encourages" actualization. Even so, the generalized transition from potentiality (what the structure encourages) to actuality requires the backing of sustaining conditions. My *actual* freedom of choice in consuming is a function of how much is in my wallet; my *actual* freedom of choice of producing assumes that I have or can find financial resources for getting myself started as a producer. Clearly, the assimilation of the market to freedom of choice is subject to important restrictions. These restrictions may indeed appear to be strictures. The fact remains that the *potential* is there; the market structure is consonant with freedom of choice for all. That much or, if one wishes, that little, cannot be said of any other known economic structure. Most of our distant as well as recent past attests to slave or slave-like labor, and certainly to infinitely less actual choosing of one's own occupation than in today's market systems. As for the nonmarket solution—collectivistic planning—it does rest on enforced occupation; it is the master mind that decides where the labor force has to go and to stay.

The above may be recast, as economists would prefer, in terms of "freedom of exchange." Even so, the same qualifications apply. It is true that the parties to a market transaction are free to enter, or not to enter, such a transaction; but this is not unqualifiedly true. The parties to an exchange are not, or may not be, of equal force; that is, their respective *power resources* (financial or other) may be highly unequal. Thus, market transactions are "free" but at the same time conditioned and "constrained" by unequal resources. They are truly free when I can refuse the exchange. They are less free, or even ultimately unfree, when I cannot. At the end we return to the conclusion that the linkage between market and individual freedom is best seen and defended comparatively, in this form: While market systems do not hamper the exercise of whatever "power of freedom" individuals have (at the moment of the exchange), nonmarket systems certainly and mightily do restrict and compress freedom of choice.

Resuming our thread, at least one more item must be added to the list of the outstanding properties of the market system. The theory of decisions, or of decision making, generally assumes "perfect information" as a standard and relates imperfect decisions to imperfect information. The market system, however, is monitored by millions or even billions of daily discrete decisions taken by individuals who certainly fall below any minimal standard of imperfect information (as set by decision-making theory). In the market, that is to say, it makes little sense to impute imperfect or wrong decisions to the "cause" imperfect information. This does not mean that the man in the market performs in utter darkness. He knows just about as little as he needs to know —and this because the market does most of the information work for him. Market competition is, as Hayek stresses, a *discovery procedure* and, in the end, an enormous *information simplifier.*[23] The market not only produces information in the form of extraordinarily simplified signals, but also authenticates (or falsifies) that information by the very feedback processes that produce it. Concretely put, all that any single producer needs to know is whether a given product "has a market" and whether he can produce at the market price or at an even lower one. All of this he finds out, at worst, by trying. If he does not get the pertinent market signals right, he is out. If he does, he is in—not only for his own self-interest but also for the generalized interests of the consumers. Organized orders impose, if they are to function, information costs and knowledge costs (to their managers). If an organized order is not understood—democracy is a good case in point—it is bound to be mismanaged. The market order does not need to be understood (it does not impose knowledge costs), and it reduces the information costs to a bare minimum.[24] The market is not only an invisible hand; it is also, to pursue the metaphor, an *invisible mind*.[25]

14.3   Capitalism, Individualism, Collectivism

To sum up, the market is *(a)* the only basis for the calculus of prices and costs; *(b)* management-costless; *(c)* flexible and change responsive; *(d)* the complement of freedom of choice; *(e)* an enormous information simplifier. This is, it cannot be denied, an impressive enumeration of assets. Those who deny them do not really do so; they simply choose to ignore them. Why is it, then, that the market system prompts so much hostility and so little recognition of its merits? The emphasis of its foes is not so much on the failures (that competition is imperfect, that efficiency pricing is not as efficient as assumed, and the like) as on the fact that the market subsystem is, at base, a private enterprise system and thereby an intrinsically wicked "capitalist" phenomenon. We shall come to this specific allegation as the discussion unfolds. At the beginning, the dislike of the market should be construed broadly: It is disliked because it runs counter to the powerful tide of the "egalitarian project."[26]

It is important to say egalitarian "project," for it would be grossly inaccurate to say that the market system is intrinsically inimical to equality as such. In truth, the defender of the market strongly defends *some* equalities — which happen to be the ones that have been for some time out of fashion. It would also be unjust to accuse the market system of being insensitive to any and all principles of justice. In truth, the market system firmly abides by the criterion of justice that reads: equal shares to equals, and unequal to unequals.[27] Yet many people who apply this criterion, i.e., "proportionate justice," to other contexts dislike it in the context of the market. Inexplicably so? Not quite, for proportionate justice acquires, in market hands, a particularly irritating feature: It allows no room for interpretation and manipulation. The market implacably determines with its own mechanisms, and without a shadow of doubt, "who is equal" and "who is unequal"—whether the interested parties like it or not.

In essence, along the sequence of equalities outlined in a previous chapter the market strongly endorses, figuratively speaking, equal laws (against sectional legislation) and equality of opportunity. Conversely, the "logic" of the market is incompatible with, and hostile to, any kind of equalization of circumstances. The reason for this is straightforward. The equalization of circumstances — even if limited to the starting points of the life race — inevitably requires unequal treatments; and this the market logic cannot accept. Unequal treatments favor the worst (subcompetitive) runner and disfavor the good one. This is the very negation of competition and of what the market is all about: economic efficiency. In a nutshell, the contrast is this: The market stands for proportionate justice, while the egalitarian project stands for redistributive justice; the market favors the "equals" (taken at their face value), while the egalitarian project favors the "unequals" (those who are less equal). The market is not intrinsically anti-egalitarian, but it must appear such to the proponents of the redistributive project.

Let us acknowledge it without bickering: The market is a cruel entity. It abides by the law of the success of the fittest. It does seek a fit for everybody, and it does motivate individuals to exert themselves as best they can. But the irremediably unfit are expelled from the market society; they are left to perish or survive on some other arrangement. To what or to whom should this cruelty be imputed? Is it the cruelty of an exasperated individualism or, as Macpherson would have it, of "possessive individualism"? We are told so to no end, but the truth is exactly the other way around: It is a social or collectivistic cruelty. The market is *individual-blind;* it is a ruthless *society-serving* machinery.[28] How this crucial point can be missed, and how it came to be stated upside down, is a most interesting matter.

In order to get the issue straight, we must be clearheaded about the real protagonist: Is it the market system, or is it, instead, the capitalist? It is here that the issue is joined; and despite tons of passionate rhetoric to the contrary, there can be little doubt about it: The master entity, the stake holder, is the market, not the capitalist. The owner of private capital is *in* the market, *part of* the market, and *subsumed* in the market. He is enriched by the laws of the market, that is, not by laws of his making but by laws to which he submits. Indeed, the capitalist is enriched as much as he is impoverished by the laws of the market; what he gains today he can lose tomorrow, and there is nothing he can do about that.[29] Remember, the market system is a spontaneous outgrowth; it was not preconceived and designed by anyone, certainly not by the capitalists. The capitalists did not invent the market; rather, the market invented the capitalists.

When private capitalism is done away with, the worry remains: What about the market system? As we shall soon see, this is what "market socialism" is centrally about. The colossal efficiency failures of collectivistic planning have brought home—regardless of ideological differences—that what matters is the market. If the capitalist must die, the market must be saved. That is to say, we would still need a mechanism for determining costs and prices, for sustaining productivity and, in general, for meeting those problems that the market system solves. After all, the dispossession of capitalists displeases only the capitalists, certainly not a voting majority in any present-day democracy. How, then, do capitalists keep themselves afloat? By corruption and conspiracy? Conspiracy theories loom large but explain little. That the market system is generated by capitalism and is under its control is a short shot that largely sidetracks the issue. The issue is confronted by recognizing that the market system mightily stands on its own feet; it defends itself by itself. In short, the market self-ordering is *the* protagonist.

If this is established, then we must make up our minds and be consistent. If we wish to argue that capitalist societies are irremediably tainted at their core by an original sin, it follows that this must be a market-rooted sin. If, on the other hand, we insist that the sin is in capitalism and the sinner is the capitalist, then it cannot be an original or even a capital sin. For the capitalist is but a whale who swims in the market sea. We may thus revert to the specific allegation that the original sin is "individualism" (possessive, unbridled, or atomistic; or all three in one). In this instance, the dilemma is: Either the villain is market-rooted (indivisible from, and nurtured by, the market), or else individualism is not an important villain (and we are wasting time in witch-hunting). So, the real question comes down to this: Is *the market* individual-serving and individual-regarding?

This is a question assessed best with reference to the notion of *economic value*. Do things have an objective, intrinsic economic value? Locke had already noted that "marketable value" had nothing to do with the "intrinsic natural worth of anything."[30] And Ricardo was just about the last major economist to believe that some kind of absolute or intrinsic value existed. Since his time, economists have given up that belief: In economics, value is above all *exchange value* (Locke's marketable value), that is, a value that lies somewhere between the price at which consumers buy and the cost at which producers are able to produce. But Marx stayed with Ricardo or, better, pursued on his own the search for an absolute value. Marx found the key to his solution in Hegel's *Phenomenology*.[31] In dissent with Hegel's Panglossian "dialectics of the Spirit," but on the basis of the analytical categories of Hegel's philosophy of labor, Marx perceived the condition of *homo laborans* in the early industrial society as an "alienation" of man into the object of his work and saw the remedy (exactly like Hegel) in "reappropriation."[32] How can this alienation be not only proved but measured? By establishing that "value" is not exchange value but *work value*: The intrinsic value of any man-made product is the amount of work it "congeals" and, in measurable terms, its cost in work time. And value as work value is the parameter—all the way up to *Capital*—of Marx's overall prognosis and therapy. From an economic standpoint, Marx was off the mark. But while the Marxian concept of value does not speak to the economist, it does speak to our conscience and, more exactly, to what "value" means in philosophy and in ethics: What is believed to be good or just. His work value has little to do with economics but a great deal to do with setting an ethical parameter: what *ought to be valued.*

Let us pause on the work-value principle. Does it imply that each worker should be compensated on the basis of his individual yardstick? For example, if a watch costs one watchmaker one day of work and the next watchmaker ten days, should the latter be compensated ten times as much? If we stick to the principle, it is hard to deny that this is what it implies *in principle.* Not in practice, however. Marx spent more than twenty years reading economists and attending to his economic theory. Marx well understood, therefore, that it was both absurd and impossible to apply his work-value principle literally. Consequently Marx resisted the interpretation (of Lassalle and of the Ricardian socialists) that the worker was entitled to the *full* equivalent of what his work produced. He also held that his work-value principle had to be *averaged;* in practice, computed as the aggregate, socially necessary labor time for producing a given commodity under given technical conditions. With reference to the example of the watch, Marx might thus have come up with this averaging: One watch is equal, for everybody, to five days of work value. Yet this is a far cry from what the market (so to speak) would say. The market would say that if a watch can be done in one day, there is no reason for paying anybody for more than one day's work time and that whoever cannot make it that fast has to face the risk of being, in the end, outmarketed.

In this comparison, then, the market comes out as being individual-disregarding, whereas it is Marx who is individual-regarding. The work-value principle cannot be applied literally, as we have just seen. Also, Marx concedes that "deductions" must be made from the social product (for the replacement and expansion of the means of production, administration costs, and the like) before paying workers for their labor; hence the work-value principle does not entail that workers receive the "undiminished proceeds" of their labor. Yet, when all the aforesaid adjustments are made, the work-value principle still speaks clear and loud to one effect: It says that each and all workers receive, under capitalism, far less than their due. The work-value principle leads, in fact, to the notion of surplus value; and surplus value is exploitation, it is unpaid labor.[33] In the end we always come back to the *principle* that work is *the* objective or intrinsic source of value. Few people read *Capital*—certainly a cumbersome if not tedious work. Almost everybody knows, however, the formula "to each according to his work," which is the formula that exactly summarizes the work-value principle and is, at the same time, the rallying slogan of Marx's *Critique of the Gotha Programme.*[34] All told, we land at this paradoxical conclusion: It is Marx who, in the name of communism, speaks for all the single individuals the market system both ignores and crushes. Vis-à-vis the market system, it is Marx who stands for "individualism."[35]

Max Weber picked up from Marx that "the market community as such is the most impersonal relationship . . . into which humans can enter with one another. . . . The reason for the impersonality of the market is . . . its orientation to the commodity and only that."[36] Impersonal it is. By the same token it is inhumane or, as I have said, cruel. But it is not impersonal and inhumane on account of its orientation to the commodity; this is a truncated explanation and one that misses the justification. Marxists stop at the commodity, the alleged "fetish" of the capitalistic era. But the commodity is not buried in a vault; it travels to the consumers, that is, to everybody; and it is the impersonal *orientation to everybody* that provides the full explanation and, with it, the justification. Market relationships are faceless and person-disregarding because the market mechanisms embody, as it were, the ethico-economic principle of collectivism: The *whole* of the consumers is more, far more, than its *micro-parts,* than the labor input of the individual producers.

Thus the market is condemned by Marx on the basis of an "individualistic" ethico-economic principle. Conversely, the market is defended by "individualists" (liberists, classical liberals, neoliberals, and libertarians) in spite of the fact that it does crush the individual producer—the *homo faber* and the *homo laborans*—for the sake of collective, indeed collectivistic, consumer benefits. Are not both flagrant inconsistencies? I believe that they are, provided that they are qualified by two underpinnings.

First, individualists are consistent with their principle in input: They assume, and wish to activate, individual self-interest as the motor of the overall market processing. They fail, however, to defend themselves from the attacks of the collectivists by retorting that, in output, they are the ones who uphold collective benefits at the detriment of individual-regarding claims. Conversely, collectivists are consistent with their principle (if it is, as assumed here, the Marxian ethico-economic value principle) as long as they attack "capitalist greed" as an individualistic perversion; but their consistency ends as soon as their therapy begins. The second underpinning is that the collectivistic final outcome of the market process is *unintended* by its single actors, who may be motivated only by their private greed; yet the general-interest outcome is a very real one. Conversely, on the basis of Marx's ethico-economic principle no collectively superior outcome appears plausible; but his *unintended* individualism has in fact benefited wage earners and protected them from the cruelty of the market. This too is a very real fact.

These qualifications notwithstanding, the paradox subsists: Marx is (unwittingly) individualist, the market is (unwittingly) collectivist; yet individualists defend the market and collectivists attack it. What went wrong? How did everything get mixed up in a sequel of ironic role reversals and equivocations? This is too big a question to be answered here in any minimally adequate fashion. I can only follow up the thread unraveled so far, namely, that the notion of capitalism overshadowed and sidetracked the one of market, with a second, additional element: The indiscriminate attack on capitalism fudges its object and somehow never puts in their right places "capital for use," on the one hand, and "capital accumulation," on the other — as we shall see in the next section.

Before moving on, let us conclude on the "imperfections" of the market. Some imperfections have to do with *outer limits* of the market, others with *obstructions* to the market, and still others with *intrinsic failures*. In the first sense the market system is imperfect in that it does not attend to everything; it "leaves out"— and this simply means that it is only a subsystem. In the second sense we say that the market is rendered imperfect, that is, "malfunctioning," by being tampered with. The market would function if it were left to function, whereas its performance is obstructed, if not crippled, by collective bargaining, trade union protectionism, sacred cows, and corporatist practices. In this case the argument is pro-market; the imperfections would disappear if the self-monitoring and self-correcting capabilities of the system were restored. In the third sense we say, instead, that the market is "intrinsically imperfect," that it centrally fails to do what it is supposed to do most. The market, far from being omnipotent, is *impotent* vis-à-vis the capitalist-king and the huge firm; monopolistic concentrations and multinational octopuses stand above the market and outflank it. This is, then, the truly anti-market stance. Among its many versions the most popular one is perhaps the one expounded by J.K. Galbraith, namely, that there are two parts or levels of the economy, and that the laws of the market apply to the lower level of "thousands of small and traditional proprietors" but no longer to the "industrial system," a label that Galbraith restrictively applies to the upper level of the "few hundred highly organized corporations."[37] Braudel concurs and comments: Here "the great predators roam and the law of the jungle operates. This . . . is the real home of capitalism."[38] And this is the stance and, indeed, indictment that needs reckoning. Since here the underlying argument is that both the huge firm and/or the huge capitalist circumvent competition, it is appropriate to pause on this notion.

Competition, it is argued, is the very essence of the market; that is, a market system without intra-market competitiveness is not a market system at all. But competition may oust competition. What if the intra-market competitors turn out to be incapable of competing, or to be competition killers? Under such circumstances, is it not the case that a market rhetoric covers up a very different state of affairs, namely, exploitative monopolies that fix their prices far above costs? Thus goes the allegation; but it is not a flawless allegation. Its weakness resides in confusing *competition as a structure,* or rule of the game, with competitiveness or, better, *degrees of competitiveness,* i.e., with how fiercely or mildly the game is played. The rule of the game is an invariant: It is as it is. The actual game, instead, varies: It can be played overcompetitively (to a quasi-suicidal point), just about right (this is what we generally mean by competitiveness), or not at all (when a player is either a monopolist or protected). How, then, does the state of the game affect the structure? In particular, can a state of subcompetitiveness cancel competition as a structure? I think not, for the structural *potentialities* remain as they are; potentially, but also effectively, the rules stand. It is definitely not the case that a monopoly can raise its prices at whim. As long as it is a *de facto* monopoly, that is, a monopoly located within a competition-structured system, by raising prices it permits entries into the market of previously subcompetitive competitors. Therefore the structure is operative even when "sufficient competitiveness" is absent, even when competitors are dormant, for a false step of the monopolist will wake them up. A market may in fact be a poor market; even so, the consumers are still defended by a *competition-structured system.*

In the end, even if the market system displays intrinsic defects and poor self-correcting mechanisms, the view that the market should be curtailed, if not dumped, must be assessed and justified vis-à-vis its replacements. The question is: How does the market system *compare,* on the same items, with nonmarket arrangements? No matter how imperfect or even dysfunctional the market may be, with respect to x, y, and z (the same items) does it function *better* or *worse* than its substitute? If, despite everything, it still performs better, then the emphasis of the anti-market stance is undue. Its criticisms may all be correct; yet they do not sustain an alternative. For example, is there a route to efficiency pricing other than to *have* a market—a real, not a simulated, market? When all is said, it should never be forgotten that the market subsystem is crucial to the productive subsystem. On this score there is little doubt that the market sustains productivity, whereas production becomes less productive under nonmarket arrangements. And to the extent that productive sectors of the industrial societies become unproductive (operate at a loss and consume, instead of accumulate, capital), to the same extent fewer jobs are created and fewer public goods can be afforded. Thereafter a morning will come when all our high hopes—distributive justice, equalization of opportunities and/or of conditions—will explode in our hands like soap bubbles. It is important, then, to have the weighing of the alternatives in order.

14.4 *Market Socialism*

Do market systems (subsystems) have a concrete, clear-cut alternative aside from total planning? It has been seen that limited planning is still market governed on at least two counts: the determination of costs and prices, and the detection of consumer preferences. In particular, limited planning has not, at least so far, brought about a different system; rather, it has altered the mixes (the proportions) of the Western economies by restricting the areas of performance of their market subsystems. Yet the answer to the above question currently tends to be: Yes, the viable alternative to existing market systems is "market socialism." In many ways this is a novelty and certainly deserves to be investigated as such. In order to do so, we must begin by clarifying the term socialism.

In the communist doctrine, "socialism" stands for the preliminary stage of the as yet unattained communist society. Thus, the Soviet Union, the Eastern European countries, and their replicas around the world call themselves socialist countries. To non-communists, however, "socialism" stands for a very different ideal and reality; and reference is made here to what socialism means to the socialists themselves and, more tangibly, to how the major Socialist parties in the free world currently conceive their own doctrine.[39] Originally, their doctrine generally was a Marxist one, albeit, more often than not, of the revisionist, "gradualist" variety vehemently excommunicated by Lenin. Today, what remains of the original Marxist impetus is essentially *anticapitalism*. This is, admittedly, a sweeping summary in need of many finessings. The gist still is that whenever a Socialist party or government feels the need to move leftward and to take a distinctively socialist stand, it will invariably call for "nationalizations."[40] The rhetoric may also include the word planning; but while nationalizations are in fact made, it is hardly the case that socialist governments have ever gone as far as establishing a system of limited planning (as defined). Anticapitalism thus translates, in actual policy, into *state ownership*—nothing else and nothing more. To be sure, the proprietor state has established itself, even at similar levels of magnitude, under non-socialist governments as well; not on grounds of principle, however, but on grounds of yielding. Most governments are incessantly pressured, by unions and owners in unholy alliance, into salvaging (by nationalizing) bankrupt plants, banks, and services. A socialist government, however, happily nationalizes profitable enterprises as well. While a non-socialist government stockpiles property out of feebleness, because it cannot resist employment-saving pressures, a socialist government "socializes" in principle, because this is the policy that combats and enfeebles capitalism.

The state's takeovers, unless they are pure and simple confiscations, are generally called nationalizations or socializations. Similarly, state ownership may be called social ownership, and by this route the argument has been that property has been collectivized and, still more acrobatically, that state property is equal to people's property. Technically, the distinctions between private, social, public, and state property do detect differences.[41] In practice, and this includes the practice of socialist governments to date, these distinctions are largely nominal, and the choice of the wording is largely a function of its glamour. In practice we seldom have (to some very minor extent) social property and we eminently have, instead, state property.[42] This is exactly and importantly the case when we ultimately come to *who controls the capital*, that is, capital accumulation, capital allocations, and the power that results. Land or even buildings theoretically can be (though very inconveniently, if not disastrously so) a *res nullius*, a thing of nobody; capital cannot. Capital (from the beginning of the industrial revolution onward) is not *there*; it must be incessantly generated, managed, and invested by somebody, not by nobody. When we come to what capital eminently is today—financial and investment capital—under whatever arrangement, control means property and property means control. It follows from this that the proprietor state is equally, and crucially, the *capital-owning* state.

This is the focus of the matter, for it reveals two points. First, it brings out that socialism does not seek state property as an end in itself or merely to extend the spoils system; it seeks it in earnest for the ulterior and better reason that, along this course, the balance shifts from private capitalism to *state capitalism*. Without state capitalism, socialism is (with respect to its ultimate goals) largely impotent; with state capitalism, it acquires potency. Second, the focus on capital owning helps establish what is eliminable and what is ineluctable about "capitalism"—indeed the crux of the matter.

The predicaments of our time all began with the invention of the machine —of all transformations, the grandest one. So long as the machine is a simple, non-costly instrument, we still have a commercial, not an industrial society. But the "mechanical machine" changed everything: It worked in place of the worker and thus, it was said, liberated man from work.[43] The other, less perceived side of the coin is that man has to work for the machine: He has to pay for it. It is here that the Marxian alternative fails us: Marx entirely misses the *dynamics* of the machine, to wit, industrial revolution. His surplus value (whatever is more than, or taken away from, work value) leads to a theory of exploitation that leads, in turn, to a stagnant technology and an overly static economy. The machine-industrial sequel of revolutions of the last two centuries hinges on *discovering* incessantly perfected technologies at market-affordable prices for meeting changing and expanding needs. Marx can neither explain nor sustain any of this. *If the problem is exploitation, it cannot be capital accumulation.* In particular, Marx can hardly allow, in his solution, for the magnitude of investments needed for paying for the escalating costs of the machinery.[44] And the point to be affixed in our minds is that this grand transformation brings about an entirely new form and notion of "capital."

In order to grasp the metamorphosis, let us draw the simplest possible distinction: the one between *wealth for use* and *wealth for investment* (capital).[45] Private wealth for use has existed since the beginning of history under all latitudes and regardless of political forms. Only extremely primitive or migratory, scarcity-plagued, small-scale societal arrangements lack a differentiation between haves and have-nots, between richer and poorer. Indeed, and contrary to current folklore, wealth for use is far less destined for "conspicuous consumption" (status and aesthetic oriented) today than in all previous times. In the ancient Mediterranean empires, in China, in India, in Europe (until the industrial revolution), the poor worked with their hands for the rich, and whatever accumulation of wealth they produced above and beyond the fixed capital needs of their time—roads, bridges, aqueducts, houses, defenses—largely went into magnificent palaces, temples, and cathedrals. It centrally was wealth for use, for status recognition, for the pleasure of the eye.[46] With the industrial revolution this kind of conspicuous consumption soon appeared to be impossibly wasteful consumption; wealth for use was nice, but wealth for investment was necessary—it was *the* prior condition of everything else. It was then that capitalism was truly born, as is borne out by the fact that "capital," "capitalist" and, finally, "capitalism" became interconnected —thus establishing by mutual reinforcement their distinctive and novel economic connotations—only during the second half of the nineteenth century.[47]

Wealth for use or for its own sake is not, then, "capital." Capital is wealth channeled into investment, production, and profit and thus destined to capital productive (and reproductive) accumulation; and it is capital accumulation (for investment) that becomes, from then onward, the sine qua non of industrial and economic growth. The rich no longer needed the poor to work for them; rather, the rich and the poor alike needed capital accumulation to work for both (the greater investment power of the former, and the creation of jobs for the latter). This entails that *capital accumulation* (of reproducible capital) is with us not only to stay but incessantly to grow—it is a function of technological developments and technological imperatives. In particular, the more we enter the "technetronic society," spoken of by Brzezinski, and the robot age, the greater, at an exponential rhythm, the amount of capital that must be set aside (accumulated) for investment. The state that Marxists call capitalist has no capital, i.e., no wealth-producing or productive capital; its income basically comes from taxation. The communist state, instead, is *the* capitalist state in the literal and central sense that it owns all the productive capital and is the sole controller of capital accumulation and allocation.

Capital accumulation is as necessary for a collectivistic economy as for a market economy. In this sense modern society as such does hinge on surplus value and, *pace* Marx, cannot be anticapitalist. Let the cant rest; the choice, at least so far, is purely and simply a choice between *private capitalists* and *state capitalism*. This and no other is (or has been) the variable. Capital for use is the trivial and in no way distinctive part of "capitalism"; capital for investment is its immensely greater and indeed distinctive part.

We are now ready to assess the novelty of *market socialism,* which has two sides. On the one hand, it resides in the fact that socialism (in democracies) has finally come to grips with the real world of economics. In particular, and centrally, "market" socialism accepts and wishes to save the market. On the other hand, and on this premise, market "socialism" proposes a solution of its own and works out new, detailed proposals that both surpass and negate state ownership (or state capitalism), that is, the socialist program as enacted thus far by socialist governments. Are market systems necessarily *private enterprise* systems? To this query socialists have generally replied no—but without much further ado.[48] Market socialists, instead, are fully aware of its centrality. The responses, to be sure, vary; that is, there are many varieties of market socialism. I shall first mention the variety outlined by Lindblom and then dwell on a mainstream version.

Lindblom suggests *market planning,* that is, a planner sovereignty *over* the market. In this proposal, planning is the subject, market the object; it is the planner, a central planner (the state), that "plans" the market. In the market system, production is directed by consumer purchases, i.e., by consumer sovereignty; in Lindblom's "planner sovereignty" blueprint, production is directed, instead, by government purchases. In essence, the government commands "by buying," and this because it is the *only* purchaser of *all* final products. In Lindblom's words, "All production, consumer goods included, would be guided by the purchases of a government that has displaced the consumer as the 'sovereign.' . . . Government authority would direct the allocation of resources of the productive process by buying or not buying final products, or by buying more or less of them." For example, "Government would signal for shoe production . . . by increasing its purchase of shoes. . . .'" As for the objection that it would be infinitely more expedient to let the shoe producers sell directly to consumers, Lindblom meets it by pointing out that "officials want outputs different from those which consumers would buy if left to themselves." Lindblom also concedes that a planner sovereignty system may well wish to suppress not only consumer but also "worker sovereignty," initially in the sense that "wage rates charged to producers would reflect planner preferences with respect to workers' job assignments" but also with respect to the ultimate implication that it would eventually become "necessary to conscript labor."[49]

The "planning of the market" formula belongs within the ambit of market socialism in that private enterprises are still the producing (though not the selling) units. This entails, at least in Lindblom's view, that what matters most—the pricing function of the market—is preserved. Nevertheless, the formula remains highly unconvincing and appears inadequately thought through. It does not happen as a matter of course that when the planner allocates more money to buying shoes, the shoemakers will be there to produce them. What are they supposed to do when shoes are not a priority? Hibernate? And, of course, shoes are the easy example. But take computers. The planners may decide, perhaps rightly, that their users are wasting them and, hence, that there is no need for more. The first thing to go, in the computer industry, would be the research budget; and if the planners do not themselves decide who has to be killed (a nasty decision to make), the whole of the computer industry would be left to vegetate, at best, in a state of semidismantlement. Five years later, it may dawn on the planners that all their computer technology is obsolete, that foreign competitors have tenth-generation computers, while they are stuck with the third generation. Will they remedy the situation by paying more for more computers? All the odds are that their "closed system" (an implication that Lindblom misses) has missed the train and will remain subcompetitive for good. Examples aside, it is very doubtful that under the planner's sovereignty any of the miracles of the self-regulating market system—as itemized earlier—would continue to happen. True, private enterprises remain; yet are they still *enterprises*? The answer is no; they are only private. By all odds, and if the wastes and bribery that endemically affect all state buying teach us anything, the planner sovereignty formula can only, and quickly, end up at a gigantic and highly rigid system of collusions between the public purchaser (who orders all the goods) and the producers that do exist (desperately seeking "private," not market, ways to stay alive). With consumer sovereignty gone, the planner is not only required never to be mistaken —for self-correcting mechanisms no longer exist—but is further required to be an incorruptible angel. If he is no angel, and if he is corruptible, no better predatory system has ever been devised for enriching by fiat pet producers at one end and the omnipotent buyer, the planners, at the other.

However that may be, the planner's sovereignty proposal can be set aside on the simple consideration that it seeks to improve collectivistic planning — the old trend — whereas the mainstream of market socialism expresses a new trend. To plan the market leaves us with total centralized control and, thereby, with a gigantic, all-powerful bureaucratic state. Instead, market socialism propounds the view that the market does best what bureaucracy does worse. Its impetus originates in the outcry: Enough with the inefficient, costly, ever-growing, all-suffocating bureaucratic state — enough, no matter whether the bureaucratic Moloch is intent on planning the market or content with accumulating state property. The immediate question is: If the bureaucratic state is to be displaced, by what can it be replaced? The answers generally point, in one way or the other, to the Yugoslav kind of industrial democracy. Market socialism has now a real-world experiment — Yugoslavia's workers' self-management — on which concretely to reflect and from which concretely to propose. In contrast to Lindblom's planning *over* the market (from above), market socialism seeks a planning *via* the market and assisted *by* the market. Market socialism is indeed — a rare event in politics — true to its name: It is what it claims to be.

My emphasis on the novelty of market socialism will prompt the learned skeptic to ask, What is new? Industrial democracy (based on the workers' self-management of their plant) was already outlined before the turn of the nineteenth century by the Webbs and subsequently by G.H.D. Cole. Furthermore, a literature on industrial democracy has been alive and around since the end of World War II.[50] This is true, except that all of this was not accepted by most socialists as socialist; unions were hostile, fearing a loss of control over their members, and Socialist parties went along, bowing to union pressure. Notice also that parties of ideological bent and origin, if they are to change course, need an ideological ancestor, that is, a legitimation from their side. And here the novelty is that while Marx fades away, Proudhon is being rediscovered.[51] Not only was Proudhon right and Marx wrong (about property, bureaucracy, and the tyrannical state that would result from the communist solution); he was also distinctly socialist in the sense that Proudhon's socialism countered, point by point, the socialism-communism mix. Then, alongside Proudhon, it was easy for socialists to revisit a long line of revolutionary (not bourgeois) authors who, while remaining Marxists, forcefully denounced the potential or actual degeneration of Marxism into bureaucratism and wholesale oppression: the "renegade Kautsky," Rosa Luxemburg, the last Trotsky—to do injustice to many more names.[52] If market socialism was in want of a pedigree, it now has one. It is secure enough by now to confront the "pure" market theorists—Mises, Hayek, Milton Friedman—with arguments. To all of this I would add that there is a major difference between having blueprints and having a real-world laboratory. There is, then, a great deal of novelty in how market socialism brings together and recombines the elements of its good society.

Ancestors aside, how does market socialism stand vis-à-vis participation and pluralism? Definitely, it accepts the *value* of pluralism and translates its pluralistic stance in the demand for "policentric planning" (something quite close to what was previously called framework planning and indicative planning) and, overall, for a generalized decentralization and diffusion of power. As for participation, it may well be said that workers' self-management is the equivalent of "participatory democracy." Yes, in the narrow but not in the broad. Pellicani says *participative market economy,*[53] but the label is qualified by noting that "self-management should not be confused with direct democracy, an exalting formula which is inapplicable at the level of large numbers. To establish self-management simply means to introduce the elective principle, that is, the mechanism of delegation of the right to command, also in the plants."[54] And framework planning is called in at this point to counteract the degenerative tendencies of a self-management left to itself, namely, to impede a corporative, plant-by-plant, self-protectionism, as well as to impede the consumption of what has to go into investment.

The argument comes to this: "First, democratic socialism cannot be built upon a fully state-owned economy; second, the socialist mode of production coincides with a market economy based on self-management and polycentric programming."[55] As for private enterprise, it is allowed to have its share and must remain, above all, an *enterprise,* an open, risk-taking exploration that is rewarded, when successful, by profits. Private property does not haunt the propounder of market socialism. After all, it was Proudhon who coined the phrase "property is theft"; yet it was also Proudhon who subsequently held that the only way to impede the crushing of man by the state was private property: "To counterweigh public power . . . and by this route to insure individual liberty, this will be . . . the essential function of property. The force of the state is a force of concentration; whereas property is a decentralizing force."[56] In essence, private property protects liberty, and so does market competition. In Proudhon's own words, "competition is the very law of the market," and this entails that "to suppress competition is the same as to suppress liberty itself . . . to bring the worker back to the system of favoritism and abuse from which 1789 had liberated him."[57]

All told, I would say that the theory of market socialism proposes an ideal realistically grafted on the facts.[58] But if market socialism fares well enough in theory, what about the practice? The practice largely rests on the Yugoslav case.[59] The existence of a real-world experiment in progress certainly is, in many ways, an asset and a source of strength for market socialism. But if the embrace becomes too close, it may also turn out to be a liability.[60] The Yugoslav experiment rests, politically and otherwise, on shaky foundations.[61] Two specific points deserve mentioning. First, we have yet to see a real case of "social property," that is, of neither private nor state property. The Yugoslav system of self-management is neither authentic enough nor backed by the social ownership of the plant by its workers: *pro capite* shares that cannot be freely sold or bought but still represent the criterion by which rewards are distributed, losses are made to hurt, and collective success is compensated.[62] Aside from principle — affirming that social property can indeed exist — the concrete problem is one of inducements, of strengthening motivations that have no long-standing substitute in participation for participation's sake. Second, and more crucially, the Yugoslav experiment does not really dispose of the "state capitalism" reality. Capital accumulation and its corollary, the allocation of capital resources, are still entirely in the state's hands. In the end we always have to reckon with this knot. Currently, not even market systems are doing well on this score; in most Western countries "consumerism" is thinning down capital accumulation to a precariously low point, and stagflation remains a worry that cannot cease to haunt the economist. The fact remains that all the nonmarket systems are doing worse. Yugoslavia has not been a convincing exception to this. Its glow of relative prosperity (by Eastern standards) has come from a private economy largely left to do its own things, and from the infusion of Western capital; not from the self-management arrangement. The question, Are market systems *necessarily* private enterprise systems? remains unresolved.[63]

Another open question is whether market socialism (in theory, aside from Yugoslav practice) can match, in terms of maximizing productivity and minimizing errors and waste, the performance of the market as such, as a self-monitoring system. If it cannot, then we have a big tradeoff to settle. On behalf of market socialism, and indeed to its great merit, at least this should be granted: It does propose a plausible tradeoff. More than this, market socialism affords to a demoralized world lacking ideas and ideals a project to which to attend. Perhaps the Hobson's choice is not solely between the cruelty of market efficiency and, at the other extreme, the senseless inefficiency of collectivistic planning. Perhaps we are finding our way toward a true "mixed system," toward a real third kind (not simply to different mixings of the same thing). To assert, with Lindblom, that all real-world systems "practice some degree of market socialism"[64] is more misleading than illuminating. The difference between economic systems is established by their *prime movers,* by their driving principles and mechanisms. As long as the policy of socialism consists simply in transfers from private to state property, along this route socialism may well succeed, in the end, in killing the market system; but it cannot succeed in establishing a new economic logic, another efficient prime mover. The present-day theory of market socialism understands this and has a grip on a handle. But market socialism exists almost nowhere; it is still, to an overwhelming degree, a project; and it is not helped in the least by being deprived of its distinctiveness.

We began with the analysis of "planning." Where have we landed vis-à-vis our start? That is, where does market socialism stand vis-à-vis the analytical distinction between limited and total planning? I would say that it provides substance and reality to a label — planning — that Westerners have so far largely abused and applied, at best, inconclusively. At the same time it is clear that the planning envisaged by market socialism still belongs to the class "limited planning" (as defined). Market socialism wishes the market, in its pluralistic-competitive aspects, to perform, to remain (even if steered and regulated) a central protagonist. Furthermore, market socialism indeed represents the response to, and the very negation of, the total planning of the communist regimes. Its democratic credentials are firm and impeccable. Its economic viability may be highly doubted by the market economists and yet represents the one option that may not fail us.

14.5 *Democratic Planning*

Throughout the preceding sections, the argument was confined basically to economic problems discussed in economic terms. An economic system is not a political system. Yet the two are interconnected, and I turn now, in order to appreciate the connections, to political problems discussed in political terms.

On economic grounds alone it is fair to say that the pro-market thesis wins. If it does not win, and indeed if it should lose, it will be on political grounds. As pointed out earlier, the market's spontaneous order, or self-ordering, runs against the powerful tide of the egalitarian project and specifically the tide of the "redistributive project." It is here that the market system finds its implacable enemies. One may note that this is at base an ethical, not a political, stance. Even so, the redistributive project hinges entirely on *political means;* it is entrusted to the public hand and, if need be, to a strongly coercive hand.

We may speak of the state that manages the economic system as an "economic state" and of the state that owns industries as an "industrial state." Nonetheless, the "political state" is still there, and it is the political agency that runs the economic one. Up until now I have discussed *plannings,* not *planners.* But plannings are not disembodied entities; they are planned by individuals empowered with the power to plan, to decide for others, who in turn are deprived of the power to decide for themselves. It is only with reference to the market system—i.e., to a self-ordering order—that we can avoid asking, Who markets? With reference to planning, Who plans? is not an avoidable question. Up until now the distinction has been between limited and total planning. In political terms, however, the distinction is between democratic planning and nondemocratic planning, and the issue thus becomes: To what extent and in what manner is planning compatible with democracy? To be sure, in a first approximation limited planning can be translated into democratic planning, whereas total planning can be said to correspond to nondemocratic planning. Nonetheless, as we switch from the economic to the political labels, we correspondingly switch to different problems.

Let us reenter politics via the question, *Who are the planners?* In a democratic system the main lines of an economic policy must be approved by parliaments and deliberated on by governments, thus falling within the province of politicians recruited through universal suffrage. On this simple consideration it is already no wonder that our democracies have made so little headway, thus far, in terms of either rational planning (the criterion) or limited planning. We can build up a mountain of regulations, counterregulations, exceptions, and nationalizations; but even an Everest of interventions does not, in and by itself, add up to "planning" in any meaningful sense of the term. Where is the coordination? Where is the overall project? Much of this, even if called planning, is in fact chaos. In like manner, and reverting to planning as "rational organization," how much rationality can we expect from legislators and governments? Granted, it is rational for the politician to pay votes with favors; and each single policy measure can be defended on some ground or other of rationality. But here reference is to planning: What is required to be rational is the overall design. And even a far from stringent underpinning of "rational planning" involves that two conditions must be met: The whole must display some inner congruence (*rationality as coherence*); and the means must be sufficient and in fact conducive to the desired ends (*means-ends rationality*).[65]

If so, the chances that such conditions are fulfilled by democratic governments are slim. The sheer calculus of the means requires a high level of professional expertise, and the coherence of the overall design must be sustained by autonomy of decision, by not having to yield to sectorial and short-range demands. The reality is, instead, that the recruitment of political personnel has little to do with the expertise in question and that politicians generally handle economic policies within a very short time horizon and by yielding to contradictory cross-pressures, by keeping a keen eye on immediate electoral costs and gains. Thus, when we ask rational planning of our politicians, we are asking for the very thing that is hardest to obtain.

The question, Who are the planners? may receive a different answer, namely, that they are *experts,* not politicians. The politicians cover up for the experts, but they are in fact advised by experts (economists and ad hoc bureaucracies) who are also, and this is the crucial point, in charge of the implementation. To the extent that this is so, the chances of rational planning (as defined) become brighter. But as soon as the expert enters the scene, we hear the complaint of the participationist democrat. This, he will say, is another step away, and indeed against, democracy—democracy as demo-power. On my criteria, however, this would be a shift from democracy *in input* (how much the voice of the people counts) to democracy *in output* (how much the people benefit), and I have held that this is not only a legitimate but also a hardly avoidable shift.[66] But I have never held that democracy in output— conceived as demo-distributions—can be entirely disconnected from democracy in input. The moment has come to look attentively into this connection, for a connection must remain.

Putting the case in a nutshell, the more we lean on the demos, the less we are likely to achieve rational planning; conversely, the more we lean on the expert, the less democratic we are in demo-power terms. This reflection compounds the problem of *democratic planning.* As I was saying, democratic planning is not the same as limited planning; it confronts us with a distinctly political set of problems.

Mannheim believed that democratic planning should ultimately presuppose and rest on a "planning for freedom" understood as a social science manipulation of the environment from which to obtain spontaneously from the individuals the appropriate and desired behavior.[67] I am not prepared in the least to go that far. The point that I intend to pursue is a much simpler one, namely, that if we speak of democratic planning, there must be something democratic about it. I have conceded that the democratic element need not be in input and that, indeed, it will have to be much more in output. Yet I must forcefully say it again: It is democracy (a power vested in the people) that must monitor and enforce demophily and demo-benefits. This means that the political structure of democracy must remain. At the same time it must accommodate experts, for there is no sense in planning by inexperts.

We are thus required to assess, in the final analysis, the role and weight of the expert. In order to appreciate the ponderousness of this problem fully, it is well to tackle it where it begins. Actually, two distinct beginnings are involved. One thread starts with the question, What is the democratic solution to the problem of power? The other thread rests on the premise that democracy does not presuppose, in any sense, competency.

14.6   Democracy, Power, and Incompetence

If there is one paramount problem that liberalism and, in its wake, liberal democracy do solve, it is the problem of *taming power*—political power, to be sure. This applies not only to the past but even more to the future. Weak and impotent as our democracies may have become, the fact remains that in the contemporary world the "power potential" has taken on magnitudes that even our imagination, in its wildest flights, finds it difficult to envision. A technological age supplies instruments that can multiply thousandfolds the material force of man—and of a single man. The power menace is in frightful increase. Hence, the problem of state power becomes more acute than ever. It is important, therefore, to ask ourselves: What is the democratic position on the problem of power? Better put, What is the liberal-democratic solution of the problem of power? Prima facie, it would appear that there is no certain answer to this query, since two opposite views are held.

The first view is that continental democracies have, historically speaking, carried forward the work of the absolute monarchies by acting as supreme leveling powers that have destroyed all *corps intermédiaires,* all intermediate powers.[68] Democracy, in this view, has meant a menacing concentration of power in the state, for once the intermediate loci of power between the citizens and the state have been dismantled, all that is left is a low plain of subjects that can be easily dominated from the only extant summit. But while some authors view with apprehension the demise of all autonomous counterpowers, other authors denounce present-day democracies for tolerating under the cover of formal equality the growth of economic inequalities, and indeed for permitting the formation of gigantic financial and capitalistic power holdings that may be stronger than the state itself.[69]

These two diagnoses appear diametrically opposed. According to the first, democracy levels everyone down into impotence. According to the second, democracy is itself impotent because it is overpowered by economic powers. In the first case it is said: By its equalizing policies, democracy makes everyone powerless before the Leviathan. In the second case it is argued: Democracy does not equalize at all—indeed, it is itself deprived of its power by *de facto* potentates. Thus, while the first thesis demands that concentrated power be dispersed, the second advocates a strengthening of the central power and, in view of this, the entrusting of economic power no less than political power to the state. But we should not fail to see that the two diagnoses refer to different problems. Those who stress the danger of an excessive concentration of power in the state worry about the *power of the sword,* whereas those who demand more power for the state worry about the *power of money.* If so, we have to make sure that each concern does not overstep its ambit of validity. On the one hand, it is consistent with the political concern (about the sword) to argue that equal amounts of infinitesimal power to each and all simply amount to a pulverization of power and hence create, within the society, a dangerous vacuum of power. Consequently, the political concern favors pluralistic and polyarchic arrangements.[70] On the other hand, the economic concern (about the power of money) is well entitled to worry about the existence of power imbalances that betray the spirit of democracy and belie its alleged equality. As the focus shifts from how the citizen relates to the state, to the relationships between poor and rich, employees and employers, our search for solutions must equally shift.

The foregoing does not attest, then, to two mutually contradictory replies to the question: What is the democratic solution to the problem of power? The two answers fall into place when they are seen in sequence. No matter how little we may care about political forms, the procedural priority remains as it is and does not advance economic democracy ahead of political democracy. One cannot solve the so-called social question simply by putting the problem of the state into brackets, for the solution of the socioeconomic problem is demanded of the state. Hence, as regards the political problem of power, it is not two solutions that are available, but one.

The referent of the word *people* is not the referent of the word *state.* We may speak of the democratic state as a "people's state" to indicate that a bridge is now connecting the two banks—but a bridge does not replace the banks, it presupposes them. No matter how much we toy with the sentence "the people are the state," the state is not *the* people but only *few* people in high place, and indeed placed *above* the people. The facts of the matter are, very simply, that the power that materially belongs to the state does not belong to the people, and that the more that power is vested in the state, the less it stays with the people. The issue thus is: What can the *outsiders,* the people, do about the state *insiders?* Clearly, we cannot all become insiders (even assuming, implausibly, that we would like to). Hence the best we can do *from the outside* is curtail the power of the insiders; and the surest way of doing so is to diffuse power. Specifically, power is held in check by counterpowers, that is, the technique for "neutralizing power" is not to allow too-powerful powers to exist. As for the "democratization of power," the ulterior requirement is that these counterpowers be, as much as possible, of a democratic kind, and that they be eminently vested in a multigroup society of truly voluntary associations, of truly participatory groups.[71]

Not only is this the democratic solution to the problem of political power, it is also the *porro unum,* the overriding priority of the entire political tradition of the West. For the whole of Western tradition has been endlessly concerned with this basic demand: that power be depersonalized, that impersonal power be substituted for personal power, that the person-in-office be absorbed into the office. In this perspective the query, Why democracy? receives the straightforward reply: Because we know of no other political formula that frees the citizens from the *fear of the persons* to whom power is entrusted. However, democracy succeeds, on the whole, in exorcising arbitrary and personalized power precisely because it is a mechanism purposely created for this end. It works with this task in view. It is effective to the extent that it serves this purpose. What of other purposes? In particular, is democracy an adequate instrument in view of the ambitions of a technological age, an age that ultimately looks forward to the "planning of history"?

If we manage to control power, this is largely because democracy works, in practice, as a device for slowing down, filtering, and decanting the processes of power. From the standpoint of the speed at which it performs, democracy entails a rather slow and halting process of decision making; and from the standpoint of its scope of action, democracy implies a somewhat restricted range of decisions. We cannot avoid paying a price and accepting certain limitations if we want to tame power. The price is a kind of temporizing inertia, often a lack of resolution and, what is more, a remarkable waste of effort. The implication is that if we demand of democracy a stepped-up process of rational and global transformation, we are asking too much.

Moving on to our second thread, a democratic system neither presupposes nor requires *competency.* If it did, how could we justify political equality, that is, the equal right and weight of each electoral voice? As Friedrich correctly points out, "Political equality is compatible only with democratic legitimacy. . . . If there is . . . a belief that the title to rule . . . rests upon special qualities, evidently political equality cannot exist."[72] Even though we generally have professional politicians, they are "professional" in knowing how to handle the game of politics, not professional in other expertises, not *experts.* As we have seen when discussing the electoral theory of democracy, there is no intrinsic absurdity in the lack of competence of electorates.[73] There is no intrinsic absurdity in this, provided that a democratic system is not asked to perform in utter disregard of the limits within which its premises hold.

In principle, it is not true that politics does not require ad hoc knowledge and competence. It is only true that a *certain kind* of politics can do without the expert; specifically, the "small politics" whose primary concern is to safeguard human beings from despotic domination. In other words, the democratic postulate that politics does not involve special qualification is valid insofar as democratic politics remains, if not "small," a middle-range politics. If a political system is grounded on the assumption that everybody is able, by birthright, to handle political affairs, then it must comply with its own assumption and thereby recognize that certain boundaries are not to be crossed. This means, in plain terms, that to the extent that democracy is based on lack of expertise, it does not provide a foundation from which to launch into the grand politics of an engineering of history. If we want democracy, we must be content with what it provides. Otherwise, if we want a preconceived and well-conceived "rational society," we shall have to call upon the experts and entrust ourselves to them. An operation requires a surgeon; if we do not want the surgeon, we shall have to do without the operation. If we partake of the ideal of the person whose ambition is to "turn the world . . . into an enormous machine, every part of which, on his pressing a button, moves according to his design,"[74] then the price to be paid for this clockwise world is democracy.[75]

The democratic postulate of no-qualification had its purest expression in the *polis,* where officials were appointed by lot. Today we apply it to a far lesser extent, since, after all, elections are expected to sort out some "elected" people, that is, to make a selection. In the framework of a democracy intent upon limited planning, that postulate will have to find a still more restricted application. And beyond this point it simply cannot be applied at all: The more total planning is sought, the more democratic incompetence must unreservedly yield to technocratic competence.

14.7 *The Role of the Expert*

I have made a somewhat long detour but a necessary one. As we muddle through the last quarter of the twentieth century, we find ourselves uneasily, and often hazily, placed between these two extremes: a government of non-experts over experts, or a government planned out by experts without democracy. If democracy is to survive, it will have to steer clear of either extreme. Yet the direction in which we have to move is an unmistakable one: It is the direction imposed on us by the benefits and burdens of technological progress. Technology truly is our *deus ex machina;* it is the god that keeps us alive, and yet it enslaves us to its *machina.* For in the end, the *deus* is no other than ourselves; it is we who have to pay for the miracles we receive.[76]

As our overall knowledge progresses, the knowledge gap between nonspecialists and specialists increases. Translated into the arithmetic of democracy, the knowledge gap is this: There is a growing imbalance between a powerless knowledge (of minute and multiple groups of specialists) and an all-powerful ignorance (of the majorities of non-specialists). Unless democracy is to become an unbearably inefficient political form, we have to reduce this imbalance, that is, we have to surrender to the need for a democracy that, without being governed by experts, importantly relies on their know-how. Actually, and despite much rhetoric to the contrary, we *are* moving toward *less* power of the people. The obvious reason is that a maximum of popular power is possible only in simple societies whose leadership tasks are relatively elementary. As the mechanisms of social and economic life become more and more complex, interlocking, and of truly gigantic magnitude, the expert's opinion must acquire a much greater weight than his vote as an elector. Even though electoral concerns may lead the politician to disregard the specialist's advice, already today the "power of initiative" is very much with brain trusts and techno-experts. This development need not alarm us, for a democracy survives as long as what is essential — and therefore *must* be controlled — is kept within the area of democratic controls. Bureaucracies, for example, are not organized in accordance with democratic criteria; yet only the participatory democrat is dismayed by this. This is still more the case with military structures (even in Greek democracy the choice of the *strategoí,* the military commanders, was an exception to the rule of appointment by lot). As Michels pointed out long ago, most of the organisms at work within a democractic system do not have and (he contended) never will have a democratic structure; nonetheless, and despite his dire predictions, democracies have survived. So, democratic planning need not pose insoluble problems — on one condition: that we give them careful thought. Instead, we seem to live deep in contradiction.

As long as democracy is conceived as a mechanism for neutralizing power, we have a democracy amenable to the requirements of planning. But if we think, instead, that men and women ought actively to govern — as we are being told by the "new" democratic theory — it is absurd to advocate any kind of planning, since planning requires that the non-expert be subordinated to the expert, that is, an increasingly governed (not self-governing) democracy. Nor does it make any sense to develop, on the one hand, a political mechanism meant to work through a minimal expertise and within the limits of a *generic reasonableness* — that is, on the basis of common sense — and to insist, on the other hand, that the same mechanism meet the demands of a specialized, *scientific reason*. In short, we cannot *have* both more democracy, i.e., a maximum of popular power, and more planning, i.e., more power for the planners. We may only *ask* for both; and this means that our head is proceeding in one direction, while our steps are going in another. A sure way of finally stumbling, I fear, in a final way.

My concern here is not with preaching goals but with signaling inconsistencies. Some of us may find the ideal of a clockwork society meticulously worked out by a supermind a palatable ideal. Even so, it should be clear that democracy is not only an inappropriate *instrument* for that goal but also the incarnation of the *contrary ideal*. On the basis of the liberal-democratic conception of life, it makes no sense that someone should be in charge of predetermining and calculating how we should achieve happiness, what we should want, and what we should value. Western man has long been brought up to believe that everybody has his own wants for his own reasons. In this *Weltanschauung,* to objectivize the world of preferences, of happiness, of goals, amounts to an ultimate form of bondage, since it means that we are treating man as an "object." In the democratic conception of life in particular, the people's interest can be determined only by the people's will. This means that there is no other way of making sure that it is the interest of the people that shall be attended to; it also means that human beings are interested in what *they themselves want,* not in what someone else wants for them. It is supremely inconsistent, therefore, to seek at the same time a world where the good life is to be chosen *subjectively,* and a world where a technological sophocracy is charged with choosing the *objective* good life.

Suppose, probably falsely, that some time in the future our know-how may make possible such a science of society as could really master the world of man. Even so, our conception of life would demand that the expert not be in charge of deciding what the good life is. The social engineer would not be asked to tell us what we should like and which goals we should seek. He would be in charge, rather, of warning us in advance about our mistakes and telling us ahead of time what we might run into if we chose to launch upon a given venture. The divide may be drawn thus: A government of experts is admissible in regard to means, not ends.

Where does this discussion leave us with respect to the distinction between democracy in input (demo-power), and democracy in output, that is, the demo-benefits demanded of democratic planning? We have seen that despite revivals of democratic primitivism, all the imperatives of a technological world run counter to democracy in input, and even more against the participatory dream. The balance between democracy in input and democracy in output has, in fact, long been shifting away from demo-power. It is equally clear that it can be struck at very different points. But a balance must remain. This balance hinges, ultimately, on how much power we are prepared to entrust to the expert. So long as he proposes and advises, this is only a necessity. But how much further are we permitted to go in the name of "democratic planning"? A way of answering is to look into the notion of a government of science.

14.8   *The Government of Science*

I have made passing reference thus far to a planning of history or an engineering of history, to a clockwork world, and to a science-molded "rational society." While these expressions are intuitively intelligible, they deserve some probing. All of them find a common matrix in the advent of science and, more precisely, in the idea that the victory of science over nature can be replicated, in due course, by an equally victorious "science of society."

Comte assigned to this science the final supremacy and the name sociology.[77] He was preceded by Saint-Simon. However, for some seven years, between 1817 and 1823, Comte acted as a ghostwriter for Saint-Simon, and a strong, common source of inspiration between the two is patent. Saint-Simon as an outsider, but Comte and nearly all of their proselytes as insiders, sprang from the fertile soil of the Ecole Polytechnique created in Paris by the Revolutionary Convention in 1794. It was a school for engineers but also, more deeply and broadly, the embodiment of the "scientific spirit" of the Enlightenment as eminently expressed by Condorcet. Very appropriately, therefore, Hayek refers to what we have come to call scientism as the "polytechnic mentality."[78] However, *scientism* is a more familiar label for pointing to an *excess of science* and specifically to an all-pervading scientific positivism (as propounded and exemplified by Comte). In our line of inquiry, what all this added up to was rendered by Ernest Renan, an eminent historian but also a Comtean: "To organize humanity scientifically, this is modern science's ultimate word, this is its daring but legitimate claim."[79] That was well over a century ago, and Renan was still speaking in a prophetic style. Today, this is no longer a loose and distant claim. Today we have a science that has leaped far beyond the wildest dreams of the early positivists. Scientists are legion, and to them a scientifically organized humanity is not only a congenial idea but an ideal that appears within reach.

Shall we settle, then, for the general label *government of science?* I am suggesting that we do, that this is a good umbrella and a telling focus. The label gives us a firm grip not only on the background of the ideal of a "rational society" but also on the intellectual impetus that pushes it to the foreground. The label recommends itself in three additional respects. First, it stands in vivid contrast to the old Platonic ideal of the philosopher-king. Second, it qualifies the notion of reason in terms of a specific kind of "scientific reason." Third, it prompts the straightforward question: Government of science or of scientists?

The Platonic ideal was sophocracy, that government be entrusted to the wise and the knowledgeable *(sophói)*. And, of course, the protagonist is here the philosopher—he who loves *sophía*. The scientist is, with respect to the traditional philosopher, an entirely new and different breed. We can still say, if it pleases us, that the government of science is a species of the genus sophocracy. But we must note important genetic mutations that have occurred along the way. *Sophía* was, above all, wisdom; whereas we do not ask of a scientist to be wise. Also, philosophy, from the Greeks all the way to the idealists, was the "knowledge of all things." The scientist has no knowledge of all things; he is, and must be, a specialist and often a narrow one. Furthermore, the very notion of knowledge is not the same in the two cases. Philosophical knowledge was (until the advent of science) speculative, often loose, always soft: It did not rest on evidence. Scientific knowledge is hard—it rests on evidence—precise, and breeds scientific rationalism, that is, a variety of rationalism that philosophy neither could or did breed. It is revealing, then, to say government of science because it tells us that we are no longer toying with the Platonic ideal: Between the philosopher-king and the scientist-king there is indeed a world of difference. It also tells us that reference is not made to reason in general but to one of its varieties.

Coming to the crucial point, Who is to be the king? Science or the scientist?[80] If the question is pressed, it becomes difficult to deny that the disembodied entity, science as such, concretely stands for *some scientists*. The interesting point is, however, that among the propounders of the "scientific organization of humanity" the question is seldom if ever pressed. What always stands in the forefront is the idea of an impersonal government of a faceless entity—whether science itself, a "scientific and positive capacity" (Saint-Simon and Comte), a "universal association," a collective spirit or mind, or, ultimately, the "government of things." If anyone, it was Saint-Simon who had concrete actors in mind. In the three bodies that were to run, in his 1819 constitutional design, the industrial system, the "chamber of inventions" was to be composed of 200 engineers (out of 300 members); the "chamber of control," the *chambre d'éxamination,* contained 300 biologists, physicists, and mathematicians; and the "chamber of execution" was to be composed entirely of industrialists, of entrepreneurs, those in charge of the productive work and, indeed, the wealthiest and most successful among them.[81] But while Saint-Simon did occasionally keep his feet on the ground, the emphasis of the Saint-Simonians was on abstract entities. Comte in particular landed at "a rational submission to the preponderance of the laws of nature," to a government (scientists) actually governed by the necessary dictates of science.[82] The soil was thus tilled for a final, clear-cut leap: the replacement of the government of men by the "administration of things." This was no longer, however, Saint-Simon or Comte; it was Engels.[83] And since, via Engels, the *government of things* entered Marxism, let this be considered the popular, slogan version of the ideal of a disembodied government.

It is interesting, though immaterial to my point, to speculate whether Engels was directly influenced in this coinage by the scientific positivism of Saint-Simon and Comte.[84] Certainly the scientism that entered Marxism comes from Engels; Marx himself was too Hegelian for that. Yet Marx, no less than Engels, proclaimed their common doctrine "scientific," thereby excommunicating all other socialisms as being non-scientific or pre-scientific. Unquestionably, with them "science" was a key word that had struck deep roots. Note also that the notion that politics was to be dissolved into "administration," indeed that government was to be replaced by mere administration, was already put forward by Saint-Simon (and probably put down in writing by Comte) in 1819-20[85] and was a familiar idea to their schools. Where lies the difference? The difference, what I have called the leap, is in saying *things*. The socialists of the polytechnic breed (indeed, of truer scientific breeding than Engels, let alone Marx) never went explicitly that far. A religion of engineers is still of engineers; they could not leave the solution simply to "things." That was very close to being their message, to being what they wished their listeners to understand; but at some point one never fails to find in their writings some concrete protagonist in charge: scientists, industrialists, a central bank (presumably with bankers). But the industrialist was, to Engels and Marx, the exploiter; and the scientist could hardly be their administrator, since in their doctrine the protagonist had to be the proletariat. There was there a Gordian knot, and Engels cut it with a sword: *die Verwaltung von Sachen,* the carrying on by things. Far too simple? Certainly—so much so that once it was said, it was left at that. But this was also the case with the notion of the dictatorship of the proletariat; it was mentioned only in passing by Marx,[86] yet it stuck and became a central notion. So did the "administration of things" —and with greater reason. The dictatorship of the proletariat is, after all, only a transitory moment, only the harsh beginning of the route to communism. But the administration of things is communism itself, the end state.

Here we have the indispensable gap-filling complement of the Marxist prediction that politics will cease to exist, that the state will wither away. Nothing ends if it is replaced by nothing at all. But the government of men will end—this being the key to the solution—*because* it will be replaced by a self-administration of things.

The question might be: Granted that *die Verwaltung von Sachen* bears, like Atlas, the weight of the communist prophecy on its shoulders, why should it be brought under the government-of-science umbrella? What have "things" to do with "science"? Nothing—had the soil not been long tilled by the joint gospels of Saint-Simon and Comte. The underlying credibility of Engels's "things" remains entrusted to the grand design of a world self-governed by Scientific Reason. Without this implicit backing, the Marxist prophecy would hardly be, after a century, still mightily with us. I shall, therefore, pursue the argument with the understanding that the "government of things" is no orphan; it represents, rather, an extreme, simplistic version of a major intellectual movement.

Resuming the main thread, what are we to make of the notion of a government of science? Would it be, if it ever will be, of science or of scientists? Let us take up first the more abstract issue. In my understanding, the notion of a government of science is a by-product of "scientism." If so, the issue concerns the faults and the limits of scientific-positivistic rationalism. What is in question and needs questioning is not, of course, the capacity of humans to "reason"—the more of it, the better. What is in question is the scientistic-physicalist variety of rationalism, its self-assurance, arrogance, and, ultimately, limitless appetite. Let us grant this specimen, since our vocabulary does not assist us otherwise, a capital letter: Reason. The grievance, or the quarrel, is, then, about science that becomes Scientism and, concomitantly, about reason that becomes Reason. Scientism extends science to everything, indeed beyond the realms to which the actual performance of science actually applies—it is a trespassing. Correlatively, the specific reason employed by the physicalist sciences becomes the only, the absolute, all-subsuming Reason—a Reason stripped, among other things, of reasonableness.

In making its estimates, Reason is often tempted to forget that when all is said and done, it is not *reasons* but *persons,* not disembodied but incarnate ideas, that are to govern us even in a world governed, as it were, by Reason. This is, of course, a very tempting omission. If governments could be depersonalized frictionless machines monitored by equations, then everything might fall into place. But governments are institutions run by human beings. Certainly, if we place the impersonal majesty of Science and Reason where the more prosaic reality of persons should be, everything may find a beautiful fit — in theory. But not in history, not when real actors replace fictitious ones. Governments will always be of persons, never of things. Hence, there is little doubt as to who will be king: If a government of science were ever to exist, it would be a government of scientists. Even so, it still is unclear what this might mean.

If we understand by "government of scientists" that scientists and (in a technological time) technocrats will replace politicians, that is, that the future politician will be recruited from experts and scientists, this is not only a very hazardous prediction but also no solution. It is a hazardous prediction because from technology to technocracy the passage is as long as the one from *logos* (knowing the technique) to *cracy,* to power. Knowing gives power over what is known; but from here to a generalized power over a whole society the leap is nearly astronomical. In any event, this would be no solution at all, for a taking over by scientists of the role of politicians would not imply that the new governors would act, in their political capacity, as scientists. Indeed, a government of scientists is likely to have little in common with a government of science, except in the displeasing sense that the "scientific politico" will use his technical know-how as a very effective *instrumentum regni,* as a highly perfected instrument of domination. However, that politicians will be replaced by scientists is a most implausible hypothesis. The plausible one is that the scientist will be put to use by the politico and that the technical skill of the former will prove very useful to who knows how to master, not knowledge, but people.

We are back to saying, then, that the idea of a government of science (thereby including the "scientific" Marxist promise of an administration of things) owes all its attractiveness to the idea of a frictionless government of Reason in which the best among the projects put together by the experts — scientists and technocrats — somehow chooses itself. But if we allow ourselves to be lulled to sleep by such a fairy tale, we are heading to bitter awakenings. The depersonalization of power has been a task to which Western man has devoted all of his political ingenuity. Yet it would be plain silly to say that we have succeeded in transforming the politician into a public administrator of the public interest, that is, into a selfless discharger of social functions. We have succeeded only in keeping him under watch. But if even this comparatively minor step unceasingly fails us, what should we say of a gigantic leap all the way to the withering away of politics itself? We can only say, I am afraid, that it is a sheer leap into outright deception. In fact, it would be a gigantic leap backward, for, let us never forget it, the self-government of "scientific reason" (or of things) has no room for a control-over-persons; this would be an impossible, inadmissible disturbance.

The notion that the problem of political power has been solved once and for all arises among people who enjoy a freedom that they did nothing to establish. Many Westerners today even refuse to see how menacingly a wholly undomesticated power—multiplied exponentially by the power of technology —has established itself all around them. But the harsh reality of politics takes its revenge on those who neglect it. It especially takes its revenge on those who put their bets on "eternal Saint-Simonism"[87] and believe in the end of politics. To be sure, "If men were good these counsels would not be good"; or, as an author of the *Federalist* wrote, somewhat echoing Machiavelli, "If men were angels there would be no need for government."[88] But men are not angels, and although we should never cease to hope in their goodness, how can we plan rational and just societies in total abeyance of the risk "human badness"?

Scientism, I said, is *science that trespasses.* It is not beyond the capabilities of present-day scientists and techno-experts to design a Rational Society targeted at scientifically warranted goals implemented by scientifically calculated means. Let us also concede, for the sheer sake of argument, perfect information and impossibility of error. Would such a Rational Society also be a "good society"? Scientism can only reply in the affirmative; it has no way of distinguishing between Rational and good. Its trespassing consists precisely in ruling out any criterion that is not its own. Hence, what is Rational must be, by definition, good. Yet, reason (non-capitalized) tells us that a society *of men,* of frail and groping human beings, may be rationally organized and monitored, and not be, in their own experience, a good society at all. Recall that in the Western conception of the world the good society, or the good life, ultimately consists in allowing each person to choose what he wishes *for his own reasons.* A society in which everything is decided for everybody by Reason is not—in this understanding of life and its values—a worthy society. True, this is only a Western *Weltanschauung.* But in the non-Western ones, infinitely different as they may be, the distinction between what is rational (a Western import) and what is good holds even more.

From Reason, we had better revert, then, to reason. This entails, above all, that "not the least important task for human reason [is] rationally to comprehend its own limitations."[89] When applied to human beings, reason works best when it knows how fallible it can be.

Notes

1. *Politics, Economics and Welfare*, p. 20 (and chaps. 1-3 passim). As if to leave no doubt as to the latitude of their definition, Dahl and Lindblom further state: "The attempt to achieve rational politico-economic action may . . . be described as economic planning whether the attempt employs the market or master mind."

2. The first major analysis was by Ludwig von Mises, *Die Gemeinwirthschaft*, published in 1922, translated and revised under the title *Socialism* (London: Cape, 1936). But see especially F.A. von Hayek et al., *Collectivist Economic Planning* (London: Routledge & Kegan Paul, 1935). This pace-setting symposium includes the initial doubts of N.G. Pierson (1902) and E. Barone (1908), the first attack of Mises (1920), and two original contributions of Hayek himself in which he expands upon the Mises thesis that the information required by economic calculation requires, in turn, market-determined prices.

3. The first label was devised by Bertrand de Jouvenel, *L'Economie Dirigée* (Paris, 1928). The Italian *dirigismo* was a calque of the French *dirigée*. The debate was a very lively one in Italy. See *La Crisi del Capitalismo* (Firenze: Sansoni, 1933), with contributions by Pirou, Sombart, Durbin, Patterson, Spirito; and especially *L'Economia Programmatica* (Firenze: Sansoni, 1933), with contributions by Brocard, Landauer, J.A. Hobson, Lorwin, Dobbert, Spirito.

4. Under this definition the welfare state, or sheer public ownership of industries, banks, and utilities, is not "planning." Despite a deluge of works in Western countries bearing the word planning in the title, the fact remains that welfare policies and programs are just that. Likewise, the sheer addition of one nationalization to another has to do with the expansion of the state sector, not with planning.

5. While I single out the pricing function and specifically the calculation of costs as the sine qua non function, it is by no means (see section 2) the sole property of market systems.

6. Limited planning is also limited, to be sure, by democratic constraints. As long as the planners perform within a democratic framework, freedom of consumption and freedom of occupation (the choice of one's occupation) are not easily trampled upon.

7. It was not, however, a demand either of Saint-Simon or of Comte. Both were socialists in the sense that they negated liberalism, individualism, democracy, and the market system. Both also advocated a radical restructuring of property. Yet, both believed that property had to be retained for "industrialism" (a term coined by Saint-Simon) to be efficient.

8. Reference is made to the Saint-Simonians rather than to Saint-Simon himself for two reasons. First, the doctrine ascribed to Henri de Saint-Simon found its streamlined formulation in a course of lectures delivered after his death by his pupils: *Doctrine de Saint-Simon: Exposition* (1829-30). Second, there are two differences between Saint-Simon and the doctrine attributed to him in the *Exposition* (compare, e.g., the *Exposition* with Saint-Simon's *Système Industriel* of 1821-22). One is that only the pupils, not Saint-Simon (see n. 7 above) requested the abolition of private property. The second difference is that the school (especially Enfantin) went further than Saint-Simon in outlining a "planned economy" managed by a "unitary, directing bank." Bearing the various paternities in mind, it is appropriate to conclude that the *Exposition*

is "one of the great landmarks in the history of socialism" and that with respect to the organization of a planned economy it carried "socialist thought further than was done for nearly a hundred years after its publication." F.A. von Hayek, *The Counter-Revolution of Science: Studies on the Abuse of Reason* (Glencoe: Free Press, 1952), p. 147. The most important history of Saint-Simonianism remains S. Charléty, *Histoire du Saint-Simonisme* (Paris: Hartmann, 1931).

9. See chapter 15, sections 1-2. The essential point is that Marx's centralization of the means of production was conceived negatively rather than positively, as a taking away, not as an economic command system.

10. Lenin engaged first, until the spring of 1921, in what was subsequently and misleadingly called "war Communism." What he had in mind was not "emergency economics," but some kind of natural economic system. Faced with collapse, Lenin retreated into the "New Economic Policy" (NEP). Lenin died in 1924, NEP lasted from 1921 to 1927, and the first Five Year Plan, the actual inception of total planning, was decided by Stalin in 1928. As Alec Nove puts it, "The word 'planning' had very different meaning in 1923-26 to that which it later acquired. There was . . . no 'command economy.' . . . What emerged from these calculations [of the Gosplan, the state general-planning commission] were not plans in the sense of orders to act, but 'control figures,' which were partly a forecast and partly a guide . . . for discussing and determining priorities." *An Economic History of the USSR,* rev. ed. (Harmondsworth: Penguin Books, 1982), p. 101.

11. This was the central objection of the 1935 symposium on *Collectivist Economic Planning* (see n. 2 above) and came to be known as the Mises-Hayek line of criticism. A good overview of the state of the debate in the late 1930s is T.J.B. Hoff (1938), *Economic Calculation in the Socialist Society* (Indianapolis: Liberty Press, 1981). Hayek wrote in 1940 another important article on economic calculation, "The Competitive Solution," now in *Individualism and Economic Order* (Chicago: University of Chicago Press, 1948).

12. Thus, Hayek's *The Road to Serfdom* (Chicago: University of Chicago Press, 1944), found a passionate response in Herman Finer, *The Road to Reaction* (Boston: Little Brown, 1945). This exchange brought to the fore, however, the political debate about planning: it bears on the politics, not the economics, of planning.

13. Oskar Lange was among the first socialist economists to confront the Mises-Hayek objection. See O. Lange and F.M. Taylor, *On the Economic Theory of Socialism* (Minneapolis: University of Minnesota Press, 1938). A very long line of literature followed. See H.D. Dickinson, *Economics of Socialism* (London: Oxford University Press, 1939); Abba P. Lerner, *Economics of Control* (New York: Macmillan, 1944); C. Bettelheim, *Problèmes Théoriques et Pratiques de la Planification* (Paris: Presses Universitaires de France, 1946); C. Napoleoni, *Il Pensiero Economico del 900* (Torino: Einaudi, 1963); B. Ward, *The Socialist Economy: A Study of Organizational Alternatives* (New York: Random House, 1967); G.M. Heal, *The Theory of Economic Planning* (New York: Elsevier, 1973); A. Nove and D.M. Nuti, *Socialist Economics* (Harmondsworth: Penguin Books, 1974); B. Jossa, *Socialismo e Mercato* (Milano: Etas Kompass, 1978). A useful reader is W.A. Leeman, ed., *Capitalism, Market Socialism and Central Planning* (Boston: Houghton Mifflin, 1963).

14. The single prominent economist who straightforwardly dismissed the Mises-Hayek objection was Maurice Dobb, *Political Economy and Capitalism* (London: Rout-

ledge & Kegan Paul, 1937). Another standard exposition is Paul M. Sweezy, *The Theory of Capitalist Development* (New York: Oxford University Press, 1942). As a rule, in the West the principles of Marxist political economy are most persuasively expounded ex adverso against the background of capitalism. See also Paul A. Baran, *The Political Economy of Growth* (New York: Marzani & Munsell, 1960); Ernest Mandel, *Marxist Economic Theory*, 2 vols. (New York: Monthly Review, 1968); and M. Dobb, *Socialist Planning: Some Problems* (London: Lawrence & Wishart, 1970).

15. C.E. Lindblom, *Politics and Markets* (New York: Basic Books, 1977), p. 325.

16. Ibid., p. 101.

17. R.A. Dahl, in S.K. Bailey et al., *Research Frontiers in Politics and Government* (Washington, D.C.: Brookings Institution, 1955), p. 46. See also *Politics, Economics and Welfare*, where Dahl and Lindblom speak of "tyranny of the *isms*" and assert: "The great issues are no longer the great issues, if ever they were" (p. 5). In *Politics and Markets* Lindblom still abides by the "anti-isms" minimizing strategy: his leitmotif is that reality smooths out what theory (erroneously, in his view) separates.

18. The metaphor of the "invisible hand" goes back to Adam Smith, who employed it, however, only twice. Smith had in mind positive "unintended consequences," the fact that individual motives ("his own gain") bring about social benefits which are "no part of his intentions" (*An Inquiry into the Nature and Causes of the Wealth of Nations* [1776] [New York: Modern Library, 1937], p. 423). The metaphor currently extends to other characteristics of the market system, as will be seen shortly.

19. Among the successes, the French *Commisariat du Plan* has mainly dealt with industrial reconstruction, and Sweden's recourse to limited planning has promoted, more than anything else, the buildup of what is now called a "corporatist state." The Netherlands can also be included in the limited planning pattern; but no planning in any specific technical meaning of the term can be attributed to most Western democracies, and even less to Japan.

20. At a minimum, the following: *(a)* patterned within-system interactions among the component elements, such that *(b)* any variation in one element will affect and/or alter the others. A system is also assumed to be bounded.

21. The objection that the huge firm or, indeed, the "huge capitalist" circumvent the laws of the market and are able to fix prices arbitrarily will be taken up in section 3, where I draw the distinction between market competition as a structure, on the one hand, and actual competitiveness, on the other hand.

22. F.A. von Hayek, *Kinds of Order in Society* (1964) (Menlo Park: Institute for Humane Studies, 1975), p. 5. The argument is more fully developed in Hayek's *Law, Legislation and Liberty*, vol. 1, *Rules and Order* (Chicago: University of Chicago Press, 1973), chap. 2. The importance of Hayek's notion of "spontaneous order" is highlighted by John H. Gray, *Hayek on Liberty* (Oxford: Blackwell, 1984), chaps. 2, 6. Gray also underscores the epistemological role attributed by Hayek to social institutions.

23. See especially Hayek's *Law, Legislation and Liberty*, vol. 3, *The Political Order of a Free People* (Chicago: University of Chicago Press, 1979), chap. 15. See also Thomas Sowell, *Knowledge and Decisions* (New York: Basic Books, 1980).

24. In essence, cognitive incompetence, as discussed in chapter 5, esp. section 7, is not a problem vis-à-vis a market system.

25. Vilfredo Pareto gave us a quantified *a contrario* illustration of all of this. He calculated that for an imaginary society of 100 persons trading in all only 700 goods

and services, it would require the solution of 70,699 simultaneous equations to equate supply and demand in the manner the free market does on its own. See *Manuale di Economia Politica* (Milano, 1909), chap. 3, sects. 201-17.

26. This is the felicitous coinage of Raymond Aron, *Les Désillusions du Progres* (Paris: Calmann-Lévy, 1969), p. 311.

27. For this and subsequent points about equality and justice, see chapter 12, sections 4 and 5.

28. This is by no means to contradict Karl Polanyi's point that the market destroyed the organic society that preceded the industrial revolution (*The Great Transformation* [Boston: Beacon Press, 1944], passim). What Polanyi described was the "historical cruelty" of the market. That devastation, I take it, has since been absorbed; hence my point refers to its intrinsic, daily cruelty. A.O. Hirschman provides a fascinating account of the various interpretations given to the market society in *The Passions and the Interests,* and in "Rival Interpretations of Market Society: Civilizing, Destructive or Feeble?" *Journal of Economic Literature,* December 1982.

29. Henri Pirenne, *Les Périodes de l'Histoire Sociale du Capitalisme* (Brussels, 1922), pointed out that merchant families generally lost their prominence in two or three generations. In contrast to noble dynasties, capitalist dynasties are short lived.

30. See H. Arendt, *The Human Condition* (Chicago: University of Chicago Press, 1958), p. 164. Her analysis of "labor" (chap. 3) and "work" (chap. 4) is extraordinarily insightful.

31. Reference is made especially to the "dialectics of the master and the slave." However, the *Phenomenology* was inspired, on this theme, by Hegel's earlier *Jena Lectures* of 1803-1804. Marx's *Economico-Philosophic Manuscripts of 1844* centrally confront Hegel's *Phenomenology* and neatly attest to a response within the ambit of Hegel's conceptualization. For the Hegelian derivation of Marx's thinking on this central point, see esp. Karl Löwith, *Von Hegel bis Nietzsche* (Zürich: Europa Verlag, 1938), pt. II, chap. 2: "The Problem of Work." That Marx's "alienation" also owes to Feuerbach is doubtlessly true. But Feuerbach dealt with religious alienation, while Hegel had already applied the concept to the work process.

32. The difference was that Hegel's "reappropriation" of the self to itself belonged to an omnitemporal dialectical process (at least in the 1831 *Philosophy of Law* section on the "system of needs," though far less so in the *Jena Lectures*), whereas Marx assigned the alienation to the present (capitalism) and postponed the reappropriation to the future (the communist society). While Marx no longer used the word alienation in *Capital,* the concept remains and is central to his entire economic theorizing. See, among others, P. Craig Roberts and M.A. Stephenson, *Marx's Theory of Exchange, Alienation and Crisis* (New York: Praeger, 1973). The argument is followed up in chapter 15, section 2.

33. The charge is reinforced by the distinction between "labor time" and "labor power." While this distinction is central to the Marxian indictment of capitalism, it does not affect the point at issue.

34. *The Gotha Critique* (1875) includes, in addition, need and ability criteria. The three formulas are assessed in chapter 15, section 1.

35. It will be seen in the next chapter (section 1) that this conclusion is not as paradoxical as it may appear and that it is perfectly consistent with Marx's anthropology. The missing, forthcoming qualification is that Marx's individualism is "organic."

The text implies only, then, that Marx's allocation of benefits is individualistic. It should also be clear that "individualism" is conceived here in contradistinction to "collectivism" and that characteriological issues (e.g., whether a market society engenders the "ugly individual") are immaterial to my argument. For such issues see the discussion of R.E. Lane, "Individualism and the Market Society," in *Liberal Democracy,* ed. J.R. Pennock and J.W. Chapman (New York: New York University Press, 1983).

36. *Wirtschaft und Gesellschaft,* vol. 1, pt. 2, chap. 6.

37. See *The New Industrial State* (Boston: Houghton Mifflin, 1967), pp. 9-10.

38. Fernand Braudel, *The Wheels of Commerce: Civilization and Capitalism 15th-18th Century* (New York: Harper & Row, 1982), 2:230.

39. The label "social democracy" became truly distinctive only in 1920 with the establishment of the Third (Communist) International. Until the Russian Revolution, Lenin and the Mensheviks were members of the "Social Democratic" grouping of the Second International, and much of the Leninist doctrine of the party was called by Lenin himself social democratic. Given these verbal vagaries, the least confusing distinction is the one between "non-communist socialism" and communism that hinges, in turn, on the non-acceptance of the twenty-one conditions set forth by Lenin in 1920 for admission in the Comintern (or Third International). Since then it is of course permissible to label all the parties of the first group "social democratic"; but this way of handling the matter obscures that two divergent souls have long survived and still do among Western socialisms. A symposium that brings out the extant complexity of socialism as an ideal is L. Kolakowski and Stuart Hampshire, eds., *The Socialist Idea: A Reappraisal* (New York: Basic Books, 1974).

40. Interestingly, "nationalization" remains to date a statutory commitment for the English Labour party, whereas "socialization" disappeared from the 1959 Bad Godesberg program of the German Social Democratic party.

41. Social ownership is meaningfully and correctly applicable to a self-management of the workers of their plant accompanied by *pro capite* shares (property titles) that draw dividends from the profits but cannot be freely sold (see n. 62, below). The notion of "public" property is, on the other hand, largely juridical. There are also technical and juridical differences between nationalization and socialization, but these distinctions are immaterial to our analysis.

42. No one better than Trotsky has made the point that nationalization of property does not, in itself, create "social property." This, he said, is "the fundamental sophism of the [Soviet] official doctrine." Actually, "State property is converted into socialist property in proportion as it ceases to be State property." *The Revolution Betrayed* (New York: Pioneer, 1957), pp. 236, 239.

43. The escalation is as follows: from the machine that multiplies the output of man's work we pass to the automated machine, which is simply watched over by man, and from here we go all the way to the machine that produces by itself other machines. See J. von Neumann, *Theory of Self-Reproducing Automata* (Urbana: University of Illinois Press, 1966). This capital is the "fixed" part of reproducible capital. The accumulation need includes also a "circulating" and financial part.

44. Remember that Marx predicted the demise of capitalism as resulting from its need to destine escalating proportions of "constant capital" (his name for fixed capital) to investments, thus bringing about *(a)* a growing pauperization of the workers, and *(b)* falling interests for the capitalists. Now, had Marx conceived capital accumu-

lation as a technological imperative, his two "laws" would equally apply to the economics of communism. This confirms that Marx had little grasp of the technological dynamics and constraints of the industrial process as such.

45. Historically, there is no reason to single out and to employ the word capital until the industrial revolution. While "capital" as an economic term can be traced back to the thirteenth century, the word has long been preeminently used in its etymological meaning (*caput,* head, as in the expressions capital sin and capital punishment). Its economic usage remained for centuries infrequent and generic: it stood, indifferently, for money, wealth, goods, property and patrimony. "Capitalist" was coined only in the mid-seventeenth century, and this word too was used for over a century (very seldom) generically, simply to mean the "moneyed men," the wealthy (not the investor or the entrepreneur). In order, then, to appreciate the important and distinctive meaning of "capital," "capitalist" and, finally, "capitalism" we must await the nineteenth century and specifically associate these notions (as I am about to do) with "wealth for investment," not with wealth for use. On capitalism, see R. Passow, *Kapitalismus: Eine Begrifflich-Terminologishe Studie* (Jena, 1918). More generally see Braudel, *The Wheels of Commerce,* vol. 2, esp. pp. 231-43.

46. Throughout the Middle Ages, and well beyond, money was simply one of the *consumptibiles,* one of the things to be consumed. And while profit seeking is indeed very old, it too was largely destined to accumulation for its own sake and consumption, and hardly conceived for investment. Money lenders and banks are only a very small exception to this generalization. In Braudel's account, between the thirteenth and eighteenth centuries there were only three occasions, in the West, of "a well advanced [banking] development which appeared to be leading . . . towards . . . some form of financial capitalism"; and all were "blocked in mid-career" and ended "in failure" (*Wheels of Commerce,* p. 392). Remember, also, that lending at interest was generally perceived as "usury" and still condemned as such by Pope Benedict XIV in 1745.

47. To be sure, the "spirit of capitalism" can be traced back to far earlier seeds. Along with Max Weber's classic *The Protestant Ethic and the Spirit of Capitalism* (1904-5), see also Werner Sombart, *Der Moderne Kapitalismus* (1905) and *Der Bourgeois* (1913); and Jean Baechler, *Les Origines du Capitalisme* (Paris: Gallimard, 1974). Braudel, *Wheels of Commerce,* criticizes both Weber and Sombart.

48. Note that my question addresses a structural arrangement, that is, whether there can be a market system without a polycentric structure of autonomous and antagonistic actors. Some Marxist economists concede, as does Sweezy, that "the market does not imply capitalism" (*The Theory of Capitalist Development,* p. 56). But this is conceded on the basis of a distinction between the market as a method of allocating resources, and capitalism as a method of distributing wealth, that misconstrues both entities. In any event, I raise a different issue.

49. *Politics and Markets,* pp. 98-99.

50. See chapter 1, section 3 (and notes 11-13). To be sure, in that literature one finds very different versions of "industrial democracy," many of which do not include self-management. For instance Clegg's *A New Approach to Industrial Democracy* (Oxford: Blackwell, 1960) — an approach largely entered in the British Royal Commission Report on Trade Unions and Employers, and in the Labour Party Report of 1967, *Industrial Democracy* — falls outside of the acceptation under scrutiny. So do the partner-

ship proposals of the English Liberal Party and the German formula of *Mitbestimmung*. Blumberg's *Industrial Democracy* (London: Constable, 1968) follows, instead, the Webb-Cole tradition. For a cross-European concise overview of legislative proposals and/or enacted reforms falling under the "industrial democracy" heading, see *Cogestione: Esperienze e Problemi* (Torino: Biblioteca della Libertà, 1976), no. 63.

51. I follow here, and in much of what follows, Luciano Pellicani, *Il Mercato e i Socialismi* (Milano: SugarCo, 1979), who more than any other present-day neo-socialist brilliantly brings together the threads of the theory of market socialism.

52. Karl Kautsky became, in Lenin's favorite slogan, "renegade" in that he came over, with his pamphlet *The Dictatorship of the Proletariat* (1918), and even more with *Terrorism and Communism* (1919), to "bourgeois democracy." Rosa Luxemburg, while sharing Kautsky's view that the Soviet dictatorship "over the proletariat" would not lead to socialism but to barbarism, expressed in *The Russian Revolution* (written in 1918 but published in 1922) a critique from, say, the libertarian extreme left. Trotsky represents yet another position. His *Revolution Betrayed* of 1937 remains one of the most lucid analyses of the deep structural reasons for the bureaucratic degenerations of communism (under Stalin); yet Trotsky never admitted that degenerations were intrinsic to the structure: he imputed them to the Stalinist aberration. (See the excellent exposé of the point by Baruch Knei-Paz, *The Social and Political Thought of Leon Trotsky* [Oxford: Clarendon Press, 1978], chap. 10: "Stalinism: The Revolution Bureaucratized.") It was Bruno Rizzi who first took stock of Trotsky's impossible self-contradiction and carried the Trotskian premises to their logical conclusion in *La Bureaucratisation du Monde* (Paris, 1939, trans. *Il Collettivismo Burocratico* [Milano: SugarCo, 1977]). Wittfogel's *Oriental Despotism* (New Haven: Yale University Press, 1957) is perhaps the most masterful historical follow-up of Trotsky's bureaucratization theme; and his conclusion that it is the absence of an economic system independent of the state that leads to total despotism is very relevant for market socialism.

53. *Il Mercato e i Socialismi*, pp. 274-77.

54. Ibid., p. 178. This is clearly far apart from the participatory democracy literature surveyed in chapter 5, section 6, herein.

55. Ibid., p. 274.

56. That property is theft is the thread of *What Is Property?* (1840); the quotation is, instead, from Proudhon's later work, *La Théorie de la Propriété*, posthumously published in 1866, chap. 5, sect. 3. The distance in views between Proudhon and Marx came to the forefront with Proudhon's *Philosophy of Misery* of 1846 (the full title is *Système des Contradictions Economiques — Philosophie de la Misère*), to which Marx quickly responded, in 1847, with *The Poverty of Philosophy*.

57. Proudhon, *Idée Génerale de la Révolution* (Paris, 1851), p. 47.

58. This conclusion, let it be stressed, applies to what I have called mainstream and would not apply to the various new lefts.

59. Largely though not exclusively. The Swedish Meidner plan (a very detailed proposal of industrial self-management), and the similar British Bullock Report are autocthonous. See R. Meidner, *Il Prezzo dell' Eguaglianza* (Cosenza: Lerici, 1976).

60. On the Yugoslav experiment the literature has become extensive. See A. Meister, *Socialisme et Autogestion: L'Experiénce Yugoslave* (Paris: Editions du Seuil, 1964); B. Horvat, *Towards a Theory of Planned Economy* (Belgrade: Yugoslav Institute Economic Affairs, 1964); S. Pejovic, *The Market Planned Economy of Yugoslavia* (Minne-

apolis: University of Minnesota Press, 1966); J. Wilczynski, *The Economics of Socialism* (London: Routledge & Kegan Paul, 1970); W. Brus, *The Market in a Socialist Economy* (London: Routledge & Kegan Paul, 1972); Morris Bornstein, ed., *Plan and Market: Economic Reform in Eastern Europe* (New Haven: Yale University Press, 1973); R. Bicanic, *Economic Policy in Socialist Yugoslavia* (New York: Cambridge University Press, 1973); J. Vanek, *The General Theory of Labor-Managed Market Economics* (Ithaca: Cornell University Press, 1970); J. Vanek, ed., *Self-Management* (Baltimore: Penguin Books, 1975); M. Drulovic, *La Democrazia Autogestita* (Roma: Editori Riuniti, 1978).

61. Among the critical appraisals, see Ota Sik, *Marxismo-Leninismo e Società Industriale* (Milano: Garzanti, 1974); and A. Garand, *L'Autogestion, l'Entreprise, et l'Economie Nationale* (Paris: France-Empire, 1974). On political grounds, the witnessing of Milovan Djilas, *The New Class* (New York: Praeger, 1957), remains important.

62. It is precisely the limitations to purchasing and selling that render a property title "social." Western experiences with partnership distributions to workers show that the recipients tend to sell their shares, considering them as an addition to their salary. A remedy to this is to permit the selling (to the firm) only when the employee leaves, and to prohibit purchases by outsiders.

63. In essence, the point in favor of property and private enterprise is that non-owned things and resources invite irresponsible behavior: What is not "myne" is not cared for. More technically put, a *res nullius,* a common property, or state property, fails to internalize, in their users, costs and benefits. For a broad appraisal, J.R. Pennock and J.W. Chapman, eds., *Property* (New York: New York University Press, 1980), contains excellent contributions. See also Alan Ryan, *Property and Political Theory* (Oxford: Blackwell, 1984).

64. *Politics and Markets,* p. 112.

65. This was, in essence, Max Weber's understanding of rationality, and specifically of *Zweckrationalität.* Mannheim called the coordination between means and ends "functional rationality." See *Man and Society in an Age of Reconstruction* (London: Routledge & Kegan Paul, 1940), pp. 52-60.

66. See chapter 8, section 6.

67. See "Planned Society and the Problem of Human Personality," in *Essays on Sociology and Social Psychology* (London: Routledge & Kegan Paul, 1953), part 4; and *Freedom, Power and Democratic Planning* (London: Routledge & Kegan Paul, 1950), passim. Mannheim himself was aware of the danger of a planning that ultimately addresses the very nature of man. Answering the question, Who plans those who do the planning? he avowed: "The longer I reflect on this question, the more it haunts me" (*Man and Society in an Age of Reconstruction,* p. 74).

68. This is notably the thesis set forth by Tocqueville's *L'Ancien Régime et la Révolution* (Paris, 1856).

69. A third protagonist here is the power of organized labor. While I must neglect this additional complexity, it should be understood that trade unionism tends to be a "state within the state" and interferes, or may interfere, in market mechanisms more powerfully than monopolies.

70. Social or societal pluralism is said to be the equivalent of the constitutional separation of powers. However, a social pluralism lacking constitutional protection is, of itself, ineffective; it implements but cannot replace constitutional pluralism.

71. This, let it be recalled, is what "social" democracy means. See chapter 1, section 3, and chapter 13, sections 5-6.

72. *Man and His Government* (New York: McGraw-Hill, 1963), p. 296.

73. See chapter 5, passim, but esp. sections 5-7.

74. Hayek, *The Counter-Revolution of Science,* pp. 101-2.

75. This was already very clear and was very clearly admitted by Saint-Simon and his school, and also by Comte. Among the founding fathers of socialism, only Proudhon refused this implication.

76. The literature on the age of technology is truly overwhelming. Among the more subtle interpretations, see Sergio Cotta, *La Sfida Tecnologica* (Bologna: Il Mulino, 1968). The influential work of Jacques Ellul, *The Technological Society* (New York: Knopf, 1964), identifies "technology" with "technique," i.e., means for achieving ends, and is, in my opinion, unconvincing.

77. Interestingly, his preferred label was "social physics." He opted for "sociology" after having accused Quetelet of having used (and spoiled) "social physics" with reference to "mere statistics." But until the fourth volume (1839) of his *Cours de Philosophie Positive* (1830-42) Comte insisted on saying social physics. "Sociology" was thus enthroned by his final *Système de Politique Positive* (1851-54), not in the earlier version of the *Système* published in 1822 (with a different title) and republished in 1824.

78. See *The Counter-Revolution of Science,* esp. pp. 105-28. See also F.E. Manuel, *The Prophets of Paris* (Cambridge, Mass.: Harvard University Press, 1962); and, more generally, M. Leroy, *Histoire des Idées Sociales en France,* 3 vols. (Paris: Gallimard, 1947-54).

79. *L'Avenir de la Science* (1849) (Paris: 1890), p. 37. The qualification is even more interesting. "The science which will govern the world," he wrote in the same passage, "will not be politics . . . but philosophy." Renan intended that "philosophy as science" (the positivistic interpretation) would govern the world.

80. Basically, this is the theme of who has power in the industrial society. With specific regard to Saint-Simon and Comte, see the careful analysis of D. Fisichella, *Il Potere nella Società Industriale: Saint-Simon e Comte* (Napoli: Morano, 1965).

81. This is the constitutional project in Saint-Simon's *Organisateur* of 1819-20. The spirit of the design was to establish a mechanism in which "decisions result only from scientific demonstrations totally independent of human will" and the leitmotif was, even here, one of impersonal, guiding "spiritual power." See *Oeuvres de Saint-Simon et d' Enfantin* (Paris, 1865-78), vol. xx, esp. pp. 50-58 and 199-200.

82. See *Cours de Philosophie Positive,* vol. 4 (1839), 2d ed. (Paris: Littré, 1864), pp. 147-48. A good English condensation of Comte's writings is *The Positive Philosophy of Auguste Comte,* by H. Martineau, 2 vols., 3d ed. (London, 1893). On Comte, the fundamental interpretation is, for our vantage point, the one of Raymond Aron, especially in his *Main Currents of Sociological Thought* (Garden City, N.Y.: Anchor Books, 1968).

83. F. Engels, *Anti-Dühring* (1878), pt. III, chap. 2. The full, original sentence is: "An die Stelle der Regierung über Personen tritt die Verwaltung von Sachen. Der Staat wird nicht 'abgeschafft,' er *stirbt ab*" (emphasis of Engels). *Verwaltung* means "administration," but is often rendered by the translators as "government." The two terms have thus become interchangeable.

84. This is suggested, very plausibly, by Hayek, *The Counter-Revolution of Sci-*

ence, esp. pt. III: "Comte and Hegel."

85. In the *Organisateur* (vol. XX, pp. 144-45, in cit. ed. of *Oeuvres*). See, very conveniently, *Henri Saint-Simon: Selected Writings,* ed. and trans. Keith Taylor (New York: Holmes & Meier, 1975), pt. III: "From the Government of Men to the Administration of Things."

86. See chapter 15, section 2 (and n. 26).

87. This is the label of W. Röpke for the ideal of a technocracy of social engineers. See his chapter "Ewiger Saint-Simonismus," *Civitas Humana* (London: Hodge, 1948). But see the qualifications by Fisichella, *Il Potere nella Società Industriale,* chaps. 6, 7, and 9: Saint-Simon and Comte were much more cautious on the matter than the notion of technocracy in itself suggests.

88. *The Federalist,* No. 51. The author is probably Madison.

89. Hayek, *The Counter-Revolution of Science,* p. 92.

15. Another Democracy?

Socialist societies have no problem with immigration, only emigration.
—J.-F. Revel

15.1 *The Good Society of Rousseau and Marx*

Democracy is, for me, the same as Western-type democracy. That is to say that throughout this work my referent is liberal democracy. Indeed, I stress that "democracy" is an abbreviation for "liberal democracy," that the liberal state came first, and that modern democracy entered the real world by becoming "liberalized."[1] Is my focus a narrow or partial one? And am I leaving out something, some part of the real world? These are the two queries that are confronted in this chapter.

My perspective is a liberal-democratic one. If it is a narrow or even a one-sided one, then there must be another perspective, a *non* liberal-democratic one. Is there? The question is addressed, to be sure, to the pace-setting authors, to the thinkers who have made history. With regard to a nonliberal democracy, the author who comes to everybody's mind is Marx. However, Rousseau is also frequently brought into the picture.

To begin, then, with Rousseau, can it be said that he provides a *counter-ideal,* an ideal that negates the one of liberal democracy? If the question is so phrased, we might be tempted to answer in the affirmative. But if we ask, more pointedly, whether Rousseau conceived and proposed a *freedomless* democracy, a democracy that does not value freedom—and specifically the "law protected" freedom that liberalism does protect—then the answer is unhesitatingly no. Recall how Rousseau posed the problem of his ideal city: "to find a form of association which will *defend* and *protect* every member belonging to it, and in which the *individual,* while uniting himself with all the others, will obey only *himself* and remain *free* as before."[2] The terms that I have italicized—the concepts of defense, protection, individual, obedience to oneself, freedom—are the basic ones of the liberal conception of life. Again, when in the *Social Contract* Rousseau put to himself the question, "In what precisely does the greatest of all benefits consist, such that it should be the object of

450

all legislation?" his reply was: "It reduces itself to two principal objectives, liberty and equality." And for Rousseau the latter objective was an implication of the first: One should pursue equality, he said, "because liberty cannot exist without it."[3]

There is not a grain of evidence that supports the contention that Rousseau, via his notion of the general will, made "the criterion of democracy the achievement of ends," thus establishing an alternative, nonliberal-democratic, interpretation of democracy.[4] Talmon imputes to Rousseau the fathering of totalitarian democracy; but this was an unintended consequence and, indeed, the outcome of a more general perfectionistic pattern.[5] Whenever Rousseau is displayed as a theorist of illiberal democracy, what is actually displayed are the loopholes in his theory. Let it be added, in fairness to Rousseau, that his alleged errors are, far more often than not, errors of his interpreters. It is we, some two centuries later, who amplify the weak points of Rousseau's construction by projecting into a historical vacuum a recipe conceived for a small, homogeneous community. Of his own accord, Rousseau put democracy where Montesquieu put the constitution; indeed, two very different solutions, but aimed at the very same end: protecting the liberty of the individual from oppression.[6] Rousseau did require direct democracy to take the place of liberal *garantisme*. However, since Rousseau unwaveringly stressed that his democracy was inapplicable to large states, we can only conclude, on his own premises, that with respect to large republics we have no choice: The insufficient and unsafe solution, liberal *garantisme*, is still better than nothing. Rousseau's witnessing cannot be stretched, if one wishes to stretch it, beyond this conclusion.

We are left with Marx. Here I propose to confine my analysis to Marx's *ideal;* the linkage between the ideal and its means will be assessed in the next section. Does Marx's good society—what he called full communism, or communism for short—express a counter-ideal? Let me defer the answer to the end of the analysis. At the outset, let it simply be pointed out that while Marx's notion of freedom is certainly not the one of liberalism, nonetheless he sought freedom, indeed "absolute" freedom. His ideal society (communism) represents the most extreme version of a pure and simple libertarian society.

In order to unravel the many underlying intricacies of the ultimate vision of Marx it is well to begin with how he conceived democracy. Up until his conversion to communism in 1845, Marx used the term democracy (in a standard meaning) appreciatively.[7] After 1845, however, the Marxian usage became ambivalent. In his theoretical writings the word seldom appeared, and it is clear that to Marx "democracy" was inferior to "communism." What disturbed Marx probably was that democracy implied *kratos,* power, whereas communism is power-free: as the wording says, communism is a state of commonality, a *Gemeinwesen,* in which any and all *kratos* has withered away. Concurrently the emphasis shifted on the identification of democracy with a state-dominated society, and specifically with "bourgeois democracy," a state that still oppressed the proletariat. On the other hand, in the exoteric writings, the ones that appealed to the general public, Marx continued to use "democracy" not only in a positive sense but also as a quasi synonym for communism. This was the case in the 1848 *Manifesto* and in *The Civil War in France* of 1871. These happen to be the two writings of Marx that have centrally affected the political course of Marxism, not only because they are among the relatively few ones published during Marx's lifetime, but also because they are the only writings in which the mature, "official" Marx does outline the traits of his ideal society. On all these considerations it is appropriate to conclude, then, that Marx did not entirely rule out "democracy"; indeed, on important occasions he used the word as a permissible descriptor of his ideal.

The standard formulation of the Marxian ideal is found in the *Communist Manifesto,* where "democracy" is defined "an association in which the free development of each is the condition of the free development of all."[8] How are we to explicate this formula? Since the *Manifesto* largely puts in clear and concise language the thoughts that Marx and Engels had cumbersomely elaborated in the *German Ideology* of 1845-46, let us first look into this text. The passage that goes to explicate the formula of the *Manifesto* is this: "In communist society, where nobody has one exclusive sphere of activity but each can become accomplished in any branch he wishes, society regulates the general production and thus makes it possible for me to do one thing today and another tomorrow, to hunt in the morning, fish in the afternoon, rear cattle in the evening, criticize after dinner, just as I have in mind, without ever becoming hunter, fisherman, shepherd, or critic."[9] No doubt, here the world of the future is pictured with disarming libertarian candor. Was this the naiveté of youth? Hardly so, because the substance of this passage bears on the division of labor and affirms that freedom (full and true freedom) requires its negation. As long as we are assigned to and constrained by "one exclusive sphere of activity," we are unfree. Now, the aversion to the division of labor precedes, in Marx, the aversion to private property; it also represents the hardest condition to meet. Private property can be abolished by decree; but nobody has yet attempted, or even shown how to do away with the division of labor. Yet the point remained a central one in *Capital* and was neatly reaffirmed in the *Gotha Critique* of 1875 as follows: "In a higher phase of communist society . . . the enslaving subordination of individuals under division of labor . . . has vanished."[10] If the ultimate ideal is also the hardest one to implement, then it can be said that communism is, above and beyond the abolition of private property, the abolition of the division of labor.

The pre-1845 writings of Marx permit us, however, to explicate the formula of the *Manifesto* at an even deeper level—indeed, at its ultimate philosophical level. The basic notion is here the one of "alienation," of estrangement. Until Hegel, alienation was largely a theological concept that Hegel himself picked up in his early theological work. And when Marx encountered Hegel (via Feuerbach), the lightning that struck Marx forever was the theme of alienation, of *Entfremdung*. Man, in the Marxian diagnosis, had increasingly come to alienate himself from himself; and if the salvation envisioned by Marx can be compressed in one expression, it is the *overcoming of alienation,* the reappropriation of any and all estrangement. Touching bedrock, this is what communism is all about: *the reinstatement of true and full freedom resulting from the termination of all alienation.*

The foregoing libertarian vision must be immediately qualified by noting that Marx's libertarianism was extrapolitical, that is, neither confined to, nor preoccupied by, politics. As a political thinker, Marx mainly confined himself to forecasting the natural extinction of politics. He was convinced that once his grand economic surgery had been accomplished, humanity's recovery from all the ills with which it had been afflicted would be automatic. His expectation was that "when . . . class distinctions have disappeared, and all production has been concentrated in the hands of associated individuals, *the public power will lose its political character.*"[11] One can say that in political matters Marx was indeed simple-minded; and I would say that for this very reason Marx's ideal was of unbeatable simplicity. Communism adds up to being a pure and simple "harmonious demos." If communism is rendered as "communist democracy" (a rendering that Marx permits, at least as a catchwording), then it can be said that Marx looked toward a stateless, self-governing coercion-free democracy without vertical structures, without power problems, without cleavage or conflict of any sort—in brief, toward the most primitive, simplistic, idyllic administration in common of the communal life.[12]

That Marx basically conceived freedom in opposition to alienation, as being the overcoming of all alienation, and that his libertarianism was extrapolitical, does not settle the problem of whether Marx conceived freedom in an individualistic or a collectivistic manner. Since one is never mistaken if, in order to interpret Marx, one goes back to Hegel, let us reformulate the question thus: Was Marx's freedom of the Hegelian kind? Yes in the tools—no in the conclusion. Hegel's philosophy of the state and of society was constructed stepwise with reference to three levels; and the important distinction for our purposes is the one between the level of the civil society (the "system of needs") and the state level (the level of *Sittlichkeit*). The former was a need-oriented individualistic sphere; the latter was the level at which the individual was called on to merge into the superior morality and universality of the state. Marx challenged this distinction by negating the superior sphere, the one of the state. Hence, the problem of how the individual (the "particular") related to the whole (the "universal") had to be resolved, for Marx, within the ambit of the Hegelian civil society: Marx compressed a two-step process into one. In Hegel the moment of individualism (of the bourgeois) and the moment of wholism or collectivism (as we would say) are analytically separated before being dialectically merged; in Marx they are simply merged, in one blow, into the notion of *Gattungswesen*, of a species-being.[13] It is unnecessary to dwell on the obscurity of this notion; it is sufficient to note that under a dialectical treatment, a dialectical *aufheben*, the individual can be *aufgehoben* into the species either in the sense of being "annihilated" in it (this is the collectivistic reading), or in the sense of being "uplifted" and "maintained" in a superior fashion in it (this is the anti-collectivistic reading). And, of course, one can have both things together.

Marx held on to a man conceived of as a "species being" whenever this anthropology was needed to sustain the picture of a stateless, harmoniously functioning society. But no sooner is this problem disposed of than his ideal of "economic liberation" of man takes on very different features. The rule of a collectivistic anthropology should be that each submits to the whole—and this is the one rule, or criterion, that Marx does not have. In the *Gotha Critique* Marx mentions three criteria: *(a)* to each according to his needs; *(b)* to each according to his work; and *(c)* from each according to his abilities. The first criterion, *to each according to his needs,* assumes a "full communism" in which no scarcity of any kind any longer persists, and thus applies to some distant end state. It is not much of a criterion either, for it simply says that under conditions of abundance and, indeed, of redundancy no distribution problem any longer exists; everybody can freely pick from the social stock of consumer commodities, since there is more than enough for all. The other two criteria are neater ones. Since we have already discussed the work-value principle—of which the maxim *to each according to his work* is a correct rendering[14]—let me simply underscore that this is the Marxian distributive criterion par excellence. This is so not only because it represents the cornerstone of Marx's economic theory but also, as we have just seen, because it is the only one that applies until free picking (according to needs) is made possible in some distant future by the end of all scarcity. The interesting remaining question is: How are we to read the criterion *from each according to his abilities?* What renders this formula a highly telling one is that it is not confined to the transition to communism; Marx explicitly assigns it, instead, to "full communism." The maxim says, then, that even at the end of the process abilities are assumed to remain different. This implies, in turn, that individuals remain different. And the fact is that the collectivistic maxim par excellence, namely, *from each what benefits the whole,* is the maxim that Marx never upholds or even implicitly endorses. There are many possible readings of Marx's three criteria—work-value, need-satisfaction, and according-to-ability—but none of the conceivable readings goes to support the collectivistic, whole-serving maxim.

Am I about to conclude, then, that Marx was ultimately, if only unwittingly, an "individualist"? No, that would be pushing the reading between the lines too far. In his youth Marx had absorbed the message of the Romantic and Hegelian organicism; and there is little doubt in my mind that the anthropology that sustains from beginning to end the ideal society of Marx bears an organic or "organismic" imprint. Marx unwaveringly combated the anarchic ideal and the anarchic version of libertarianism. But Marx equally criticized "primitive communism" because "it negates in all respects the personality of man" and "violently sets aside talent."[15] Without the backing of an organic *Gestalt,* this is a difficult course to steer; but with its backing, there was no reason for Marx to conceive communism as a uniform and uniformity-seeking society; he could equally afford (without fear of yielding to the anarchic view) to conceive communism as a society of differentiated individuals. This is even more the case when an organic totality is dialecticized. As already noted, a dialectical *Aufhebung* accomplishes in one two things: an annihilation that deprives the ego of egoism, and an uplifting that happily conjoins the *ego* with the *alter.* Thus the social individuals of Marx, unlike their predecessors in the rough or primitive visions of communism, still are individuals. His good society does not call for "identical equals." It is, instead, a society in which all the potentialities of human beings are finally "liberated," a society in which, for the first time in history, no limitation is set to human free creativity.[16] As Kolakowski exactly sums it up, the "prime task of socialism is to liberate all the powers latent in every human being and develop his personal abilities to the utmost in the social context."[17]

But when all of the above is acknowledged, we still obtain an *organic individualism* that has nothing to share with *liberal individualism.*[18] The correct conclusion seems thus to be that Marx was able to entertain a libertarian ideal in its most extreme form—and yet different from the anarchic one—because his libertarianism was of the organic kind.

We may now assess the *counter-ideal* of Marx. First, Marx opposed de-mocracy-as-state and bourgeois democracy, but was prepared to concede that communism was "full democracy." Second, Marx fought the freedom of liber-alism, but in the name and for the sake of an infinitely greater freedom. Third, Marx rejected the (economic) freedoms of liberism—freedom of property, free-dom of exchange, etc.—precisely because they appeared to him forms of en-slavement. As we turn from the negations to the ideal stated in the positive, the Marxian good society is a stateless, spontaneously harmonious commu-nity instituted by economic plentiness. Politically speaking, total freedom is achieved (by communism) via the disappearance of politics. Economically speaking, total freedom is achieved (by communism) as a liberation from all economic constraints—and this is akin to saying that the solution lies in the disappearance of economics. Indeed, if there is no "necessity," no scarcity, no need, no *labor* (fatigue, effort, pain), then the realm of economics has withered away just as much as the realm of politics.

As everything melts and withers away, we are simply left with a heavenly city. The counter-ideal actually is a *supra-ideal* that hovers far above the ideals it combats. And the earth is no match for heaven. In order to have a match we must ask: How is the Marxian supra-ideal brought down, from its heaven-ly location, back to earth? That is to say, by what means and ways can the Marxian heavenly city become an earthly one? Before turning in the next sec-tion to this question, the point that bears stressing is that the good society of Marx results from a course of *liberation,* not of equalization. Equality never is, in Marx, the driving force of the process; it is an entailment, an implica-tion. His salvationist message is libertarian, not egalitarian. Marx proposed a counter-ideal that was the libertarian ideal in its most extreme and millen-aristic form. Today, writers who extol a freedomless conception of the good life, who are prepared to sacrifice liberty to equality, are legion. But their credentials cannot be found in Marx. Marx certainly rejected liberal democ-racy, but in the name and for the sake of a total liberation, of a demos freed from everything and absolutely free in everything.

15.2 Democracy and the State in Marx and Lenin

Thus far I have looked only into the ultimate ideal of Marx. But communism is also related by Marx to a set of provisions. And Lenin did inaugurate on earth the Marxian city, in 1917, in compliance with the provisions set forth by Marx. Our inquiry must thus be extended, at the least, to Lenin.

Marx, we have seen, held on (despite mental reservations) to democracy as a good word on important occasions. In the 1848 *Communist Manifesto* the proletariat was assigned the task of arriving "victoriously at democracy," and the association in which "the free development of each is the condition of the free development of all" was called by Marx "democracy." As far as democracy goes, that was it. The *Manifesto* had more to say, however, regarding economic measures. Even if such measures are familiar ones, it is well to recall them: *(a)* expropriation of landed property, *(b)* heavily graduated income tax, *(c)* the abolition of all right of inheritance, *(d)* the confiscation of emigrants' and rebels' property, *(e)* the centralization of credit in the hands of the state, *(f)* centralized control of the means of communication and transportation, *(g)* increase in the number of state-owned factories, *(h)* equal liability of all to labor, *(i)* combination of agriculture with manufacturing industries, *(j)* free public education. Would these provisions, when fully enacted, also and *eo ipso* achieve democracy as defined, i.e., as the freedom of each and all? This inference is certainly permissible. If so, in the *Manifesto* the term democracy has no political referent and indeed no distinctive political meaning.

Nothing was added to the 1848 outline of what was required in order to establish a communist society during the following decades, that is, until 1871. It was the revolutionary experience of the Paris Commune that shifted Marx's attention from economics to politics and, specifically, to how the revolution of the proletariat was to unfold itself. In the writings on the Paris Commune brought together under the title *The Civil War in France,* the political form of the proletarian society took shape as resulting from the following measures: suppression of the standing army, police, and bureaucracy; universal suffrage; brief duration and revocability of appointments; elective judges subject to recall.[19] These measures of the Commune furnished, according to Marx, the "foundations of *true democratic institutions.*"[20] That Marx's account had little to do with what really happened in Paris between 18 March and 28 May 1871, is immaterial. It is also immaterial that Marx was critical of the men of the Commune. The point is that in the text in question he had no reservation whatever about the exemplary value of that event (as he reconstructed it), which attested to the "tendency of a government of the people on the part of the people."[21] The secret of the Commune, wrote Marx, "was this: it was essentially a working-class government . . . the political form at last discovered under which to work out the economic emancipation of labor."[22] It should also be borne in mind that Marx perceived the event as a "communal" experience, a "communal regime" to be multiplied and repeated across all "the great industrial centers of France." As a result, the "old centralized government would, in the provinces too, have to give way to the self-government of the producers."[23]

The interpreters have long been wondering whether this is the "true" Marx. The novelty or the deviation of 1871 does not reside in the elimination of the state, for this is the Marxian stand all along. But should the state be destroyed *immediately* and in its *entirety?* The immediate and wholesale destruction of the state was the thesis of Proudhon and even more consistently of Bakunin. The fact that Marx endorsed the thesis of his enemies in 1871 (as he doubtlessly did) does not detract from the fact that, both before and after, Marx relentlessly attacked it. The crucial implication is that if the state is fully and immediately dismantled, it logically and practically follows that there is no "centralizer" left; hence what has immediately to follow is, inescapably, a fully "decentralized" horizontal society, the literal self-management of the proletariat. However, in the *Manifesto* (as its provisions show) and elsewhere Marx upheld a centralizing state, a state that would expropriate private property and capital owners, and hence a state that concentrates the economy in its own hands. So, what is the import of the writings on the Paris Commune in the overall thinking of Marx? Which is the true Marx?

It seems to me that Marx never was, on the point, clearheaded and of one mind only. Certainly his prevalent thesis is that the state must first be conquered and then maintained, if only transitionally, as the state in charge of the state holdings. On the other hand, the thesis that the state should be smashed (Marx's favorite word was *zerbrechen*) is not confined to the Paris Commune writings. In the *Manifesto* Marx makes reference to "all production . . . concentrated . . . in associated individuals": a doubtless reference, then, to the stateless, decentralized formula loudly underwritten in 1871. Concurrently, the immediate breaking up of the state was the thesis advocated in 1851 in the last chapter of the *18th Brumaire of Louis Bonaparte.*[24] It is difficult to hold, therefore, that the Marx that advocates decentralization and self-management is "occasional" or insincere. Admittedly, this is not the major strand; but maybe it is a minor one because most of his thinking is polemical, that is, because Marx wishes above all to affirm his distinctiveness against Bakunin, Proudhon, and the anarchic doctrine.[25] Be that as it may, the sure thing is that in endorsing the Paris Commune Marx is in perfect tune with his ultimate libertarian ideal. It is not, then, that *The Civil War in France* contradicts the overall thinking of Marx; rather, in his overall thinking there is a standing contradiction. While Marx himself neither confronted nor resolved it, I believe that the interpreter can.

Marx had in mind two kinds of state that he never disentangled: the *political state,* a sheer instrument of oppression, and the *economic state,* the one in charge of the state holdings. The political state had to be conquered and destroyed as quickly as possible. How quickly? In the main (and despite the 1871 writings), not as quickly as the anarchist proposed. In the main Marx held that the force of the state (the "old" state that had been conquered) had to be used against its former users, and therefore that the political state had to survive for the duration of the actual revolutionary process. Even so, the political state was for Marx not only a provisional necessary evil but a mere *aftermath state,* a tail end of the evils of the past. This is, I believe, a basic stand.

The waverings of Marx bear, instead, on the economic state. It is with reference to the latter that Marx holds, more often than not, that a state must survive: the state that "centralizes" in its own hands what was hitherto decentralized in the hands of the capitalists. While Marx upheld an aftermath political state, he never endorsed the *rebuilding* of a new *centralized political state.* What had to be done *politically* was to be done (we shall see shortly) by the revolutionary process itself. But Marx did uphold, more often than not, a *centralized economic state.* What had to be done *economically* had to be done (in his prevailing view) by a proprietor-state of the means of production: a semi-state, if one wishes, but still a state. However, even the *economic semi-state* was to be a relatively short-lived one. It cannot be doubted that in the long or longer run also the economic state was destined to wither away. Marx had no institutionalized and permanent "planned economy" in mind; he never conceived anything else beyond "centralization." That is to say that the centralization that Marx advocated was a *negative centralization,* i.e., a negation (a dialectical negation) of itself; not, then, a centralization that would sustain a new economic Moloch but, rather, a dispossessing centralization conducive to a "natural" economic life (as opposed to a capitalistically distorted one).

While there are indeed two Marx's—the anti-centralist and the centralist —that do contradict each other, the interpreter can resolve that contradiction by showing that *(a)* Marx refuses in principle the political state, even though he readmits it, in practice, as a temporary necessary evil; *(b)* endorses (with exceptions) a partial economic state, though not forever or as a final solution; and therefore that *(c)* Marx ultimately advocates the abolition of the state in its entirety. Ultimately, therefore, Marx is consistent and true to his final ideal when he upholds the Paris Commune as the "political form" of the "economic emancipation of labor." As communism is fully realized, full decentralization is also realized.

We are now in a position to address the notion of the dictatorship of the proletariat. Throughout his copious writings Marx let himself say "dictatorship of the proletariat" just about on six occasions in all[26] and importantly only in the 1875 *Gotha Critique,* where one reads: "Between the capitalist and the communist society there is the period of revolutionary transformation from the one to the other. What corresponds to this is a period of political transition in which the state cannot be anything else than a *revolutionary dictatorship of the proletariat.*" The expression, then, was not used by Marx in 1871. Yet the most famous and ill-famed notion of Marx enters Marxism with reference to the Paris Commune—via Engels, however. It was Engels who, after Marx's death in 1883, concluded his Introduction to the 1891 edition of Marx's *Civil War in France* with these words: "The German philistine has lately been thrown once again into wholesome paroxysms by the expression 'dictatorship of the proletariat.' Well, gentle sirs, would you like to know how this dictatorship looks? Then look at the Paris Commune. That was the dictatorship of the proletariat."[27] Would Marx himself have approved? The *Gotha Critique* and the other rare occasions on which Marx did say "dictatorship of the proletariat" offer no ground for suspecting otherwise. That Marx himself showed no particular liking for the expression attests, if anything, to the fact that it did not have, in his mind, any special meaning. In any event, Lenin cannot be faulted for having largely built his interpretation of Marx (as we shall soon see) on *The Civil War in France* and on Engels's witnessing that the Paris Commune was the dictatorship of the proletariat. The fact is, then, that from the turn of the century onward Marxism does impute to Marx the notion of dictatorship of the proletariat, does elevate it to a key notion, and does assume that such a dictatorship consisted, for Marx, of the measures implemented by the Paris Commune: in essence, and most importantly, the suppression of the preexisting army, police, and bureaucracy.

The crucial question remains: Is a state that cannot be "anything else than" a revolutionary dictatorship of the proletariat still a state? On the basis of the distinction that I have drawn between political state and economic state, it is clear that the dictatorship of the proletariat does not address the latter but the former: the state that Marx signaled for quick if not immediate breaking. Let it also be recalled that Marx *always* resolved the problems of politics by dissolving politics, that is, by the very act of eliminating the state (to be sure, the state as instrument of oppression). On both counts the implication is that Marx did not conceive the dictatorship of the proletariat as still being a state. Marx's dictatorship of the proletariat was not the establishment of a state dictatorship but the destruction of the state by means of the proletariat-as-dictator. Dictatorship, for Marx, was simply another word for "revolution"; it meant only *use of force.* Mind you, not a gentle or limited use of force: Marx intended "terror," a total revolution that was a totally regenerating revolution. His "proletarian army," the proletariat in arms, was both to liquidate its class enemies and to destroy all the hitherto existing institutions. The old

Engels who survived Marx for some twelve years (he died in 1895) possibly came to believe in a natural, peaceful transition to socialism. Marx did not: The revolution was necessary, and the revolution entailed, in sequence, the seizure, utilization and, thereinafter, the smashing of the state (the political state). My conjecture is that Marx used the expression dictatorship of the proletariat as sparingly as he did because his emphasis was on the action, on "revolution." In any event, what is sure is that Marx intended the expression *literally:* not to mean dictatorship in *favor of* the proletariat but the direct exercise of force *by* the proletariat itself.[28] Proletariat, in other words, is the subject.[29] The point bears stressing: The dictatorship of the proletariat was for Marx the actual revolution of the proletariat in arms, nothing other than "the proletariat organized as the dominating class"[30] employing its force to dissolve the state and defeat its enemies — not to remake another state, another instrument of oppression, to which to give itself again.

If a state is still needed in order to run a public economy, the state in charge of the state holdings (the one eminently envisaged in the *Manifesto*) is certainly not, for Marx, the dictatorship of the proletariat. As far as the latter goes, its peculiarity, indeed its anomaly, is precisely that of being a stateless dictatorship. "The Commune," Engels pointed out, "was no longer a State in the proper sense of the word."[31] Lenin confirmed in 1917: "The Commune ceased to be a State . . . in the place of a special repressive force, the whole population itself came onto the scene. All this is a departure from the State in its proper sense. And had the Commune asserted itself as a lasting power, remnants of the State would of themselves have 'withered away' within it."[32] The gist is this: The dictatorship of the proletariat is in Marx the emergency self-government (for the period of overt class war) of the proletariat itself, and nothing more.

We may now turn to Lenin. It was especially in *State and Revolution* that Lenin set for himself the task of providing the authentic reading of Marx's ideas on democracy, the state, and the dictatorship of the proletariat. The contention often goes that Lenin betrayed Marx. On the crucial point of how the party relates to the proletariat, I believe that he did. Interestingly, this is the one point on which *State and Revolution* is silent. In this text Lenin attempts above all to bring together and systematize Marx. By doing so Lenin brings out — unwittingly, to be sure — that Marx cannot be streamlined, let alone systematized. It is precisely because Lenin reads Marx very well that he ends up with producing a masterpiece of elusiveness.

One may impute the disorder and obscurity of *State and Revolution* to haste. The pamphlet bears the closing date of August 1917 and was written between the February 1917 "first revolution" of the Liberals (the *Kadets*) and the October Revolution, the one that Lenin was about to unleash and win. Yet *State and Revolution* stands far above these contingencies.[33] It represents the major and last attempt at establishing how Marx really intended, when it comes to politics, the deployment of the victory of the proletariat. The last attempt because from that year onward the innocence of theorizing would have been lost forever. Lenin himself would soon have to reckon with, and bow to, the force of facts. During the summer of 1917, however, he could still afford to establish, alone with himself, the orthodoxy. That he did so in haste does not imply that he would have done better without haste. Lenin did very well—within the constraints of what Marx had said, gainsaid, and left unsaid. The question of democracy is examined by Lenin in relation to three phases: the capitalist, the socialist (inferior or incomplete communist phase), and the communist. This tripartition should not make one believe that the discussion proceeds in an orderly fashion and that Lenin illustrates three notions of democracy, one for each context. To the contrary, the discussion proceeds haphazardly, and in order to unravel the tangle it is helpful to distinguish between a basic idea and a series of minor strands.

Basically, the idea of democracy was associated in Lenin with the existence of the state. Democracy, he wrote, "is a form of the State, one of its varieties." Which form? Which variety? To Lenin it did not matter. To him the state, any state, was "an organization of violence for the suppression of some class"; it was a "special apparatus for coercion," or a "special machine for repression."[34] But if this is so, then "democracy" does not qualify any specific type of state: All states are alike, they all oppress the demos, and they all are antidemocratic. It should follow that in this connection it is useless to concern oneself with democracy. If the notion of democracy still retains a meaning, one must seek it elsewhere, outside the realm of the state. Not so. To Lenin that "democracy equals state" was the basic, steadfast, and unchanging association. His leitmotif was: Since the state is bad, democracy is bad too. From the premise that democracy "is a form of the State, one of its varieties," Lenin cavalierly drew the conclusion: "Consequently it, like every State, represents . . . the organized systematic use of violence against persons."[35] Therefore—and this was the gist of Lenin's argument—democracy is to be destroyed by the same token by which the state is to be destroyed.[36]

The significant point about this demonstration is that Lenin never indicated that in speaking of democracy-as-state, and thus of democracy as something to be rejected wholesale, he was alluding to bourgeois democracy. Lenin admitted in subordinate hypothesis that democracy is also something else. But he did not say that his criticism of democracy qua state system ended where the capitalist conception of democracy ended. He spoke of democracy as the "organized systematic use of violence" in the absolute, as if to say: This is an intrinsic characteristic. We shall see why. At the moment it is of interest to note that his conception should have brought him to a swift, clear-cut conclusion: that he repudiated democracy and that communism had nothing to do with democracy.

But when Lenin came to the second phase, the dictatorship of the proletariat, he changed his tune. He maintained that the dictatorship of the proletariat was "more democratic" than bourgeois democracy. If he meant that in this case the exercise of violence was more intense and systematic than before, one cannot object; his logic would be faultless. But instead he now used "democracy" in a different and positive sense. In a capitalist society, Lenin argued, democracy is democracy for a minute minority; whereas the dictatorship of the proletariat is a democracy for the vast majority, and is a dictatorship only as regards a minority of (former) oppressors. The text goes thus: "The dictatorship of the proletariat, i.e., the organization of the vanguard of the oppressed as the ruling class for the purpose of suppressing the oppressors, cannot result merely in an expansion of democracy. *Simultaneously* with an immense expansion of democracy, *which for the first time* becomes democracy for the poor, democracy for the people, and not democracy for the money bags, the dictatorship of the proletariat imposes a series of restrictions on the freedom of the oppressors, the exploiters, the capitalists. We must suppress them . . . their resistance must be crushed by force; and it is clear that where there is suppression, where there is violence, there is no freedom and no democracy."[37]

The passage is interesting for three reasons. First, Lenin's touch on the party's role is here a very light touch; the "vanguard" is displayed as the mere "organization of the oppressed"– a far cry from how Lenin had conceived the party on many other occasions and as far back as 1902. Since this is the one point where Lenin does "betray" Marx, a short digression is in order. Marx was not a party man. He participated in party-like organizations for a few years only, first in the Communist League that commissioned the 1848 *Manifesto,* and subsequently in the First International between 1864 and 1873. With regard to the latter, Marx stood for a democratic, open organization based on majority vote; and he would later criticize Lassalle and the German Social-Democratic party for being too disciplined and dogmatic. One may suspect that Marx stood for intra-party democracy because he was not in control. On many occasions, moreover, Marx expressed contempt for the peasants and the workers. The fact remains that in the *Manifesto* Marx referred to the communists as the most "conscious" part of the proletariat and that, in his doctrine, he never went further than conceiving both himself and a communist party as midwives of history.[38] Lenin was instead a true party man and forger. In *What Is to Be Done?* (1902) Lenin superimposed the party on the proletariat (whose "spontaneousness," he asserted, led to a bourgeois consciousness), and his "vanguard party" was such not because it represented the proletariat but because it embodied the true and correct ideology. This is much more than changing "class" (the proletariat as a whole) into "classconscious vanguard of the class"; it amounts to establishing that the party is, by definition, the proletariat in its right mind, regardless of what the real proletariat (as it exists) might believe or wish. Gramsci's "new Prince" is thus a direct heir of the Leninist conception of party. In *One Step Forward, Two Steps Back* (1904) Lenin added that, since the notion of building the party from the bottom upward was "false democracy," it followed that the party had to be built from the top downward.[39] Clearly, Lenin does change the protagonist, the very bearer of the revolution. Marx's "class," the proletariat in its entirety, becomes with Lenin the "vanguard" *over it*. This is not Marx, but it is not the Lenin of 1917 either.

I was saying that the quotation from *State and Revolution* was interesting for three reasons. The second one is that here the emphasis tends to be more on the nondemocratic than on the democratic aspect of the dictatorship of the proletariat. And the third one is that now Lenin means by democracy the opposite of what he did before. In effect, he says definitely that the use of repression, the use of violence, is not democracy. What, then, is Lenin's laudatory interpretation of democracy? The quotation shows that now Lenin is using democracy in its literal sense of power of the people, and that democracy is associated with liberty. If we search the entire booklet carefully, we shall find here and there, incidentally, those features that are familiar to us: that democracy is equality, that it is subjugation of the minority to the majority, and even the proposition that "we cannot imagine democracy, even proletarian democracy, without representative institutions."[40] All this, it is true, is conceded in passing, somewhat reluctantly, and always surrounded by evasions and reservations.[41] The fact remains that we find in Lenin a positive meaning of democracy only to the extent that he associates the term with its traditional "bourgeois" connotations. But with a paradoxical twist: To the democracies of the Western type, Lenin applies the characteristics of dictatorship (restriction of liberty and use of force), whereas to the dictatorship of the proletariat, he attributes the characteristics of what Westerners call democracy (liberty for the vast majority).

One might object that this is not a paradox because, even if Lenin's exposition is hard to follow, the substance is that ours claim to be democracies but are not, whereas in socialism our falsehoods become true, since in the dictatorship of the proletariat the vast majority has the power and the liberty. We need not ascertain whether these are the facts, for the fact is that this was not at all Lenin's logic. If it were, then in the third phase, that of communism, Lenin should have said that with the withering away of the dictatorship of the proletariat true and complete democracy would be achieved. Neat and simple. Not so. As soon as Lenin puts his foot into the realm of the future, he shuffles the cards again. Read this: "Only in communist society, only then 'the State ceases to exist,' and it 'becomes possible to speak of freedom.' Only then will there become possible and be realized a truly complete democracy, democracy without any exceptions whatever. And only then *will democracy begin to wither away*. . . . Communism alone is capable of giving really complete democracy, and the more complete it is, the more quickly will it become unnecessary, and wither away of itself."[42] The thesis now is that communism will cause even the truly complete democracy to wither away. Clearly, Lenin is returning to the primary association, that is, to the thesis that the existence of democracy is tied to the existence of the state. And that is why Lenin, when he repudiated democracy-as-state, was very careful not to place this meaning in the context of bourgeois democracy.

At this point, however, Lenin has to dismiss a democracy about which he had shortly before (with reference to the dictatorship of the proletariat) spoken favorably. Therefore, he mitigates his tone, mixing together the basic no with a yes dictated by circumstances. Prima facie, Lenin says and gainsays. But in substance he supports the no. Lenin's ultimate ideal is a suppression of the state, which, by reason of his *idée fixe* that democracy equals state equals oppression, is the elimination of democracy as well. He warned: "It is constantly forgotten that the abolition of the State means also the abolition of democracy; that the withering away of the State means the withering away of democracy." He insisted: "The more complete the democracy, the nearer the moment when it begins to be unnecessary."[43] This game of saying and gainsaying reflects, I believe, an underlying consistency. Communism is "true democracy" because Marx said so on two important occasions, and Lenin had to say what Marx said. But Lenin was not convinced. He sensed, one suspects, that he had succeeded in identifying democracy in a positive fashion only by the same criteria that are valid for bourgeois knowledge. For its part, Marxism as anti-bourgeois knowledge offered him only criteria for refuting democracy. Therefore Lenin rebels, in the final analysis, at the idea of bringing communism back to democracy, even to true democracy.

In the adding up, then, Lenin had to perform as circuitously as he did. In the context of bourgeois democracy, democracy (since it exists only for the few) *does not exist* by definition; in the context of the dictatorship of the

proletariat, there is more democracy than before (which is no large concession, since before there was none at all), but all the same real democracy still
cannot exist; and in the context of communism, democracy *should not exist*
because it is superfluous. "Democracy" bounces from one phase to the next
phase; and when it reaches the final stage, one is told that there is no further
point in bothering with it. Basically, democracy means to Lenin exactly the
same thing as dictatorship (exercise of force and repressive violence); in the
context of socialism, democracy means what it means for the capitalists; and
in the context of communism, it means nothing.

Now, all of the foregoing is Marx, that is, based on Marx. The difference,
aside from emphasis, is that when the bits and pieces of Marx are pieced
together, we are left with a monument of obfuscation and evasiveness. It is
small wonder that whoever is brought up in the Marxist-Leninist tradition
understands near to nothing of the liberal democracy that he so much despises
and rejects. Nonetheless, to the extent that "democracy" had, either in Marx
or Lenin, a positive substance and meaning, it is the same meaning given to
the word by liberal democrats. When other meanings are intended, they are
derogatory ones; and when democracy is finally resolved into communism,
the word retains no meaning at all. The pyrotechnic display of Lenin admir-
ably suits, however, the purpose of enabling the Marxist-Leninist to argue
that he is always, automatically, democratic (or more democratic) than his
opponent and, conversely, that his opponent is always, automatically,
nondemocratic. But the expediency value of Lenin's piece of bravura will become salient only decades later. In the summer of 1917 it was not "democracy"
but the entire blueprint of *State and Revolution* that was about to be set in
motion.

While the word democracy has been my thread, it is obvious that Lenin
had far more pressing and important matters in mind. In 1917 he was asking
himself once again what to do with the state and what was the dictatorship
of the proletariat — and this is to ask *how* the revolution, the action, is to unfold. In *State and Revolution* Lenin brings Marx together under the searchlight
of what is to be done. He is not interested in Marx as a thinker but in the revolutionary Marx, in what Marx had to say regarding *the means,* the actual
implementation and achievement of socialism. This is what *State and Revolution* — as the title clearly says — is eminently about. The extraordinary thing,
if one pauses to reflect, is that on the very eve of a revolution that Lenin was
on the verge of winning he was still buying wholesale the program of action
that Marx had derived from the experience of the Paris Commune. The months
that followed amply attested to the fact that Lenin truly believed in his Marx.
But the locomotive of history almost immediately began to make a U-turn.

As Lenin conquered and dismantled the tsarist state, it was not the theory that shaped the practice but the practice that swept away the theory. Let this be stressed: It was the very "revolutionary theory," the practice-oriented one, that backfired and blasted into Lenin's own hands. The only recipe that worked, that passed into reality, was the non-Marxian one: the party as Lenin had conceived it. All the rest, whatever was sought by Lenin in Marx's name, did not happen and actually materialized in the reverse. The withering away of the state lasted from 7 November 1917 until 19 July 1918 (when the new constitution came into effect). By March 1921 it was the workers' control in industry that had withered away, and the Leninist state acquired its constitutive characteristic: It was already an oppositionless, full-fledged dictatorial state. Between 1922 and 1924 the apparat state slipped from the enfeebled hands of Lenin into the heavy ones of Stalin; but, in truth, it already was an unshakable apparat state. And the hitherto banned word "state" was officially reinstated in the 1923 constitution, where one reads that the "Union of the Soviet Socialist Republics is a single Federal State." What stood behind the word was (in Lenin's own expression) a "bureaucratic cancer" that, far from withering away, was in the process of devouring the creature to which Lenin had given birth. Lenin was spared only the sight of a rampant, omnipotent police establishing itself as the very pillar of the ironically called State of the Soviets. But that too was soon to come.[44] The heavenly city of Marx was descended by Lenin on earth; but the transplant implanted an inferno.

15.3   *Popular Democracy*

As regards the notion of democracy, the twenty years between Lenin's death in 1924 and Stalin's sweep over Eastern Europe at the end of World War II are uninteresting. Lenin leaves us, we have seen, with a pyrotechnic display that puts the Marxist-Leninist always on the "more democratic" side of the battle; but this was to be grasped from the late 1940s onward. Under Stalin's regime the exercise was pointless, since democracy was simply a banished word—until 1945. In that year, however, a new label was coined and launched: popular democracy. We may resume our thread from there.

To be exact, "popular democracy" was applied to the East European countries under Soviet control, not to the Soviet Union itself.[45] World War II was won in the name of democracy; nor was dictatorship quite the right word to advertise (no matter how many qualifications were attached to it) at a time of liberation from dictatorships. Popular democracy was thus the "good wording" that the circumstances required or at least recommended. An additional reason for the coining of a new label was that since the Soviet Union had labored for decades in establishing "socialism," it could not be, in the Soviet perception of matters, that socialism could be established overnight in other countries. The understanding thus was that while socialism was already affirmed, already a firm reality in the guiding state, "popular democracies" were something less. Yet once we grant that copies are not as good as the prototype, copies also speak for the original. I shall, therefore, employ the label somewhat extensively, that is, also for the purpose of revisiting the state of affairs in the Soviet Union.

It is self-evident that "popular democracy" is a verbal redundancy. Since the word democracy already means, by itself, popular power, the new coinage must be rendered in full as "popular power of the people" or, if one wants to be facetious, *bipopular power*. Marx observed that "it is not by linking the word people and the word State in a thousand ways that one will make the solution of the problem a hair's breadth nearer."[46] Similarly, it is not by saying "popular democracy" or (why not?) "popular democracy of the people" that the problem will be changed by a hair's breadth. The last expression would be doubly tautological but would not for this reason indicate a differentiating characteristic of *tripopular power* with respect to the point of departure, the pure and simple concept of democracy. Of course, one can say that "popular" is introduced in antithesis to, and in order to mark the difference from, "capitalist." But this is a feeble defense. Marxists say anyhow, and have said for well over a century, "capitalist democracy" in order to leave "democracy," the true or authentic one, to their own consumption. On this score the new label hardly finds a justification. Does, then, the label stand for direct democracy, i.e., the superseding of representative democracy? No. Since Lenin had been very clear about what direct democracy meant, on that score he had produced a damage beyond repair. Direct democracy consisted, for Marx, in what the Paris Commune did; and Lenin repeated Marx to the letter. Hence, in the face of totalitarian planning and a rampant total bureaucracy, even a purely nominal, a purely facade resurrection of "direct democracy" appeared, in the 1940s, unthinkable. To be sure, if naive Westerners read popular democracy to mean a direct, or more direct, or participatory democracy, so much the better. But this was not how the label was explicated by its original propounders.[47] Even so, it is clear that the label is, and intends to be, suggestive of a *greater democracy*. Can this suggestion be sustained?

For reasons that will soon be apparent, the question is best answered on structural grounds and should thus be reformulated as follows: What are the real-world characteristics of so-called popular democracies? In particular, are they structurally any different from the real-world features of the prototype, of the guiding "socialist" state? The East European regimes are not different from the Soviet Union with respect to the characteristic "dictatorship"; that is, all the polities that claim to be communist, or moving toward communism, are all dictatorships—and this structural feature, being the common one, will be looked into in the next section. However, so-called popular democracies differ from the Soviet prototype with respect to another structural characteristic: They do not, or may not, enforce unipartism—the single-party monopoly —as rigidly as the guiding state does. Their distinctiveness resides in this feature.

The Soviet Union itself is a single-party state that allows voting only on a single, party-dictated list of candidates. The argument is, in this respect, that multipartism (Western bourgeois democracy) corresponds to a society of classes and, therefore, that multipartism becomes unnecessary once classes are abolished. Actually, a classless society entails that everybody comes to be of the same opinion; hence, it is unipartism that expresses true democracy.[48] Kelsen shrewdly formulated the objection by pointing out that if "a political party were nothing but 'a part of a class,' and if more than one party could only exist where antagonistic classes exist, there would be no reason not to grant complete freedom to political parties in Soviet Russia."[49] Conversely, "if one asserts that . . . 'the Soviet Union is a classless society' one must conclude . . . 'therefore the Soviet Union must not display *any* party.'"[50] Let it also be pointed out that the Soviet theory mirrors the ever-returning ideal of a monochrome world, and that a return is thereby made to the old position that variety is incompatible with authority, that only unanimity and not dissent can be the safe basis of the state. Be that as it may, the point of interest is that the Soviet Union has allowed some kind and degree of party multiplicity to the East European regimes. Why so? And to what degree?

Taking a step back to the 1945-48 years, the fact that Eastern Europe was occupied by Soviet troops implied that the Marx-Leninist theory of revolution did not apply as envisaged. Indeed, a violent, revolutionary seizure of power was not only unnecessary but tactically unwise. Remember, also, that a number of East European countries had had, in their past and unlike Russia, a liberal-democratic experience. On their liberation it was only natural for a multiplicity of parties to emerge in Czechoslovakia, Hungary, Poland, and East Germany. On all these counts the immediate postwar governments did materialize as coalitions ("national fronts" or national unity fronts) in which bourgeois parties did participate, at the outset, on a somewhat equal footing. Their equal (if conditioned) footing lasted only a few years. But when the communist takeovers or coups took place, it appeared, or had been discovered, that some parties could be permitted to survive; they did no harm while maintaining a semblance of "democracy" on display. It should be clearly understood, however, that from 1948 onward no "secondary party" has ever been permitted to compete oppositionally with the Communist ruling party. To be given a share in the distribution of posts does not entail that the power is also shared—it is not. Even when the aforesaid secondary parties have not been mere sham, puppet parties, what has emerged is, at best, an arrangement that I have called "hegemonic."[51] Nor can the revolts in Hungary, Czechoslovakia, and Poland be attributed, not even in small part, to the existence of hegemonic arrangements. The East European regimes are indeed full of cracks; but their cracks do not result from relaxations of the uniparty straitjacket.[52]

All in all, the variance in party structure—the fact that satellite parties may be tolerated and licensed by the master party—has been of no practical consequence. In practice the existence of more than one party amounts to pure and simple window dressing or to little more than that. Nor does the toleration of secondary, satellite parties affect principles. In the Soviet theory, "popular democracy" is inferior to "socialism," just as socialism is in turn inferior to "communism" (when fully achieved). Hence, the allowing of some facade multiparty outlet simply attests to a non-achieved classless society, to the fact that the guided states are lagging behind, are only imperfect copies, of the guiding state. Insofar as the theory goes, the "conclusion can only be . . . that the ideal of a people's democracy can be no contribution to a new theory of democracy, or to supplementing the older theory of democracy."[53]

15.4   *The Theory of Democratic Dictatorship*

As one looks at the real-world structural features of the so-called socialist countries, their truly central feature—the dictatorial structure—allows for no variance. All the communism-pursuing countries around the world are, on their own admission, dictatorships. Of course, their claim is to be dictatorships *of* the proletariat, and the implied claim is thus that they are *democratic dictatorships*. It is time to assess what can be made of such a claim.

We already know how "dictatorship of the proletariat" was intended by Engels and, in Marx's name, by Lenin. A dictatorship is *of the proletariat* if, and only if, it is not a dictatorship *of the state*. This is a peremptory condition—also for Lenin. When Lenin made reference to the dictatorship of the proletariat, he set aside the vanguard function of the party. Also for Lenin a dictatorship of the proletariat had to be, if democratic, a dictatorship of the class, of the proletariat in its entirety, of the proletariat in person.[54] The reason that makes the dictatorship of the proletariat "democratic" is, in effect, this: An "outward dictatorship" employing violence against the minority of the former oppressors is an "internal democracy" for the majority, for the proletariat itself. This is, in Lenin's own argument, the condition that enters "democracy" into the picture. Therefore, and clearly, on Marx's and Lenin's own criteria what at present exists in the communist countries is definitely not a democratic dictatorship. Since the state has grown a hundredfold, Marx and Lenin would doubtless have to admit that what actually exists is a state dictatorship, or *a dictatorship pure and simple*.

What is a dictatorship pure and simple? Marxists tend to dodge the question. When they realize that they cannot hold on to the dictatorship *of* the proletariat fiction, they fall back on a second line of argument: Dictatorship for dictatorship, they say, the one of the proletariat is more democratic than the one of the bourgeoisie.[55] However, as stated the argument does not hold, for no dictatorship *of* the proletariat has yet materialized; the ones that exist are *state* dictatorships *over* the proletariat. So, how can a nonexistent actually be "more than" something else? A nonexistent is simply *not existent;* it cannot perform "more democratically than," because it has yet to begin to perform. The argument can make sense only if restated, in full, as follows: Since the proletariat everywhere is, without exception, under the clutch of a dictatorship, the communist (nonbourgeois) dictatorship over the proletariat is better than, and preferable to, the bourgeois (capitalist) dictatorship over the proletariat. As restated, the argument is permissible because we now seemingly have a comparison among existents, and because "more democratic" has been ruled out *ex hypothesi* and replaced by "better than."

But if the argument is now permissible, is it plausible? On what evidence has the Soviet dictatorship been better than the bourgeois dictatorships? Khrushchev's estimate was that Stalin "liquidated" during the 1930s some 8 million people; and this is a very low figure.[56] Notice also that Stalin's purges and deportations had nothing to do with "war communism" or with the civil war; it was a peacetime, cold-blooded massacre. Now, the alleged dictatorship of the bourgeoisie never (and nowhere) exterminated anybody, never deported millions of people to concentration camps, never terrorized the citizenry by means of an omnipotent secret police, and indeed cannot imprison or condemn with secret and sham trials. Lenin declared the freedom of the press a "bourgeois deceit," the Menshevik newspapers were closed down as early as 1919, and no press other than the official one has reappeared since. Trade unions were immediately regimented as "state organizations" and remain such to date. Universities lost their autonomy in 1921, and education has ever since been "indoctrination" of the sole truth embodied by the party doctrine. By and large, "opposition thought" was already suppressed by 1920, and since that time the Soviet system has been a system of "thought control."[57] Now, and once again, no bourgeois parliamentary state has ever done any of this.

The alleged dictatorship of the bourgeoisie allows all the freedoms that Lenin, let alone Stalin, canceled out of existence. Dictatorship for dictatorship, there is no doubt about it: It is the bourgeois dictatorship that has been and is incommensurably better, incommensurably milder—in short, an infinitely lesser dictatorship.

Of course, the retort to the above is that I miss and misunderstand the Marxist meaning of "dictatorship." Let us come to that. Marx, Engels, and Lenin did speak of the bourgeois state as a dictatorial state; but on account of its being *bourgeois,* not on account of its *structure.* As a rule, the founding fathers used the word dictatorship as a synonym for exercise of violence and/or defined the term sociologically. The latter was certainly the case with reference to the dictatorship of the bourgeoisie. This expression did not make reference to a form of state but to the imputation that the parliamentary state (as they frequently called it) was in fact a cover-up for the "dictatorship by a class." However, with this class definition of dictatorship we can travel only until the early 1920s. Indeed, in 1920 Lenin already came up with the "scientific" definition of dictatorship that has been generally adopted ever since. "The scientific term dictatorship," he wrote, "means nothing more nor less than authority untrammeled by any laws, absolutely unrestricted by any rules whatever, and based directly on force."[58] This does not deprive Marxists of the right to define a dictatorship *also* on sociological grounds. But they can no longer deny that "dictatorship" *also* points to a form of state, to a political structure. Present-day Marxists definitely know that the term stands not only for "class dictatorship" but also for a state in which the dictator (a single person or a very small clique of persons) exercises absolute power. They definitely know that Stalin, Hitler, and Mussolini are classified as dictators on that account (by class origin, they were all proletarians); they definitely know that dictatorship denotes a system of government *legibus solutus* in which all power is concentrated, unchecked and beyond checking, in the *locus imperii.* They know it so well that their literature endlessly denounces all non-Marxist dictatorships as "dictatorships" in the meaning just defined: as states characterized by an arbitrary, force-based, and oppressive wielding of power.

I asked what pure and simple dictatorship was. It can now be replied that aside from, or in addition to, special meanings, the term has one core meaning for everybody—even for Marxists. It means, quite simply, a power structure that permits absolute rulership. Therefore the conclusion cannot be escaped that the alleged dictatorship of the bourgeoisie (of a class) is an infinitely lesser dictatorship than the Soviet dictatorship (of a state). Actually, the very comparability of the two things comes into question. How can the so-called capitalist states be compared with the so-called proletarian states by saying "dictatorship for dictatorship"? The former are *not* dictatorially structured states; the latter *are* states characterized by a dictatorial structure. Once this very basic difference is established, one can go on to discuss to what extent it is true that within bourgeois democracies the hegemonic class is the bourgeoisie, and whether it is true that within the Soviet-type dictatorship the proletariat is really the hegemonic class—provided that it remains clear that this discussion changes nothing with regard to the form of the state, which remains as it is.

The class definition of dictatorship and the "hegemonic class" issue can make us believe that the question of the form of the state is unimportant, but it does not allow the assertion that the bourgeois democracies are not democracies or that the Soviet dictatorship is not a dictatorship. In particular, the Marxist argument cannot sustain the assertion that there is no difference or little difference between a state in which political power is controlled and shared, and a state in which it is uncontrolled and concentrated. It is furthermore the case that the Marxist sociological notion of dictatorship is irrelevant vis-à-vis the reality born under Marxist auspices. In that reality—says Kolakowski—the "natural progression" has in fact been this: "The dictatorship first exercised over society in the name of the working class, and then over the working class in the name of the party, was now applied [circa 1920] to the party itself, creating the basis for a one-man tyranny." This is a natural progression because it naturally flows from how Lenin had conceived the party since 1902: as a "party distinguished by . . . the conviction that it represents the interests of the proletariat whatever the proletariat itself may think."[59] On this conviction alone, the case for a proletarian hegemony (and, thereby, for the class understanding of dictatorship) was lost and buried before it was even put to the test.

Where do we go from here with regard to the democratic claim of the Soviet, or Soviet-type, dictatorships? We can always defer it, to be sure, to the future. This was how the founding fathers ultimately and fundamentally put it. Indeed, they would not have endorsed the present-day claims of the apologetics of the Soviet system. Engels was very explicit on the point: "It is pure nonsense to talk of a 'free people's State'; so long as the proletariat still uses the *State* it does not use it in the interest of freedom but in order to hold down its adversaries, and as soon as it becomes possible to speak of freedom the State as such ceases to exist."[60] Lenin said it even more clearly: "While the state exists there is no freedom. When there is freedom there will be no State."[61] All of this we already know well. The interesting question is how short the "transitional" dictatorship was supposed to be, or, which is asking the same, how long had the future to be waited for. On the eve of the revolution, Lenin declared: "The proletarian State will begin to wither away immediately after its victory."[62] A year later, in 1918, he conceded that the extinction of the state might require some ten years. In a speech of 1 May 1919, he declared that the majority of the people between thirty and thirty-five years of age would see the dawn of communism. Eventually Lenin went as far as conceding that "ten or twenty years sooner or later make no difference when measured by the scale of world history." But this was his maximal concession.[63]

Needless to say, nothing is easier than to be wrong in time predictions. Still, abundantly more than half a century has gone by, and the future promised by Lenin is farther removed from sight today than it was in the early 1920s. Perhaps the moment has come for asking ourselves whether it will ever be. Perhaps the prophecy *is* undermined by an original sin, by a constitutive error.

I submit that this is the case. The entire construction stands on a highly dubious premise and on an impossible, unworldly promise. The dubious premise is that an ultimate, greater despot is needed to put an end to despotism, that if the bourgeois state is not replaced by a dictatorship, the state as such cannot perish. On this premise we are delivered a dictatorial state. In essence, then, the entire construction hinges on a *promise:* the verbal assurance that the "exercise of violence" will be confined to and limited by the assignment of destroying the classes. But how can a dictatorship be held to a promise? In particular, how can it be held to the promise that it will destroy itself by itself? The reply is unbeatably simple: It cannot. A dictatorship is, by definition, a state *out of control;* it controls its subjects without being controlled by them. Therefore, and patently, with regard to a dictatorship no assurance can ever hold; any promise is void *ex hypothesi.* Since a dictatorship is such in that it allows discretionary and unbounded power, its very nature excludes *a limine* the possibility of assigning it a temporal limit and mortgaging its development. Promising a liberty that must first pass through the tunnel of a dictatorship is like burning the money needed for tomorrow's payment. The credibility of a promise of the sort is just about zero. With this, we are left not only to wonder but even more to despair about human credulity.

15.5 *Democracy and Demophily*

Rather than a counter-ideal, we have found in Marx a "supra-ideal," a flight unto a libertarian heaven where both politics and economics have withered away. We have not found, in Lenin, any concept or definition of "communist democracy." We have only found, in the notion of "popular democracy," a verbal redundancy. Finally, the theory of a "democratic dictatorship" simply does not hold, not even by Marx's and Lenin's own criteria. What is left? The last-resort reply is, in the wording of Bertrand Russell, this: While the Western definition of democracy "is that it consists in the *rule* of the majority, the Russian view is that it consists in the *interests* of the majority."[64] While this solution drops any claim of superiority of one of the two formulas over the other, it does appear to outline an alternative: One democracy asserts demo-power (rule of the people), another democracy provides demo-benefits (interests of the people). What are we to make of this alternative? Does it establish "another democracy"? I very much doubt it.

The Greek tyrant already governed (so he claimed) in the interests of the populace. Enlightened despotism, when enlightened, did govern in the interest of the governed. Present-day democrats sneer at paternalism, although they would not deny that paternalism is benevolent, that it does attend to the interests of a collectivity of beneficiaries. In sum, it is from Plato onward that we incessantly hear about governing *for,* for the sake and benefit of the governed; but this has invariably been the argument in favor of the autocrat. Not government *of* the people, since the people do not know enough to recognize their real interest; but government *over* the people, despite the people, in the *interest* of the people—this is the standard justification of all tyrannies, of all the regimes that are required (*ex defectu tituli,* out of lack of title) to justify themselves.

If real-world democracy were as easy as that, if it consisted only in promising to govern "in the interest of the people," it would not have taken us some twenty-five centuries to establish democracy in deed (not merely in promise). The insurmountable objection to Russell's facile formula is in this invariable rule of life and politics: No interest is ever protected if the interested party cannot decide for itself and defend its interest. Guicciardini brought out the point with unsurpassed conciseness: *Quelle sicurtà che sono fondate in sulla volontà e discrezione di altri sono fallaci*—the assurances (safeties) that are based on the discretionary will of others are deceptive.[65] It is indeed a very, very long way to go from assurances to actual safeties; what matters are the safeties; and there is no safety as long as assurances are entrusted to the discretion of others. John Stuart Mill added (his time was a better one than Guicciardini's sixteenth century) the assertive element: "The rights and interests of every and any person are only secure from being disregarded when the person interested is himself able, and habitually disposed, to stand up for them. . . . Human beings are only secure from evil at the hands of others in proportion as they have the power of being, and are, *self-protecting*."[66]

Let us trust human beings more than Guicciardini and Mill were willing to trust them; let us admit, that is, that demophily—a sincere, authentic, dedicated love for the people—does exist. Even so, there is an abyss between *demophily* and *democracy*. Since real-world democracy consists (this is what renders it real) of a democratic machinery, democracy can do without demophily. If it is implemented by demophily, by good motives, so much the better; but the machinery assures demo-benefits even if demo-love is absent—and this is the *security* that the democratic machinery provides, that gives real, not deceptive, existence to actual democracies. And this is precisely the element that disappears when democracy is defined, purely and simply, as a government in the interest of the people.

In defense of the formula, Macpherson endows it with Aristotelian credentials. Marxists, in his view, speak of democracy as Aristotle did: Their definition is his "original" definition.[67] But this is, to begin with, a strange defense. To Aristotle, democracy was a degenerated form of the polity. Therefore, if Aristotle is summoned as a favorable witness, what should be explained is how Aristotle's badness becomes "goodness" on the basis of the same view, i.e., Aristotle's view. In the second place, Aristotle defined a stateless, direct democracy; and here what should be explained is how his definition is applicable to the most immense of all the states that ever existed. However that may be, Macpherson is, quite simply, untrue to Aristotle. As has been correctly observed, "Macpherson's view that democracy meant originally 'rule by or in the interests of the hitherto oppressed class' is doubtful. It would be a truer account . . . to say that it has meant rule by and *therefore* in the interests of the poor."[68] Aristotle developed his argument causally: He said that democracy was a rule in the interest of the poor (and/or the many) *because* democracy—the direct Greek democracy—was a government *by* the poor, i.e., a self-government *of* the poor. Hence, Aristotle said what has been said ever since: The interest of the poor, or of the many, is affirmed when the poor or the many can themselves affirm it. Aristotle does not support, but indeed disconfirms the notion that a government can be *in favor of* those who are excluded from government. That democracy could be "in the interest of the people" without being people-based is certainly not Aristotle's view.

Reverting to Bertrand Russell, is his alternative correctly formulated? Certainly it says all that can be said on behalf of the Russian view; but it is a distortive oversimplification of the Western view. "Rule of the majority" is the formula at which this work started;[69] and we have come, with reference to Western modern democracy, a long way away from a primitive, initial "etymological democracy." As both its explication and deployment progressed, it became apparent that our democracies have largely shifted from demo-power (democracy in input) to demo-benefit (democracy in output). Therefore, the alternative is not as Russell phrased it. The correct alternative is between a first definition in which democracy is *both* majority rule (in input) and major-ity-interests rule (in output), and a second definition in which democracy is *halved:* an output without input. So, "democracy"—the only one that has been found, thus far, to exist—comprises both demo-power and demo-benefits, i.e., both horns of Russell's dilemma; and what is being opposed to it and proposed as its alternative is only a tail (demo-benefits) without a head (demo-power).

Bluntly put, we have not progressed an inch, in our search for "another democracy," from where we started. The so-called alternative is like the Arab Phoenix chanted in the enchanting verse of Metastasio: *Che ci sia ognun lo dice, dove sia nessun lo sa*—that it exists, everybody says; where it exists, nobody knows.[70] Nobody knows on two counts. The first is that "in the inter-est of the people" is only a promise without warranty. Assuming (for the sake of the argument) that the promise may be honored, in such case what we would have is demophily; and demophily is not, it bears reiteration, democracy. Democracy begins with demo-power and, on that beginning, does not require demophily in order to produce demo-benefits. Demophily is, instead, a sheer possibility. If we are lucky, demophily leaves us with a benevolent despot; but what if we are unlucky? Why should we leave to chance what can be en-trusted to safeguards? To be sure, everything can be said to be possible—in some sense or other of the word. It is possible that the sun will not rise tomor-row. Maybe, but it is highly improbable (with reference to tomorrow). It is possible that a baboon seated in front of a typewriter will produce a novel; but the probability is dismally low. Likewise, it is possible that in a despotic and professedly anti-liberal state the subjects will be pampered by a benevolent despot wholly dedicated to altruism. However, the connection between dic-tatorship and philanthropy is a highly "improbable possible," whereas the con-nection between demo-power and demo-benefits is a built-in, highly probable possibility.

The second count touches bedrock. Possibles and hopes aside, does our Arab Phoenix exist? Revel caustically observes that "unlike capitalism, social-ism . . . does not enjoy the asset of being forever in 'crisis,' because first it would have to exist. . . . Until now the only crisis socialism has experienced is the crisis of non-existence."[71] Revel's point actually adresses the comparison between capitalism and socialism in their respective economic performances; but it can be enlarged and refocused on the liberal versus communist ver-sions of democracy. The question thus is: Does "another democracy," different from and opposed to liberal democracy, have a real-world existence? This is a straightforward question, and yet a question that is systematically circum-vented by the answer that the matter is not of fact but of definition; hence, the Soviet regime exists as a democracy as a function of the Soviet definition of democracy, just like Western polities are democracies as a function of the Western definition of democracy. I am the last person that would belittle the importance of defining—and I shall revert to this shortly. On the point, however, let the point be that not all definitions are equal.

The theory of democracy expounded and discussed in this work contains, it will be remembered, prescriptive definitions *and* descriptive definitions. The two stand side by side, thus allowing a cross-referencing and a linking of the ideal with the real. The linking (and likeness) may be tenuous and, if so, we shall declare: This is a poorly democratic, if not undemocratic, polity. Conversely, we may find sufficient resemblances between the ideal and the real, and in such case we shall say: This is a democracy. Democracies are declared such, then, by *comparing their ideals to their practice,* and on the basis of whether the prescription does translate itself in some conforming manner into the reality. But no such probing can be found or can be pursued with regard to the claim that communist regimes are, by their own criteria, democratic. Here we *always and only find prescriptions*—the description is never provided. Therefore the communist doctrine does not allow for its verification (or falsification). Hence it cannot demonstrate that Soviet-type regimes *exist as democracies* by their own criteria. The criteria themselves do not exist. The claim that communist systems qualify as democracies on the basis of their own definition of democracy is baseless. The communist doctrine simply *smuggles ideals as facts.* This—it must be admitted—is quite a feat, considering that a major claim of Marxism is that it alone achieves the unity of theory and practice. On such claim, Marxism is immediately self-confirming or self-negating, and Marxists should be especially versed in submitting their theory to the witnessing of practice. But this is what they unwaveringly never do.

Bringing my nets ashore, I have held that *(a)* unlikely possibilities are not to be preferred to likely ones, and that *(b)* communist-type democracies do not exist by their own criteria (or their lack). Remember, also, that "another democracy" cannot be contrasted to Western democracy by comparing and pairing an ideal with a reality. The match of facts is with facts, just as the match of ideals is with ideals.[72] But the main point to note before coming to a close is that a theory of democracy—if theory is intended seriously—cannot leave "democracy" undefined. And the minimal requirement of defining is to declare what something *is not,* that is, to declare when a term or concept ceases to apply. *Omnis determinatio est negatio,* every determination involves a negation. A negation is, thus, due. No matter how many people may speak of popular, progressive, or communist democracy, to speak of something does not suffice to prove that such a thing exists. Nobody questions the towering reality of the USSR and of a number of states modeled after it; yet are such states, in any demonstrable sense, democracies? That was the question—and to that question I flatly answer no. It is and remains my stand that the analysis of Western-type democracy coincides with the analysis of democracy *tout court.* "Another democracy" is only, in my probing, a phantom alternative. A name does not suffice to give credibility, let alone reality, to something named democracy.

15.6   *The War of Words*

The discussion conducted so far would have been unnecessary, if not inconceivable, in the 1930s. Neither Stalin nor Hitler nor Mussolini—the standard spectrum of the dictators in the modern usage of the term—made any claim that their regimes were democracies. Actually they scorned "capitalist" democracy, or (as in Mussolini's favorite expression) "pluto-democracy." From the middle of the nineteenth to the middle of the twentieth centuries, the labels liberal democracy and, for short, democracy stood for a finite set of polities, and there was widespread consensus on what the term denoted. Democracies were happy with being democracies, and nondemocracies felt no guilt complex about not being what they were not. What has dramatically changed since 1945 (circa) is hardly the real-world nature and variety of political forms but the value connotation of the word democracy. Democracy emerged from World War II as a good word, a word that elicited praise, indeed a word that *was* praise. Thus the clash of arms had barely ended when a war over the word was started. It was, and remains, a war for winning over "democracy" on one's own side.

Yet, no lesser authority than Karl Popper asserts: "We need not quarrel about words, and about such pseudo-problems as the true or essential meaning of the word democracy. *You can choose whatever name you like* . . . [as] this is not a quarrel about words."[73] Of course the real quarrel is not "about words." But can the substance (the real quarrel) be divorced from the wording? Popper, as well as many other scholars, is ill advised in downgrading the *power of words.* While the quarrel is certainly not about words, it does go on *by means of words.* Words are an inseparable part of what we quarrel about. If ideas have consequences, then words too must have consequences, for the idea is the hand of which the word is the glove. A certain idea is conveyed by a certain word. And to name a thing in a certain way is the same as to suggest how to interpret that thing. Words are not only blinders that lead us to see this and not that, to look here and not there; words are also *thought molding.*[74]

Marx "overturned" Hegel's philosophy; it stood, he claimed, on its head and had to be put on its feet.[75] Since then, we have "overturned overturnings" so many times that nobody any longer quite knows, it would appear, who stands on his head and who on his feet. In vulgar Marxism, thought is a mere "reflection of matter,"[76] that is, ideas are a copy, a sheer epiphenomenon, of the material world. We may make this materialism less vulgar, less heavy-handed; still, there is no denying that historical materialism, or dialectical materialism, is an *Unterbau* philosophy, a philosophy of the subsoil that scorns at "idealists," at the *Oberbau* philosophies that give primacy to ideas. Nonetheless, it is the materialist of Marxist persuasion who has fully grasped the power of words; it is the materialist who really masters, far more than the idealist, the art of persuasion, the ancient art of rhetoric. Conversely, the idealist — he who believes in the intrinsic force of ideas — reveals himself in the test of debate, on the ground that should be his own ground, a poor debater. He is the one who believes in ideas; yet he yields on the language that expresses ideas and is happy with leaving the terminological initiative to the materialist. In a world ever more pervaded by mass media bombardment, in which the "media word" is the fact, he tells us that words are unimportant, that it does not matter which word we use. Who stands on his head, the materialist or the idealist? I cannot tell.

Possibly the idealist (as defined) speaks only to an aristocracy of high-powered intellectuals who cannot be misled by words because they follow the idea, or the concept, under whatever verbal form or disguise. But democracies are not sophocracies, and the demos is not made of high-powered intellectuals; it is made of simpler minds for whom words do matter. The ordinary citizen knows about his and other polities just about what *words* tell him. If a polity is called a "democracy," the ordinary citizen is left to believe, and indeed is entitled to believe, in what the word says. Likewise, if a democracy is called "popular" or "progressive," a normal *animal loquax* is brought to believe that it is such. Or are we demanding of him that he should first study politics for several years and then travel across the world, for another several years, and check in person?

No matter how much we may disagree, on theoretical grounds, on the import of semantics — literally, the indicative function of words — still a theory of democracy must account for "the people" as they are. If, moreover, we do care about them, by the same token we should see to it that the people are not deceived by deceptive words. Difficult? Not at all. A *deceptive meaning* does not assume, and is not established by reference to a metaphysical, ontological, or essentialist *correct meaning*. Even if words had only conventional meanings, even so a word is deceptive — used deceptively — when the speaker does not intend the meanings attached to it by the listeners. If the speaker employs a word whose referents (its real-world counterparts) have none of the characteristics the word semantically conveys (and, therefore, conveyed to the listeners), then the speaker is, wittingly or unwittingly, a deceiver; his usage is incorrect in that it is mystifying. As Jeane Kirkpatrick curtly puts it, whoever associates a slogan like " 'For a Lasting Peace and a People's Democracy' with neither peace nor popular movements nor democracy" is guilty of "corrupting language to obscure reality," of a "systematically perverse use of language."[77] As I was saying, whoever so performs is a deceiver.

To illustrate, suppose that I write a treatise on monarchy in which the monarch is defined, in premise, as a head of state elected periodically by universal suffrage. It is an easy guess that most reviewers would turn me down by noting that I am confusing a monarchy with a republic. It would do me no good to reply that I am entitled to stipulate my own meaning of "monarchy." On the contrary, my best defense would be to say that my reviewers ignore the etymological, literal meaning of monarchy, which is the meaning that I had in fact used: rule by the one. However, that was my initial definition. Suppose now that my treatise ended by defining monarchy as a "government of the people." How would my reviewers react to that conclusion? How many would say that my work is most innovative, creative, and original? My guess is that nobody would say that. Everybody would say, I suspect, that I do not know what I am saying, that "monarchy" can only denote a government over the people exercised by one person (through a court or the agency of the few). Am I finally beaten? Not at all. I had all along a hidden trump. I would get back to my reviewers by asking, Why am I not permitted to do with the word monarchy what everybody has long been doing with the word democracy? This is a good question, and I would not wish my critics to spoil it with a bad answer. Let me reply for them. The answer is this: Monarchy is uninteresting in the war of words, for it is not a word that anybody is interested in winning over. Hence, with "monarchy" the normal rules of intellectual discourse apply; defining at whim is not permitted. Not so with "democracy." The difference is, then, that here we have a word of interest to the war of words.

The war of words bears on their emotive properties.[78] Its basic rule is to conquer the "good words" and shell the "bad words" into the enemy's camp.[79] Lenin mastered this rule to a perfection surpassed only, in imagination, by Orwell's "newspeak." Relatively few people know Russian, and therefore relatively few people know that *bolshevik* and *menshevik* are simply, and respectively, the Russian terms for majority and minority. At the 1903 congress held in London, the Leninist faction lost on the substantive issues but managed to win a small majority in the central committee elected at that congress. In truth, this was the first and last time that Lenin ever obtained a majority within the social-democratic groups (as they called themselves at the time) or in a true election.[80] Yet Lenin seized the word majority *(bolshevik)* for himself and never let it go. It did not matter that the alleged majority never was a real majority; what mattered was the make-believe, the suggestive power of the word. The *mensheviks,* the true majority, lost their first train by giving away the word to which they were entitled.

But there is more to the war of words than this benign illustration conveys. Words—some key words, to be sure—must be drained of all their informative content, let alone their heuristic value. At a minimum, they should have no verifiable meaning; and some special words should be manipulated further, that is, reduced to sheer "signals" that automatically trigger hate-love reactions.[81] The intent is, in essence, to short-circuit thinking, to make sure that the audience should have as little chance as possible to stop to think. To the word warrior, *words are weapons*—words, not ideas. And since the word warrior well knows that in the end what sticks are names (and nicknames), not the demonstrations or explanations given for them, his technique is to coin epithets and repeat them incessantly. The ruse is to label *libeling.* It has been, let us face it, a most effective technique. Would it be a gross exaggeration to say that four words of contempt—"bourgeois," "capitalist," "reactionary," and "fascist"—weigh more heavily on the destiny of our time than all the works cited in this work? I am not sure that it would.

Whether we like it or not—and I certainly do not—the war of words is a reality; and by refusing to confront it we simply allow the word warrior, the war wager, to win. As he advanced, the Western "neutral" scholar withdrew. With respect to the word democracy, his typical answer has been, over the last decades, of this sort: To anyone who defines democracy with reference to its Western exemplars, the "other democracy" is a counterfeit; but to anyone who defines democracy in the Eastern manner, it is our democracy that fails to pass the test. But if this is, as alleged, a "matter of definition," then definitions are to be taken seriously and looked into. However, the more I have been looking for the definition of "another democracy," the less I have found one.

For the sheer sake of the argument, I am prepared to concede that liberty and respect for each individual person are irrelevant to a democracy and to admit that "popular power" is all that is required. But I do not see how one can stipulate a definition such as this: Democracy is a system of decision making in which the demos decides nothing. This is, I believe, a fairly accurate distillation of how the Soviet system actually works. But then, why "democracy"? To deceive? With the term monarchy (my previous imaginary example), nobody would permit an arbitrariness of such magnitude, nobody would admit monarchy to be defined as a government of the people. By the same token, I resist on "democracy." To manifest one's dissent, to transfer one's vote from one option to another, to select freely one's governors, to decide for ourselves what we like and to press for it—all of this may be considered frivolous and unimportant. But if it is unimportant, then neither the *demos* nor its *kratos* are in any way in the picture.

Does all depend on how something is defined? I would say that much depends on definitions, but not all. If the thesis is that everything depends on definitions, then I would reverse it. I would say: Everything depends on *non-defining*. In the case at issue, the alternative of another democracy is not sustained by another definition; it is sustained by indefiniteness. What is all-important, in the war of words, is the pure and simple word, the *undefined word*. Hence I insist that, as a matter of intellectual integrity, we should neither accept nor divulge mystifying words—words that are bound to be deceiving. As a matter of intellectual integrity, it is dishonest to fool people, to call demo-power what is, in fact, *demo-impotence*.

Notes

1. See especially chapter 13, herein.

2. *Contrat,* I, 6 (my italics). For how Rousseau conceived democracy and liberty, see chapter 11, sections 4 and 5.

3. *Contrat,* II, 11. See also Rousseau's Second *Discours.* That Rousseau spoke in the language of individualism has been emphasized by, among others, Leo Strauss, *Natural Right and History* (Chicago: University of Chicago Press, 1953); A. Cobban, *Rousseau and the Modern State;* and in Derathé's works (see nn. 41 and 47, chapter 11, herein).

4. This is the contention of C.B. Macpherson, *The Real World of Democracy* (Oxford: Clarendon Press, 1966), p. 29. That Rousseau theorized an "immobile" democracy governed by unchanging laws (the exact contrary of an end-seeking dynamics) is abundantly documented, I trust, in my chapter 11, herein.

5. Talmon's conclusion reads: "Totalitarian democracy early evolved into a pattern of coercion and centralization not because it rejected the values of eighteenth-century liberal individualism, but because it had originally a too perfectionist attitude toward them. . . . Man was not merely to be freed from restraints. All the existing traditions, established institutions, and social arrangements were to be overthrown and remade, with the sole purpose of securing to man the totality of his rights and freedoms, and liberating him from all dependence." *The Origins of Totalitarian Democracy,* p. 249.

6. As exactly noted by Kelsen, "his attack against the English parliament shows to what degree freedom was for him the foundation of his political system." *Vom Wesen*

und Wert der Demokratie, chap. 1.

7. E.g., in 1843 Marx wrote: "In a democracy the constitution, the law and the state itself are only a self-determination of the people" *(Critique of Hegel's Philosophy of Law).* Marx's entire comment of Hegel's par. 279 (from which I quote) is worth reading.

8. *Manifesto,* II.

9. *The German Ideology* found no publisher at the time, and its first complete edition appeared in 1932. An incomplete one was published by Bernstein in 1903. The quotation is from pt. 1, the section on "Ideology in General, and Specifically German Philosophy." Engels, *The Origins of the Family, Private Property and the State* (1884, rev. 1891), echoed very much, some forty years later, the same theme. As S.A. Lakoff aptly comments, "Marx and Engels apparently felt irresistibly attracted to the notion of paradise regained . . . communism was the original (and idyllic) state of humanity." *Equality in Political Philosophy,* p. 225.

10. *The Gotha Critique* addressed the formation, in 1875, of the German Socialist Worker's party and was first published by Engels in 1891. The quote is from the New York translation of 1938, p. 10.

11. *Manifesto,* II. The most used English translation inexplicably and distortingly reads "a vast association of the whole nation," where the German says *Assoziierten Individuen,* "associated individuals" (as my text reads). See also Marx's reply to Proudhon: "The working class will substitute . . . for the old bourgeois order an association which will exclude classes and their antagonism, and there will no longer be political power, properly speaking, since political power is simply the official form of the antagonism in bourgeois society." *The Poverty of Philosophy* (1847), pt. II, 5.

12. That this was a "primitive" ideal of democracy was underscored by Lenin himself. Polemizing against Bernstein, who had criticized Marx's ideal as a "primitive stage of democracy," Lenin replied: "Under Socialism much of the 'primitive' democracy is inevitably revived, since for the first time in the history of civilized society, the mass of the population rises to independent participation, not only in voting and elections, but also *in the every-day administration of affairs.* Under Socialism, *all will take a turn in management* [government], and will soon become accustomed to the idea of no managers at all. . . . Socialism will . . . create such conditions for the majority of the population as to enable *everybody,* without exception, to perform State functions" *(State and Revolution,* VI, 3; my italics). See also the *Party's Program* of 1919, in which Lenin insisted on the need of having every member of the Soviets participate in turn and always in different capacities to the administration, so that finally the entire population would be included in the state-no-longer-state.

13. See especially Löwith, *Von Hegel bis Nietzsche,* pt. II, chap. 4: "The Problem of Humanity." An excessively broad treatment is the last work of John Plamenatz, *Karl Marx's Philosophy of Man* (Oxford: Clarendon Press, 1975); a too narrow one is Bertell Ollman, *Alienation: Marx's Conception of Man in Capitalist Society* (Cambridge: Cambridge University Press, 1971). See also chapter 14, nn. 31 and 32, herein. The philosophical anthropology of Marx (and his *Gattungswesen*) is expounded especially in *The Jewish Question* of 1843, and in the subsequent *Economic and Philosophic Manuscripts* (1st mns., XXIV).

14. See chapter 14, section 3, where Marx's work-value principle is compared to market collectivism.

15. *Economic and Philosophic Manuscripts of 1844* (3d. mns., add. xxxix). That men remain different, under communism, in their abilities or talents is reaffirmed (we have just seen) in the *Gotha Critique,* and is also a central theme of *The German Ideology,* where one reads: "Only in community *(Gemeinschaft)* do the means exist for every individual to cultivate his talents in all directions. Only in the community is personal freedom possible" (pt. 1, section on "The Division of Labor").

16. The most forthright translation of this vision into a definition of freedom is in *The Holy Family* (1844), where Marx and Engels assert that man's freedom is the "positive power to assert his true individuality" (chap. 6, sect. d).

17. *Main Currents of Marxism* (Oxford: Clarendon Press, 1978), 1:307.

18. D.F.B. Tucker, *Marxism and Individualism* (Oxford: Blackwell, 1980), goes as far as to maintain that Marx is both an "ethical" and a "methodological" individualist that pursues a Kantian-like "autonomy." This interpretation misses the organic-dialectical context of Marx's anthropology.

19. *The Civil War in France,* Address II. I quote from *Capital and Other Writings of K. Marx,* trans. Max Eastman (New York: Modern Library, 1932), pp. 403-5. Lenin summed up the essence of these measures in his first *Letter on Tactics,* April 1917 (with reference to the dictatorship of the proletariat) as follows: "I . . . uphold the necessity of the State in this period, but, in accordance with Marx and the experience of the Paris Commune, not of an ordinary bourgeois parliamentary State, but of a State without standing army, without police opposed to the people, without bureaucracy placed above the people."

20. *The Civil War in France,* in *Capital and Other Writings,* p. 407 (my emphasis).

21. Ibid., p. 412. The fact that a few months later, on 25 September 1871 (see n. 26 below), Marx said that "the Commune was not in a position to discover a new form of class government" hardly implies a retraction; it is, rather, an explanation (that was doubtlessly due) of why the Commune failed and lasted, in all, seventy days only.

22. Ibid., p. 407.

23. Ibid., p. 404.

24. This is a point that Marx calls to the attention of Kugelmann in a letter of 12 April 1871; clearly, an endorsement.

25. The basic difference between the Marxian and the anarchic tempo and sequencing is exactly rendered in a letter of Engels to Van Platten of 1883, as follows: "Marx and I have upheld since 1848 . . . the gradual dissolution and the final elimination of the political organization called State. . . . However . . . the proletariat must first seize the political organized force of the State and use it for eliminating the resistence of the capitalist class and for reorganizing the society. . . . The anarchists reverse the matter. They say that the proletarian revolution must *begin* with the abolition of the political organization of the state." The notes of Marx on Bakunin's book *State and Anarchy* add up to making the same point.

26. Hal Draper, "Marx and the Dictatorship of the Proletariat," *New Politics,* 1962, pp. 91-104, counts eleven "loci in which Marx and Engels used the term." If Engels is set aside, my counting is that the expression appears a first time in the second *Address* of 1850 of the Communist League (where he says, however, "dictatorship of the proletarians"); a second time in the *Class Struggle in France from 1848 to 1850,* but merely in a polemical, anti-Blanquist sense; a third time in a letter to Wedemeyer

of 5 March 1852; a fourth time at a banquet allocution of 25 September 1871, that celebrated in London the seventh anniversary of the International; a fifth time in an article against Bakunin of January 1873 that was published only in Italian (where he merely says that the working class is to replace "the dictatorship of the bourgeoisie with its own dictatorship"); and for the last time, the historically important one, in 1875.

27. In *Capital and Other Writings*, p. 381. The Institute Marx-Lenin of Moscow substitutes "the social-democratic philistine" for "the German philistine." Yet the traditional text seems to fit better in the general sense of Engels's *Introduction*, which refers to the "superstitious faith in the state" that is characteristic of the Germans in general, not only of the social-democratic philistine.

28. This is well confirmed by the fact that Marx and Engels generally used "dictatorship of the proletariat" in counterpoise to the Blanquist conception (a revolution made by a small conspiratorial group, i.e., a putsch), and precisely in order to stress that their notion called for a "class dictatorship," for the domination *(Herrschaft)* of the "entire revolutionary class." See Draper (n. 26 above), esp. p. 95, where Engels is quoted.

29. The ulterior issue is whether the "real subject" is the proletariat *an sich* (as it is in fact) or *für sich,* as an abstract entity called upon to "realize the philosophy" that Marx himself (as a Hegelian "cosmic" interpreter of the *Weltgeist*) expressed. For the latter view, see L. Pellicani, *I Rivoluzionari di Professione* (Firenze: Vallecchi, 1975), esp. chap. 3. However, this issue does not affect the notion of dictatorship of the proletariat but bears on the justification of the vanguard role of the revolutionary intelligentsia, and/or of the party, vis-à-vis the masses (see n. 38, below).

30. It was Lenin who linked this phrase of the *Manifesto* to the dictatorship of the proletariat: "Here we have a formulation of one of the most remarkable and most important ideas of Marxism on the subject of the State, namely, the idea of the 'dictatorship of the proletariat.'" *State and Revolution,* II, 7.

31. Letter to Bebel, 18 March 1875. In the same letter Engels proposed, and here he was doubtlessly true to Marx, "to replace the word State, wherever it was mentioned, by *Gemeinwesen*" (community). Recall that Marx's own term, in the writings on the Paris Commune, was "communal regime."

32. *State and Revolution,* IV, 3. On the point one can go on quoting Lenin at length. Again in *State and Revolution* he wrote: "In the first place, the proletariat, according to Marx, needs only a State which is withering away, i.e., a State which is so constituted that it begins to wither away immediately, and cannot but wither away" (II, 1). A little later he added: "Once the majority of the people *itself* suppresses its oppressors, a 'special force' for suppression *is no longer necessary*. In this sense, the State *begins to wither away*. Instead of the special institutions of a privileged minority . . . the majority can itself directly fulfill all these functions; and the more the discharge of the functions of State power devolves upon the people generally, the less need is there for the existence of this power" (III, 2).

33. Indeed, in Lucio Colletti's view, it is Lenin's "greatest contribution to political theory." *From Rousseau to Lenin* (New York: Monthly Review Press, 1972), p. 224.

34. *State and Revolution,* V, 4; II, 1; and V, 2.

35. Ibid., V, 4.

36. Lenin affirmed it insistently: "Democracy is *also* a State, and . . . consequently democracy will *also* disappear when the State disappears" (*State and Revolution,* I, 4).

Again: "Democracy is . . . the organization of violence systematically applied," and therefore the "suppression of the State is at the same time the suppression of democracy" (IV, 6).

37. *State and Revolution,* V, 2.

38. Reference is strictly made to the doctrine as it stands. As a matter of inference it can and has been often argued that "in spirit" Marx was very close to Lenin and that he would have approved the Leninist conception of party. Since Marx was doubtlessly (as we would say today) an elitist, the inference is plausible. Yet Marx's "elitism" was philosophical, not organizational (see n. 29, above). The point thus remains that the party doctrine of Lenin is not in Marx.

39. For a more extensive overview on the party point, see David McLellan, "Marx, Engels and Lenin on Party and State," in *The Withering Away of the State?* ed. Leslie Holmes (Beverly Hills: Sage, 1981), pp. 7-31; and Klaus von Beyme "Karl Marx and Party Theory," *Government and Opposition,* Winter 1985. See also, and *contra,* L. Pellicani, *I Rivoluzionari di Professione,* esp. chaps. 3-5.

40. *State and Revolution,* III, 3. This, however, is a most rare admission. In the *Civil War in France* Marx observed, obscurely, that "the Commune was to be a working, not a parliamentary body" (in *Capital and Other Writings,* p. 404). Lenin commented: "The way out of parliamentarism is to be found, of course, not in the abolition of the representative institutions and the elective principle, but in the conversion of the representative institutions from mere 'talking shops' into working bodies. 'The Commune was to be a working, not a parliamentary body, executive and legislative at the same time.' 'A working, not a parliamentary body' [Lenin exclaims triumphantly] — this hits the vital spot of present-day parliamentarianism" (*State and Revolution,* III, 3). What this is supposed to mean in practice is what Lenin does not say.

41. See, e.g., in V, 4, the twisted treatment of the notion of equality; and in IV, 6, the specious distinction with respect to the relationship between majority and minority, where Lenin exclaims: "No, democracy is *not* identical with the subordination of the minority to the majority. Democracy is a *State* recognizing the subordination of the minority to the majority, i.e., the organization for the systematic use of *violence* by one class against the other." Thus Lenin deviates toward his favored argument without concluding on the point.

42. *State and Revolution,* V, 2. The two phrases Lenin quotes are from Engels.

43. Ibid., IV, 6, and V, 4.

44. On the early period of the Soviet regime the major study remains E.H. Carr, *The Bolshevik Revolution 1917-23,* 3 vols., and *The Interregnum 1923-24* (New York: Macmillan, 1950, 1954). See also Leonard Schapiro, *The Origin of the Communist Autocracy* (New York: Praeger, 1965); Alfred Meyer, *Leninism* (New York: Praeger, 1962); Adam Ulam, *Lenin and the Bolsheviks,* 2d ed. (London: Fontana-Collins, 1969).

45. The label was first used by Tito merely to mean his own form of the dictatorship of the proletariat; but its more interesting elaboration was, between 1945 and 1947, in the Soviet-occupied countries. An early study is Michel-Henry Fabre, *Théorie des Démocracies Populaires* (Paris: Pedone, 1950). But see, especially, Z.K. Brzezinski, *The Soviet Bloc: Unity and Conflict,* rev. ed. (Cambridge, Mass.: Harvard University Press, 1967); Francis J. Kase, *People's Democracy: A Contribution to the Study of the Communist Theory of State and Revolution* (Leiden: Sijthoff, 1968); and F. Fejtö, *A History of the People's Democracies: Eastern Europe Since Stalin* (New York: Praeger, 1971).

46. The sentence, also quoted by Lenin in *State and Revolution,* v, 1, is in the *Critique of the Gotha Programme.*

47. It is revealing in this connection that in the Soviet *Petit Dictionnaire Philosophique* (French trans., "Editions en Langues Etrangères," Moscou, 1955), the entry "direct democracy" is not even listed. There are instead twelve columns devoted to "popular democracy."

48. I paraphrase from Stalin, *Leninism, Selected Writings* (New York: International Publishers, 1942), p. 395. But Lenin would have agreed.

49. H. Kelsen, *The Political Theory of Bolshevism* (Berkeley: University of California Press, 1948), p. 57.

50. M. Duverger, *Les Partis Politiques* (Paris: Colin, 1954), p. 293. For why "partyless" solutions are replaced by "party-state" systems, see Sartori, *Parties and Party Systems,* esp. pp. 39-42.

51. In *Parties and Party Systems,* chap. 7.

52. The pluralistic looseness, so to speak, of Eastern Europe as measured against the USSR is underscored by G. Ionescu, *The Politics of the European Communist States* (New York: Praeger, 1967). Ionescu emphasizes, at the same time, the "apparat nature" of all the regimes in question. However, my focus is on structural characteristics that may define "democracy," not on the loosening up. See also the overview edited by L. Holmes, *The Withering Away of the State? Party and State under Communism;* and M. Drachkovitch, ed., *East Central Europe: Yesterday, Today, Tommorrow* (Stanford: Hoover Institution Press, 1982).

53. J. Barents, *Democracy, an Unagonized Reappraisal* (The Hague: Van Keulen, 1958), pp. 28-29.

54. It cannot be held that this is true only for *State and Revolution.* Lenin died obsessed by the bureaucratic Leviathan that was growing under his eyes, and his warnings, from 1920 to his death, against "bureaucratic distortion," "the deplorable state apparatus," and the "cancer of bureaucracy" rest precisely on the above premise. On the point, see M. Lewin, *Lenin's Last Struggle* (New York: Pantheon Books, 1968).

55. This was also, remember, Lenin's fallback position, not only in *State and Revolution* (chap. 6), but also in the 1918 pamphlet *The Proletarian Revolution and the Renegade Kautski.*

56. Robert Conquest, *The Great Terror* (New York: Macmillan, 1973), pp. 699-713, estimates that some 20 million people were either executed or perished in the labor camps; Andrei Sakharov suggests from 10 to 15 million; Solzhenitsyn (in the *Gulag Archipelago*) as many as 60 million. Whatever the correct figure, the entire history of humanity never witnessed a blood bath of such magnitude.

57. This is the wording and the thread of Robert Conquest's *The Politics of Ideas in the U.S.S.R.* (New York: Praeger, 1967).

58. "Contribution to the History of the Question of the Dictatorship of the Proletariat" (1920), now in Lenin's *Collected Works* (Moscow: Progress Publishers, 1963), 31:353.

59. *Main Currents of Marxism,* 2:489, 396.

60. Letter to Bebel of 19 March 1875.

61. *State and Revolution,* v, 4. This cogently follows from the premise that "Every State is a 'special repressive force' for the suppression of the oppressed class. Consequently, *no* State is free or a 'people's State' " (1, 4).

62. Ibid., ii, 2.

63. See E.H. Carr, *The Bolshevik Revolution 1917-1923,* 1:241. It should be underscored that Lenin pictured the process of the extinction of the state, regardless of its duration, as a continuous one. This is not only the conception of *State and Revolution* and of the *April Theses,* but also the sense of all of Lenin's subsequent anathemas against bureaucratization. Even when the principle of "socialism in a single country" and the experience of power induced Lenin to postpone the dismantling of the state, he never posited that the state had first to grow, and to decrease only subsequently.

64. *What Is Democracy?* (London: Phoenix, 1946), p. 14.

65. *Ricordi,* 27.

66. *Considerations on Representative Government,* chap. 3 (p. 43 in the Liberal Arts Press ed., New York, 1958).

67. See Macpherson, *The Real World of Democracy,* pp. 5, 12, and passim.

68. Jack Lively, *Democracy* (Oxford: Basil Blackwell, 1975), p. 34.

69. See chapter 2, especially sections 1 and 4.

70. *Demetrio,* ii, 3.

71. Jean-Francois Revel, *The Totalitarian Temptation* (Garden City, N.Y.: Doubleday, 1977), p. 236.

72. The proviso that cross-regime comparative evaluations require correct pairings of descriptions with descriptions, prescriptions with prescriptions, and so forth across the board, is set forth in chapter 1, section 4, herein.

73. Cited in Cranston, *Freedom,* p. 112 (my italics).

74. See chapter 9, sections 1-3. But see esp. my "Guidelines for Concept Analysis," in Sartori, *Social Science Concepts,* pp. 15-22. Popper downgrades the power of words on account of his belittlement of definitions. See, e.g., *The Open Society and Its Enemies* (London: Routledge & Kegan Paul, 1952), 2:9-21.

75. In the Preface to the 2d ed. (1873) of *Capital.* Reference is specifically made here to Hegel's dialectics, but the point can be generalized.

76. So in the official *History of the Communist Party of the Soviet Union* (1939), chap. iv, 2. The text in question was also published separately under Stalin's name, with the title *Dialectical Materialism and Historical Materialism* (New York: International Publishers, 1940).

77. J.J. Kirkpatrick, *Dictatorships and Double Standards* (New York: Simon & Schuster, 1982), p. 135.

78. A standard work on the emotive use of language is Charles L. Stevenson, *Ethics and Language* (New Haven: Yale University Press, 1945). The point at issue, however, belongs to the studies on propaganda.

79. In this connection Kirkpatrick, *Dictatorships and Double Standards,* perceptively points out that communism no longer grows "by disseminating and winning support for its own values. . . . Communism grows by identifying itself with the prestige symbols of competing movements and so blurring issues, stakes and alignments." The Communist movement "systematically conceals its identity," and advances "by tactical incorporation of the symbols of the opposing groups" (p. 136).

80. The only free election with universal suffrage ever held in Russia was the one for the Constituent Assembly in November 1917. At that election the Bolsheviks (at the peak of their popularity) received just about one-quarter of the vote. The Assembly was dispersed, upon being convened, by the force of arms; and this is how

the Bolsheviks, since 18 January 1918, established to date their majority status.

81. A study that strongly stresses this element with reference to Pavlov's theory of conditioned reflexes is S. Chakhotin (or Tchakhotine, as in the 1939 French ed.), *The Rape of the Masses* (New York: Alliance, 1940). My emphasis, however, is on the "manipulative use" of ideas, as in Max Lerner, *Ideas Are Weapons* (New York: Viking Press, 1939). But see especially Marcello Taddei, *Il Crampo Mentale e la Società Totalitaria* (Firenze: Casati, 1985).

16. The Poverty of Ideology

Ideas, always a part of reality, have today acquired power greater than that of reality.

— Michael Novak

16.1 *The Exhaustion of Ideals*

The hedonistic value attached to goods is a function of their rarity; and this applies to "good things" as well. When we have *satis,* i.e., enough, we are satisfied; but having enough, satisfaction, breeds dissatisfaction: Enough of something makes us desire something else. Currently the Westerner has enough liberty, seeks well-being and security, and thereby "values" a protective state that will take care of his needs. However, the spiral of need is limitless and has virtually no end, for, in the end, it is no longer the needs but the desires that would have to be satisfied. Along this path the Western ideals are both transformed and attenuated.

Daniel Bell's *The End of Ideology* (published in 1960) carried the subtitle *On the Exhaustion of Political Ideas*. What, then, was on the wane? Ideologies or ideas? The ensuing debate hardly clarified the issue.[1] Since there was neither agreement nor probing of the *idea* of ideology, participants in the discussion largely talked past each other. The debate subsided with the campus revolution, and in the late 1960s the tacit consensus was that an ideological surge had falsified the prophecy. As we muddle through the 1980s, we face again the question: What is it that is exhausted? If it is not the reservoir of ideologies, is it the reservoir of ideas? I shall come to ideas shortly. But first things first. And the one process of exhaustion that has been with us steadily for some two centuries is the exhaustion of *ideals*. The Western ideals are less and less "ideals" i.e., value beliefs, in the moral meaning of the term. That is to say that at bottom, and in the beginning, the crisis of ideals—the one that cannot be doubted—is the crisis of ethics.

For a great number of reasons, none of them fully convincing, the last forceful Western philosophy of man as a "moral being" was the ethics of Kant. Perhaps morality does not fare well on its own, that is, detached from religion.[2] Perhaps progress (the ideal) swayed us onto a different track, and technological progress allowed us to proceed increasingly as utilitarian and self-serving animals. When all the reasons are given, the fact is that Western man has become, from one generation to another, more and more economic minded. The protagonists of the Glorious Revolution, of the Philadelphia Convention, of the French Revolution, and of the 1848 Revolutions can hardly be described as men who conceived politics as "who gets what, how"— as Lasswell did.[3] But when Lasswell reduced politics to a problem of "getting," nobody was particularly dismayed by the harshness of this view; this was the way it was. In the 1950s, when Raymond Aron provided a rationale for the end of ideology prophecy, nobody was particularly struck by the fact that his argument was entirely economic. "In an economy of growth," Aron wrote, "the problem of distribution takes on a meaning that is totally different from the one it has had for centuries. General wealth used to seem an almost fixed quantity. . . . If some one had too much, it meant that it had been taken away from someone else. But when the wealth of the collectivity steadily grows each year by a certain per cent, the rhythm and speed of the increase is more important than the problem of redistribution, even for the non-privileged."[4]

In essence, the argument was this: On one side we have a cake, and on the other side we have the problem of who cuts it how. The size of the cake is the concern of economics, the cutting—i.e., the distribution—is the concern of politics. If the ratio between the size of the cake and the number of eaters remains about the same, then the political problem of how it should be divided is the major problem, or at least the only one that allows for different solutions. But if we can easily supply more cakes, or a bigger cake, then the economic problem of making a larger cake supplants the political problem of who is to have the greater share. Hence, politics and particularly ideological politics will be less important in the world of tomorrow. In the long run, everybody will realize that what matters most is not the class struggle but the size of the cake. The argument crucially assumes, then, that the cake grows at a perceptible rate, and indefinitely, in excess of population growth. But can the cake grow indefinitely and fast enough? Has an era of affluence arrived to stay? And can the industrial-technological revolution sustain, and spread across the world, increasing wealth for all? The logic of the argument may well be impeccable (though I doubt it), but its factual premises have been all along as shaky as can be.

Growth implies a fast-growing consumption of resources and, above all, of a finite stock of non-renewable resources. In particular, as one industrial revolution followed another, fossil energy resources (coal, oil, and gas) have been used up at an exponential pace. In the long view we knew all the time that cheap energy had to end in a matter of decades. Whether future supplies were to come from as yet undetected deep fossil reserves, from nuclear plants, or from technological invention (i.e., from renewable energy drawn from winds, water, and solar heating), in all cases it was very clear that the cheap energy that had kept the machinery of industrial progress moving for some two centuries was about to become expensive; and costly, let alone scarce energy, is alone a sufficient reason for not projecting into the future the trends of the past. The point is reinforced by noting that growth has also been depleting our renewable resources: forests that are simply destroyed; hitherto fertile land that is turned into desert; rivers, lakes, and even seas that are polluted; water that will increasingly be in short supply. We not only have to reckon with the end of cheap energy; it is also the case that the fantastically high bill of the externalities and, indeed, of ecological disasters is coming due. And this is certainly a bill that will have to be charged on affluence.

How is it, then, that so many reputed economists have been telling us — at least until shocked by the oil shock — that "organized scarcity" had been replaced for good or, in any event, for the foreseeable future by a civilization of plenty?[5] It would seem that economists have all been predicting sustained growth and affluence without ever seriously accounting for the long-range resource conditions and resource limits of growth.[6] This leaves us, today, with little more than the hope that we shall be saved by scientific discovery and technological innovation. Since hope is all we have, let us indeed hope so. If so, however, time is of the essence; and the point thus becomes that accelerated growth "consumes" more rapidly the time that we may desperately come to need for science and technology to save us in time. Zero growth and steady-state societies certainly are unappealing prospects and may be said to have the only merit of buying time — time for scientific advances to permit the substitution of non-renewable with renewable resources. But if time is of the essence, buying time is also of the essence.

If growth economists have been shortsighted and largely off the mark, social scientists have not performed better. Whatever was intended by the end of ideology prophecy, it was easy to note from the outset — unassisted by hindsight — that it was a short-range conjecture strictly limited in space and time. It is limited in space because the only reconciled societies are, or will be, those whose economic output significantly surpasses their demographic growth. And it is temporally limited because Marxism is not, by any necessity, the last of the ideologies, and we must not confuse the decline of a specific ideology with the disappearance of ideology as such. Indeed, we must distinguish between the genus and the species, that is, between ideology as a conceptual category and its historical expressions, such as, today, Marxism and national-ism. And, for that matter, in the underdeveloped countries the tide of national-ism and political messianism is probably on the surge. Nor, on the other hand, can we afford to confide wholesale in the long-term duration of industrial peace in the privileged industrial democracies. It is plausible that an affluent society whose major problem is no longer *labor* — in the original meaning of effort, fatigue, pain — but leisure is less vulnerable to the onslaughts of ex-tremism. However, we should not assume that the first reaction to the plen-tiful life will be the reaction of the generations who will have become ac-customed to it. Perfectionism and disillusionment arise in the wake of eco-nomic development (not at the lower stages of deprivation), and the "great emptiness" of an age of leisure is bound to create new rebels, new protest attitudes, and still other unforeseen difficulties. For leisure permits us to store energy that we do not know where to expend. If we have, or shall have, nothing to do, what shall we do?[7]

Perhaps, then, we are approaching the end of surrogates and, by the same token, of illusions, of ersatz-sustained illusions. As the cake no longer leaps ahead of its eaters (it never has, in fact, in most of Latin America, Africa, and Asia), it should dawn upon us that there is no economic cure for noneco-nomic ills and, more generally, that an amoral (post-moral) person can hardly produce a good society. We have gone far too far in assimilating political be-havior to economic behavior, in telling ourselves that politics boils down to *getting,* and in pursuing what Kincaid vividly terms "the politics of the body," that is, a good life whose criteria "are pain and pleasure."[8] Since man does not have a nature in the naturalistic sense but is what he thinks he is, it is perfectly possible to make him into nothing but an economic animal. In fact, we have been trying very hard to do just that. On Kant's account, the realm of morality is the realm of self-rewarding "disinterested actions," of a behavior not motivated by material rewards. Social scientists tell us, however, that "inter-est" means "motivation" and, henceforth, that a disinterested action is non-sense, that it amounts to inaction (for we do not act unless we are motivated).[9] Ethics is not the domain of "exchanges"; the moral man gives in exchange for nothing. But we are told that everything is exchange. The maxim of the moral man is that one should not do to others what he does not wish others to do to him.[10] We relentlessly maneuver, instead, in order to shift on to others the burdens we do not like for ourselves. No society has ever entertained the notion that its members have no duties or obligations. But we entertain more and more the notion that we are "entitled," entitled to receive; the revolution of rising expectations has quickly generated the society of entitlees.

As the moral man was pushed into the backstage, it was the "rational man" that came to the fore. Indeed, the utilitarian tradition rationalizes ethics as being nothing but the enlightened, long-range self-interest of each individual.[11] For sure, Kantian ethics too belongs to the rational (not to the religious or sentiment-based) theories of morality. It could be held, therefore, that what is accomplished via moral motivations is equally accomplished via rational argument. For instance, if we need economic growth, we must see to it—as rational and calculating animals—that growth is not slowed down to a trickle by an increasing distributive and consuming appetite. In like manner, it can be rationally argued that societal benefits have societal costs and therefore that rights without obligations, getting without giving, are irrational postures. So they are; but in the aggregate, and in the very long run—certainly beyond our individual station and horizon. As rational, calculating egoists it is not rational to be civic minded; it may be irrational, for example, to waste time in voting, and it would be irrational to pay for a public good that we can have for free. Similarly, the larger an organization, the less it is rational for its members to share its burdens and further its collective goals.[12] In short, it is "rational" (in cost-benefit terms) for each individual to be a social parasite; he will be better off by exploiting others.

I was saying that we are approaching the end of surrogates, that we have reached the end of the line of the *Ersatzen*. Among them, I submit, is the notion that it is rational to be moral. It simply does not work that way. As we demand of the rational man to replace the moral man, we burden both with impossibly high standards. The long-deferred moment of truth has arrived, and the truth is that there cannot be a good society without "good," that is, where politics is reduced to economics, ideals to ideologies, and ethics to a calculus. If politics is not ethics, nonetheless the social fabric does require a moral man (alongside the political one). The exhaustion that we are surely witnessing is, therefore, the one of the ethico-political ideals that have nurtured the Western civilization and brought about, in its wake, our liberal democracies.

Certainly, technological progress is per se a powerful concomitant to the exhaustion of ideals. But I would not say, as is commonly said, that "the malaise lies in the industrial basis on which our civilization is based" and that "a society dominated by the machine process, dependent on factory and office routine, celebrating itself in the act of individual consumption, is finally insufficient to retain our loyalty."[13] That our society is "dominated by the machine process" is true enough; but why? Lest we put the cart before the horse, we are machine dominated because we are, to begin with, excessively economic minded; because we have lost, losing ethics, the loyalties that do retain us. Therefore, I would stress that technological progress is a powerful concomitant (not a prime causal factor) to the exhaustion of our ideals in two other respects. First, the affluence of the advanced industrial societies creates a soft, nerve-lacking, "seated" society. Second, technological progress brings about overpopulation and superorganization, that is, a setting in which the individual is reduced to a mere cipher and feels increasingly powerless and stifled. Let us face it: These are conditions that are conducive to ideals of rejection and rebellion, to negative ideals rather than positive ones. The open society or, as Dahrendorf would have it, the "chance-offering" society,[14] assumes a non-saturated society, hardly the one in which we live.

In addition, history has tried us severely, perhaps too much. We are weary, maladjusted, anxious, and, let us admit it, frightened. The religion of progress has turned, in the phrase of Kingsley Martin, "into a gospel of acceleration." Since the time of the French Revolution and the first industrial revolution, we have been in a rush; and rapid, incessant change gives no time to readjust. Furthermore, a "rapid movement was exhilarating and men forgot . . . to ask in what direction they were hurrying."[15] On top of all this, we have been grievously tried by the carnage of two world wars; and we have emerged from a state of war, real warfare, only to be plunged straightaway into the wearing atmosphere of the cold war and, soon after, into a peace hinged on an equilibrium of nuclear terror. Our nervous systems are shaken, we live in fear of the morrow, indeed of a terrifying morrow in which the prospect of man's self-destruction is certainly not science fiction. Hobbes's *Leviathan* appeared in 1651 after the bloodshed of a cruel civil war. To Hobbes and many of his contemporaries the supreme goal seemed to be social peace; to attain it, Hobbes theorized the omnipotence of the state. After making due allowances, a number of analogies could also apply to our situation. We too, in our exhausted state, want peace at all costs. And as the gospel of acceleration has brought us not moral but only material progress, we clutch desperately at this tangible benefit. Cost what it may, we ask for a protected existence; and in order to achieve these benefits we may well be once again disposed, as were Hobbes's contemporaries, to entrust our fates to whoever promises to dispose of Armageddon and to take care of us.

In the final analysis, it may be that the ultimate reason for the crisis, let alone the distemper, of liberal democracy is that we are spoiled, dominated by "bodily needs," and frightened. If this were so, there is no real point in all the fuss and fury about "real" democracy, "complete" liberty, and "true" justice. These are the closing fireworks of a party that is over. The truth of the matter is a different one. It is not real liberty that concerns us; it is simply that we no longer appreciate liberty as such. It is not true democracy that matters to us; it is, instead, the benefit-dispensing, need-serving state. We are unconcerned about liberty and democracy because we are soft, we are materially minded, we are weary and, on top of all this, *noti nulla cupido,* we are bored with the familiar. However, I am not at all sure that this is the ultimate diagnosis.

16.2   *Inevitables and Evitables*

If we distinguish between ideals and ideas, and if it is the case that we are scoring poorly with ideals, then we certainly are in trouble. Since ideals are, or are held as, value beliefs, there is no known therapy for their demission. Yet, man is an ideal-seeking animal.[16] An ideal-less life is a dull life. The rebellion of the young in the 1960s was an explosion of "idealism." The youth culture, or counterculture, also attested, however, to the poverty of ideals that basically consist of negations. The lesson to be learned from that experience is that there is no quick fix for the rejuvenation of ideals.[17] The protest against the great emptiness was an even greater emptiness.

To distinguish between ideals and ideas is not to say that the two realms do not communicate. Ideals do not fall upon us from heaven; they are part and parcel of a culture. Specifically, the liberal-democratic ideals were long toiled by philosophers and were born in the course of elaborating ideas. And ideas are amenable — far more manageably than ideals — to redressing and improvement. The crisis of ideals reflects, at least in part and in the long run, faulty ideas. Let me thus turn to what might be called, for the sake of symmetry, the *crisis of ideas.*

Ideas are not whatever comes to anybody's mind. In the serious meaning of the word, ideas are the end result of reasoning, indeed of "consistent reasoning," as Bertrand de Jouvenel puts it in contrasting the intellectual of the past to the present-day one. "Until the late eighteenth century — he writes — the secular intelligentsia was not numerous; its average intellectual level was therefore high. Moreover, its members were educated in ecclesiastical schools where they received a strong training in logic, which the 'scientific education' of our day seems unable to replace. Therefore these minds were prone to consistency; it is remarkable how common a quality of consistent reasoning was in their works, as compared to those of our contemporaries."[18] In his usual graceful manner de Jouvenel is saying that the discipline of reasoning (theoretical reasoning, to be sure) has lost its discipline. As the ease with which the mainstream theory of democracy was tattered in the 1960s goes to show, he is right. If we compare ourselves, across the centuries, to the classics, there is little doubt that our "quality of consistent reasoning" is of lower quality. However, this is a bias for hope — for a consistent reasoning that has been lost can also be recuperated.

I take the view, then, that while a crisis of ideals is beyond immediate repair, a crisis of ideas can be remedied in the shorter run. This view clearly implies that I do not believe in determinism or historical materialism. Not that I underestimate the impact of material changes and environmental pressures. I have also held that some inevitables are indeed inevitable. For instance, whether or not we like technology and a technetronic world, we cannot escape it; whether or not we like atomic energy, we cannot refuse it. But I cannot see that the destruction of liberal democracy is brought about by "objective inevitables." As all of humankind's history shows, *homo sapiens* is capable of responding to the environment in many ways: We have the power of determining determinations. Whether or not man is endowed with an ultimate freedom of the will, man escapes predetermination for the unmetaphysical reason that he lives a mental life, that he is a symbolic animal. Hence the last word, with an *animal loquax,* always comes from the word. As a member of the zoological realm, man is given birth and dies; but as long as he is alive, and as a thinking animal, man is a highly adaptable and highly resourceful being.

If that much is granted, then it is unwarranted to explain our present plight by invoking the inexorable march of events and other such remote and convenient alibis. The sea has its nature, but if we are shipwrecked because we lack a pilot and we are not looking at the compass, we are not entitled to say that it is the sea's fault. Even if our crisis is brought about by deep-seated, formidable forces, such forces have been unleashed by us and may, by the same token, be released and returned under our control. Once we have acknowledged that there are many causes and reasons for our drifting, one of these—a crucial one—is to be found in the fact that we have been increasingly exposed, to an unprecedented scale, to a bombardment of stupidities. However, stupidities find their remedy in being recognized for what they are. One such stupidity, a fundamental one, is the witch-hunting of ideas themselves—to which I now turn.

16.3   The Witch-Hunting of Ideas

It took Mannheim, a writer who can hardly be accused of idealistic leanings, to coin the pregnant expression "idea-struck age" and to note that liberal democracy is the typical product of it.[19] Democracy, we could say, is the fruit of an *ideocracy,* meaning by this that no historical venture of man has depended in so pronounced and hazardous a manner on the force of ideas, and therefore on our capacity for employing them and on our ability to master the symbolic world.[20] It is small wonder, then, if democracy suffers more than any other ethico-political formula from mental confusion. If, in addition, we no longer believe in the value of ideas, it is hard to see how a democratic reality can decently survive. And it is in fact the case that the sphere of critical knowledge itself—which is also the kitchen in which the menus of the future are being prepared—is deeply affected, almost to the point of paralysis, by a suspicion of ideas, or an indictment against ideas, set in motion by that modern version of witch-hunting which is the denunciation of an *ideological bias*.[21] The extent and pervasive quality of the atmosphere of suspicion generated first by Marx and subsequently substantiated by Mannheim[22] is revealed by the frequency with which people today write "ideology" where before they wrote "idea" (and derivatives). It is true that non-Marxists use the word ideology simply because it is in fashion, and thereby in an innocent and diffuse meaning. Nonetheless, words have consequences; and ideology certainly is a word of consequence when used by Marxists: It is their most insidious key word in the war of words. Is this a reason for not using it at all? Certainly not. It is, however, a reason for employing "ideology" with reason and without carelessness.

The more the word ideology is substituted for things formerly called philosophy, theory, doctrine, ideas, ideals, beliefs, creeds, myths, utopias, and still other neighboring terms, the more we create a Leviathan-word, an all-eating monster—an unholy package that must be, in my steadfast opinion, unpacked. Hence, throughout this work I have *substituted the substitutor* (ideology) by calling ideas "ideas," ideals "ideals," beliefs "beliefs," and so forth. As this unpacking proceeds, "ideology" acquires a distinctive meaning and is brought to signify what no other word (neighboring word) signifies. It is at this point, I submit, that the word is employed with reason and to the advantage of reasoning. By the same token, when the word ideology is added to—instead of overstretched over—its set of neighboring terms, it becomes possible to specify what *is not* ideology, thus rendering the concept amenable to empirical assessment. To illustrate, one does not need the word ideology to say idea, but it is well to have a term for the "conversion of ideas into social levers."[23] Likewise, we do not need the word ideology to say "philosophy," but it is useful to have a word for the mass dissemination of philosophical conceptions, that is, for denoting the "philosophical vulgarizations that bring the masses to concrete action, to the transformation of reality."[24] Similarly, nothing is gained if the term ideology simply replaces "belief" and the expression belief system, whereas the argument is sharpened if one distinguishes between "ideological beliefs" and beliefs of other kinds, e.g., religious or traditional.

In order to cast light on the aforesaid unpacking it is important to distinguish, in a preliminary fashion, between *ideology in politics* and *ideology in knowledge.* With regard to the first domain, the question is what we mean by "ideological politics" and "ideological mentality" and, to be sure, what it is these notions explain. In such cases the contrary of ideology generally is (waiting for a better one) pragmatism, that is, pragmatic politics and pragmatic mentality.[25] With regard to the other domain, the question is, essentially, whether and to what extent our knowledge is ideologically conditioned or distorted. In such cases, the contrary of ideology is "truth" and, derivatively, science.

The distinction between ideology in politics and ideology in knowledge is, in principle, a neat one. In the first case, our focus is on actions and the issue is one of *efficacy;* in the second case, our focus is on thinking and the issue is one of *validity.* In some instances the distinction may turn out to be thin, as when we apply the notion of ideology to liberalism, democracy, socialism, and communism. Yet, even these entities can and, indeed, should be decoupled, for they consist of elements that are eminently mobilization-oriented *and* of elements whose nature is eminently cognitive. The pure and simple pronouncement that liberalism, socialism, and the like, are ideologies is not only untelling but stands on the way of our asking to what extent political doctrines have, or do not have, truth value and, correlatively, to what extent they are action activators whose import lies in their efficacy. However that may be, our subject matter here is ideology in knowledge, that is, the Marxist or Marxist-derived allegation that our knowing is inescapably conditioned and distorted by socioeconomic biases.

There are many versions of this allegation, and I shall make reference to the more sophisticated one, that is, to the "existential conditioning" of thought expounded by Karl Mannheim (rather than to the cruder notion of "false consciousness" set forth by Engels). The unifying trait is this: Whenever the notion of ideology is brought to bear on knowledge, the problem is no longer one of judging an assertion with respect to its validity but of judging it in relation to the motives for which it is uttered. The inquiry, Is this assertion true? is replaced by, Why is he making it? As Merton points out in his examination of Mannheim's sociology of knowledge, in this approach "one no longer inquires into the content of beliefs and assertions to determine whether they are valid or not, one no longer confronts the assertions with relevant evidence, but introduces an entirely new question: How does it happen that these views are maintained? Thought becomes functionalized; it is interpreted in terms of its psychological or economic or social or racial sources and functions."[26] To be sure, the question, Why does he say what he is saying? is not new. But up to now it was mostly used to explain error, whereas today it is used to devalue the truth value of thinking. Thus an impersonal world of knowledge that seeks a common truth-seeking dialogue is replaced (in Mannheim's version) by a fragmented multiplicity of individuals who — being simply the echoes of their own existential situation — propound their particular ideology within the framework of their "total" ideology.

Now, if I have hidden motives, so has my contender. If my motives are sinister ones, how can my contender prove that his motives are noble? Certainly not by saying so; on top of every other reason, because the motivations in question are characterized by unawareness; they are, ultimately, subconscious ones. Under the ideological indictment we are truly all equal. There is absolutely no way — despite all attempts to the contrary — to divide the world into the ideologically biased and the ideologically unbiased. The old objection applies: If all truth is relative, so also the assertion that truth is relative is "relative." If all truth is ideologically distorted, so also the assertion that truth is distorted is "distorted."[27] If we agree to enter this kind of game, what is opposed to a bias is only a counter-bias; and it cannot be shown that a counter-bias is any better, in any sense, than the bias it denounces.

Thus the ideological witch-hunting of ideas adds up to being a self-devouring circularity that is conducive, on the one hand, to a "reinforced dogmatism"[28] and, on the other hand, to an "intellectual nihilism."[29] In Hayek's argument, recourse to the sociologico-Marxist explanation of thought is based on a super-rationalism that prepares the ground for a thorough irrationalism. In the first respect, one must postulate a privileged supermind, an infallible, unconditioned mind that represents an exception — for reasons that will ever remain mysterious — to the rule of ideological conditioning; and so we arrive at reinforced *dogmatism*. And in the second respect, "if truth is no longer discovered by observation, reasoning and argument, but by uncovering hidden causes which, unknown to the thinker, have determined his conclusions, if whether a statement is true or false is no longer decided by logical argument and empirical tests, but by examining the social position of the person who made it . . . reason has been finally driven out"— and so we arrive at mental and intellectual *nihilism*.[30]

To my mind it makes no sense to *reduce* the theory of knowledge — gnoseology and epistemology — to a sociology of knowledge.[31] In itself, a sociology of knowledge is a perfectly respectable endeavor that certainly adds (like, in a parallel fashion, psychoanalysis) to our understanding of ourselves. We are all the wiser if we are aware of the conditionings that both limit and prompt our intellectual pursuits. Even so, Jon Elster appropriately points to the following limitations: First, "there is no reason to suppose that beliefs shaped by a social position tend to serve the interests of the person in that position"; second, "there is no reason to suppose that beliefs shaped by a social position tend to serve the interests of the ruling or dominant group"; third, "there is no reason to suppose that beliefs shaped by interests tend to serve these interests."[32]

Be that as it may, the crucial point is that when we come to the *creativity of thinking,* we come to the point at which an existential and socioeconomic explanation of thought no longer explains. Given a need, a situation, and an interest, the creative mental response that will follow is not given. No sociology of knowledge can explain Marx or Mannheim; it can only explain *the success* of Marx and Mannheim. Those who fall prey to the fascination of the sociologico-Marxist rendering of thought forget the very important difference between receiver and inventor of culture, and thus between the spreading of thought and its formation. The Mannheimian deludes himself into believing that he addresses the genesis of mental products. Actually, "Mannheim's law" is valid for quite another purpose: to explain by what criterion the receivers of culture *choose between* the mental products submitted to them. A sociology of knowledge cannot tell whence the creativity of thought springs, or how to judge the correctness of thought. It shows us instead for what motives the non-thinkers or the non-thinking (those whose profession is not that of thinking) adhere to other people's thoughts. In short: A sociology of knowledge provides a criterion for the fortune of an already-created thought — not for thinking it.

If this is so, we are left with no reason at all for injecting the notion of ideology into the sphere of mental creation. In particular, why should philosophies be rebaptized ideologies? Certainly, philosophies can and do assume the form of ideology with respect to the way in which they may be abridged, simplified, and emotionally slanted at the level of common discourse for mobilizational intents. But the philosophies that are disseminated as ideologies are such on arrival, not on departure, not *qua philosophia.* If ideology serves to connote the fall or popularization of thought, it cannot be applied to the opposite process, the emergence or creation of thought. If it is used in connection with a quest for "certainty" (the certainty that gives ideology its efficacy), then it cannot be used to refer to the quest for "truth." If ideology is — as it appears very much to be —"a system of ideas about which no one thinks any longer,"[33] a dogmatized system of ideas, then let us not use the term for ideas-in-thinking. Remember, we are dealing here with ideology *in knowledge* (not with ideology in politics); a context in which the word does imply (unless it is used meaninglessly) that ideas and ideals are specious justifications, and does distract our attention from the substance of thought to what is prior to and behind thought. And the peremptory objection to this is that "if we knew how our present knowledge is conditioned or determined, it would no longer be our present knowledge. To assert that we can explain our own knowledge is to assert that we know more than we do know, a statement which is nonsense in the strict meaning of the term."[34]

In the end, we simply stumble in, and fumble with, the "liar's paradox" with which logicians have long delighted and puzzled themselves. Its stringent form is: What I state is false. And the paradox is this: If the assertion is true, then it is false (what I declare false is not-false); and if the assertion is false, then it is true (what I declare false is true). In similar fashion, if all statements are ideological falsehoods, is this very statement true or false? In either way, we contradict what we assert.

Despite all objections, the game of unmasking ideas as ideologies will of course continue. By its rules anyone can reject any argument without arguments. How convenient! But why should those who *have* arguments join in the game? And why should they accept the word that introduces and legitimizes it? Replying for myself, the reply is this: I persist in believing that ideas (of philosophers no less than of scientists) are to be understood and not unmasked, and that our first task remains to inquire whether they are true or false, verifiable or unverifiable, consistent or contradictory. The unveiling of self-interests, hidden motives, and conditionings does not dispose of an argument—it leaves it exactly as it is, warranted or unwarranted, valid or invalid. To make of thought a matter of discussing "who benefits" from what is being said is, ultimately, a way of concealing poor thinking and of cheating with sound thinking. And such a way of reasoning is indeed a sinister omen, as much for the fate of culture as for that of an experiment in reasonableness such as democracy. Let this be clearly understood: Liberal democracy ends the very moment an "idea-struck age" passes away, killed (be it repeated) not by material factors but by a cultural pattern of distrust and suspicion of ideas. Once we have sacrificed ideas and ideals on the altar of ideology, nothing can await us but a sheer "outburst of energies," to use another telling expression of Mannheim.

16.4 *Novitism and Beyondism*

Every generation wants to be new, to be original; it feels that it has to say something not yet said and challenge what has already been said. If this were not so, life would seem purposeless to us, and history would lack dynamism. But it is not easy to be original. The easy way of being original is to know little. As the elite learned society of the past gives way to the "Great Conversation" that everybody enters,[35] a *docta ignorantia* (knowing that we do not know) is easily replaced by the arrogance of ignorance, by people who feel that there was no light in the world until they lit their torch. Such people, when they perform at their best, simply rediscover the umbrella. Most of the time, however, they unknowingly attempt what has already been attempted, repeat perennially unsuccessful undertakings, and repeatedly incur costly mistakes.

Then there are those who seek originality in extremism. But the extremist, as Ortega pointedly noted, is a "born falsifier," someone who substitutes exaggeration for creation and innovation. Exaggeration "is the opposite of creation, it is the definition of inertia. The immoderates are always the inert of their age. The creative man . . . knows the limits of original truth and, for this very reason, is on the alert, ready to abandon it the moment it begins to turn into untruth."[36] The intellectual extremist, instead, lives by stealing the ideas of others and presenting their distortion as an innovation. Thus, his originality lies mainly in noise, in decibels, in using inflated words—an immoderate vocabulary whose repercussions, as the extremist himself discovers only too late, have actually gone beyond or even counter to his intentions.

Both characteristics—knowing little and exaggerating truth into untruth—enter the description of the intellectual in revolt of our time, of the revolutionary intellectuals that we have come to label intelligentsias.[37] The intelligentsia is an altogether new specimen. Its first full-fledged portrait was outlined in 1928 by Julien Benda in his renowned outcry against *La Trahison des Clercs*.[38] Benda contrasted *the laymen*, those whose "function consists essentially in the pursuit of worldly interests," and *the clercs*, that class of men "whose activity essentially is not the pursuit of practical aims." Over the millennia the clerks had been either entirely indifferent to "political passions" or "gazing as moralists" from above, and in opposition to, these passions. The clerks were, to be sure, "unable to prevent the laymen from filling all history with the noise of their hatreds and their slaughters"; yet, "thanks to the clerks, humanity did evil for two thousand years, but honored good. This contradiction was an honor to the human species, and formed the rift whereby civilization slipped into the world." But at the end of the nineteenth century, Benda pointed out, "a fundamental change occurred: the clerks began to play the game of political passions. . . . Today . . . the clerks exercise political passions with all the characteristics of passion—the tendency to action, the thirst for immediate results, the exclusive preoccupation with the desired end, the scorn for argument, the excess, the hatred, the fixed ideas." The portrait of Benda applied, to be sure, to the clerks that "had betrayed"—not to all intellectuals. It can be ennobled by noting that intelligentsias are not necessarily "passionate" for passion's sake, but because they pursue an earthly paradise, hence a paradise to be achieved by political means. The fact remains that since the beginning of our century, these intellectuals have first exorcised and then justified paradises in whose name whole peoples have been led into infernos of misery and slaughter—indeed, cruelties that outdistance even the ones of the wars of religion.

I was saying that the intellectual in revolt is a new, unprecedented breed. It was a breeding of the Romantic explosion. The intelligentsia's claim to the ancestry of the *philosophes* of the Enlightenment is hard to sustain. The Encyclopedists distinctively devoted themselves to Cartesian truth, to clear, distinct ideas; their mission was to enlighten by spreading knowledge. Quite a different thing, then, from the attitude of the intelligentsias, which originate from the historicism of the Hegelian left, whose urge is to rush headlong into action because they have to be "historical at all costs"; meaning by this that one should always be abreast of the future, on the high tide of time, that one should frantically anticipate the movement of history. To listen to them, one would think it necessary only to act, always to act. In effect, theirs is not so much spasmodic action as spasmodic talk. Thus, for well over a century we have exaggerated in exaggerating. As a result, the atmosphere of our time is permeated by hubris, by the pursuit of excess, of what is beyond proportion precisely because it despises proportion. A hubris that may be said to have— new phenomena need new words for them—two intertwined faces: *novitism* and *beyondism*. Novitism is the urge of being new at all costs, indeed at whatever cost. The "novitist" is thus characterized by the frenzy of "surpassing," of superseding everything and everybody. Hence, the novitist generates beyondism, to wit, "the refusal to accept limits, the insistence of continually reaching out . . . a destiny that is always *beyond:* beyond morality, beyond tragedy, beyond culture."[39]

Certainly we must go forward—not stand still or, even worse, go back.[40] But "forward" and "backward" with respect to what point of reference? History is the myth of Sisyphus; every generation has to start anew. None of us is born civilized; our real birth certificate bears the year zero. Our historical maturity of men of "our time" must always be reconquered; and each time we have to cover a longer distance. Civilization or, better, a progress in civilization resembles an uphill climb where the hill becomes steeper and more slippery at each step. Has the line of Western tradition become too long? Do we still have the energy and ability to travel its full length? From time to time I am struck by the uneasy feeling that the house is more civilized than its inmates and that civilizations crumble because they end by being ahead of their inhabitants. Are we really pregnant with the future, or are we in effect unable to keep pace with our time? Who are the vanguards? Maybe, those who more vociferously claim to be already living in the future are actually a rearguard that has long since lost touch with the present. And if going forward means going ever farther away from liberal democracy until one loses it, I prosaically number myself among those who pursue it wherever it is. I do not care to know whether liberal democracy is doomed. In whatever case, I stand with the utterance of the hero of Corneille: "Do your duty and leave the rest to the Gods."[41]

16.5 *Epilogue*

Political systems are all human-made, but only "modern" polities can be meaningfully said to be intentful, that is, driven by the deliberate pursuit of a better life (in common). It is notoriously true that outcomes seldom are as intended. Indeed, the inherent risk of the "willed polities" is to backfire on themselves, to result in the very reverse of what was intended. But this has not been the case with liberal democracies. Our democracies disappoint but do not betray. This is so because the theory of liberal democracy is the one theory of politics that includes a theory of its practice, that comprises ends *and* means. Still, ends can always devour their means. Surely, liberal democracy cannot be taken for granted. Slavery, said Burke, we can always have: "It is a weed that grows in every soil."[42] Liberty, instead, we can always lose: It is a seed that needs toiling. Still more, our democracies perform along a delicate tightrope of ideas, ideals, and real-world feedbacks that somehow implement and sustain one another. How did this near-miracle, this virtuous circle, come about? In particular, how did the ideas and ideals of liberal democracy acquire the virtue of translating themselves in real-world accomplishments? That virtue originated from a long and slow process that was not, in itself, miraculous at all: It consisted all along of trial-and-error testing. The mainstream theory of democracy that I have sought to reconstruct is a theory eminently shaped by experience, by being tried out. The retort to the facile (and misleading) dictum that words have arbitrary meanings is, thus, that the vocabulary of politics consists of "experience reminders," of words (concepts) whose meanings incorporate historical learning.

Though "what is past is prologue,"[43] it is only prologue. As new generations take charge and new circumstances emerge, new thoughts must also be thought. So how does each generation handle its problems and seed the future? The one lesson of the 1960s is that we are still neophytes, if not apprentice sorcerers, in the craft that I have called the management of ideals. The problems that loom ahead are mighty problems; far too mighty to be met simply by reaffirming a pure and purely normative theory of democracy. Ideals and values may either mold the real world or succumb to its vendetta, depending on whether we know how to handle the "opposite danger" and on whether we realize that principles pushed to extremes tend to operate in the reverse. So, again, how can we best advance into the future? Still by trial and error? In a way, yes. But the more immense and complex the buildup—the edifice of the civilization we inhabit—the more we should see to it that trial replaces error. By now errors can be horrors, errors that are truly too costly to bear. But if we affix our minds, as I think is necessary, on error minimization, then we are required to look carefully into the *applicability* of our programs and into *ends-means congruities,* into which means are conducive, how, to what ends.[44] Neither the applicability probing nor the calculus of means have enjoyed, of late, much popularity with the theorists of democracy. I would hope both return to fashion.

Notes

1. The originators of the debate were Edward Shils, "The End of Ideology?" *Encounter,* November 1955; S.M. Lipset, *Political Man* (Garden City, N.Y.: Doubleday, 1960), chap. 13; Raymond Aron (see n. 4, below); and, of course, Daniel Bell. For the debate itself, see M. Rejai, ed., *Decline of Ideology?* (Chicago: Aldine, 1971); and C.I. Waxman, ed., *The End of Ideology Debate* (New York: Funk & Wagnalls, 1968).

2. Religion is difficult to define, and certainly monotheism is not a defining property. But no matter how loosely we conceive of religion, Confucianism seems to contradict the conjecture that ethics needs a religious support.

3. See H.D. Lasswell, *Politics: Who Gets What, When, How* (New York: McGraw-Hill, 1936).

4. In Aron, G. Kennan, R. Oppenheimer, et al., *Colloques de Rheinfelden* (1960), trans. *World Technology and Human Destiny* (Ann Arbor: University of Michigan Press, 1963), p. 6.

5. See, to stand for all, J.K. Galbraith, *The Affluent Society* (Boston: Houghton Mifflin, 1958).

6. The major warnings came from non-professional economists, such as the "Club of Rome" group. See D.H. Meadows et al., *The Limits to Growth* (New York: Universe Books, 1972); and M. Mesarovic and E. Pestel, *Mankind at the Turning Point* (New York: Dutton, 1974). To this day, the literature that reckons with the conditions of growth and discusses its implications can hardly be said to belong to the mainstream of economics. See R.L. Heilbroner, *An Enquiry into the Human Prospect* (New York: Norton, 1975); W. Ophuls, *Ecology and the Politics of Scarcity* (San Francisco: Freeman, 1977); H. Daly, *Steady-State Economics* (San Francisco: Freeman, 1980); R.J. Barnet, *The Lean Years: Politics in the Age of Scarcity* (New York: Simon & Schuster, 1980).

7. See, in general, E. Larrabee and R. Meyersohn, eds., *Mass Leisure* (Glencoe: Free Press, 1958). On this point Georges Friedmann introduced the distinction between "freed time," a mere emptiness, and "free time," i.e., the filling of the former.

8. See J. Kincaid, "Resource Scarcity in Western Political Theory: The Contest of Body and Soul," in *Scarce Natural Resources,* ed. S. Welch and R. Miewald (Beverly Hills: Sage, 1983).

9. This transformation of the concept of interest entered the social sciences with Arthur Bentley and has been largely adopted by the behavioral persuasion in politics. An illuminating, historical reconstruction is provided by the reader edited by L. Ornaghi, *Il Concetto di "Interesse"* (Milano: Giuffrè, 1984).

10. This is the Christian precept that Kant universalizes, in the first categorical imperative, as follows: Act only on that maxim that you can will to be a universal law.

11. This applies to both "act-utilitarianism" and "rule-utilitarianism." Whether the question is which action, or which rule, has the greatest utility is immaterial to my point; but I would certainly grant that rule-utilitarianism is more likely to bring about a "well understood" interest.

12. On this specific point, see Mancur Olson, *The Logic of Collective Action* (Cambridge, Mass.: Harvard University Press, 1965). In general, and for a number of variations on the theme of individual action and collective consequences, see Brian Barry and Russell Hardin, eds., *Rational Man and Irrational Society? An Introduction and Sourcebook* (Beverly Hills: Sage, 1982).

13. Heilbroner, *An Enquiry into the Human Prospect,* pp. 159-60.

14. In my opinion, Dahrendorf's *Life Chances* is a most felicitous rendering of the liberal creed, and is more to the point than Popper's open society, which is "open," at base, epistemologically.

15. K. Martin, *French Liberal Thought in the Eighteenth Century* (London: Turnstile, 1954), p. 278. The passage refers to the Age of Enlightenment, but is even truer for us.

16. See chapter 3, esp. section 1, where I argue at length against the "bad realism" forgetful of the *ought* element of politics.

17. Too much has been made, in this connection, of the emergence of a youth culture seeking "post-materialist values." The thesis is spelled out by Ronald Inglehart, *The Silent Revolution: Changing Values and Political Styles among Western Publics* (Princeton: Princeton University Press, 1977). Harold L. Wilensky, in *Working Life,* ed. B. Gardell and G. Johansson (New York: Wiley, 1981), correctly points out that, in addition to weaknesses in measurement, Inglehart's very data show that "the issues that excite Western public are overwhelmingly economic performance and political order" (p. 260). Futhermore, fear of scarcity, or the simple end of affluence, easily brings post-materialists back to material concerns. Post-materialist values have not been, it would seem, realigning.

18. In F.A. Hayek, ed., *Capitalism and the Historians* (Chicago: University of Chicago Press, 1954), pp. 112-13.

19. See *Ideology and Utopia,* p. 192, and chap. IV, 3, passim.

20. As results implicitly from the text, I am using "ideocracy" literally as a concomitant of the literal meaning of ideology (discourse on ideas); not in Lasswell's and Kaplan's politicized meaning, i.e., to denote "any body politic in which the predominant forms of power are those resting on the manipulation of symbols." *Power and Society* (New Haven: Yale University Press, 1950), pp. 212-213.

21. "Ideology" was coined by Destutt de Tracy in 1796 to indicate, innocently, a science of the formation of ideas. Already Napoleon gave it a negative meaning, saying "ideologists" to allude to harebrained speculations based on nothing concrete. Marx gave ideology an opposite negative sense, that is, not of ideas existing in a vacuum but of ideas rooted in class interests. Lenin contradicted Marx on the question of the

superfluity of ideologies (for he defended the necessity of a mobilizing "socialist ideology"), keeping, however, for the label "bourgeois ideology" the value of anathema that Marx gave it. Also, in Hitler's powerful propaganda machine ideology was used in a disparaging sense with reference to capitalistic and democratic ideologies.

22. See, in general, Walter Carlsnaes, *The Concept of Ideology and Political Analysis: A Critical Examination of Its Usage by Marx, Lenin and Mannheim* (Westport: Greenwood Press, 1981). A very broad treatment is Hans Barth, *Truth and Ideology*, trans. (Berkeley: University of California Press, 1976). On the debate within Marxism (up to Lukacs and Gramsci), see Martin Seliger, *The Marxist Conception of Ideology* (Cambridge: Cambridge University Press, 1977). Specifically on Mannheim, see Jean Maquet, *La Sociologie de la Connaissance* (Louvain: Nauwelaerts, 1949); Robert K. Merton, *Social Theory and Social Structure*, rev. ed. (Glencoe: Free Press, 1957), chaps. 12 and esp. 13; and P. Simmonds, *Karl Mannheim's Sociology of Knowledge* (Oxford: Clarendon Press, 1978).

23. Daniel Bell, *The End of Ideology*, rev. ed. (New York: Collier Books, 1962), p. 400. The point is exactly made by Carl Friedrich: "It is confusing . . . to call any system of ideas an ideology. . . . Ideologies are action-related systems of ideas." *Man and His Government*, p. 89.

24. Antonio Gramsci, *Quaderni del Carcere* (Torino: Einaudi, 1975), n. 10, part 2, sect. 2. This is essentially the Leninist conception.

25. This is the theme that I pursue in "Politics, Ideology and Belief Systems," *American Political Science Review*, June 1969. The article also expands on the rationale for a restrictive, fairly precise, and manageable definition of ideology. See, *contra*, M. Seliger, *Ideology and Politics* (London: Allen & Unwin, 1976), which is an elaborate, albeit unconvincing, defense of the "inclusive conception." In his argument the fact that all politics has a normative-moral component (a premise I share) demonstrates "the inseparability of all politics and ideology" (p. 135). But Seliger should demonstrate (though he never does) that "ideology" is equal to "values"—an assimilation to which I take strong exception.

26. *Social Theory and Social Structure*, p. 457.

27. Mannheim grappled at length with this problem. In order to resolve it he abandoned the original (Marxist) thesis of *Ideology and Utopia* (1929) that thought is "class situated" to land at a post-Marxist "existential conditioning of knowledge," a *Seinsverbundenheit des Wissens*. His solution was that intellectuals, being a non-class free from class conditionings, escape the Marxist indictment. However, Mannheim's exception kills the rule: If only non-thinkers (non-intellectuals) think ideologically, we are no longer dealing with thinking. See, more extensively, G. Sartori, *La Politica: Logica e Metodo in Scienze Sociali* (Milano: SugarCo, 1979), pp. 101-18.

28. Popper, *The Open Society and Its Enemies*, 2:215.

29. Merton, *Social Theory and Social Structure*, p. 503.

30. Hayek, *The Counter-Revolution of Science*, p. 90.

31. This applies to Mannheim and his school. It should be recalled that Max Scheler and P.A. Sorokin (whose *Social and Cultural Dynamics* extends for four volumes) have expounded a sociology of knowledge in which "ideal factors" condition the existential ones. In this latter approach the gnoseological issue does not arise.

32. *Sour Grapes: Studies in the Subversion of Rationality* (Cambridge: Cambridge University Press, 1983), pp. 143, 147, 156. Elster claims that his secondary aim "is to

provide microfoundations for the Marxist theory of ideologies" (p. 142). In truth I find his argument compelling and, by the same token, difficult to reconcile with a Marxist point of view.

33. W. Weidlé, "Sur le Concept d'Idéologie," *Le Contrat Social* 2 (1959): 77.

34. Hayek, *The Counter-Revolution of Science*, p. 89.

35. The expression (capitalized) is of Jacques Barzun, *The House of Intellect* (New York: Harper, 1959), pp. 15 and passim.

36. Ortega y Gasset, *Revés de Almanaque* (1930), III, in *Obras* (Madrid, 1932), p. 742.

37. The word is of Polish and Russian coinage. Concerning its origins, see A. Gella, "An Introduction to the Sociology of the Intelligentsia," in *The Intelligentsia and the Intellectuals*, ed. A. Gella (Beverly Hills: Sage, 1976); and Hugh Seton-Watson, "The Russian Intellectuals," in *The Intellectuals: A Controversial Portrait*, ed. G.B. de Huszar (Glencoe: Free Press, 1960), pp. 41ff. See also, in the same reader, the excerpts from Dostoyevski and Berdiaev, pp. 106-12. An overall discussion is Pellicani, *I Rivoluzionari di Professione*.

38. Translated with the title *The Treason of the Intellectuals*. The quoted passages are from pp. 139-43 of the French 1958 edition.

39. Bell, *The Cultural Contradictions of Capitalism*, p. 50. While Bell himself does not use "beyondism," I owe him the inspiration.

40. While I cannot enter the issue of progress, two works that make for fascinating reading are R. Nisbet, *The History of the Idea of Progress* (New York: Basic Books, 1980); and G. Almond, M. Chodorow, and R. Harvey Pearce, eds., *Progress and its Discontents* (Berkeley: University of California Press, 1982).

41. Horace, 710.

42. *Two Speeches on Conciliation with America*, Second Speech, 22 March 1775.

43. Shakespeare, *The Tempest*, II, I.

44. The *Federalist Papers* are an outstanding illustration of what I have in mind. I dwell on the two recommendations in *La Politica*, pp. 38-39, 73-75, 125-130.

Name

Pareto, V., 46-48, 57, 58, 143-44, 157, 161, 174, 175, 250, 442
Parrington, V., 395
Parry, G., 124, 128, 175
Partridge, P.H., 124
Passerin d'Entreves, A., 57, 294, 334, 363
Passow, R., 445
Pateman, C., 124, 179
Pearce, R.H., 510
Pejovic, S., 446
Pellicani, L., 36, 84, 423, 446, 486, 487
Pennock, J.R., 37, 85, 124, 128, 171, 172, 363, 444, 447
Perelman, C., 362
Pericles, 281
Pestel, E., 507
Peters, B.G., 181
Peters, R.S., 276
Petrocik, J.R., 127
Piane, M. delle, 56, 57
Pierson, N.G., 440
Piovani, P., 57
Pirenne, H., 443
Pitkin, H.F., 37
Plamenatz, J., 104, 124, 208, 289, 363, 395, 484
Plato, 60, 157, 292, 297, 338, 340, 362
Plutarch, 286
Pohlenz, M., 294
Polanyi, K., 443
Polanyi, M., 85
Polsby, N.W., 84, 127, 128, 175, 211
Popper, K., 210, 479, 509
Powell, G.B., 20
Presthus, R., 175
Prewitt, K., 175
Prothro, J.W., 127
Proudhon, P.J., 150, 394, 422, 423, 446, 458
Przeworski, A., 207
Pufendorf, S., 292, 332
Putnam, R.D., 176
Pye, L., 125

Quadri, G., 208

Rae, D., 138, 173, 183, 251, 363, 364, 365, 466
Raiffa, H., 250
Ranney, A., 251
Rapoport, A., 19
Rawls, J., x, 169, 181, 250, 340, 362, 363, 364, 365, 386
Rees, J., 365, 366
Rejai, M., 507
Renan, E., 434, 448
Rensi, G., 293
Revel, J.-F., 27, 36, 212, 450, 477, 489
Rhenman, E., 18
Ricardo, D., 412
Riesman, D., 36, 148, 175
Riggs, F.W., 207
Riker, W.H., 173, 175, 248, 250
Riley, P., 333
Rizzi, B., 446
Roberts, P.C., 443
Robespierre, M. de, 288
Robinson, R., 18, 275
Röpke, W., 449
Rorty, R., 275
Rose, R., 181
Rossi, P., 129
Rossiter, C., 303-4, 329
Rousseau, J.J., 24, 29, 33, 53, 86, 92, 137, 157-58, 167, 178, 179, 204, 247, 282, 293, 295, 306, 310-19, 331, 332, 333, 334, 337, 359, 382, 397, 450-51, 483
Roussopoulos, D., 129, 179
Royer-Collard, P.P., 138, 329
Ruggiero, G. de, 293, 335, 375, 383, 384, 395, 397
Runciman, W.G., 19, 128, 129, 173, 362
Russell, B., 397, 475-77
Rustow, D.A., 125, 175
Ruyer, R., 83
Ryan, A., 447

Sabine, G.H., 395
Saint-Simon, C.H. de, 434-36, 440, 448, 449
Sakharov, A., 488

Subject

Democracy *(continued)*
  pluralist theory of; *see* Pluralism
  polis, 280-83
  political; *see* Political democracy
  and polyarchy, 7, 154-55, 156, 175,
    167, 169
  popular, 467-70, 488n.47
  populistic, 115, 121, 129n.62
  post-liberal, 383
  power and, 428-30, 432
  prescriptive definition of, 7-8, 12,
    13, 59, 70, 153, 159, 162, 163, 171
  procedural, 152, 357, 385, 388-89
  proof of; *see* Proof
  as property concept, 183-84
  public opinion and, 86-89, 96,
    98-99, 101-2, 110, 120-21
  rational, 51-55
  rationalized, 269
  realism and, 13, 44-46, 48, 80,
    240-41
  referendum, 14, 111-12, 115-20, 162,
    246-47, 283
  representative, 29-30, 33, 110, 111,
    119, 155-56, 158, 164-65, 170, 280,
    283
  republic vs., 287-88, 295nn. 40-42,
    296n.43
  revolution and, 77
  role of expert in, 431-34
  in Schumpeter, 152-54
  in segmented societies, 238-39
  selection and, 140-41, 143-44,
    166-67
  semi-direct, 283, 293n.17
  sham, 123
  social, 8-9, 11, 386, 444n.39,
    447n.71
  totalitarian, 392, 451, 483n.5
  value support and, 4-6, 8, 141, 165,
    168-71
  vertical, 14, 132, 137, 142, 147, 153,
    154, 164, 165, 167, 171
  as word, 4, 7, 12, 479, 481-83
Democratic
  planning, 425-28
  pluralism, 92, 125n.23

as a property concept, 183-84
Demo-distribution, 234-37, 427
Demolatry, 25
Demonstration democracy, 88-89,
  245-46
Demophily, 25, 474-79
Demos
  kratos and, 28-29, 234
  meanings of, 21-24
Deontology, 18n.8, 67, 70, 71
  misunderstanding of, 58, 59
Description vs. prescription, 7-8, 13,
  15-16
Despotism, 194, 198, 203-4, 287-88,
  475
  democratic, 372
  elective, 133
Dialectical materialism, 480
Dictatorship, 185, 193, 202, 204-5,
  212nn. 68, 71, 472-73
  of bourgeoisie, 472-73
  class definition of, 205, 472
  in decision making, 217, 220
  of the proletariat, 204, 436, 459-66,
    470-72, 485nn. 19, 26, 487n.45
  Roman, 185, 204, 207n.5
  theory of democratic, 470-74
  totalitarian, 202, 203
Diminishing consequences, principle
  of, 320-21
Direct democracy. *See* Democracy,
  direct
Discrimination, compensatory,
  365nn. 34, 36
Dissensus, 92, 125nn. 15, 17
Dutifulness, 242, 494

Eastern Europe, 391, 392, 467-70,
  488n.52
Economic democracy. *See* Democracy,
  economic
Economic equality, 344-46, 360-61
Economic planning. *See* Planning,
  economic
Economic system
  market as subsystem of, 405-7
  state ownership of, 360, 401-3

Experts
  role of, 427, 431-34
  science and, 434-39
Exploitation, 419
External payments, 232. *See also* Side
  payments
External risks, 216-23, 243
Extremism, 118-19, 129nn. 69, 71,
  504

Facts, ideals and, 78-79, 81. *See also*
  Evidence
Fact-value tension, 8, 46
Fascism, 44, 48, 178n.66, 189, 195,
  209n.30, 210n.31, 242, 375
Feedback
  rule, 71, 72, 77, 80
  theory of democracy, 152-54
Force, power and, 187. *See also*
  Violence
Form, meanings of, 353-54
Foundations of political system,
  267-70
Frankfurt school, 82n.7
Freedom
  autonomy and, 310, 315-20
  capacity and, 303-4, 306
  of choice, 305-6, 408
  complete, 303, 305
  in Croce, 45
  democracy and, 367-68
  equality and, 340, 342, 357-62,
    366n.50, 383, 390-91, 451
  external vs. internal, 300-301, 316-18
  fear of, 28
  formal, 390-91
  Greek criterion for, 291
  individual, 32, 33, 283, 284-87, 291,
    293n.19, 299
  kinds of, 298-301
  law and, 306-8, 315, 322, 327-28
  liberalism and, 306, 307-9, 380
  limited majority and, 32-33
  in Marx, 451
  permissive, 300
  philosophical, 299-300
  political; *see* Political freedom

  power and, 28-29
  as priority value, 272-74, 328
  process of, 300-301
  protective, 301-3
  relational, 301, 327
  stages of, 300
Free market. *See* Market system
French Revolution, 52, 67, 76, 137,
  287-88, 302, 343, 361

Game theory, 224, 231, 249n.25,
  250n.36, 261-62
Gemeinschaft, 26, 36n.6
General will, 24, 87, 178n.70, 311-14,
  332nn. 44, 45, 333nn. 54-56
Gesellschaft, 26, 36n.6
Gettysburg Address, 34-35, 38n.31
Glorious Revolution of 1688, 85n.41
Good life, 433
Good society, in Rousseau and Marx,
  450-56
Governing democracy, 86, 121, 122
Government
  as committee, 228-29
  by consent, 87-89
  intervention in economic system,
    399, 401, 426
  by leadership, 147-48
  moral functions of, 241-43
  of opinion, 87, 88-89
  people and, 30, 34-35, 86
  representative; *see* Representation
  by rulership, 145-46
  of science, 434-39
  vs. state, 53
  of things, 436-37
  see also Self-government; State
Greek democracy, 13-14, 25, 111, 157,
  241, 278-92, 309, 342. *See also*
  Greeks
Greeks, 16, 21-22, 39, 137, 203, 263,
  307, 339, 435
Group
  committee, type of, 228, 236,
    249n.22, 250n.29
  decisions, 214, 217
  small, 251n.39

Lightning Source UK Ltd.
Milton Keynes UK
UKOW06f0839011215

263870UK00002B/124/P